Increase Supply, Reduce Demand and Punish Severely

GESCHICHTE - ERINNERUNG - POLITIK
STUDIES IN HISTORY, MEMORY AND POLITICS

Edited by Anna Wolff-Powęska & Piotr Forecki

Vol. 37

PETER LANG

Maria Pasztor / Dariusz Jarosz

Increase Supply, Reduce Demand and Punish Severely

A Contextual History of Meat in Communist Poland

Translated by Alex Shannon

PETER LANG

Bibliographic Information published by the Deutsche Nationalbibliothek
The Deutsche Nationalbibliothek lists this publication in the Deutsche Nationalbibliografie; detailed bibliographic data is available in the internet at http://dnb.d-nb.de.

Library of Congress Cataloging-in-Publication Data
A CIP catalog record for this book has been applied for at the Library of Congress.

The Publication is funded by Ministry of Science and Higher Education of the Republic of Poland as a part of the National Programme for the Development of the Humanities. This publication reflects the views only of the author, and the Ministry cannot be held responsible for any use which may be made of the information contained therein.

NATIONAL PROGRAMME
FOR THE DEVELOPMENT OF HUMANITIES

Cover illustration courtesy of Benjamin Ben Chaim.

ISSN 2191-3528 · ISBN 978-3-631-82590-7 (Print)
E-ISBN 978-3-631-83509-8 (E-PDF) · E-ISBN 978-3-631-83510-4 (EPUB)
E-ISBN 978-3-631-83511-1 (MOBI) · DOI 10.3726/b17571

Peter Lang –Berlin · Bern · Bruxelles · New York · Oxford · Warszawa · Wien

This publication has been peer reviewed.

www.peterlang.com

Table of Contents

Introduction

Can meat have its own history? As shown by many publications in Western historiography,[1] the answer to that question is no doubt *yes*. Usually, however, analysis of this matter has come in the context of broader deliberations on the history of everyday life, nutrition (including the cuisine of different nations), food supply, and poverty. Research on commodities located within various social, anthropological, and cultural contexts is grabbing increased attention and arouses ever more interest. However, such interest is still quite weak in Polish historiography; indeed, the idea that meat should be considered a matter of not only postwar Poland's social or economic history but also its political history, has not resulted in more exhaustive analyses (though some interesting contributions have been made on this subject).[2] That having been said, the old joke summarizing the history of the Polish People's Republic (PRL)[3] in two words ("no meat") indicates that it may be worth considering this phenomenon and analyzing it in various research contexts. In this monograph, we try to approximate an answer to questions tied to Poland's "meat problems," to the attitudes that communist authorities and Polish society took toward these problems, and, in

1 See Madeleine Ferriéres, *Histoire des peurs alimantaires. Du Moyen Âge à l'aube du XXe siecle* (Paris: Edition du Seuil, 2002), which also includes a great amount of literature on the subject.

2 See, among others, Jerzy Kochanowski, "'Serdelki oczywiście zostają', czyli jeszcze jeden dowód na polityczną rolę kiełbasy (w 1956 r.)," in *Kuchnia władzy. Księga pamiątkowa z okazji 70-tej rocznicy urodzin Andrzeja Garlickiego*, eds. Włodzimierz Borodziej and J. Kochanowski (Warszawa: Czytelnik, 2005), 131–144; Kochanowski, *Tylnymi drzwiami. "Czarny rynek" w Polsce 1944–1989* (Warszawa: Wydawnictwo Neriton i Instytut Histroyczny UW, 2010), 158–202; Kochanowski, "Das 'Problem Nummer 1' und seine Protagonisten. Fleisch und Fleischspekulanten in Polen 1944 bis 1989," *Unsere Feinde. Konstruktionen des Anderen im Sozialismus* (Lepzig: Leipziger Universitätsverlag, 2004), 455–464. See also Kathy Burrel, "The Political and Social Life of Food in Socialist Poland," *Anthropology of East Europe Review* 21 (2003); David Crowley, "Warsaw's Schops: Stalinism and the Thaw," in *Style and Socialism: Modernity and Material Culture in Post-War Eastern Europe*, eds. Susan E. Reid and David Crowley (Oxford: Berg, 2000), 1–22.

3 The Polish People's Republic (PRL) is the official name of the Polish state in the years 1952–1989. For our purposes here, we use it (and its abbreviation) conventionally, along with the term People's Poland, to cover the entire period 1944/1945–1989.

particular, to meat shortages in the broader context of the issue of food in Poland in 1944–1989.

The starting point for our considerations is the so-called Wawrzecki case. At the turn of 1964 and 1965 in Warsaw, the trial took place of persons accused in the so-called "meat affair." As a result of this trial, one of the high officials dealing in the distribution of meat in the Polish capital – Stanisław Wawrzecki – was sentenced to death, a sentence that was carried out in March 1965. This fact became a widely discussed matter both within the Polish legal community and in broader public opinion.

For us, the Wawrzecki case serves as a pretext to draw conclusions not only about the significance of the "meat issue" in terms of the regime that ruled Poland after the Second World War and how it functioned but also about social attitudes and behaviors. Many of the topics discussed here touch on the essence of the communist system in Poland and the responses that broad social groups had toward that system's policies.

This book consists of two parts. The first part ("Control over Meat") contains our findings regarding the systemic and political determinants of food supply problems, including those related to meat shortages in the years 1944–1989. We deal with various measures taken by state and party leaders aimed at increasing the supply and limiting the consumption of meat. We also analyze how communist authorities presented meat in state propaganda.

A separate current in our considerations is analysis of the Wawrzecki case itself. We argue that the severe punishment that Wawrzecki received was the third path – alongside increasing supply and reducing demand – that Poland's postwar rulers took to solve food supply problems. We consider Warsaw's meat affair in broader terms, the most important of which relate to the mechanisms behind corruption and economic fraud, political control of the justice system, and committee supervision over party propaganda and the party apparatus.

The second part of this book ("Meat as a Problem for Ordinary People") is devoted to various socio-economic issues tied to the PRL's meat problems. This part includes an analysis of postwar Polish society's colloquial awareness, attitudes and behaviors in relation to the supply of meat. We focus on, among other things, how meat shortages shaped social discontent, including strikes and workers' demonstrations. We tried to determine what role the food supply (including meat) played in the everyday lives of Polish families, what the most important social strategies were for mitigating difficulties caused by food shortages. We also tried to place punishment for fraud in the distribution and trade of meat in a sociological and legal context by addressing, among other things, Polish attitudes toward – on the one hand – severe punishments applied in so-called "affairs," and – on the other hand – cases involving minor theft of social property.

Working on this book, we strove to ensure that we discussed all of the above-mentioned aspects of the topic based on sources and studies covering the longest possible chronological periods of time. For this reason, we cover the period from the beginning of People's Poland (1944/1945) to the year 1989. The beginning of the system transformation and the end of the PRL not only changed the political rules by which the Polish state functioned but also represented a transition to a market economy in which meat ceased be a scarce commodity.

Our research approach thus defined required a broad base of sources made up mainly of documents from the most important Polish party and state institutions. For the full list, see the bibliography.

Most importantly, we were able to make use of the documents from the Wawrzecki case, preserved in the Archives of the District Court in Warsaw, which allowed us to reconstruct the most important legal aspects of the trial. They also contain a great deal of interesting material for our analysis of how those involved in the production and trade of meat in Warsaw functioned.

Conclusions regarding the basic mechanisms of the meat affair and, more broadly, the phenomenon of economic crime in postwar Poland were based primarily on the files of the Ministry of Justice and the General Prosecutor held in the Archiwum Akt Nowych (AAN) in Warsaw. For this purpose, we also made use of documents from state audit and oversight institutions: Audit Office of the State Council (Biuro Kontroli przy Radzie Państwa), Ministry of State Supervision (Ministerstwo Kontroli Państwowej, MPK), Supreme Audit Office (Najwyższa Izba Kontroli, NIK), and relevant agencies of the Ministry of Food Industry and Purchase (Ministerstwo Przemysłu Spożywczego i Skupu, MPSiS).

Because state authorities attached such importance to the matters under examination here, they appointed a staff, under order no. 057/64 of the Minister of Internal Affairs, dated 8 May 1964, that would "direct operational and investigative activities into crimes in meat processing and marketing," headed by the chief of the Investigation Department of the Headquarters of the Citizens' Militia (Komenda Główna Milicji Obywatelskiej, KG MO) Colonel Bogusław Łamacz. We managed to gain access to the minutes of this staff's meetings in the former Central Archives of the Ministry of Internal Affairs and Administration (Centralne Archiwum Ministerstwa Spraw Wewnętrznych i Administracji, CAMSWiA), which are now preserved in the collections of the Institute of National Remembrance – IPN), and which contain highly important information not only about the course of the investigation but also about decisions made at the outset that established the course of the investigation.

One of the most important aspects of our work, concerning the mechanisms by which the party managed actions taken in the meat scandal – in particular the inquiry, investigation and trial of the main defendants – would be impossible without access not only to documents from prosecutors' offices and the Ministry of Justice indicated above, but above all the materials produced by the Central Committee of the Polish United Workers' Party (Komitet Centralny Polskiej Zjednoczonej Partii Robotniczej, KC PZPR). Important party organs were keenly interested in the meat affair and influenced the decision-making process. For this reason, their files contain rich documentation on this subject, some of which was produced by a number of other state institutions. We also used the files of the Warsaw PZPR Warsaw Committee, district committees, and some factory and local committees from the capital; therefore, we were able to examine the affair's repercussions within the party.

Our findings regarding various socio-economic repercussions tied to meat problems in the PRL were based on several basic types of sources, the first of which involves information collected by party committees at various levels. Materials collected by the Organization Department (Wydział Organizacyjny) of the KC PZPR were of the greatest importance. They contain, among other things, information, conveyed to higher officials by lower-level party members with opinions about food shortages, food price rises, and public reactions to those realities.

The second type consists of materials produced by the structures of the Ministry of the Interior (Ministerstwo Spraw Wewnętrznych, MSW), in particular by the KG MO, where we found both opinions on the matters in question here and information about specific behaviors caused by the difficult material situation (involving, among other things, difficulties with food supplies) in which large groups of society found themselves.

To the third type of sources were conclusions drawn by academic investigations offering insights, directly or indirectly, into the material situation of Poles, their food supply and quality of life. For this purpose, we have primarily used the findings of sociologists.

We treated letters sent to central state institutions as important testimony to the colloquial thinking[4] of contemporaneous Poles regarding their material situation, most of which were found in the Archive of the Center for Documentation

4 We defined colloquial thinking along the same lines a drawn by Piotr Sztompka, namely – as "beliefs diffused throughout a given group, spontaneous and intuitive beliefs" that are not ordered or systematized, do not logically follow from one to another, which does not mean that "they do not accurately contain some truth

and Program Collections (Archiwum Ośrodka Dokumentacji i Zbiorów Programowych, AODiZP) of TVP S.A. (Poland's state television station), or more precisely – in bulletins preserved there containing correspondence send to the Polish Radio and Television. We found a similar information, though much less extensive, in documents preserved in the files of the KC PZPR.

This book also includes the results of our research on meat production, processing and trade in the communist shortage economy.[5] Of course, we based these results on the existing professional literature (see the bibliography below), but also on the archival materials found in the Ministry of Internal Commerce (Ministerstwo Handlu Wewnętrznego, MHW), Ministry of Foreign Trade (Ministerstwo Handlu Zagranicznego, MHZ), Ministry of Provisions (Ministerstwo Aprowizacji, MA), Ministry of Food Industry and Purchase (Ministerstwa Przemysłu Spożywczego i Skupu, MPSiS), and State Commission for Economic Planning (Państwowa Komisja Planowania Gospodarczego, PKPG), located in the AAN. These materials allowed for a better understanding of what meat meant in Polish society and of the problems of food supply in the Polish economy after the Second World War.

While preparing to write this book, we also examined Polish press materials. On this basis, we tried to recreate the propaganda climate that accompanied events surrounding the meat affair.

The interdisciplinary nature of this work required the authors to read and interpret sources and studies belonging not only to various disciplines within history but also to the field of sociology, law, or criminology. We were able to develop these last themes thanks to the kindness and assistance of specialists in these fields, especially the late Professor Andrzej Murzynowski. The final shape of this monograph was also significantly influenced by discussions on selected topics carried out at sessions of the Pracownia Dziejów Polski po 1945 of the Institute of History at the Polish Academy of Sciences, headed by Prof. Dr. Hab. Tomasz Szarota. We wish to express our gratitude to their participants.

---

about world." See Piotr Sztompka, *Socjologia. Analiza społeczeństwa* (Kraków: Znak, 2002), 295.

5 We used this term in the meaning given to it by János Kornai in *Economics of Shortage* (New York: North-Holland Pub. Co, 1980); for the Polish version, see *Niedobór w gospodarce* (Warszawa: Państwowe Wydawnictwo Ekonomiczne, 1985).

Part I: Control over Meat

Chapter 1: Meat in a Shortage Economy

It is impossible to explain the role played by meat in the history of People's Poland without understanding the broader socio-economic context in which postwar Poland, and indeed the entire Central and Eastern Europe (in the Soviet sphere of influence), functioned. The economies of the countries in this region were best characterized by János Kornai, who used a language which was central to his discipline, but which is understandable to historians. As Kornai emphasized, the state played a large role in these economies. As that role grew, and as state redistribution of household incomes became increasingly important, the importance of measures designed to allocate goods and services through rationing also increased, and waiting time in queues grew longer. State domination of the economy and the consistent erosion of market forces and private enterprise led to a chronic shortage of goods and services, especially food. In this situation, state authorities employed methods to ration them – i.e. to distribute them according to non-supply-demand criteria, which required selection according to such complicated criteria as: urgency of need, merit, family situation, social status, political attitude, personal connections, and remuneration for services provided to the entity making the allocation, and corruption. To obtain a product in short supply, one had to wait in a queue, though even this did not guarantee success. Setting aside the detailed complexities of economic theory, it should be noted that, according to Kornai, the distribution of food in the so-called "real socialist" countries of Central and Eastern Europe in the first years after the communist revolution, in the period marked by civil war or war with an external enemy, was primarily non-market in nature. Market allocations conceived in this way, in which an effective price played some kind of role, was applied at the time only to certain products. They dominated in "relatively calm" periods within the "traditional economy management system."[6] In the economy described in Kornai's work, there was no obvious regularity in the market economy, according to an increase in real demand would cause an increase in supply. In a centrally planned socialist economy, price increases and demand reduction were not generally sufficient to eliminate shortages,[7] which did not prevent the economic authorities from occasionally using such a tool as price increases to regulate demand for food products, such as price increases.

6 Kornai, 550–584.
7 Ibid., 651.

Chapter 2: Meat as a Problem for Politicians

Systemic supply shortages, including those involving meat and meat products were – strange as it may sound – the "daily bread" of both the ruled and rulers of Poland since 1944. Analysis of source materials produced by key institutions of the communist state indicates that there was no period in the history of the PRL in which not only the rulers but also the governed, believed that the social needs tied the consumption of meat and meat products were/had been fulfilled. Even in the "golden period" of the first half of the Gierek decade,[8] documentation of meetings of the Politburo of the KC PZPR – the supreme authority in Poland at that time – indicates that Polish leaders estimated that meat and meat product shortages were smaller than in the 1960s, but that they still existed. A report entitled "Assessing the progress of the implementation of the National Economic Plan in the first half of 1972," presented at a Politburo session in July 1972, stated that "foodstuffs were assured in full supply," but there were "local shortages of meat, butter and vegetables."[9] Analysis by the Ministry of Internal Commerce and Services (Ministerstwo Handlu Wewnętrznego i Usług, MHWiU) was slightly less laconic; according to this analysis, in the first half of 1972 there was a high demand for food products, with the exception of some items. "Supplies of meat and butter did not cover demand,and there were difficulties in meeting the demand for vegetables, potatoes, pastries, chocolate and chocolate products, domestic wines, processed fruit and vegetables (May-June), and some food concentrates (e.g. coffee [. . .])."[10]

8 The Gierek decade refers to the period of PRL history between 1970 and 1980 and to Edward Gierek, the First Secretary of the KC PZPR. An important feature of this period was rapid economic development, largely based on loans taken in the West, which contributed to socio-economic crisis and finally led to Gierek's fall in 1980. The years 1971–1975 were marked by a consumer boom unprecedented in the history of the PRL, which manifested itself in, among other things, increased meat consumption.

9 Archiwum Akt Nowych [hereafter cited as AAN], Komitet Centralny Polskiej Zjednoczonej Partii Robotniczej [hereafter cited as KC PPR], mikrofilm 2929 [dawna sygnatura 1760], Ocena przebiegu realizacji Narodowego Planu gospodarczego w pierwszym półroczu 1972, Warszawa, lipiec 1972, p. 29.

10 Ibid., Ocena sytuacji rynkowej w I półroczu i przewidywanego zaopatrzenia rynku w I półroczu 1972, Ministerstwo Handlu Wewnętrznego i Usług, Warszawa lipiec 1972, p. 82.

This sense that consumer needs were not being met forced authorities to perform an extremely complicated balancing act, especially around Christmas, when purchases of meat and cold cuts increased. The resolution of these problems was a matter to be dealt with by ministerial and party bureaucratic structures. Already in the 1940s and 1950s, before Christmas, on May Day, during Easter, and especially at Christmas time, authorities organized larger quantities of meat and cold cuts, along with other food items (eggs, butter, poultry, fish, etc.), which were then delivered to stores.[11]

The fact that this type of "pre-Christmas campaign" was repeated later is demonstrated by the protocol from a conference attended by deputy directors of the Provincial Union of Meat Industry Enterprises for Production and Trade (Wojewódzkie Zjednoczenie Przedsiębiorstw Przemysłu Mięsnego ds. Produkcji i ds. Handlowych), which was held in Warsaw on 9 November 1965, and whose focus was "production and supply policy in November and December to secure the Christmas market supplies and other current production and trade matters."[12]

Guidelines were established for "economizing supplies for increased tasks involving Christmas provisioning." The idea was for Poles to be able to buy before Christmas (a holiday that is extremely important in the Polish national tradition) at least a greater number of higher quality meats and cold cuts. Recommendations were for, among other things, "the allocation of whole ham and shoulders from the last ten days of November and the first half of December, and about 50 % of the ham supply from 10–15 December, to be use for smoked meats." At the same time, "in order to create an atmosphere of a fully saturated market" it was recommended that the following be delivered to a network of butchers: "hams with bone as of 5 December; smoked hams and shoulders without bones – as of 10 December; cooked hams and shoulders – as of 16 December." High demand for hotdogs "should be satisfied by producing as much as the supply of intestine skins will allow." Shortages were to be supplemented by the largest possible deliveries of "pork sausages, hotdogs and breakfast sausages." The demand for white sausage "should be satisfied by deliveries over the course of four days before Christmas and four days before New Year."

11 Michał Jastrząb, *Puste półki. Problem zaopatrzenia ludności w artykuły powszechnego użytku w Polsce w latach 1949–1956* (Warszawa: Wydawnictwo Szkoły Przedsiębiorczości i Zarządzania im. Leona Koźmińskiego, 2004), 274–275.

12 AAN, Ministerstwo Przemysłu Spożywczego i Skupu [hereafter cited as MPSS], 1/209, pp. 10–11.

Even in the abundant year of 1974, information provided by the Minister of Internal Commerce and Services presented at a meeting of the Politburo "on supplying people and about work in trade during the pre-Christmas period" stated that the supply of poultry was full ("local turkey and geese shortages have occurred"), and that supplies of beef, pork, offal and popular types of cold cuts were "sufficient," but there was a shortage of "higher quality cold cuts and meats" (which were especially sought after!) and a severe lack of herring (especially on the rural market). The Minister boasted that an "influx of an appropriate number of employees was organized to improve consumer services. Retired people, family members, and above all students from higher grades in schools were employed and were preparing for trade and services." Work taking inventory was suspended for the pre-Christmas season, as were shop renovations. Shops that stayed open on 15 and 22 December were hailed as a success and example of self-sacrifice. It is worth remembering, however, that this state of relative satisfaction of needs was achieved even at this time thanks to the fact that about 45 % of the monthly "meat accumulation" was allocated for the pre-holiday period.[13]

Two years later, on 9 December 1976, by which time difficulties tied to provisioning had gotten significantly worse, the Politburo, having received the relevant information, recommended "strict compliance with the guidelines for the distribution of foodstuffs," which meant that the market supply during the pre-Christmas period should be "at such a level so as not to deviate too much from the level expected for the first quarter of next year, especially for those articles whose shortage will be felt over the longer term.[14] Polish authorities were clearly concerned that social dissatisfaction with food shortages, pacified in the period before Christmas, might "accumulate over time" and might not explode thereafter. This fear was particularly great given the memorable events of June 1976.[15] Most likely for this reason, fearing the outbreak of social discontent, he

---

13 AAN, KC PZPR, mikrofilm 2903 [dawna sygnatura 1782], Informacja Ministra Handlu Wewnętrznego i Usług E. Sznajdera o zaopatrzeniu ludności i pracy handlu w okresie przedświątecznym, Warszawa, 28 grudnia 1974, p. 19.

14 AAN, KC PZPR, mikrofilm 2908 [dawna sygnatura 1794], Protokół nr 45 z posiedzenia Biura Politycznego w dniu 9 grudnia 1976 r., p. 367.

15 In June 1976, the Polish authorities attempted to raise the prices of basic food products, including meat. In response, street demonstrations took place in many cities (the largest in Radom, Płock and Ursus just outside of Warsaw). The authorities retreated from these prices rises and took repressive measures against the protest participants. The so-called June Events led to the emergence of one of the most important political opposition organizations in the PRL – the Workers' Defense Committee (Komitet

Politburo, at a meeting on 21 December 1976, discussed once again the question of supplying the internal market in the first quarter of 1977, and decided to purchase imported market goods for PLZ[16] 402 million, of which PLZ 332 million would be for foodstuffs. Participants emphasized that the supply of fats, meat and poultry was of the utmost importance within the cost limits set for this purpose.[17]

This pattern of thinking, as if in some kind of campaign, and such attempts to improve the social mood before what Polish authorities viewed as "dangerous" or important in terms of propaganda, required that stores be better supplied with meat and sausages before the next pseudo-elections, that such foodstuffs be "throwing" onto the market during important national holidays (especially May Day), etc. Such behaviors led to the conviction that, for the price of better provisioning, Polish leaders could "buy" increased social peace.

The fact that there was always too little meat, and that – for doctrinal reasons – there could be no change in the rules that governed the shortage economy, does not tell us that Polish authorities had no methods at their disposal to deal with meat shortages. The means used to solve this problem can be divided into three basic groups: increasing the supply of meat, limiting the demand for meat, and punishing those who had committed fraud in its production, processing and distribution.

1. Increasing Supply

Methods to increase supply underwent numerous changes. Their milder version consisted primarily in creating conditions for the development of agricultural production[18] and of the food industry. As elements in this process, one can point to the gradual departure from the system marked by the compulsory supply of

---

Obrony Robotników, KOR). For more, see Paweł Sasanka, *Czerwiec 1976. Geneza przebieg konsekwencje* (Warszawa: Instytut Pamięci Narodowej, 2006).

16 PLZ – the official currency of the Polish People's Republic (PRL), changed to PLN after redenomination in 1995. A common term for both is "zloty."

17 Ibid., Protokół nr 46 posiedzenia Biura Politycznego w dniu 21 grudnia 1976 r., p. 428; Ibid., Informacja o przewidywanej sytuacji pieniężno-rynkowej i dostawach towarów w I kwartale 1977 r., p. 431–436.

18 We write more about these matters below. At this point, it is worth explaining that the system of compulsory deliveries (which, starting in the years 1951–1952, encompassed animals for slaughter, grains, potatoes and milk) involved the state forcing peasants to sell part of their agricultural production at reduced prices. Supply quotas were constructed in such a way that a disproportionately large part of that production was to be delivered by the largest farms, run by what were called (using Soviet terminology)

agricultural products, including livestock (from 1972), periodic increases in prices tied to pig and cattle contracting, and importation of the means for agricultural production and meat. This last instrument was used particularly often in the seventies. On 15 February 1971, the Politburo decided to ask the Soviet leadership for a loan for the import of food, and in particular meat, at a value US $ 100 million.[19] In February 1971, the Politburo decided to import 160–165 thousand tons of pork.[20]

The import of meat was particularly large (in kg per capita) in 1971 – 4.6 kg; in 1977 – 3.1 kg; and in 1978 – 1.6 kg. The collapse of livestock production from 1981 meant that imports were increased to 5.1 kg to meet regulatory needs. The crisis years of the 1980s influenced the reduction of meat exports; if in 1975 it constituted 8 % of domestic production; in 1980 – 6 %; and then later – around 4 %.[21]

An important instrument for increasing meat production was feed import, which was especially large in the 1970s. It is estimated that while between 16–19 % of meat production in 1971–1975 was based on imported feed, that value was 24–28 % in the period 1976–1980. In the years 1982–1986, as a result of limitations in foreign exchange, that value decreased to 9 %.[22]

In cases where, for macroeconomic or political reasons, the above-indicated methods for increasing the meat supply proved to be ineffective, an increasingly important role was played by other, rather bizarre ways to most rationally manage inadequate – as they put it in official documents – "meat accumulation," which found frequent expression in attempts to maneuver around whatever meats and cold cuts were available in various ways, including through the creation of new recipes for these products.

Central authorities came up with an original idea in 1964. At a meeting held on 13 January of that year, the Politburo discussed a note presented by the Central Committee's Economic Department. The plan was to economize in the consumption of meat intended for the production of some cured meat products

---

"kulaks." Such a system served to destroy these farms, which during the Stalinist period were treated as the largest "internal enemy" in the countryside.

19 AAN, KC PZPR mikrofilm 2914 [dawna sygnatura 1745], Protokół nr 35 posiedzenia Biura Politycznego i Prezydium Rządu w dniu 15 lutego 1971 r., p. 658.

20 Ibid., Protokół nr 39 posiedzenia Biura Politycznego w dniu 9 marca 1971 r., p. 831.

21 Bożena Gulbicka, Wanda Sztarbałło, Barbara Chmielewska, Aleksandra Dyka, *Samowystarczalność żywnościowa Polski* (Warszawa: Instytut Ekonomiki Rolnictwa i Gospodarki Żywnościowej, 1990), 48.

22 Ibid., 49.

by introducing the soy into the ingredients. Research had found that attempts to produce some types of sausages, in which "10 % of the class II and III pork meat was replaced by soy brought positive results. In addition to the savings that came with replacing the more expensive raw material (pork) with cheaper raw material (soy), the process achieved a 15 to 30 % higher yield of the finished product." Estimated savings came to about PLZ 147 million per year. Officials advised the introduction of 2 or 3 new kinds of sausages with soy additives, whose price would be symbolically lower. Introduction of these sausages was to take place "on an experimental basis" – i.e. in select localities at first so that "public opinion" could be gauged. "Caution is necessary because we have not produced soy sausage before." In addition, officials pointed out that it was necessary to extend to another four kinds of sausages the policy to overcome shortages of pork with beef. This policy had already been applied in 30 types of cold cuts, with the total now reaching 40.[23] Immediate implementation of these plans turned out to be difficult because the National Economic Plan for 1964 did not call for soy imports, but the discussion of such ideas suggests that authorities of that time were searching desperately for ways to increase the supply of cold cuts for Polish consumers.

Officials entertained similar ideas before[24] and after that time. In the 1970s, officials gave a great deal of thought to methods – as they put it – to narrow the "sausage sales front" formed by consumers.[25] The idea of "increasing meat accumulation" was largely effective in the development of poultry production in large farms, built on the basis of Western loans and licenses. At the beginning of 1975, the Politburo decided that, in the next five-year plan, an at least 1 kg increase in meat consumption per capita/per year would be covered by the increase in poultry production.[26] As a result of these activities, an increase in per capita meat consumption of 21 kg was achieved in 1980 in large part due to a greater (by

23 AAN, KC PZPR, V/77 [mikrofilm 2894], Załącznik do protokołu nr 92. Notatka w sprawie zmian zaopatrzenia rynku w mięso i wyroby mięsne, Wydział Ekonomiczny KC, 16 grudnia 1963, p. 78.

24 In 1949, the relevant authorities decided that cold cuts should not contain more than 25 % of meat. Jastrząb, *Puste półki,* 131.

25 AAN, KC PZPR, mikrofilm 2918 [dawna sygnatura 1749], Informacja Ministerstwa Handlu Wewnętrznego o przewidywanym zaopatrzeniu rynku wewnętrznego w okresie wrzesień – grudzień 1971, Warszawa 14 września 1971, pp. 156–157.

26 AAN, KC PZPR, mikrofilm 2903 [dawna sygnatura 1782], Protokół nr 143 z posiedzenia Biura Politycznego w dniu 28 stycznia 1975 r.

7.7 kg) consumption of mainly broilers (poultry intensively fattened) produced using industrial methods and with imported feed.[27]

It was also in the 1970s that the highest party authorities recommended the Ministry of Agriculture and the MPSiS, among others, further increases in meat processed with "added protein substitutes," the acceleration of work on the "introduction of new technologies for obtaining meat substitutes," and consideration of the purchase in the U.S. of a "complete soy protein production plant."[28] In addition, authorities ordered officials to economize the management of "meat based resources."[29] A similar set of proposed actions also appeared in documents issued in the 1980s by the MHWiU.[30]

According to the recommendations made by state authorities, large enterprises decided to carry out animal husbandry in the context of side deals, which they viewed as an opportunity to improve the supply situation for their employees. From the 1940s, factory managers, with the full participation of trade unions, created workplace canteens (buffets) and factory shops (cooperatives) with food products (including meat and meat products).[31]

Similar solutions were used by the Employee Holiday Fund (Fundusz Wczasów Pracowniczych, FWP) – an institution operating within trade union structures which, in the first half of the 1950s, held a monopoly over so-called organized recreation. From 1950, Fund centers maintained a network of pig farms. There were such farms at 12 centers at the beginning of 1951, and at every center by the end of that year. Although the report materials indicate we should be cautious

---

27 Gulbicka, Sztarbałło, Chmielewska, Dyka, *Samowystarczalność żywnościowa,* 46.

28 AAN, KC PZPR, mikrofilm 2903 [dawna sygnatura 1782], Protokół nr 143 z posiedzenia Biura Politycznego w dniu 28 stycznia 1975 r.

29 AAN, KC PZPR, mikrofilm 2905 [dawna sygnatura 1786], Kompleksowy program racjonalizacji spożycia żywności z uwzględnieniem form oddziaływania na konsumenta do 1980 roku, MHWiU, Warszawa wrzesień 1975, p. 383.

30 AAN, Ministerstwo Handlu Wewnętrznego i Usług [hereafter cited as MHWiU], 10/8, Warunki odejścia od reglamentowanej sprzedaży mięsa i jego przetworów, Warszawa, czerwiec 1987, Ministerstwo Handlu Wewnętrznego i Usług, pp. 1–2.

31 See Jan Naumiuk, *Na początku trudnej drogi. Ruch zawodowy w Polsce Ludowej w latach 1944–1949* (Kielce: Wydawnictwo Łódzkie, 1985), 199; Aleksander Kochański, *Polska 1944–1991. Informator* historyczny, vol. 2 (Warszawa: Wydawnictwo Sejmowe, 2000), 473, 560.

about their economic effects, these farms undoubtedly played a positive role in diversifying the holiday menu.[32]

Interestingly, this idea was used again in a later period and served as a recommendation from central authorities to combat meat shortages, a fact that is evidenced by the minutes of a meeting of the Politburo held on 19 October 1977. During discussions on the subject of the organization of workers' rest, participants in that meeting postulated that "all larger work establishments run their own breeding farms, supplying meat to, among other place, company holiday locales."[33] This idea that enterprises would run breeding farms was, at that time, one of several ideas for overcoming difficulties tied to food supplies recommended by the Politburo shortly after the workers' violent demonstrations in June 1976.[34]

However, authorities did not always limit themselves to mild and low-risk methods when they wanted to increase meat supplies during food shortages. In the Stalinist period, they employed more drastic, extortive means (with varying degrees of success) to increase meat production. As the war was coming to an end, in August 1944, the new authorities in Poland introduced compulsory deliveries of in-kind provisions, which were lower than the wartime quotas enforced by the German occupier, but their implementation caused a great deal of trouble. Problems stemmed, on the one hand, from economic exhaustion on peasant farms and, on the other hand, from reluctance on the part of peasants to fulfill the government's demands. According to data from the Ministry of Provisions in the fiscal year of 1944/45, the government's demand for grains amounted to 1,131,891 tons, but only 700,109 tons was delivered. Meat deliveries in this period amounted to 101,450 tons, the demand being 102,334 tons.[35] In the 1945/46 fiscal year, meat deliveries amounted to just over 10,000, while their demand was over 95,000 tons. Under the resolution of the Council of Ministers

---

32 Archiwum Ruchu Zawodowego [hereafter cited as ARZ], Centralna Rada Związków Zawodowych [hereafter cited as CRZZ] Sekretariat Z. Wasilkowskiej, 28, Protokół z analizy bilansu zbiorczego Funduszu Wczasów Pracowniczych za rok 1953 r., pp. 21–23.

33 AAN, KC PZPR, mikrofilm 2911 [dawna sygnatura 1801], Protokół nr 80 z posiedzenia BP 19 października 1977, p. 299.

34 E. Gierek spoke about this topic during a meeting with journalists on 7 October 1976. See AAN, KC PZPR, XIA/439, Stenogram ze spotkania z dziennikarzami w dniu 7 października 1976, p. 3.

35 AAN, Ministerstwo Aprowizacji [hereafter cited as MA], 202, Wymiar i realizacja świadczeń rzeczowych w roku gospodarczym 1944/45 (dane uzgodnione z Wydziałem Świadczeń Rzeczowych), p. 1.

passed on 6 June 1946, these compulsory deliveries were ended, effective on 1 July of the same year, but shortages continued to pile up; on 28 February 1948, they amounted to 11,649 tons of grain and 750 tons of meat.[36]

After a period of relative improvement in supplies in 1946–1949, the model of economic development adopted in the next year, which favored the development of heavy industry, meant an increased burden for farms. At the same time, the implementation of a new policy toward the village, which consisted of forced collectivization and limits on the production capacity of private large-scale farms, resulted in increasing provision difficulties. In response, officials (in 1951–1952) introduced a system of mandatory supplies of potatoes, milk, cereals, and slaughter animals. In practice, this meant farms were drained of produce.[37] In the modern "peasant war" flared up over mandatory deliveries, nearly 0.5 million peasants were punished (mainly fines) in the years 1953–1955, of which over 115,000 were punished for failure to deliver live cattle.[38] In later years, the scale of repression in this respect was incomparably smaller in the village, but the system in its basic version (which included potatoes, grains and livestock) remained in effect throughout the entire period of Władysław Gomułka's rule[39] as the method used – alongside contracting – to secure food supplies in the PRL.[40]

2. Reducing Demand

In view of the constant shortage of meat, a variety of methods to reduce demand were applied in a way that complemented along with methods applied to increase its supply. When economic conditions were relatively good, the mildest method of achieving this goal was to stimulate consumption of products other than those based on meat and of industrial goods.

In the "classic" version, the search (largely unsuccessful) for what was usually referred to as the "mythical balance of goods and money" took place in the

---

36 Ibid., Przebieg świadczeń rzeczowych w latach gospodarczych 1945/46 i 1946/47, p. 8.

37 Stefan Felbur, *Analiza układu cen produktów rolnych w Polsce* (Warszawa: Państwowe wydawnictwo Naukowe, 1962), 75, tab. 17.

38 Dariusz Jarosz, *Polityka władz komunistycznych w Polsce w latach 1948–1956 a chłopi* (Warszawa: Wydawnictwo DiG, 1998), 228–231. W 1950 r. liczba gospodarstw chłopskich w Polsce jest szacowana na ok. 3,1 mln.

39 Władysław Gomułka (1905–1982) became the First Secretary of the KC PZPR in October 1956 and was forced to resign in December 1970, after the bloody suppression of the workers' rebellion on the Polish Coast.

40 Mandatory milk deliveries were abolished in 1957, and those of cereals, potatoes and slaughtered animals in 1971.

1970s. The decision taken in February 1971 to withdraw the price increases implemented in December 1970,[41] and to increase the lowest wages, family benefits, and pensions, resulted in – as the Komisja Planowania przy Radzie Ministrów (Planning Commission of the Council of Ministers_ predicted in March 1971 – increased purchasing power for the broader population by about PLZ 20 billion. Because this improvement in income went largely to the lowest earners, Polish authorities rightly counted on the fact that the increased purchasing power would be directed mainly at the purchase of meat and fats.[42] According to the findings of the MHW in September 1971, the actual average increase in personal income amounted to 9 % in the first half of that year. The ministry predicted that for all of 1971, income would be by an amount greater than PLZ 8 billion. more than amount assumed by the revised plan, and it would 9.1 % higher than the average income in 1970. In this situation, at its meetings on 16 July, 20 August, and 6 September, the Council of Ministers, seeking to provide consumers additional purchasing power, ordered all ministries and heads of the Provincial National Councils (state bodies at the local level) to increase the supply of goods to the market.[43] In connection with this, an accelerated search for possibilities to sell industrial goods began, the supply of which was sufficient at the time and could be increased. For this purpose, in 1972, "cooperation between wholesale and retail entities was improved." Officials responsible for interior trade wrote with clear pride about the supply of these goods beyond working hours to the "retail network." The authors pointed to the development of "non-store sales" – that is, sales taking place at workplaces and fairs, and door-to-door sales (mainly in rural areas, especially on market days, fairs) and the establishment of additional sales stands. It was at this time that so-called "collective

41 The so-called December events in Poland involved the bloody suppression of a workers' rebellion on the Polish Coast, initiated by strikes in Gdańsk and Gdynia. Their direct cause was the increase in the prices of basic food products, which was announced on 12 December 1970. As a result of clashes with the army and the militia, over 41 people died and more than 1,100 were injured. The new party-state authorities, headed by Edward Gierek, initially did not want to retreat from the price increases introduced in December. They did so only in February 1971, under the influence of a new strike wave, which included textile factories in Łódź.

42 AAN, KC PZPR, mikrofilm 2914 [dawna sygnatura 1745], Notatka opracowana w Komisji Planowania przy Radzie Ministrów w sprawie zaopatrzenia rynku w mięso i tłuszcze oraz inne artykuły spożywcze w 1971 r.

43 AAN, KC PZPR, mikrofilm 2918 [dawna sygnatura 1749], Informacja Ministerstwa Handlu Wewnętrznego o przewidywanym zaopatrzeniu rynku wewnętrznego w okresie wrzesień – grudzień 1971, Warszawa 14 września 1971.

purchases" were started for workplaces in cities and villages. The sale of TV sets began for residents of small towns, allowing the customer to check the set's operation and make a purchase decision within ten days (delivery and installation of the equipment at the buyer's home was free). Sales were expanded using the post office and via rural representatives, etc. In cities, television rental outlets appeared: on a contractual basis, the customer could use a TV set for a monthly subscription fee for half a year, after which he had to decide to return or purchase the set. In the latter case, monthly payments were deducted from the price. For advertising purposes, demonstrations of the use of mechanical equipment were organized along with lectures given by instructors in mass women's organizations (the Women's League, Household Committee), qualified sellers, etc. In the Furniture Trade Center stores, customer records and telephone delivery information were introduced, which – the claim was made – led to increased sales. As a result of these and similar activities (if one can believe official information on this topic), sales of refrigerators, radios, tape recorders and turntables also increased. The same objectives were served by extending the scope and forms of installment sales, which at that time included, among other items, refrigerators. In installments one could buy, among other things, automobiles, certain mopeds and motorcycles, coffee makers, fishing equipment, and telescopes.[44] This way of thinking played an important role in calculating the price and procedures for the sale of the most popular small-engine automobile – the Fiat 126p in 1972.[45] The decision to make a prepayment for such an automobile was often mentioned as one of several methods for combating the "emerging difficulties in supplying the market with certain articles" recommended by the Politburo at a meeting on 21 September 1971.[46] As a market balance was becoming increasingly difficult to maintain under these conditions, the state increased the prices of goods and services. For this reason, the Fiat 126p from 1976 could no longer be bought at

44 AAN, KC PZPR, mikrofilm 2929 [dawna sygnatura 1760], Informacja o środkach podejmowanych przez handel w roku 1972 dla aktywnego kształtowania sytuacji rynkowej, p. 101 ff.

45 AAN, KC PZPR, mikrofilm 2932 [dawna sygnatura 1763], "Założenia sprzedaży samochodów osobowych Polski Fiat 126 P," Warszawa 19 X 1972, Ministerstwo Finansów, p. 321. The Fiat 126 p was a small car produced in Poland under the license of the Italian concern. In order to buy it, one had to make an appropriate prepayment, which was registered in the so-called "car book." This requirement was an anti-inflationary procedure aimed at weakening pressures to purchase deficit food products.

46 AAN, KC PZPR, 1749 (mikrofilm 2918), Protokół nr 62 posiedzenia Biura Politycznego w dniu 21 września 1971, p. 103.

its initial price of PLZ 69,000, but rather at PLZ 87,000. At the same time, the cost to purchase of other car brands available on the Polish market at the time also increased.[47]

The shaping of a new consumption model was also served by changes in the scope of housing construction. Thanks to a decisive increase in construction (especially by cooperatives subordinate to the state) it was easier to find a flat. To secure such a flat, one had to gather an appropriate financial housing deposit, which officials increased, and which in turn was supposed to force people to set aside a larger portion of their income for this purpose using special housing ledgers.[48] Authorities expected to achieve the same goal by gradually implementing a project to significantly expand the sale of apartments using foreign currency.[49]

Another, relatively mild, and even persuasive, method for limiting the demand for meat, present in the thinking and actions of Polish authorities throughout the period of People's Poland involved propaganda designed to change the model of nutrition into one that was less meat-centered. Many times during discussions on food supply problems held by members of central decision-making bodies, Polish leaders focused on the wider implementation of – as they described it in relevant documents – "deepened meat production" and the promotion of rational forms of nutrition.[50] From this viewpoint, of particular interest is the discussion at the meeting of the Politburo on 30 September 1975 on a "comprehensive program of rationalization of food consumption, taking into account the impact on the consumer until 1980," presented by the Undersecretary of State at the MHWiU Edward Wiszniewski. The recommendation that came out of this meeting was "gastronomy and factory canteens consistently enforce compliance with orders to adopt more widely dishes made from eggs, milk, vegetables and fish, to increase the choice and variety of dishes that could be an alternative to traditional meat dishes, to study the recipe of dishes in terms of calorie content." On television and radio, let alone women's magazines, "one should consciously

47 AAN, KC PZPR, 1793 (mikrofilm 2908), Notatka w sprawie dwukierunkowych zmian cen detalicznych niektórych artykułów, Warszawa, 20 sierpnia 1976 r., p. 187.

48 AAN, KC PZPR, 1781 (mikrofilm 2902), Informacja o realizacji uchwały V Plenum KC PZPR w sprawie perspektywicznego programu mieszkaniowego, Warszawa, listopad 1974, p. 540.

49 AAN, KC PZPR, 1771 (mikrofilm 2940), Protokół nr 84 z posiedzenia Biura Politycznego w dniu 4 września 1973 r., p. 436.

50 See AAN, KC PZPR, 2902 (mikrofilm 2902), Protokół nr 127 z posiedzenia BP w dniu 3 września 1974, p. 49.

and thoughtfully 'create a fashion for various kinds of dishes that do not require meat.'" In addition, the decision was made to not promote the reduction of animal fats consumption on a wider scale, but to introduce onto the market flavored grades of lard in modern and appealing packaging.[51]

This tendency toward the more or less (depending on the historical period) "discrediting" of meat can be found in official documents[52] and cookbooks from this period. Quite clearly, this advice was tied to the problems involving food supplies.

The authors of a book on family nutrition published in 1948, Zofia Czerny and Maria Strasburger, in their descriptions of various types of foods, wrote that while milk and other dairy products were:

> [...] perfectly suited to replace meat, meat cannot take their place, because meat does not contain as many vitamins as milk, nor is it so rich in important minerals. So we see that milk and cheese are even higher-value foods than meat. The same can be said for eggs, which contain as much protein as meat, but are much richer in minerals and vitamins.

They admitted that meat is a filling food, that it has an "attractive taste and smell," but it should not be eaten in large quantities: "A small addition of meat perfectly complements those foods in which only the protein is lacking. This is the best way to use meat in homes and group households, because meat is the most useful for us not when we eat a large piece of roasted pork or cutlet, but when we add a small piece of meat to vegetable or flour-based dishes."[53]

In their next book, published in 1957, the same authors threw similar accusations against meat: its lack of certain vitamins and contained insufficient amounts of calcium. They claimed that the only meat products "rich in vitamins are offal – i.e. the internal organs of animals, such as the liver, kidneys, heart – and pork, which contains a lot of vitamin B1." Hence, the practical conclusions: "Eat meat, but not in excessive quantities, and let us not forget about the great value

---

51 AAN, KC PZPR, mikrofilm 1786 (2905), Protokół nr 172 z posiedzenia BP w dniu 30 września 1975, p. 375.

52 Andrzej Zawistowski argued (*Bilety do sklepu. Handel reglamentowany w PRL*, Warszawa: PWN, 2017, 107) that in 1951, the Ministry of Internal Trade issued circular letters regarding the restriction of the use of meat in the collective diet and its replacement by fruit, cheese and pasta.

53 Zofia Czerny, Maria Strasburger, *Żywienie rodziny. Wiadomości ogólne. Przepisy potraw* (Warszawa: Czytelnik, 1948), 21. Spełnieniem tych zaleceń były "przykładowe jadłospisy dla rodzin pracujących stołujących się w domu" zawarte w *Książce kucharskiej* Z. Czerny (Warszawa: Polskie Wydawnictwa Gospodarcze, 1954).

of offal. [. . .] A normal daily portion of meat should not exceed about 100 g, or 10 dkg."[54]

Authors of another book, published in 1959 under the title *Praktyczna kuchnia* (Practical kitchen), assessed the value of meat in a similar way, and they recommended especially the consumption of offal. One important novelty here was the "critical" evaluation of white meat, especially veal. The authors wrote that it was wrong to think that white meat is more valuable than "dark meat, for example beef." White meat has a finer texture, and thus more easily becomes tender during cooking. In terms of nutritional value, however, there are no differences. Boiled beef is just as valuable as boiled chicken or veal. Still, as they went on to observe in this book, "Overloading meals with meat dishes and eating large portions of meat at every meal is harmful to the body."[55]

We find a much wider set of arguments about the high value of meatless and half-meat dishes in Polish circumstances in a book by Zofia Zawistowska published 1965. As she wrote,

> [. . .] Meatless and partial-meat dishes have not been widely recognized and have not yet become popular. Especially in the culinary repertoire of housewives working professionally outside the home. And yet they deserve to take their proper place in our kitchen and receive their due recognition by the household members. To be sure, some of them are more labor-intensive, but they are usually cheaper than meat. And in the overall balance of the housewife's time, you can easily see the profit: The additional amount of work is compensated with interest, avoiding the loss of time standing in line. Cheaper types of meat can be obtained almost always. In many Polish families, a meal without meat is considered a low-level meal. Such a view is incorrect and does not correspond to reality. In the culinary repertoire of rich societies, a number of meatless dishes are among the most valued. The famous spaghetti with parmesan cheese or pizza are, for example, the most popular dishes in Italian cuisine.[56]

A similar conclusion can be found in the textbook *Modern Family Nutrition* from 1966: "The recommended daily portion of meat is not at all high. [. . .] Excess meat is not indicated for reasons that are not only economic but also health-related. To meet our body's needs, we do not need to buy the most expensive types of meat, cheaper versions are equally valuable, and sometimes even more

54 Czerny, Strasburger, *Gotuj smacznie i zdrowo* (Warszawa: Państwowy Zakład Wydawnictw Lekarskich, 1957), 48.

55 Maria Dudzik [et al.], *Praktyczna kuchnia* (Warszawa: Państwowe Wydawnictwo Rolnicze i Leśne, 1959), 25–26.

56 Zofia Zawistowska, *Potrawy bezmięsne i półmięsne* (Warszawa: Wydawnictwo Przemysłu Lekkiego i Spożywczego, 1965), 32.

valuable." In addition, the authors of this book advised readers that managing meat as a valuable but relatively expensive product would be reasonable. For this reason, they recommended that families separate the daily ration of meat into two or even three meals, and that they make greater use of half-meat dishes.[57]

In the period of "Gierek prosperity," this anti-propaganda surrounding meat was replaced by a more rational evaluation of meat's nutritional value. In *Kuchnia polska* (Polish Cuisine) from 1974, we read that:

> [...] meat is one of the highly valuable food products. It is a main source of protein characterized by high nutritional (biological) value, calorie content, digestibility, and fat content. [...] Meat as a typical protein product is very low in carbohydrates, therefore meat dishes must be supplemented with dishes prepared from products with a high carbohydrate content, such as flour, grains, sugar, and potatoes."[58]

The economic crisis of the 1980s influenced the way culinary guides treated meat. In a cookbook by Zawistowska and Małgorzata Krzyżanowska published in 1982, we read that Poles "still" treated "meat and fatty foods," animal fats, sweets, and sugar to be particularly attractive in their diet. "As a consequence, the frequency of twentieth-century civilizational diseases is increasing, such as obesity, atherosclerosis, tooth decay, cardiovascular deficiencies, diseases of the liver and the digestive system. We pay very dearly for the satiety we have achieved. The main and most important reason for this state of affairs is ignorance regarding proper nutrition."[59] This way of treating meat is confirmed by findings regarding the content of cookbooks published in the 1980s that were addressed to an individual reader. The author of these studies did not find among them independent publications devoted to the preparation of dishes from beef, pork, or poultry. At the time, many books appeared referring to the subject of meat, but mainly as a kind of "spectrum." The author writes that "these books include: *Białko nie tylko w mięsie* (Protein not only in meat) by Zofia Zawistowska, *Wartościowe potrawy bezmięsne* (Valuable meatless dishes) by Anna Kołłajs-Dołowy and Ewa Siemaszko," and *200 potraw półmięsnych* (200 half-meat dishes) by Jadwiga Celczycka. It is no coincidence that authors at the time also propagated rabbit

57 Feliksa Starzyńska, Zawistowska, *Nowoczesne żywienie rodziny* (Warszawa: Państwowy Zakład Wydawnictw Lekarskich, 1966), 140–141.

58 *Kuchnia polska* (Warszawa: Państwowe Wydawnictwo Ekonomiczne, 1974), 445–446.

59 Zawistowska, Krzyżanowska Małgorzata, *Książka kucharska* (Warszawa: Watra, 1982), 9.

and rabbit-meat dishes.[60] Researchers also detected this tendency in advice sections in the pages of contemporary magazines.[61]

The "savings" that came with the careful use of meat in the kitchen found expression in concrete culinary proposals. For example, in the most popular women's magazine *Przyjaciółka* in 1949, editors proposed the following set of lunches for the entire week:

> Sunday. Barley soup; stuffed cabbage with meat, potatoes. Monday. Vegetable soup; dumplings with cheese. Tuesday. Pumpkin soup with noodles; fried fish, potatoes. Wednesday. Pea soup with croutons dumplings with plum jam. Thursday. Red borscht with potatoes; groats, cabbage salad. Friday. Potato soup; Potato cutlets. Saturday. Cucumber soup; beets with potatoes.[62]

In other weekly proposals put forward by *Przyjaciółka*, meat as one of the ingredients in dishes appeared at most twice in the early fifties.[63] In the same magazine in the 1960s and 1970s, in a permanent column entitled "Obiady" (Lunches), meat as part of the weekly menu (obligatory also in the form of so-called half-meat dishes) occurred more often, even five times a week. However, printed recipes there were dominated by vegetable and half-meat dishes and the popularization of the cuisine of other countries.[64]

Obviously, these "gentle" methods of limiting demand did not always result in a socially acceptable improvement in meat supply. For this reason, these methods often co-existed with – or were overshadowed by – methods that can be conventionally called administrative-restrictive.

Among such measures, meatless days introduced in 1946 deserve attention. On 1 February of that year, pursuant to a decree issued by the Prime Minister, "serving and selling meat in any form except for poultry, fish, rabbit and venison" was prohibited on Tuesdays, Wednesdays and Thursdays in restaurants and other "gastronomical enterprise." On Fridays, Saturdays, Sundays and Mondays it was allowed to serve and sell meals containing a maximum of 200 grams of

---

60 Agnieszka Witkowska-Krych, "Coś z niczego, czyli przepisy kulinarne w dobie kryzysu. Analiza treści wybranych książek kucharskich wydanych w ostatniej dekadzie PRL," *Wyzwoleni, ale nie wolni. Studia z historii najnowszej* 2 (2015): 79.

61 See B. Bieniecka, "Kuchnia oszczędna (Zielone surówki zielone sałatki)," *Magazyn Rodzinny* 97 (1982): 35; Bieniecka, "Kuchnia oszczędna (Co z kilograma żeberek?)," *Magazyn Rodzinny* 103 (1982): 35; Bieniecka, "Kuchnia oszczędna (Co z łopatki?)," *Magazyn Rodzinny* 96 (1982): 35.

62 "Gotujemy," *Przyjaciółka* 8 (1949).

63 See *Przyjaciółka* 29 (1953), 33 (1953).

64 See *Przyjaciółka* 27 (1964), *Przyjaciółka* 4 (1974)

meat, though only one dish could be sold to each person. The number of dishes served with meat or meat products was limited to four, specified in the menu. On Tuesdays, Wednesdays, and Thursdays it was also forbidden to do any business with meat and meat products (except poultry, rabbit, fish, and wild game) in butcher shops, grocery stores, gastronomical enterprises in general, taverns, street stalls, etc.[65] In April 1946, this prohibition was further strengthened. In its new version, it was forbidden on Wednesdays, Thursdays, and Fridays to do any business in meat, meat products, and animal fats; in turn, it was allowed on the other days of the week to sell meat dishes with a maximum weight of 100 grams. Moreover, some punished three times for ignoring these rules faced losing their concession to run a business.[66] In July 1949, the Minister of Internal Trade softened these provisions slightly by allowing certain lower grade meats to be sold on non-meat days until 15 October 1949.[67] Meatless days were ended by late November 1949.[68]

The Gomułka team's invention in this respect was the so-called meatless Mondays, introduced by order of the Minister of Internal Trade dated 29 July 1959. On this day, the sale of meat dishes in restaurants and canteens was prohibited; only offal, headcheese, black pudding, pork fat and lard could be sold in stores.[69] In October 1959, during a period of extreme meat shortages, officials restricted the sale of meat from so-called farm slaughterhouses (i.e. those run by peasants on farms) on Mondays (this rule was repealed in June 1962).[70]

---

65 Rozporządzenie prezesa Rady Ministrów z dnia 1 lutego 1946 r. w sprawie spożycia potraw mięsnych w przedsiębiorstwach przemysłu gastronomicznego i gospodniego oraz ograniczenia obrotu handlowego mięsem i jego przetworami, pochodzącymi z uboju zwierząt rzeźnych, Dz. U. 1946, No. 9, Item 68.

66 Rozporządzenie prezesa Rady Ministrów z dnia 24 kwietnia 1946 r. w sprawie ograniczenia obrotu mięsem, jego przetworami oraz tłuszczami zwierzęcymi, Dz. U. No. 18, Item. 121.

67 Zarządzenie ministra handlu wewnętrznego z dnia 12 lipca 1949 r. w sprawie dopuszczenia niektórych rodzajów wędlin do obrotu w dni bezmięsne, Monitor Polski, No. A-48, Item 652. Jastrząb, *Puste półki*, 33–34.

68 Rozporządzenie Ministra Handlu Wewnętrznego z dnia 29 listopada 1949 r. w sprawie zniesienia dni bezmięsnych, Dziennik Ustaw 1950, No. 2, Item 5.

69 Kochański, *Polska 1944–1991. Informator historyczny*, vol. II, 174; Marcin Zaremba, *Społeczeństwo polskie lat sześćdziesiątych – między "małą stabilizacją" a "małą destabilizacją"* in *Oblicza Marca 1968*, eds. Konrad Rokicki, Sławomir Stępień (Warszawa: Instytut Pamięci Narodowej, 2004), 32.

70 Kochański, *Polska 1944–1991. Informator historyczny*, vol. II, 183.

Regulations of trade in meat, usually issued by the Ministry of Internal Trade, were a permanent part of demand control and were applied until the 1980s.[71]

A much more effective practice for limiting this demand was direct administrative rationing[72] of the supply of meat and meat products.

Such rationing after the Second World War was not peculiar to Poland. Indeed, rationing systems covering basic food products (most often involving bread, meat, cereal products, fats and sugar) were in force during the First and Second World Wars everywhere in Europe, as well as in the USA, and they were still quite common in the 1940s and early 1950s.[73] Rationing policies also existed in interwar Poland until the beginning of the 1920s and during the Second World War.[74]

Among other items, the ration card system covering meat was introduced through instructions issued by the Economic Bureau of the Presidium of the Polish National Liberation Committee (Polski Komitet Wyzwolenia Narodowego, PKWN)[75] dated 27 September 1944, and from 1 May 1945 to 1 January 1949 that system covered the entire country.[76] In 1946, the number of people using such a provisioning amounted to 9,689,000 (41 % of the total population of the country), and in 1947 it amounted to 4,262,400 (34 %).[77]

After this system was abolished, six types of fat vouchers were introduced in some parts of the country (finally abolished on 1 July 1950). In 1949, rationing was introduced ad hoc in particular voivodeships and only for a defined period of time.[78]

Rations cards for meat, meat products and fats appeared once again in August 1951. Employees of selected plants received them, decisions regarding which were made by the PZPR Voivodeship Committees. All in all, after the groups

---

71 Ibid., 186.

72 Zawistowski, *Bilety do sklepu,* 22–23; Jacek Kurczewski, *Umowa o kartki*, in *Umowa o kartki*, ed. J. Kurczewski (Warszawa: Trio, 2004), 213.

73 Zawistowski, *Bilety do sklepu,* 36–38.

74 Ibid., 42–45.

75 The PKWN is the first quasi-governmental body formed with Stalin's approval by Polish communists in July 1944. On 31 December 1944, it was renamed the Provisional Government.

76 Zdzisław Zblewski, *Leksykon PRL-u* (Kraków: ZNAK, 2001), 69; Zawistowski, *Bilety do sklepu*, 55.

77 AAN, MA, 202, Ludność korzystająca z zaopatrzenia kartkowego w roku 1946 i 1947, pp. 58 ff.

78 Zawistowski, *Bilety do sklepu,* 103; Jastrząb, *Puste półki,* 127–134.

entitled to collect them were expanded, so-called vouchers were used by approx.. 4.5 million out of a total of 5.3 million working Poles. The list of rationed goods also gradually increased (for instance, stockings, soap, detergents, sugar and sweets).[79] This rationing program was in force until 3 January 1953. It was ended on that day, and for to "effectively combat these kinds of crime, which are practiced by anti-social entities in order to earn illegal profits by exploiting consumer interests," officials issued a decree on the protection of purchasers' interests was soon passed. At the same time, as this program was ended, officials raised prices significantly.[80]

Decisions from 1953 basically closed the matter of rationing consumer goods for 23 years. During this period, officials around the country made sporadic and spontaneous attempts to ration goods, but they were opposed by central authorities.

Despite the difficulties the government faced in supplying meat to the market, the Gomułka team did not decide to implement a ration card system. Why? It seems that a member of the PUWP Central Committee Political Bureau, Stefan Jędrychowski, explained the reasons behind this position clearly during a conference 10 October 1959 attended by PZPR first secretaries and secretaries of the economic Voivodeship Committees, the issue being the meat price increase. Answering questions in this matter, he argued:

> First of all, the card system can be imagined as total rationing – i.e. with a total ban on trade in this article, and then a black market rises up, illegal instead of based on a free market – or as the existence of cards [. . .] parallel to the market, with the existence of a free market with higher prices than card prices. And then the price of these articles, the price of that part of the commodity mass that would be sold without cards, would have to go up far higher, the span would have to be far higher with all that it entails, and what would result is speculation, leaks, etc. In addition, the card system is a known system: it is a system that is constantly expanding, i.e. at the beginning there is a limited number of people entitled to cards, some groups are excluded etc. and then it is constantly expanding, there is still pressure to add new categories and then more. With the card system – as experience suggests – it is not possible to maintain a diverse assortment of goods, the system is disorganized and degenerates, because in the end only one type of good is sold using these cards. The card system is a type of project used during wartime or in warlike situations, and therefore, if it can be avoided, then it of course should not be started.[81]

79 Zawistowski, *Bilety do sklepu*, 111 ff; Jastrząb, *Puste półki*, 87 ff.

80 AAN, Ministerstwo Sprawiedliwości [hereafter cited as MS], 2147, Uzasadnienie do projektu dekretu o ochronie nabywców w obrocie handlowym, p. 45.

81 AAN, KC PZPR, 237/V/458, Narada I Sekretarzy i Sekretarzy Ekonomicznych w sprawie podwyżki cen mięsa w dniu 10 października 1959, p. 248 ff.

Under pressure, PRL authorities introduced sugar ration cards (in 1976), but they considered further expansion of meat rationing a bad option, one which was to be avoided despite the fact that, in September 1976, as many as 60 % of the people polled were in favor of such a solution.[82] Leaders at the center of power gave consideration to such a variant, but they rejected it, mainly because of an insufficient supply of meat and meat products on retail market, especially the best varieties (hams, sirloins, smoked hams), and also too large of a difference in supplies among voivodeships.[83] Reasons tied to the regimes image could not have been without significance; after all, expansion of the ration system meant PRL officials were admitting that the socialist system, built with great effort, could not solve the Polish people's basic problems.

In 1981, communist authorities in Poland were forced to admit that "the king had no clothes." Once again, and for the last time in the history of the PRL, the authorities introduced the rationing of meat and meat products – this time on the basis of a resolution of the Council of Ministers on 20 February 1981. And, despite numerous changes in coming years, this rationing program was ended only with the start of Poland's systemic transformation in 1989.[84]

A program introduced at the beginning of 1981 to ration meat and other food and industrial products was the result of the deteriorating "money-market situation," but this time it was not the authorities who had taken the initiative, but rather the striking workers of the Gdańsk Shipyard, who on the night of 16–17 August 1980 formulated in point 11 of their draft demands for the August Agreements: "Impose on the meat and food cards or vouchers (until the situation on the market was under control)."[85] The appropriate guidelines for the possibility of meat rationing were introduced into the August Agreement.[86] Their

82 Zawistowski, *Bilety do sklepu*, 193.

83 AAN, KC PZPR, XIA/535, Sytuacja na krajowym rynku mięsnym w roku 1976 i przewidywania na rok 1977, Warszawa, 20 VIII 1976, p. 23.

84 Małgorzata Fuszara, "Prawne aspekty reglamentacji," in *Umowa o kartki*, ed. Kurczewski (Warszawa: TRIO, 2004), 124–131.

85 Zawistowski, *Bilety do sklepu*, 189.

86 "August Agreements" is the name given to documents signed by state authorities and strike committees in Szczecin (30 August 1980), Gdańsk (31 August), in Jastrzębie-Zdrój (3 September) and Dąbrowa Górnicza (11 September). These agreements enabled the creation of independent, self-governing trade unions (in September they adopted the name "Solidarity") led by Lech Wałęsa. They marked the beginning of the so-called Solidarity carnival, which ended with the introduction of martial law in Poland (13 December 1981) and repression of trade union activists.

implementation was increasingly urgent, because the supply situation in Poland was deteriorating and authorities knew it. In one document on this subject, preserved in the files of the KC PZPR from the beginning of October 1980, we read that the fourth quarter of that year would be particularly difficult because, on the one hand, an accumulation of production losses and, on the other hand, an additional influx of money onto the market. Officials estimated the resulting supply gap in this quarter at around PLZ 50 billion. The food supply problem was expected to worsen as a result of disrupted supplies and the decrease in purchases, which in the case of milk and meat in the first decade of October 1981 was smaller than a year earlier by 10–15 %. This forced state authorities to import (for "emergency relief," both from capitalist and socialist countries) 1.5 billion tons of grain, 50,000 tons of meat, 20,000 tons animal fat, 3,000 tons of butter and 10,000 tons of fish and preserves. Despite this, food supplies on the market decreased by around 16 % since the beginning of the year, which meant that it was not possible to ensure the continuous sale of basic food products. What is worse, forecasts regarding the purchase of slaughtered animals for the next year indicated the possibility that meat supplies would continue to decline. This study's conclusion was unequivocal: "[. . .] we have no other choice but to introduce the rationing of meat and fat sales (card system)." Without rationing, "there is no chance of survival in the food market in 1981–1982."[87]

This tragic situation continued to worsen at the beginning of 1981. According to a special team under the leadership of First Deputy President of the National Bank of Poland, Stanisław Nieckarz, on the basis of PLZ 1000 of monetary income in the period January-February 1981, the value of supplies intended for market fell to the level of PLZ 793 compared to PLZ 910 a year before and PLZ 889 two years before. The average monthly wage in January and February 1981 amounted to PLZ 6,335, which meant it was 21 % (PLZ 1,103) higher than in the corresponding period of 1980. In February 1981, even more so than in previous months, there were difficulties in maintaining the continuity of sales of many goods, in particular such basic necessities as (beyond meat and meat products, which was assumed!) sugar, butter, milk, vegetable fats, cheese, potatoes, washing powders and soaps.[88]

87 AAN, KC PZPR, XI/504, Sytuacja pieniężno –rynkowa [październik 1980], p. 11 ff.

88 AAN, KC PZPR, XIB/484, Informacja Ministra Finansów dla członka Biura Politycznego KC Tadeusza Grabskiego o sytuacji pieniężno-rynkowej w okresie styczeń – luty 1981, Warszawa, 17 marca 1981. Opracował zespół pod kierownictwem I zastępcy Prezesa NBP Stanisława Nieckarza, aprobował Minister Finansów Marian Krzak, pp. 2–7.

On 1 April 1981, the rationed sale of meat and its products began, and soon after that many other food items.[89] All of this was preceded by regional and local rationing introduced by the authorities at lower levels before Christmas in 1980.[90] The decision to introduce a rationing program was adopted with the understanding that it came with disadvantages. Officials later considered canceling the program, but they decided against doing so despite the fact that – as they assessed the situation – the years 1984–1986 were marked by an improvement in the meat supply for market. In 1987, MHW estimated that ending the meat rationing system would entail an average price increase of 50–60 %. Officials abandoned this idea though they were fully aware of the negative effects of the current system, such as the cost of services (ration card printing, transport, distribution, etc.), barriers to rationalizing meat consumption (each of those entitled to receive cards had a predetermined quantity of meat and meat products regardless of the meat supply), exciting demand among groups of buyers who until then had not attempted to fulfill that demand, and the consolidation in some social groups of the view that only a rationing system can ensure safe levels of consumption and access to a commodity.[91]

The system of direct meat rationing is only the most expressive form of a wider, lasting method of administrative management of this commodity. This system consisted of regulating supplies using top-down criteria, including primarily (though not only) territorial criteria, related both to the character of the locality (the size of an urban center, a town, or a village) as well as its socio-professional structure. In other words, officials defined the possibilities for buying meat depending primarily on where the meat consumer lived, where he worked and what job he performed.

Already within the framework of the card system introduced in 1944, the largest group among the nearly 7 million people supplied with food in this way in February 1948 were state employees (1,027,000) and employees of state (or state managed) enterprises (4,340,000).[92] Already at that time, supply standards (including in meat) were higher in the so-called main cities (which, in February

---

89 Krystyna Świetlik, *Znaczenie reglamentacji w procesie racjonalizacji wyżywienia* (Warszawa: Instytut Ekonomiki Rolnictwa i Gospodarki Żywnościowej, 1991), 5–15.

90 Zawistowski, *Bilety do sklepu,* 308 ff.

91 AAN, MHWiU, 10/8, Warunki odejścia od reglamentowanej sprzedaży mięsa i jego przetworów, Warszawa, czerwiec 1987, Ministerstwo Handlu Wewnętrznego i Usług, pp. 1 ff.

92 AAN, MA, 202, Zestawienie wyników ankiety w sprawie podziału na grupy osób zaopatrywanych kartkowo według stanu z lutego 1948 r., pp. 124 ff.

1945, included Warsaw, Łódź, Poznań, Kraków, Katowice, Częstochowa, Bydgoszcz, Chorzów, Gdynia, Lublin, and Białystok) than in smaller cities and towns. Functionaries in the Citizens' Militia (Milicja Obywatelska, MO) and the Ministry of Public Security (Ministerstwo Bezpieczeństwa Publicznego, commonly abbreviated UB, meaning Department of Security [Urząd Bezpiecześtwa]) received separate and higher allocations.[93]

The ration program introduced in 1951 was particularly selective. The commission appointed by the KC PZPR in September 1951 to study how this program would function stated that, although it covered more than 2 million workers and white-collar workers in 290 cities and residential areas, it was not introduced at all in such large cities as Białystok, Olsztyn, and Koszalin. In Lublin, meat distribution was carried out on the basis of a list of names. In Szczecin, its sales were made through shops and kiosks, located in workers' quarters and on the outskirts of the city, or by transporting meat, sausages, and fats to workplaces. As a result of the introduction of such a system in Łódź and Warsaw, the number of employed people covered by the vouchers was estimated at 65–85 %; in the Kraków and Łódź Voivodeships – 34–42 % (i.e. 25 % of the total meat pool); and in less-industrialized voivodeships (in addition to those already mentioned, i.e. Białystok, Olsztyn, and Koszalin) – 15–30 %. The flaw here, as perceived by the authorities, was "injustice" through the division of employees of a given city into "privileged and unprivileged." In addition, the system did not include the allocation of benefits according to the number of family members. We read in the relevant document that "in some cities [. . .] employees in particular institutions were divided into blue-collar and white-collar workers, giving the first the right to provisions, and omitting the other." Use of a canteen could offer "certain privileges."[94]

The unquestionable priority throughout this period (and not only when direct administrative rationing was in effect) was the improved provision of large urban areas with a large number of workers at the expense of towns and villages and so-called green areas (which had the advantage of being agricultural). It is true that some documents created by those in power contain recommendations for a

93 Łukasz Kamiński, *Polacy wobec nowej rzeczywistości 1944–1948: formy pozainstytucjonalnego, żywiołowego oporu społecznego* (Toruń: Wydawnictwo Adam Marszałek, 2000), 143.

94 AAN, Państwowa Komisja Planowania Gospodarczego (hereafter cited as PKPG), 5478, Notatka Komisji powołanej przez Komitet Centralny PZPR dla spraw związanych z zaopatrzeniem bonowym w mięso i tłuszcze wieprzowe, złożona na ręce wicepremiera H. Minca w dniu 27 IX 1951 r., pp. 1 ff.

gradual reduction of these disparities. However, in a situation marked by permanent shortages, and especially given their cyclical aggravation, such a reduction was difficult to implement.[95] In 1976, sales of meat and meat products per capita were the largest in the Warsaw Voivodeship (96.5 kg), the Łódź Voivodeship (85.3 kg), and the Katowice Voivodeship (75.5 kg) – i.e. Poland's most important industrial centers at that time – and the smallest around Zamość (19.4 kg), Łomża (19.5 kg), and the Bialskopodlaskie region (21.9 kg), which were generally agricultural regions.[96] Information on meat deliveries (per capita in kg) in 1978, 1980 and 1985 indicates some changes in these proportions. Granted, the following voivodeships still held the highest positions: Warsaw (106.7 kg, 109.9 kg, 52.5 kg, respectively), Katowice (89.9 kg, 98.9 kg 51.6 kg) and Łódź (87.2 kg, 88.7 kg and 49.6 kg), and the lowest positions were held by Bialskopodlaskie (21.8 kg, 23.7 kg, 24.2 kg) and Łomża (19.2 kg, 21.2 kg and 23.1 kg), the fact is that the discrepancy in supply levels was small in 1985 than it had been in 1980.

Above all, what we see here is the effect of the rationing program for meat and meat products.[97] Detailed research, covering the years 1982–1987, showed that the tendency established by rationing, by which regional differences and privileges enjoyed by large urban centers (as a product of the rationing rules) were limited, was of a rather permanent nature. The voivodeships with the highest rates of market consumption of products with high nutritional value (meat, fish, milk) belonged to northern voivodeships (Koszalin, Szczecin, Olsztyn, Elbląg, Gdańsk). "Highly urbanized voivodeships, such as Katowice, Warsaw, Łódź, Wałbrzych, and Jelenia Góra – which, in the first half of the 1970s, were characterized by the highest living standards and at the same time a high quality daily diet – lost their position regarding both the level of market consumption and

95 See AAN, KC PZPR, 1745 (mikrofilm 2914), Protokół nr 39 posiedzenia Biura Politycznego w dniu 9 marca 1971 r., p. 831; AAN, KC PZPR, 1749 (mikrofilm 2918), Informacja Ministerstwa Handlu Wewnętrznego o przewidywanym zaopatrzeniu rynku wewnętrznego w okresie wrzesień – grudzień 1971, Warszawa 14 września 1971, p. 156; AAN, KC PZPR mikrofilm 2921, Ocena sytuacji rynkowej w końcu IV kwartału 1971 r. i przewidywanego zaopatrzenia rynku w I półroczu 1972, MHW, Warszawa styczeń 1972, p. 461; AAN, KC PZPR, 1768 (mikrofilm 2937), Protokół nr 69 z posiedzenia Biura Politycznego w dniu 17 kwietnia 1973, p. 12.

96 AAN, KC PZPR, XIA/535, Sytuacja na krajowym rynku mięsnym w roku 1976 i przewidywania na rok 1977, Warszawa, 20 VIII 1976, p. 23.

97 AAN, MHWiU, 10/8, Warunki odejścia od reglamentowanej sprzedaży mięsa i jego przetworów, Warszawa, czerwiec 1987, Ministerstwo Handlu Wewnętrznego i Usług, p. 27.

the satisfaction of their nutritional needs."[98] In the 1980s, agricultural provinces attained the top position in terms of food provisioning. Why? Because workers' households located there were able to beset fulfill the so-called defensive consumption model. In these agricultural regions, residents had a greater opportunity to supplement food market purchases by acquiring food on the open market, a situation that was quite different from that experienced by working families in large cities: Katowice, Warsaw, or Łódź, where the market had well-stocked with food products in the 1970s. In the 1980s, these cities failed to defend the high level of food consumption because they were more dependent than the agricultural regions on poor and unstable supplies of food to the city's stores.[99]

One matter that requires further study is the question when and to what extent officials considered ad hoc political reasons in the construction of this distribution list. It is known, for example, that between June and September 1981 a particularly large additional pool of meat, one that exceeded quantities tied to the rationed sale system by 1500–1800 tons, was directed to the Katowice Voivodeship. This move was – as we read in a note drawn up in the Ministry of Mining and Energy (Ministerstwa Górnictwa i Energetyki) – an element of the social-living standard "package" aimed at improving the overall mood in mining region of Silesia. Considering the fact that, in 1981, those working in the coal mining industry lost their housing preferences for the first time in the postwar period, fears for social unrest in this region seemed fully justified.[100] This way of "extinguishing" the actual or expected social unrest by "throwing in" extra amounts of meat was used quite widely.

Needless to say, the most socially troublesome method used to limit the demand for meat was the price rise. This matter has been addressed in a wide body of historical and economic literature. At this point, it is only worth noting that this propensity to raise food prices (introduced in 1953, 1959, 1967, 1970, 1976, 1980, and 1982), motivated by the desire on the part of the government to balance supply and demand, caused great social tensions mainly because food expenses played an important role in the Polish family's budget. But price increases, to the extent that they could be carried out, led only to a temporary restoration of the supply-demand balance, which was mainly the case in 1959

98 Elżbieta Lorek, *Zmiany w strukturze konsumpcji w Polsce w układzie przestrzennym* (Katowice: Akademia Ekonomiczna, 1993), 187.

99 Ibid., 188 ff.

100 AAN, KC PZPR, XIC/33, Ministerstwo Górnictwa i Energetyki, Sprawy socjalno-bytowe w przemyśle węgla kamiennego, Warszawa wrzesień 1981, p. 7.

and in February 1982. This second increase (officials increased food prices on average 340–350 %!) allowed the government to withdraw from the rationing of most of them (with the exception of meat and some confectionery and dairy products).[101]

After the experiences of December 1970 and June 1976, when price increases for basic food products were one of the most important causes of mass social unrest, the tendency to use this tool to restore market equilibrium decreased, despite the fact that its necessity became more and more obvious. This fact is evidenced by, among other things, a report put together by a special party team and presented at a Politburo meeting on 13 December 1977, whose focus was the development of pricing policy principles for basic foodstuffs. The authors of this document stated that prices have not changed for several years, and took note of the fact that the last price increases for meat, meat products and pork fat had been introduced in 1967. Rapeseed oil prices in force in 1978 had gone unchanged since 1953; some varieties of flour and groats – since 1955; and the price of basic types of bread – Mazovian, which constituted more than half of the general supplies of this article – had been in force since 1964; and in the case of sugar, the price had even gone down, from PLZ 15 in 1953 to PLZ 12 in 1954 and PLZ 10,50 in 1967. All of which made these articles cheaper in relation to other goods, which did not support the government's desired changes in the consumption structure, and which led to the detachment of basic foodstuff prices from the costs of their production. As calculated, each increase in the income of the population by 1 % then resulted in an increase in demand for food by 0.6 %, and demand for meat and its products by 0.8 %. Poles wanted to spend on food, indeed increasingly on meat, but they could not spend sufficiently because of insufficient supply.

The authors of the report wrote that, in the years 1971–1973, the rapid increase in incomes was accompanied by a rapid increase in food consumption based on personal income. In 1975, the growth of animal production was stopped. Officials estimated that, at the beginning of 1978, subsidies for PLZ 1 spent on the purchase of meat products amounted to over PLZ 0,70. Granted, subsidy systems employed for the production of food were common throughout the world, but officials in Poland used them in conditions marked by a gross detachment from production costs. Authors of the above-cited document expressed the essence of

101 Czesław Bywalec, *Wzrost gospodarczy a poziom życia społeczeństwa polskiego* (Warszawa: Instytut rynku Wewnętrznego i Konsumpcji, 1991), 87–88; Świetlik, *Znaczenie reglamentacji*, 9.

the Polish problem regarding food prices in the conclusion of their report. They found that a major part of society

> [. . .] is particularly sensitive to the problem of basic food prices. In its understanding, this is not only an economic and social problem but also a political one. Therefore, any decisions regarding this problem must be accompanied by the necessary political conditions.

For this reason, when constructing the policy to shape food product prices, "economic reasons require confrontation with social and political reasons, which together tend to maintain these prices for some time at the current level."[102] The final conclusion was a clear expression of the philosophy behind policies pursued by the ruling Gierek team.

The failure to make difficult economic decisions in the face of the expected social conflict led to increased food shortages. Escaping these difficulties by making unpopular decisions about price increases for some meat and cold cuts was one of the reasons for the strikes in July and August 1980[103] and for the emergence of Solidarity. The new political team, led by Wojciech Jaruzelski, drastic increased food prices in the social and political conditions created by martial law (introduced on 13 December 1981), when possibilities for social protest against these decisions were significantly limited. Nevertheless, food subsidies in the late 1980s consumed about 30 % of the state budget. In mid-1989, in order to maintain cold cut prices, they were subsidized by 211.4 %; pork by 220.7 %; and beef by 276.8 %.[104] In this way, Polish authorities bought social peace, though as it turned out – unsuccessfully. The raison d'être of the economy was usually difficult to reconcile with the rationale felt by a large part of society.

3. Punishment: The Wawrzecki Case and More

As we attempted to show above, methods used to increase supply and limit demand for meat proved to be ineffective and politically costly and dangerous for the government. In order to channel social dissatisfaction, officials used another strategy, one which involved punishing those whom they considered perpetrators of economic fraud in the "meat industry," who would become

---

102 AAN, KC PZPR, 1802 (mikrofilm 2912), Protokół nr 85 z posiedzenia BP w dniu 13 grudnia 1977 r. Sprawozdanie z prac partyjno- rządowych zespołów problemowych powołanych przez IV plenum KC PZPR, Warszawa styczeń 1978, p. 210.

103 Jerzy Holzer, *"Solidarność" 1980–1981. Geneza i historia* (Paryż: Instytut Literacki, 1984), 89.

104 Kochanowski, *Tylnymi drzwiami*, 163.

scapegoats as the government sought the causes of food supply shortages but was unwilling to admit that the main cause was "real socialism's" inefficient economic system. The most notable example of this method was the Warsaw meat scandal. However, before we try to present the details of this case, we need to describe its broader context. In order to better understand the case, it is worth considering the role that corruption and economic fraud played in the economy of the PRL.

3.1. Historical Context: Corruption and Economic Fraud in the PRL

Corruption, bribery and theft of state property were manifestations of the social pathology that characterized Poland even in the very early postwar period. State authorities at the time recognized that the battle against the above problems using existing legal instruments was ineffective. For this reason, by virtue of a decree of 16 November 1945, the Special Commission to Battle Fraud and Economic Sabotage (Komisja Specjalna do Walki z Nadużyciami i Szkodnictwem Gospodarczym, KS) was created. We read in article 1 that this new institution was established to "detect and prosecute crimes affecting the State's economic and social interests, in particular: misappropriation, plunder of property belonging to the public and under public administration, corruption, bribery, speculation and so-called looting."[105] The scope of this commission's activities increased significantly after 1947 in connection with the so-called battle over trade.[106] Until 1950, the Commission had powers to find and investigate crimes. After that, its functions were limited to adjudicating matters at the request of the prosecutor, who also managed the execution of these judgments.[107] The fact that the Special

105 Dekret z 16 listopada 1945 r. o utworzeniu i zakresie działania Komisji Specjalnej do Walki z Nadużyciami i Szkodnictwem Gospodarczym, Dz. U. No. 53, Item 302.

106 The "battle over trade," started in April 1947, meant the destruction of private shops and wholesalers and their replacement by a state network. Specially established committees set obligatory prices and margins in trade. The private sector was also affected by the system in which concessions were increasingly difficult and expensive to obtain. State-owned wholesalers were supervised by a growing bureaucracy. The Public Department Stores (Powszechne Domy Towarowe, PDT), as standard socialist trade outlets, were to become the "new" symbol of trade. Private shops, destroyed by intentional fiscal policy, decreased number. In 1950, there were 43,388 of them (including stalls and so-called mobile sales points); in 1951 – 31,999; in 1953 – 16,544 and in 1955 – 14,059. See: Janusz Kaliński, *Bitwa o handel 1947–1948* (Warszawa: Książka i Wiedza, 1971).

107 *Komisja Specjalna do Walki z Nadużyciami i Szkodnictwem Gospodarczym (1945–1954). Wybór źródeł*, ed. and intro. Jarosz, Tadeusz Wolsza (Warszawa: Główna Komisja

Commission's activities within its specified powers was quite intense is demonstrated by the number of judgments referring to a labor camp (Table 1).

As the below data indicates, Polish officials used punishment in a labor camp most often to combat speculation, clerical crimes (bribery) and actions against monopolies. In total, those sent to labor camps through KS rulings number about 90,000. It is worth remembering, however, that this institution and its regional delegations also used fines as an additional and basic punishment. According to what is admittedly incomplete data, the number of people who received fines in 1947 was around 21,890; in 1948 – 44,865; in 1949 – 3,223; in 1951 – 30,377; in 1952 – 50,608; in 1953 – 34,624; in 1954 – 13,119. Beyond, in 1945–1949 in almost 10,000 cases, Commission authorities issued a decision forcing the accused to forfeit property.[108]

As the data cited below shows, not all crimes that the commission prosecuted can be classified as corruption or economic fraud, categories that did not cover, for example, so-called hostile propaganda ("whispering" – that is, the expression of opinions critical of state authorities and their policies, including in private conversations), which the Commission prosecuted after 1950 as an action aimed at "provoking panic in order to harm the interests of the working masses." "Hooliganism" can also not be included under these categories. Beyond that, the Commission was a flexible element in steering economic life in Poland through its ability to adjust both the scale and severity of repression to the current needs of policy makers. Quite apart from the politicization and clear abuse of the law, the Commission rulings indicate that economic crimes were a widespread phenomenon in Poland in 1945–1954.

At the end of the 1940s, the Commission dealt with at least a few cases whose importance, due to the scale of the fraud involved, should be considered particularly large.

In the years 1948–1949, one subject of interest to the Commission involved fraud in the trade of rationed coal. In 1945–1948 employees of the Central Production Office of Coal Products (Centrala Zbytu Produktów Przemysłu Węglowego) had reportedly received bribes from representatives of private coal companies in exchange for raw material of a higher quality, from more

Badania Zbrodni przeciwko Narodowi Polskiemu Instytut Pamieci Narodowej, 1995), 5–7; Jarosz, Wolsza, "Komisja Specjalna do Walki z Nadużyciami i Szkodnictwem Gospodarczym (1945–1954)," *Biuletyn Głównej Komisji Badania Zbrodni przeciwko Narodowi Polskiemu* 36 (1993): 8–17.

108 Jarosz, Wolsza, "Komisja Specjalna do Walki z Nadużyciami i Szkodnictwem Gospodarczym (1945–1954)," 27.

Table 1. Decisions of the Special Commission on referral to a labor camp in the years 1946–1954, arranged by type of crime

Type of Crime	YEAR																	
	1946		1947		1948		1949		1950		1951		1952		1953		1954	
	No.	%	No.	%	No.	%	No.	%	No.	%	No.	%	No.	%	No.	%	No.	%
Bureaucratic offenses	216	15.5	900	20.7	1211	23.4	1588	17.4			1190	11.2	1947	8.6	1470	7.8	333	4.3
Speculation	256	18.3	518	11.9	621	11.9	1072	11.6			2862	27.1	2672	11.9	4531	24.1	2462	31.7
Plundering and misappropriation of social property	170	12.2	207	4.8	331	6.4	-	-			-	-	-	-	603 a)	3.2	108 a)	1.5
Looting	120	8.6	209	4.8	-	-	-	-			-	-	-	-	-	-	-	-
Bribery	-	-	20	0.5	38	0.7	57	0.6			-	-	-	-	-	-	-	-
Foreign currency crimes b)	106	7.6	180	4.2	189	3.6	196	2.1			99	0.8	118	0.6	-	-	78	1.0
Border crossing and smuggling	-	-	151	3.5	428	8.3	1516	16.5			124	1.3	354	1.6	-	-	-	-
Actions against State monopolies	93	6.6	1016	23.4	509	9.8	1278	14.0	-	-	1260c)	12.1	1401c)	6.3	1127d)	6.0	250 c)	3.3
Fraud tied to aide from the UNRRA	85	6.1	29	0.7	-	-	-	-			-	-	-	-	-	-	-	-
Illegal trade in skins	21	1.5	270	6.2	735	14.2	709	7.7			473	4.6	588	2.6	-	-	507	6.6
Illegal slaughtering	-	-	-	-	314	6.1	2119	23.1			2094	19.8	3741	16.7	742	3.9	-	-
hooliganism	-	-	-	-	-	-	-	-			395	3.8	4121	18.4	3471	18.5	2697	34.8
Hostile propaganda	-	-	-	-	-	-	-	-			322	3.1	1262	5.7	2704	14.4	91	1.1

Others	330	23.6	835	19.3	810	15.6	599	7.0			1715	16.2	6194	27.6	4159	22.1	1213	15.7
Totals	1397	100	4335	100	5186	100	9134	100			10534	100	22398	100	18807	100	7739	100

a) crimes prosecuted under the decree of 4 March 1953 on the protection of social property against petty thefts
b) also trade in foreign currencies
c) illegal production and trade in alcohol
d) illegal production and trade in alcohol and tobacco

Source: *Komisja Specjalna do Walki z Nadużyciami i Szkodnictwem Gospodarczym (1945–1954). Wybór źródeł*, ed. and intro. Jarosz, Tadeusz Wolsza (Warszawa: Główna Komisja Badania Zbrodni przeciwko Narodowi Polskiemu Instytut Pamięci Narodowej, 1995).

conveniently located mines, a process that bypassed the established order. One aspect of this case involved fraud at the City Fuel Works (Miejski Zakłady Opałowe, MZO) in Warsaw, whose management the Commission accused of illegally selling of coke to private recipients and, in the process, taking bribes. Based on the prosecution filed by the KS Executive Bureau, the District Court in Warsaw sentenced the director of the MZO to death, his deputy to life in prison, and two employees to 4 and 10 years in prison.

The Commission's authorities in 1949 investigated fraud in the "Bacutil" company which involved the illegal sale of technical animal fats, offal, and other post-mortem waste to private entrepreneurs.

In the same year, KS dealt with fraud in the sale of yarn, leather, knitwear, and finished goods in craft supply institutions (mainly at the Craft Center [Centrala Rzemieślnicza]). At the same time, attempts were made to explain the emergence of rationed articles on the open market, such as stearin, glycerin, bone oil, etc. originating from fat-processing plants. In 1950, the Commission dealt with fraud in woodworking plants and sawmills, as indicated by the emergence of more rationed wood in free circulation.[109]

The scale and reach of fraud during this period is also reported in documents produced by other state institutions. Here are some of them.

In May 1946, the Presidium Office of the temporary postwar parliament – the State National Council (Krajowa Rada Narodowa, KRN) – was informed that in January of that year, the Treasury Protection Brigade (Brygada Ochrony Skarbowej) in Gdynia discovered barrels filled with herring in the yard beyond a house bearing the stamp of the United Nations Relief and Rehabilitation Administration (UNRRA).[110] They had been sold on the free market from a

---

109 Ibid., 22–23.

110 The UNRRA was an institution that financed aid for war-ruined European and Asian countries. About 70 % of UNRRA funds came from the USA. The UNRRA's assistance to Poland came in the form of supplies of goods, the value of which in the years 1945–1947 – according to government estimates – amounted to approx. 474 million PLZ, of which about US $ 100 million was allocated to meet the needs of children and young people. For more, see Juźwik, Aleksander, *Od ratownictwa do etatyzacji. Opieka nad dziećmi i młodzieżą w działalności organizacji społecznych w Polsce w latach 1944–1950*, a doctoral work written at the Instytut Historii PAN, directed by D. Jarosz (Warszawa 2017); Juźwik, "Zagraniczna pomoc charytatywna dla dzieci i młodzieży w Polsce w latach 1945–1950," *Polska 1944/45–1989. Studia i materiały* 11 (2013): 93–118; Zaremba, *Wielka trwoga. Polska lat 1944–1947. Ludowa reakcja na kryzys* (Kraków: ZNAK, 2012).

"Społem" warehouse. An investigation revealed that from the beginning of November 1945 to 23 January 1946, workers at this warehouse had sold 60 barrels of herring on the open market, 100 kg of tea, and 60 kg of cheese. On 27–28 March 1946, an *ad hoc* court in Gdynia sentenced these workers to prison terms of 2–3 years.[111]

In October and November 1947, a trial was held at the District Court in Warsaw against two high-ranking officials from the Ministry of Labor and Social Welfare (Ministerstwo Pracy i Opieki Społecznej, MPiOS). Prosecutors presented evidence that they had robbed people of their gifts and benefits. The accused were sentenced to 10 and 13 years in prison.[112]

At the beginning of 1954, the Voivodeship Headquarters of the MO in Zielona Góra started an investigation into the management of the Textile Central warehouse, which was accused of fraud, theft and speculation in textile materials. Thirteen people were arrested who allegedly had systematically appropriated surplus material, sold it to speculators at exorbitant prices directly from wholesalers, and delivered only the money to stores. By the time of their arrest, they had seized about 870 m of textile materials worth about PLZ 400,000. The investigation showed that a system of legalized theft existed throughout the entire country and involved the appropriation of material surpluses. Investigators found that there was a complicated procedure for the transfer of money to wholesale and retail outlets instead of scarce goods, which were subject to speculation. As a result of an extensive investigation, it was established that "speculative elements" supplied themselves watches from smugglers living on the Baltic Coast (Gdańsk, Gdynia, Sopot[113]) and were also the main recipients of currencies laundered out of the country for smuggled goods.[114]

---

111 AAN, Biuro Prezydialne Krajowej Rady Narodowej (hereafter cited as BP KRN), 214, Notatka Naczelnika Wydziału Prawnego Biura Prezydialnego KRN I. Klajnermana z 6 maja 1946 r., p. 12. Przekonanie potoczne o kradzieżach dostaw UNRRA zawierał dowcip z 1948 r.: "Co to jest: Po wodzie płynie, na lądzie ginie? -? –UNRRA". Qtd. after *Nie tylko do śmiechu. Dowcipy z czadów Peerelu 1948–1989. Z wieloletniej kolekcji Bronisława Saludy* (Warszawa: Omnipress, 1991), 15.

112 AAN, Biuro Kontroli przy Radzie Państwa (hereafter cited as BKRP), 220, Dyrektor Biura Kontroli przy Radzie Państwa inż. Jan Grubecki do pana Prezydenta Rzeczpospolitej Polskiej, 29 stycznia 1948 r., p. 58.

113 These were the largest port cities in Poland, located on the Baltic Sea coast.

114 Instytut Pamięci Narodowej Biuro Udostępniania (hereafter cited as IPN BU), Ministerstwo Bezpieczeństwa Publicznego (hereafter cited as MBP), 1572/579, Dodatek dotyczący realizacji przeprowadzonych przez organa MO, Warszawa, 25 II 1954, p. 301.

In January 1954 alone, the MO accused 8,312 people throughout all of Poland who had committed crimes to the detriment of the national economy. Most of them, at least according to state data, were committed in small industries – 1,004; in construction – 694; in state urban trade – 1,182; in rural trade – 768, on State Agricultural Farms (Państwowe Gospodarstwa Rolne PGR)[115] – 836; and in forestry – 1,164. In addition to perpetrators acting individually, the MO revealed 179 groups involved in organized crime.[116]

In 1951, the Ministerstwo Bezpieczeństwa Publicznego (Ministry of Public Safety, MBP) investigation apparatus conducted a total of 676 cases involving 1,511 people suspected of economic crimes (very broadly defined). Among them, the largest group was peasants defined a medium-sized farmers (25 %) and "kulaks" (14 %). 36 % of all those arrested were bureaucrats/officials (in this group, the basic accusation was bribery) and 18 % were workers. The rest were mainly engineers and technical specialists. As of 1 January 1952 the total number of people detained for "sabotage and economic sabotage" by the MBP investigation apparatus was 335 (17 % of all arrests), and as of 31 December 1952 that number was 542 (about 20 %). The vast majority of these people were arrested for "economic sabotage."[117]

In his analysis of the increase in state property crimes in 1955 compared to the previous year, the PRL Prosecutor General, Stefan Kalinowski, claimed that such crime was particularly widespread in the so-called auxiliary craft cooperatives, especially in industrial voivodeships (Katowice, which at the time was called Stalinogród,[118] Wrocław, Łódź, and Warsaw). They obtained orders from industrial enterprises for supplies, services and works in the context of large-scale scams, including those that ate into the business of the Bolesław Bierut,[119] Nowa

115 The State Agricultural Farms (PGR) were created in 1949 from the merger of State Landed Real Estate organization, created after the war, and the State Horse Breeding and State Plant Breeding Establishments. The farms represented the state-owned form of agriculture production, and they were characterized by low efficiency and high production costs.

116 IPN BU, MBP, 1572/579], Notatka w sprawie nasilenia walki z przestępczością w gospodarce narodowej za miesiąc styczeń 1954, Warszawa 24 II 1954, pp. 292 ff.

117 IPN BU, MBP, 1572/2382, Sprawozdanie z pracy aparatu śledczego BP za okres od 1 stycznia do 31 grudnia 1952, p. 82.

118 The Silesian city of Katowice was renamed Stalinogród in connection with the death of Joseph Stalin in March 1953. It returned to its original name in December 1956.

119 Bolesław Bierut (1892–1956) was the Polish President in the years 1947–1952; in the years 1952–1954, he was Prime Minister; and from 1948 until his death in 1956, he was head of the PZPR. His name was given to the steelworks in Częstochowa.

Huta,[120] and "Dalmor"[121] steelworks. There was an increasing number of crime cases involving orders involving academic institutions and project-cost estimate work which would be carried out in a manner contrary to applicable regulations and which exposed the national economy to losses. As an example, Kalinowski gave the "Biprostal" Office of Studies and Construction Design in Kraków, which had commissioned the Kraków Polytechnic Institute for design-cost estimates which were then carried out by "Biprostal" employees. The Polytechnic Institute's role consisted of calculating the mark-up for scientific-service works to the amount of 100 %. In the capital city, the Center of Technical Research "Metro" commissioned the Department of Industrial Construction of the Warsaw University of Technology to perform an inventory of a mineshaft; the latter accepted the order by handing over the work to "Metro" employees.

"Unplanned losses in construction," Kalinowski claimed "reaching tens of millions of zlotys are almost the rule." Such losses resulted from the misappropriation, waste and theft of building materials, from the falsification of processing plans, and from criminal machinations of employees in construction companies.

In the socialized trade,[122] Kalinowski recognized that cash-commodity shortages were most dangerous. Investigations of about 170 people were under way in local agricultural cooperatives in eight voivodeships, whose crimes consisted of the purchase by speculators of material and clothing products from homeworkers as well as from the Center of the Folk and Artistic Industries. The value of these goods amounted to PLZ 50 million, but they were sold to both cooperative and state-owned stores at prices about 100 % higher than the

120 Nowa Huta, built after 1949 near Kraków, was one of the largest industrial investments in Stalinist Poland.

121 A deep-sea fisheries company that was established in 1946.

122 In this work, where necessary, the following terms are used: socialized economy, socialized enterprise/factory, socialized trade, socialized industry. In these cases, the term "socialized" – according to the understanding adopted in the economics of the so-called "real socialism" – state or cooperative ownership is opposed to private ownership. In the case of Poland, this "socialization" of industry and trade took place in the years 1946–1948. In spite of great pressure applied by authorities, it was possible to "socialize" only a small part of agriculture during the collectivization of 1948–1956. From 1956, the pressure to liquidate private peasant farms weakened. Poland was the only country in Central and Eastern Europe (other than perhaps Yugoslavia) which maintained a dominant private sector in agriculture up through 1989.

purchase prices. The crime was facilitated by a thicket of rules, sometimes conflicting with each other, regulating trade in goods.[123]

Some of the economic fraud discovered in the sixties had a "genealogy" dating back to the early 1950s. This was the case of scams carried out by employees of the District Grain Plants (Powiatowe Zakłady Zbożowe) in the Kielce Voivodeship, which were detected in 1963. It turned out that the falsification of the purchase documentation for grains and grasses began there in 1950.[124]

The mechanism at work in most of these examples of fraud, especially the largest ones, indicates a certain regularity. At that time, big scandals were particularly frequent at the intersection between the state and private sector in the economy.[125] Measures taken to limit the development and licensing of private enterprises and shortages of necessarily rationed goods and services – these were the most important factors that favored corruption and other economic fraud in the communist economic system. Fraud also arose where officials decided to distribute goods free of charge, and they were encouraged by all the non-market or quasi-market procedures used for the sale and purchase of goods (restrictions, obligatory supplies of agricultural products, quotas, etc.).

Did the changes of October 1956[126] affect the nature and scale of economic fraud in Poland? By way of an interesting attempt to answer this question, we can examine an analysis, carried out by the Supreme Audit Office (Najwyższa Izba Kontroli, NIK[127]) in 1957, of eighteen cases of fraud that most often ended

---

123 AAN, Ministerstwo Kontroli Państwowej (hereafter cited as MKP), 1/110, Stefan Kalinowski, Warszawa 24 lutego 1956, pp. 40 ff.

124 See *Katalog niektórych spraw: kryminalnych, gospodarczych, dewizowych i innych prowadzonych przez jednostki Milicji Obywatelskiej na terenie kraju* (Warszawa: Wydawnictwo KG MO, Oddział Kontroli, Badań i Analiz, grudzień 1966), 63.

125 For the same opinion, see Witold Pawełko, *Zapobieganie przestępstwom gospodarczym* (Warszawa: PWN, 1971), 67 ff.

126 Polish historiography describes the political events that took place in October 1956 as the October transformation, when – as a result of the decision of the VIII plenary of the KC PZPR and despite resistance from the Soviet leadership – a former Stalinist prisoner, Władysław Gomułka, came to power in Poland. He assumed the position of the First Secretary of the KC PZPR and introduced temporary liberalization of the system.

127 In its postwar form, the Supreme Audit Office was established based on the act of 9 March 1949 on State Control as a body formally independent of the government and subject to the Council of State. In 1952, it was transformed into the Ministry of State Audit subordinated to the government and the prime minister, which destroyed

with an indictment against state-owned, cooperative and private production companies, shops, service and purchasing institutions, PGR, universities, and municipal enterprises. NIK confirmed in particular the corruptive nature of the contact of state-owned enterprises with craft enterprises and small private producers activated after October 1956. Despite the differences in methods, forms, means and objects of the crimes involved, it was possible, according to inspectors, to identify certain common phenomena. The most common types of fraud involved in the analyzed cases were:

1. the purchase of goods or the acceptance services at exorbitant prices, directing them to a specific supplier who took personal gain;
2. fictitious purchases (issuing fictitious invoices for undelivered goods); in these instances of fraud a special role was played by rural cooperative stores and municipal commission stores;
3. misappropriation of purchased goods and materials by purchasers;
4. fraud in the area of wages (fictitious payment of wages, fictitious or minimal performance of remunerated activities – funds for commissioned work, renovation funds, loans for training, etc. were exploited in particular; falsification of production results for undeserved bonuses; wasteful use of funds for rewards. "In brief, however, it can be said that this [fraud] mainly manifested itself in the clear falsification of payroll documents, in the listing of non-existent people, so-called dead souls, the falsification of receipts or the extortion of receipts for wages not received or received but in amounts lower than listed." The harm caused by these activities also consisted in the fact that they involved a wide range of employees and therefore had a particularly demoralizing impact on the personnel;
5. thefts in greater amounts, especially when the enterprise directors were involved in the fraud.

According to the analysis, most of the perpetrators of fraud emerged from the so-called criminal cooperation within so-called private initiatives involving dishonest employees in the state and cooperative apparatus. There was a group

its appearance of independence (the law on state control of 22 November 1952). Pursuant to the act of 13 December 1957, the Supreme Audit Office was restored as the highest audit institution in the state. In its new form, it cooperated with the Sejm, and the Council of State played its supervisory role as specified by the Act. See Andrzej Sylwestrzak, *Najwyższa Izba Kontroli* (Warszawa: Zakład Narodowy im. Ossolińskich, 1990), 110–199.

of cottagers and other small producers using craft or industrialized methods, whose products were purchased by state and cooperative organizations, and sometimes directly by state-owned production companies, for which in certain situations they were the only source of supply. "Speculators-agents, characters who normally work nowhere and who are not registered in financial and trade departments, who do not pay taxes – are the ones who buy products from these small producers and, using criminal methods, sell them at far higher prices to purchasing companies or direct users."

In the opinion of NIK auditors, cooperatives played an important role in economic crime. "It is not the best people gathered in the management apparatus of cooperatives. A large number of administrative employees of the cooperative, usually in managerial positions, have proven to be susceptible to all kinds of schemes and have been willing – for a decent bribe – to allow the cooperative to engage in various kinds of speculation. Some of these employees have even been the instigators of serious fraud themselves."

Analyzing the social background of perpetrators, officials concluded that, contrary to the prevailing judgments, crimes were generally not committed by people from particularly difficult life circumstances. The overwhelming majority were upper and mid-level employees whose wages were relatively high and who, moreover, also benefited to a large extent from commissioned work and rewards. The list of criminals in eighteen examined cases included mainly: directors of central unions and their deputies, directors of enterprises and their deputies, heads of voivodeship enterprises, leading engineers, leading mechanics of central unions and enterprises, presidents and managers of cooperatives, managers of state and cooperative stores, and factory masters. Less frequent among them were warehousemen, cashiers, department heads, and very rarely – workers, usually in the role of passive helpers (apart from minor thefts). "Private-cooperative schemers" were usually in league with corrupt government officials who had known each other for a long time. Employees of enterprises, bribed by speculators, became not only participants but also "agitators for bribery in their immediate surroundings or in other factories known to them."

In a subsequent part of the document, officials presented the criminal mechanism as a fraudulent type of supply and service transaction: "As if officially, it was a cooperative that emerged as a supplier, in whose name employees were involved in the essence of the transaction. This cooperative, at a fairly high price, would buy the given goods from a private person, paying for them immediately (or in stages) in cash, and then delivering these items to the state enterprise with a sizable margin and collected payments due. It fell to employees of state-owned

Table 2. Private trade outlets and gastronomic establishments in Poland in 1948–1957

Year	1948	1951	1952	1953	1954	1955	1956	31 I 1957
No. of private trade outlets	127, 877	31,999	27,154	15,771	16,472	13,761	17,823	18, 588
No. of private gastronomic establishments	13, 849	2,035	1,494	853	780	479	863	1,515

Source: AAN, Polskie Towarzystwo Ekonomiczne (hereafter cited as PTE), 167, Przegląd bieżącej sytuacji gospodarczej kraju i zadań stojących przed polityką gospodarczą, Warszawa, April-May 1957, p. 63.

enterprises to ensure that all documents required to complete the transaction were prepared and any unforeseen obstacles (incomplete and untimely deliveries) were removed. At the same time, they forged a number of documents, such as payrolls, receipts, orders, and many others, depending on the fraud's specific purpose. Due to the need to circumvent a number of rules regarding deliveries, the execution of some transactions sometimes required highly complex schemes, which meant that a handful of dishonest employees, in order to gain benefits for themselves personally, started the true avalanche of crimes."[128]

Economic crime was no doubt encouraged by the growth of private enterprise after 1956. In the period between December 1956 and December 1957 alone, the number of craft workshops in Poland increased from over 96,600 to over 133,350. This growth was in large part the result of changes in the organizational forms of work cooperatives. In the liberalized economic system, obtaining a concession for such an enterprise was much easier than it had been in the Stalinist period, though to actually produce, raw materials (meat, steel, building materials, wood, etc.) were required, and these were in short supply. For this reason, organizations often resorted to supply sources that were, from the point of view of current law, illegal.[129]

We observe a similar growth in private enterprise during this period in trade and gastronomy (Table 2).

---

128 AAN, Najwyższa Izba Kontroli (hereafter as: NIK), 17/57, Analiza dokumentów, dotyczących osiemnastu spraw przestępstw gospodarczych [1957], pp. 46–54.

129 Archiwum Dokumentacji Historycznej PRL (hereafter as: ADH PRL), Kolekcja S. Jędrychowskiego, J I/53, Główne problemy sytuacji gospodarczej kraju. Ogólna ocena roku 1957, p. 261.

Before we try to answer the question about how we can estimate the scale of economic crime in Poland after 1956, it is worth pointing out that such crime included a wide variety of enterprises and institutions belonging to many branches of the economy, which is evidenced primarily by numerous examples of detected frauds, of which only a part were disclosed to the public. Here are some of them.

In 1957, the PZPR Central Committee was informed about the operational conclusions made by the MO at the Warsaw Praga Północ District Headquarters, which showed that, in the years 1956–1957, six passenger cars built at the Passenger Automobile Factory (Fabryka Samochodów Osobowych, FSO) in Żerań (within the borders of Warsaw) had been stolen from that plant. The report contained a detailed description of how the scheme played out. Officials made arrests in this case.[130]

However, they were not able to deter FSO employees from committing theft later. In May 1964, the MO opened an investigation into a group of individuals who had stolen car parts and car assemblies from this factory. Twenty-eight people were arrested, including 19 FSO employees (including 2 PZPR members). They had stolen car components: gearboxes, ignition switches, sensors, clutch discs, etc. – that is, everything that was in short supply in car workshops.[131]

Fraud in the automotive industry had a much greater range. According to incomplete data presented at a meeting on 20 August 1963 at the KG MO, militia authorities were conducting 61 investigations in this sector involving more than 800 people, of which 254 had been arrested. One hundred and seventy-eight people had been arrested on charges at "Motozbyt," which was a state-owned enterprise dealing in, among other things, the supply of spare car parts. Private entrepreneurs were also investigated. One of them involved the owner of several locksmith-car workshops in Warsaw and the Warsaw Voivodeship who owned 6 villas, 2 outlets, and 2 automobiles (including one super-modern Mercedes). Officials found 19 kg of gold and gold products. The cause of this crime was primarily the paralysis within the field of automotive services. In 1962, the demand for spare parts for "Star" trucks was satisfied by only 54 %, and for M-20 "Warszawa" and Syrena passenger cars by 60 %. The supply of

130 AAN, KC PZPR, XI/281, Notatka służbowa dotycząca sytuacji na terenie Fabryki Samochodów Osobowych w Warszawie, Warszawa dnia 11 listopada 1957, p. 253.

131 Archiwum Państwowe w Warszawie (hereafter as: APW), 30/VII-43, vol. 25, Informacja nr 21/IX/507 z 25 IX 1964 dot. ujawnionej grupy złodziei w Fabryce Samochodów Osobowych na Żeraniu, p. 15.

subassemblies for imported automobiles was no better. At the same time, there was an increase in the number of private automobile workshops and private companies trading in automotive parts who were seeking illegal ways to meet the needs of their growing number of clients.[132]

On 5 September 1957, based on materials collected by the KG MO, officials initiated an investigation into employees in the Central Administration for Wholesale Fancy Goods Trade "Centrogal" (Centralny Zarząd Handlu Artykułami Galanteryjnymi "Centrogal") who had taken bribes from private producers in exchange for orders for the sale of their goods. In this case, among others, three heads of departments and two senior economists of "Centrogal" were arrested. The investigation encompassed 27 people at the time, including 9 officials and 18 producers or their intermediaries, 14 of whom were indicted.[133]

In 1958, authorities were on the trail of a huge scandal in the leather industry. They visited Radom – a city with some of the largest shoe factories in Poland. In their report for the PZPR Central Committee, they wrote: "There are many signs confirming the general opinion that Radom is one of the 'richest cities' in Poland." Data from the Municipal Economic Planning Commission (Miejska Komisja Planowania Gospodarczego) for 1957 indicated that the city's income amounted to PLZ 1,294 million, and its expenses were PLZ 1,633 million! Such an imbalance was achieved through a simultaneous small increase in savings deposits in the Universal Savings Bank (Powszechna Kasa Oszczędności, PKO) bank[134] and significant expenses made by "a certain portion of the population outside of Radom, such as for example the purchase of passenger cars (the number of passenger cars currently in Radom in 391, including 124 luxury taxis; in 1957 and the first 5 months of 1958, the number of private passenger cars doubled compared to December 1956)." The high purchasing power of "certain strata of the population" was also evidenced by the turnover at a local jewelry

132 IPN, KG MO, 35/3658, Wystąpienie w dyskusji ppłk Zbigniewa Gabińskiego Naczelnika Wydziału II Oddziału IV na odbytej w dniu 20 sierpnia 1963 r. naradzie naczelników KW MO i równorzędnych, poświęcone niektórym formom przestępczości występującej w produkcji, remontach, obrocie częściami i akcesoriami samochodowymi.

133 ADH PRL, Kolekcja Stefana Jędrychowskiego, J I/11a, Notatka służbowa w sprawie nadużyć dokonanych przez pracowników Centralnego Zarządu Handlu Artykułami Galanteryjnymi "Centrogal" w Łodzi.

134 The PKO was established on 1 January 1950 from the transformation of the Postal Savings Bank, which was created in 1919. It held savings contributions of PRL citizens mainly on the basis of so-called PKO savings books.

store (PLZ 1 million per month, i.e. as much as at the most prosperous jewelry store in Warsaw) and at resale stores. The managers of jewelry shops claimed that Radom was the best city in which to sell foreign watches, supplied by enterprises in Gdynia, Gdańsk, Łódź and Warsaw. Those possessing cash invested their cash in "valuable objects like jewelry and foreign currency, not in a visible way, e.g. in construction." Tanners, the surplus of which in the local labor market was about 2,500, contributed to the corruption and fraud. All of them – the authors of the cited document claimed – "threw themselves" into illegal trade. Necessary products (raw hides, tanning agents, chemicals) were obtained from fences as a result of theft at local state-owned enterprises. One of the most well-known people in the criminal world in this field was Shaja Lengleben, who was "living in disguise." The secretary of the Party Committee on Radom Footwear Producers (Radomskie Zakłady Obuwia, RZO)[135] and members of the committee who were questioned on these occasions, "reported openly that "everyone at [RZO] steals, both party members and non-party members." There were cases that "when a newly admitted controller manages to find a skin at the gate – he is pushed away by a thief. None of the more than a thousand workers present at that moment tries to prevent the suspect from escaping. Often controllers are attacked on the street and beaten for their zealous service." The MO was met with a wall of silence from the crews of businesses tolerating corruption and theft.[136]

The situation at the RZO was not exceptional. In the case of Radom, investigations resulted in a trial of those accused of corruption. In January 1960, the Provincial Court in Kielce issued a summary judgment against Bolesław Dedo, head of supply and sale at the tanning cooperative "Przyszłość" (Future), who was sentenced to death (the sentence was not carried out). Together with 16 co-accused, he had committed fraud causing losses in the amount of PLZ 20 million from 1948 to 1959.[137]

In the years 1960–1962, more than 300 employees of tanning factories, footwear enterprises, central purchasing centers, the National Union of Tannery

---

135 The RZO was founded in 1947 as a state-owned enterprise. In 1959, the Zakłady Przemysłu Skórzanego "Radoskór" was founded on the basis of five tanneries and two shoe factories from the prewar Bata company, which were nationalized in 1945.

136 AAN, KC PZPR XI/281, Prezydium Centralnego Zespołu do Walki z Nadużyciami, Warszawa czerwiec 1958, pp. 26–32.

137 AAN, KC PZPR, 237/XIV-273, Ryszard Strzelecki do Władysława Gomułki, I sekretarza KC PZPR, Warszawa, 22 III 1961, pp. 1 ff; Irena Majchrzak, *Pracownicze przestępstwo gospodarcze i jego sprawca* (Warszawa: Wiedza Powszechna, 1965), 49. A broader discussion of the legal and political aspects of the case can be found below.

Cooperatives, among others, were indicted in the so-called leather affair. Investigators had found fraud not only in Radom but also in Warsaw, Żyrardów, Kraków, Nowy Sącz, and Kielce.

The most prominent case after Dedo's was that of Eugeniusz Galicki, director of the Warsaw Tanneries, where investigators found evidence that theft and the illegal trade in leather had taken place since 1953. It was proven that he and another accused individual had stolen social property valued at nearly PLZ 8 million. In this case, 13 villas and single-family homes were "secured," along with four automobiles, a motorcycle, jewelry, Persian rugs, foreign currency, and other items. The trial, took place ad hoc before the Provincial Court in Warsaw, ended on 3 October 1960 with convictions and life sentences for the main accused and two others.[138]

After the revelation of scandals in the leather industry, NIK carried out investigations in 1961–1962 regarding trade in sheep wool and yarn in state-owned enterprises and cooperatives. As a result of these inspections, 188 proceedings were initiated by 1 December 1962. Among the 624 people tied up in this investigation were 23 directors, 35 cooperative presidents, 30 accountants and 212 department heads. By 15 December 1962, the courts had examined 46 cases brought against 293 people, including 9 cases in summary proceedings against 70 people.[139]

Based on analysis of the above materials, it appears that it was the trade sector that was particularly vulnerable to fraud. This conclusion is also confirmed by the information contained in documents produced by KG MO at the end of the 1950s. In total, in 1956 the MO initiated 16,025 cases of trade crime, and in 1957 that number was 13,084. In those two years respectively, 1,429 and 1,689 people were arrested. A detailed breakdown of these cases, ordered by type of enterprise in 1957, is contained in Table 3.

In 1963, prosecutors and the MO completed collecting evidence in 6,886 cases involving offenses under the act of 13 July 1957 on combating speculation and defending the interests of purchasers and agricultural producers in trade. In

138 Majchrzak, *Pracownicze przestępstwo gospodarcze*, 48–49; AAN, KC PZPR, 237/XIV-305, Notatka informacyjna w sprawie poważniejszych nadużyć w gospodarce mięsem, w piekarnictwie, w nasiennictwie i w zakładach przemysłu skórzanego przesłana przez Prokuratora Generalnego PRL Kazimierza Kosztirko do sekretarza KC PZPR Ryszarda Strzeleckiego, Warszawa 17 września 1964 r., pp. 65 ff.

139 AAN, KC PZPR, VII/149, Załącznik nr 1 do Biuletynu nr 115 Biura Sekretariatu KC PZPR, 16 maja 1963. List Wydziału Organizacyjnego KC i CKKP do I sekretarzy KW, p. 251.

Table 3. Cases related to trade crimes initiated by the MO in 1957

Type of Crime	Cases initiated	People arrested	Total losses in PLZ
Urban Retail	3,127	454	14,884,253
State Department Stores	381	54	852,270
Trade Centers	1,881	336	12,341,726
Urban Meat Trade	639	60	900,158
Food Cooperatives	3,927	495	13,577,171
Workforce Supply Units[a]	646	80	5,232,907
Food Establishments	1,976	111	5,424,776
Fruit and Vegetable Trade Enterprises	507	99	4,825,639
TOTAL	**13,084**	**1,689**	**58,038,900**

[a] Workforce Supply Units were established in 1951 in large plants in selected key branches of industry. They dealt with, among other things, canteens and employee buffets, auxiliary farms, service outlets and nearby stores.

Source: Archiwum Instytutu Pamięci Narodowej (hereafter cited as IPN), KG MO, 4365, Notatka dotycząca sytuacji w handlu, Warszawa, 10 marca 1958.

addition, the State Trade Inspectorate (Państwowa Inspekcja Handlowa, PIH), conducting its own preparatory proceedings, submitted to the courts an indictment in 1,236 cases. In total, in 1963, 8,122 preparatory proceedings were concluded in cases involving speculation and subject to prosecution under criminal. In addition, PIH directed 5,470 cases to the penal-administrative councils.[140]

In 1963, according to MO data, trade crime accounted for 22 % of all cases of economic crimes. "The most alarming phenomenon in crime in the trade apparatus," we read in the Bulletin of the General Prosecutor (Biuletyn Generalnej Prokuratury), "is the fact, recently confirmed in some institutions, that almost everyone involved in retail trade in a given company, including its management, participate in fraud. Fraud revealed in regional service and trade cooperatives dealing in automotive equipment indicate that all of the cooperatives of this type in the country had been involved criminal activity."[141]

140 Penal-administrative councils were appointed at the presidia of national councils and had the right to punish perpetrators of criminal offenses. In 1971, they were renamed the criminal case councils. Marian Kallas, Adam Lityński, *Historia ustroju i prawa Polski Ludowej* (Warszawa: Wydawnictwo Lexis Naxis, 2003), 253.

141 Z. Naumowicz, "Przestępstwa w handlu," *Biuletyn Generalnej Prokuratury* 12 (1964).

Table 4. "Cash shortfall" cases sent to prosecutors in 1961–1966

Year	No. of Cases
1961	10,248
1962	7,904
1963	6,916
1964	6,333
1965	5,519
1966	5,519
3rd quarter of 1966	3,853

Source: AAN, Prokuratura Generalna (hereafter cited as PG), 1/11, Informacja dotycząca spraw o przestępstwa z Art. 286 k.k. Fr. Rafałowskiego, Prokuratora Prokuratury Generalnej, 4 November 1966, pp. 13–18.

Another category of crimes to which trade was exposed involved cash shortfalls. The number of cases of this type received by prosecutor's offices in 1961–1966 gradually decreased (Table 4).

By September 1964, nine serious scandals related to the distribution, storage and processing of flour had been revealed in Warsaw and in the following voivodeships: Katowice and Opole. Losses tied to these cases amounted to PLZ 4,300,000. One-hundred-ten people were caught up in fraud cases valued at PLZ 50,000 or more, of whom 37 were sent to the court for indictment. Above all, these cases involved mixing rye and wheat flours not in accordance with recipes, using fewer eggs and less yeast and milk for baking, and more water, all of which allowed for increased production, which was sold socialized stores. Bakery managers, in consultation with store managers, delivered bread at higher prices than those registered. Part of the "savings" thus produced was sold without any documentation. The resulting profits were divided according to an agreed formula.[142]

The most serious and at the same time case of crime in the food industry was the fraud case brought by the Regional Prosecutor's Office in Warsaw against employees of the "Praha" bar in Warsaw – one of the largest establishments of this type in Poland. They started their criminal activity immediately after its opening in the spring of 1959, with the participation of buffet employees, cashiers and room managers. The fraud consisted in the fact that the managers of 12 buffets (out of

142 AAN, KC PZPR, 237/XIV-305, pp. 63 ff; AAN, Prokuratura Generalna (hereafter cited as PG), 4/31, pp. 60 ff.

14 there) "fraudulently" created "merchandise and cash surpluses, deliberately giving consumers smaller portions and increasing the volume of prepared kitchen meals by adding water and using various additives prepared 'privately' by kitchen employees." These surpluses were sold, and money was then withdrawn from cash registers by reusing receipts, by buffet managers receiving money not taken through the cash registers, by not handing over money collected from tour managers, etc. The income obtained from the buffet managers was shared with the subordinate staff as well as with the room manager and the bar director. The first indictment in this case was brought to the Provincial Court in Warsaw on 14 April 1962. In a verdict handed down on 6 August 1962, three people were convicted of abusing their authority and failure to perform official duties. They were sentenced to prison terms of between 3 and 6.5 years and a fine of PLZ 50,000, 40,000 and 30,000. Twenty-two people were convicted of cheating buyers and sent to prison from between10 months and 4 years and fined from PLZ 3,000 to 40,000.[143]

The parameters of the affair grew wider. Officials detected the greatest instances of fraud at the Warsaw Gastronomic Factory (Warszawskie Zakłady Gastronomiczne, WZG). In this case, 14 separate preparatory proceedings were conducted, involving more than 400 people suspected of fraud. By December 1966, 268 people were charged, of which 145 were put in pre-trial detention. In 1966, investigators referred 9 cases and associated files to the Court, cases which involved 106 people, of whom 99 were arrested. They were accused of stealing social assets worth 5.5 million PLZ, and of other crimes valued at 4,600,000 PLZ. Indictments were directed at, among others, 4 WZG directors, 2 deputy directors, 42 plant managers, 38 canteen managers, 2 chefs and 2 warehouse keepers.[144] Fraud in the food industry was also detected in other cities.[145]

One sector of the economy where abuses were commonplace was the already-mentioned construction sector. The character and mechanisms of this fraud was described by, among other institutions, the General Prosecutor's Office,

---

143 AAN, PG, 4/590, Informacja dotycząca niektórych zagadnień. . ., p. 155; AAN, PG, 1/24, Notatka w sprawie nadużyć w barze "Praha," Warszawa 16 maja 1963, p. 180.

144 AAN, KC PZPR, 237/V-615, Informacja dotycząca nadużyć popełnionych w państwowych zakładach gastronomicznych opracowana przez zespól towarzyszy w składzie: dep. Gen. Prok. P. Hachulski, dyr. Zespołu Obrotu Towarowego NIK N. Radziwiller, szef Oddz. IV KG MO Neldner i po szefa Oddz. Dochodzeniowego Grzelak, 2 grudnia 1965, p. 120; AAN, PG, 1/24, Kazimierz Kosztirko do prezesa Rady Ministrów Józefa Cyrankiewicza, marzec 1967, p. 65–69.

145 AAN, PG, 1/24, p. 66–68; Kary dla łapowników z gastronomii, *Trybuna Robotnicza* 1964, no. 139.

which provided information based on materials tied to indictments in 130 of the most serious cases brought in 1960 by district and voivodeship prosecutors to voivodeship courts. This information shows that in most cases related to construction, criminal activity lasted for a period of 6 months to 2 years, and in 24 cases it lasted over 2 years. Crimes consisted primarily of theft of social property, and their perpetrators were mainly "persons exercising direct investment-construction or financial supervision, or persons supervising the manager of the enterprise or an individual (investor) – related to each other in criminal mafias or gangs." The overwhelming majority of examined cases concerned offenses that were actually carried out. Only a few concerned the crimes in the planning-cost estimate phase (inflating cost estimates and their approval without formal verification, without additional cost estimates prepared by the contractor himself as work was being carried out, and not verified by the client). A greater number of crimes were committed in cases involving commissions issued to private enterprises (giving orders for bribes, commissioning works without bids, without specifying the value of orders and without indicative cost estimates, valuations of materials, etc.). Fraud usually consisted of the falsification of invoices and bills for works completed, for supplies and services; of the misappropriation of part of workers' and suppliers' claims through the falsification and forging of their signatures on payroll lists and on delivery notes and through the use of double documentation; of the theft of materials and money by moving them out of the records mostly by falsifying accounting documents and accounting operations involving the management of materials and finances. In addition, it was possible to organize work "on one's own account" by persons employed in socialized enterprises by means of equipment, workers and sometimes materials of a "socialized enterprise."[146]

The fuel sector was also not free of fraud. The MO detected instances of such fraud in the second half of 1963. By 30 June 1965, 289 investigations had been carried out regarding crimes of considerable significance. The prosecution encircled 1,210 people, including 349 employees of Petroleum Products Center (Centrala Produktów Naftowych, CPN) – mostly sellers at petrol stations and 861 managers of socialized transport companies. Petrol stations served as a place for liquefying both "saved" surplus fuels and products stolen from distribution warehouses, which were sold to owners of private automobiles outside the register, on the seller's own account. The largest instances of fraud were detected in

146 AAN, PG 1/25, Informacja o najpoważniejszych przestępstwach gospodarczych w budownictwie (na podstawie aktów oskarżeń), p. 350.

construction transport, and the most common practice was the destruction and damage of mileage counters and the fictitious increase in vehicle mileage.[147]

High officials in the Polish foreign trade centers were also accused fraud and mismanagement. The greatest publicity was given to affairs described by Walery Namiotkiewicz, Jan Olszewski, and Jerzy Ambroziewicz in the series of articles entitled "Błoto i dolary" (Mud and Dollars) and published from the end of September 1956 in the weekly *Po prostu*.[148] More than 100 letters were sent to *Po prostu* offices showing the behind-the-scenes mechanisms of these instances of fraud.[149] In 1964, investigating authorities requested that the prosecutor's office bring to justice the former director of Foreign Trade Center (Centrali Handlu Zagranicznego, CHZ) "Motoimport" and directors at that headquarters who, having failed to perform their official duties, exposed the state treasury to large losses when purchasing coolers and spare parts for Fiat buses. In the same year, the Interior Ministry brought to light attempts by the Foreign Trade Center "Elektrim" to conclude an unfavorable contract with the Brazilian company "Talamaca" for the export of assembly shops and telephone sets. A department manager at that Center was dismissed from the foreign trade department for having attempted to extort bribes from foreign buyers.

In 1964, arrests of members of organized smuggling gangs continued. At that time, the Department II of the General Prosecutor's Office (dealing with economic crime) oversaw 64 investigations of smuggling and currency fraud, which involved 344 people (including 248 arrested) suspected of illegal trade with "foreign exchange assets" and smuggling of goods to the tune of 25,644,000. Forty-four indictments were filed with the court, and 243 people were charged with illegal currency trading and smuggling of a value of $ 1,350,000 (according to the PKO exchange rate at the time, PLZ 95,200,000).

On 26 January 1965, the Security Service (the PRL secret police, Służba Bezpieczeństwa, SB) uncovered a group of people involved in the smuggling of twenty-dollar gold coins to Poland. For their transport, a safe deposit box was organized in one of the Warsaw-Berlin train wagons. In it banknotes were taken

147 AAN, KC PZPR, 237/V-615, KG MO, Informacja nr 12, 30 września 1965, p. 103–106.

148 At this time, the weekly *Po Prostu* was one of the most important magazines critical of Stalinism and calling for de-Stalinization. Its "revisionist" character aroused increasing criticism from the new Gomułka party leadership, which took power in October 1956. The dissolution of this weekly by authorities in October 1957 caused student protests, which were suppressed by the militia.

149 For more on this subject, see Adam Leszczyński, *Sprawy do załatwienia. Listy do* Po prostu *1955–1957* (Warszawa: TRIO, 2000), 71–75.

from Warsaw, and gold coins were brought from Berlin. By that date, 35 home searches had been carried out across the country, 22 people had been detained for 48 hours. During the search, 115 twenty-dollar gold coins, 68 other gold coins, 70 dkg of gold bars, $ 5,000 in banknotes, PLZ 711,000. in cash and registered PKO booklets, and a few dozen pieces of jewelry. The organizer of this group was arrested, among others.[150]

Some of the perpetrators showed unusually artful in carrying out these crimes. Here is an example in 1964. The Łódź Regional Court considered the case of smugglers who took over US $74,000 out of the country and smuggled about 30 kg of gold into Poland.

> The method of operation consisted of placing illegally purchased thousand-dollar banknotes into hollowed-out meat, then sending them to the addresses of persons residing abroad. From there, the perpetrators received parcels containing various articles, including cans of cocoa. These cans, with the company label and a weight corresponding to the basis weight specified on the package, contained – beside cocoa – a certain amount of gold, ground and cocoa-colored. This fact could not be detected organoleptically. A dental technician separated the gold from the cocoa through a thermal method used in dentistry [. . .]. The perpetrators deposited the income gained using this method, in the form of dental products, in France, where they intended to emigrate.[151]

---

150 IPN BU, MSW II, 1585/2256, Biuletyn Wewnętrzny nr 26/65, 1 lutego 1965, p. 65. A report by the Ministry of Justice shows that in total 332 people were sentenced in 1964 district courts for foreign currency crimes (of which 219 were sentence to prison time), and in 1963, that number was 386. The most common type of crime was illegal trade in foreign currencies. Such crimes were encouraged by "exchange rate differences in the capitalist markets and the illegal domestic market. In capitalist markets, the price of one $ 20 coin ranges between US $42 and $44 in cash. Importing such a coin for illegally exported dollar banknotes and selling it on the so-called 'black market' inside Poland brings about $ 10–12 in profit to traders. Also differences in the exchange rates of gold coins on the domestic market facilitate this activity. The price paid by the only institution authorized to buy gold in the country, which is PP 'Jubiler,' differs significantly from the prices quoted in the illegal market. The State Enterprise 'Jubiler' pays PLZ 3,464 for a $. 20 coin. Depending on the economic situation, the price of such a coin on the 'black market' gets is between 5,800 PLZ or $56 in cash." AAN, MS, 1434, Przestępstwa dewizowe w praktyce sądów. Opracowanie Departamentu Nadzoru Sądowego Ministerstwa Sprawiedliwości, Warszawa październik 1965, pp. 4 ff.

151 Ibid., p. 6.

In 1963, as a result of actions taken by the SB, eighteen crew members of the ship M/S Batory 18 were arrested for complicity in smuggling.[152] Employees serving international trains were also involved in smuggling.[153] In 1957 alone, officials pursued a total of 2,000 cases of customs crimes involving about PLZ 4 million of goods smuggled into Poland, not including gold and foreign currencies, which were handed over to the National Bank of Poland (NBP) without valuation. This represented only a small part of the real total smuggling. According to inspectors' findings, the crews on many Polish Merchant Navy vessels used their stays in foreign ports for smuggling purposes.[154]

What was the scale of economic crime in Poland in the period when the meat affair broke out? Specialists dealing with this issue argue that it is extremely difficult to determine its size. Estimates on this subject can be based primarily on several categories of materials. For the years 1945–1954, a certain view of this matter is provided by information previously cited and tied to KS operations. For a later period, data contained in criminal records kept by the Ministry of Justice (which is not always exact and does not include multiple-object and multi-person crime configurations) are usually used for this purpose, as well as MO statistics regarding registered crimes and reports filed in their regard to prosecutors' offices. This data usually does not correspond to the scale of actually committed crimes, especially in terms of so-called minor theft of social property. It is difficult to determine the so-called "dark number" that criminologists use to determine the disproportion between the number of crimes actually committed and those that come to light.[155] Nevertheless, in order to be aware of the minimum scale of the phenomenon, it is worth acquainting ourselves with statistics concerning the number of persons covered by indictments in the most important groups of economic crime cases (Table 5).

The damage caused by the detected crimes of theft of social property amounted in 1957 to PLZ 456,940,000; in 1958 to PLZ 406,090,000; in 1959 to 391,041,000 PLZ; and in 1960 to PLZ 344,594,000. A separate group consisted of those found guilty of shortages, whose value in 1959 amounted to PLZ 726.6 million, and in

---

152 IPN BU, KG MO, 1585/492, Informacja o pracy SB MSW za IV kwartał 1963, p. 6.

153 APW, 30/VII-43, t.25, Informacja nr 9/X/529 z 10 października 1964 Sektora Informacji Wydziału Organizacyjnego KW PZPR dot. zebrania POP w "Warsie," p. 74.

154 AAN, KC PZPR, XI/281, Uchwała Zespołu przy Prezesie Rady Ministrów do Spraw Zwalczania Spekulacji i Nadużyć Gospodarczych z dnia 13 kwietnia 1958, pp. 107–111.

155 See Leszek Lernell, *Przestępczość gospodarcza. Zagadnienia społeczno-ekonomiczne* (Warszawa: Wydawnictwo Prawnicze 1965), 77–85.

Table 5. Number of people charged in cases involving economic crimes in the years 1957–1960

	Year			
	1957	**1958**	**1959**	**1960**
Total No. of people	128,994	139,823	127,449	114,045
Including: Theft of social property	95,622	104,499	95,392	84,827
Clerical crime	25,172	23,705	19,863	20,567
Speculation	8,200	11,619	12,194	8,651

Source: Jacek Marecki, *Ekonomiczne i organizacyjne problemy przestępczości gospodarczej* (manuscript, Warszawa, 1962), 14–15.

1960 to PLZ 680.7 million.[156] MO statistics in 1964 estimated losses resulting from offenses tied to theft of social property at over 417,572,000, and clerical crime – PLZ 317,409,000.[157] This amount was greater than the annual investment outlays for higher education in that year (PLZ 521 million) or spending on nurseries (PLZ 521 million). At that time, the national income was estimated at approx. PLZ 497 billion.[158]

The fact that the actual losses in this regard were much greater is evidenced by, among other things, research carried out by the Institute of Internal Trade and the Department of Economic Crime Studies of the Main School of Planning and Statistics (Szkoła Główna Planowania i Statystyki, SGPiS, now the Warsaw School of Economics) in 1961–1964 involving the purchase of various everyday food articles voivodeship cities, districts and locales, and the average "fraud rate" calculated on this basis. That rate was, on average, 1.9 % of the total value of the transaction, but when the sale of meat and cold cuts was involved, it increased to 3.16 %; and coffee, to 20–30 %! The consumer losses calculated on this basis were estimated at PLZ 1.5 billion annually.[159] Only in July 1961, out of 179 stores in Warsaw where "monitored" purchases were made, in 83 % were found to be fraudulent to the consumer's disadvantage.[160]

---

156 Marecki, *Ekonomiczne i organizacyjne problemy*, 16, 25.

157 Helena Kołakowska-Przełomiec, Edward Syzduł, "Przestępstwa gospodarcze w Polsce w świetle statystyki milicyjnej za lata 1962–1965," *Państwo i Prawo* 9 (1966): 346.

158 Data from *Rocznik Statystyczny GUS* (Warszawa: GUS, 1965) 70, tab. 4 (88), 92, tab. 10 (117), 495, tab. 9 (692).

159 See Lernell, *Przestępczość gospodarcza,* 83; Marecki, "Na niekorzyść konsumenta," *Życie Gospodarcze* 28 (1964).

160 Marecki, *Ekonomiczne i organizacyjne problemy*, 38.

Data from MO statistics shows that the number of detected economic crimes in 1962 was 124,386 (i.e. 29.3 % of all revealed crimes); in 1963 – 153,469 (29.7 %); in 1964 – 133,863 (28, 9 %); and in 1965 – 134,892 (27.7 %). However, this data needs to be supplemented with some comment explaining the dynamics which comes into play here. In 1962, a change in the statistical registration system was implemented by MO, which meant that in 1962 there were far fewer preparatory proceedings counted from the end of previous year. However, the decline in the total number of all crimes, including economic crimes in 1964, was the effect of an announced amnesty. Despite this, the tendency was clearly visible in these years, according to which the share of economic crimes in the total number of crimes in Poland was about 30 %; about 70 % of them were property thefts.[161]

How did the proportions and sizes of crime in particular sectors of the economy shape up?

Due to the limited representativeness of data on this subject, a precise answer to such a question is difficult. According to Jacek Marecki, based on data from NIK, shortages in trade in 1959 amounted in total to 57.5 %, and in 1960 – 59.7 %; in industry – 25.1 % and 20.8 %; in construction and communal economy – 5.75 and 5.4 %; in transport – 4.6 % and 5.7 %, in agriculture – 4.5 % and 5.4 %; and in other sectors – 2.6 % and 3 0 %. The actual value was much higher, although it is impossible to make a precise calculation. According to Marecki, those involved in construction argued that in the early sixties, material "leaks" reached 2–3 % of the total investment value. Involving a total value of about PLZ 60 billion, in 1960 that amounted to about PLZ 1.5 billion, while documented shortages in construction in that year amounted to PLZ 36.7 million. The situation was probably similar in other sectors of the economy.[162]

This trend is confirmed by other sources. According to information on economic crime in 1960, presented to the offices of the KC PZPR that oversaw enterprises where a particularly high number of crimes involving social property were committed, investigators revealed 11,000 cases of theft in the Ministry of Construction and Construction Materials (the vast majority involving construction companies); the Ministry of Agriculture (10,000 thefts, mainly at PGR), the Ministry of Food Industry and Purchase (8,000, 50 % of which were in the meat industry); and the MHW (about 8,000).[163]

161 Kołakowska-Przełomiec, Syzduł, "Przestępstwa gospodarcze w Polsce," 340–341.

162 Marecki, *Ekonomiczne i organizacyjne problemy*, 186–190.

163 ADH PRL, Biuletyn Informacyjny Biura Sekretariatu KC PZPR nr 98, 4 lipca 1961, załącznik 2 (Informacje o przestępczości gospodarczej w 1960 r.), mat. nieuporządkowane.

Table 6. Adults convicted by common courts for crimes of an economic nature in the years 1959–1965

Type of crime	1959	1960	1961	1962	1963	1964	1965
Total*	280,761	301,927	328,490	298,090	271,545	191,933	222,323
Including:							
Involving social property, including:	66,691	59,889	66,849	59,928	53,164	37,867	43,072
Social assets	31,715	32,370	41,614	37,829	36,273	27,963	31,374
Petty theft	30,696	24,617	21,574	18,469	14,036	8,000	9,529
Clerical crimes, including	14,360	14,719	16,682	15,081	12,063	7,072	4,862
Cash shortfalls		3,541	3,303	2,507	2,828	1,523	1,116
Bribery	603	586	626	742	920	767	755
Crimes against state economic interests, including:	21,514	25,634	23,244	19,152	16,533	11,196	13,270
Speculation	6,948	7,083	7,179	5,937	4,904	3,427	4,201

*** adults convicted in general by common courts for all types of crimes (not only economic crimes)**

Source: *Rocznik Statystyczny GUS 1961* (Warszawa: GUS, 1961), 426, tab. 12(655); *Rocznik Statystyczny GUS 1967* (Warszawa: GUS, 1967), 591, tab. 14(898).

Table 6 contains data from the Central Statistical Office (GUS) regarding the number of those convicted for committing crimes of an economic nature in the period 1959–1965.

The above data shows that convicted crimes against social property accounted for approx. 1/5 of the total number of those convicted by common courts in the specific period under discussion here. The number of those convicted of clerical crimes was much smaller (from 5 % in 1961–1962 to 2.2 % in 1965) and to the detriment of the state's economic interests (from 5.8 % in 1964 to 8.5 % in 1960). These figures differ significantly from statistical data on those suspected of such crimes. It is even more difficult to handle these figures in terms of real proportions of behaviors punished in this way. They came about as a result of the interplay of many factors, among which there were the penal policy in force at the time and the contemporaneous cultural norms.

Who were the perpetrators of these crimes, socially speaking? Partial answers to this question have already been provided through previously-mentioned materials. Based on the analysis of materials from government oversight and justice institutions from 1959–1960, J. Marecki claimed that "minor crimes, unfortunately on a massive scale, are committed by rank-and-file workers (e.g. minor worker thefts in industrial plants). [. . .] More serious crimes are usually committed by employees who are materially responsible, managing the operational branches (shops, construction), increasingly often in connection with the management, supervisory and control apparatus, and sometimes even in cooperation with employees of another enterprise." Among the total number of white-collar workers who committed economic crimes in 1959, 9.8 % were directors and managers (in 1960 that percentage increased to 13.2 %), and 15.3 % were accountants and warehouse attendants (in 1960, 16.0 %).[164] Data collected by the MO (Table 7) indicated the same trend.

The above-cited data, especially regarding serious abuse by officials, is understated since not all of it was included in the MO statistics. It also did not cover a significant part of the fraud against consumers committed by store personnel, which was processed in a simplified manner.

In the later years, the general tendency toward the dominance of minor thefts among economic crimes did not change. The share of perpetrators as individuals in managerial positions was also at a similar level. According to the General Prosecutor's Office in 1964, 2,965 (3.5 %) directors and managers of socialized workplaces were involved in cases concerning the theft of social property, 1,983 (2.3 %) store managers and salespeople, and 922 (1.1 %) accountants. The share of directors and managers in the total number of suspects increased compared to 1963 by approx. 2 %, as was the case with store managers, including sellers.[165]

So far we have carried our analysis of economic crime in the PRL up into the mid-1960s – i.e. until the period when the authorities decided to highlight the Warsaw meat affair. However, it is worth trying to answer the question about how such crimes developed over the course of the next two decades – i.e. to the period of systemic transformation in 1989. We can make certain conclusions in this regard using data from GUS.

---

164 Marecki, *Ekonomiczne i organizacyjne problemy*, 195–196.

165 AAN, PG, 1/25, Informacja o wynikach ścigania przestępstw gospodarczych w 1964 r., Warszawa 7 IV 1965, pp. 303–307.

Table 7. Perpetrators of crimes against social property discovered by the MO in 1958–1960 by profession, position and social group

Profession-position	**1958**		**1959**		**1960**	
Social group	**No.**	%	**No.**	%	**No.**	%
Total	169,286	100.0	174,734	100.0	143,301	100.0
Socialized econcomy, including:	103,623	61.2	109,776	62.8	89,873	62.7
White-collar workers, including:	40,010	23.6	43,802	25.1	35,812	25.0
Directors and supervisors	4,559	2.7	4,315	2.5	4,718	3.3
Warehouse attendants and accountants	5,810	3.4	6,698	3.8	5,722	4.0
Shop workers	12,690	7.5	12,659	7.3	9,109	6.4
Other officials	16,951	10.0	20,130	11.5	16,263	11.3
Blue-collar workers	63,613	37.6	65,974	37.7	54,001	37.7
Non-socialized economy, including:	65,663	38.8	64,958	37.2	53,428	37.3
Free professions	2,876	1.8	2,996	1.7	1,095	0.8
Peasants	31,168	18.4	24,853	14.2	20,461	14.3
Private initiative	4,304	2.5	4,301	2.5	3,072	2.1
Non-working	27,315	16.1	32,808	18.8	28,800	20.1

Source: ADH PRL, Biuletyn Informacyjny Biura Sekretariatu KC PZPR nr 98, 4 lipca 1961, załącznik 2 (Informacje o przestępczości gospodarczej w 1960 r.).

However, the above data requires a few comments. First of all, it should be noted that in this period, the criteria for statistical registration of these crimes changed, a new category of *shortage* appeared. Speculation was defined in various ways, and our ability to compare crimes classified as such in the fifties, sixties and

Table 8. Selected, confirmed economic crimes in Poland in the years 1956–1989

Year	Theft of public assets	Shortages***	Crimes* involving speculation
1957	124,461**		20,900
1958	116,904**		23,138
1960	109,881**		14,022
1965	98,100		5,440
1967	83,400	5,313	3,506
1970	64,040	4,180	2,921
1972	53,980	2,495	2,851
1975	49,915	2,344	3,410
1977	50,302	2,225	4,351
1980	48,682	2,072	5,229
1981	40,559	1,651	5,729
1982	43,047	1,472	14,943
1985	51,016	2,072	24,171
1989	37,199	846	6,819

*** for the years 1969–1989: Art. 221–224 p.c. and the act dated 25 IX 1981.**
**** theft of social property**
***** a category introduced in the p.c. as of the year 1969.**

Source: Grażyna Grabarczyk, *Przestępczość gospodarcza na tle przemian ustrojowych w Polsce* (Toruń: Towarzystwo Naukowe Organizacji i Kierownictwa "Dom Organizatora," 2002), 76–99; *Rocznik Statystyczny GUS 1959* (Warszawa: GUS, 1959), 382, tab. 1 (618*); Rocznik Statystyczny GUS 1982* (Warszawa: GUS, 1982), 470, tab. 8 (767); *Rocznik Statystyczny GUS 1961* (Warszawa: GUS, 1961), 422, tab. 1(644); *Rocznik Statystyczny GUS 1971* (Warszawa: GUS, 1971), 621–622, tab. 1(924) and 2(921).

later is limited. And it is difficult to establish on this basis the above-mentioned dark number of crimes committed.[166]

Despite these differences, a tendency is clearly visible, according to which the first years of Gomułka's rule represent a period of intensified economic crime. It weakened in the 1960s, both on a global scale and in terms of basic types of speculation and theft (misappropriation) of social property. Basic GUS data seems to indicate that at least certain types of economic crimes intensified in the 1980s.

166 See Lernell, *Przestępczość gospodarcza*, 77–85.

Such trends find confirmation in data published after 1989 by the Institute of Justice (Instytut Wymiaru Sprawiedliwości) involving the years 1970–1990. What results from them is the conclusion that the economic crime rate per 100,000 people in this period was the smallest in 1981 (163 – i.e. 58,568 crimes recorded), and the largest was in 1985 (351 – i.e. 130,647). In the years 1971–1980 that rate fluctuated slightly between nearly 300 in 1971 to around 200 in 1980.[167]

These observations can be supplemented with the results of detailed and unsystematic criminological tests concerning developments the Gomułka era. They indicate that economic crimes made up around 30 % of the total crimes committed in Poland, and that about 70 % of them involved property theft.[168] Even if we believe that the draconian penalties which officials applied to the perpetrators of the largest economic crimes in the 1960s had some effect and led to their reduction, this tendency was not permanent.

3.2. The Mechanism of Fraud in Warsaw's Meat Economy

3.2.1. The Method of Detecting Fraud

The disclosure of fraud in the Warsaw meat affair was, on the one hand, the actions taken by those within the structures subordinated to the Ministry of Internal Affairs and, on the other hand, complaints flowing into the central state institutions. According to the confidential information of the Ministry of the Interior on 7 September 1964,[169] crimes in the Warsaw meat economy were detected as a result of actions taken in mid-1963 by the Warsaw MO, which provided information about thefts in the "Służewiec" Meat Plant and the Municipal Slaughterhouse, whose employees sold stolen meat in stores within the Municipal Meat Trade (Miejski Handel Mięsem, MHM) network[170] and "the

167 *Atlas przestępczości w Polsce*, ed. Andrzej Siemaszko (Warszawa: Oficyna Naukowa, 1994), 30. In this study, the category of economic crimes includes: the theft of social assets, criminal mismanagement, shortages, speculation, foreign exchange crime, and certain other tax offenses.

168 Kołakowska-Przełomiec, Syzduł, "Przestępstwa gospodarcze w Polsce," 340–341.

169 AAN, KC PZPR, 237/XIV-306, Informacja o ustaleniach śledztwa dotyczącego przestępstw w gospodarce mięsnej w m. st. Warszawie na dzień 7 września 1964, p. 83.

170 The first six state enterprises of the Municipal Trade in Meat (MHM) in the capital city – Warszawa –Zachód, Warszawa – Północ, Warszawa – Południe, Warszawa – Śródmieście, Warszawa – Praga – Południe i Warszawa – Praga – Północ – were established by the resolution of the Presidium of the National Council in 1953 replacing the previously existing "Municipal Meat Trade in Warsaw." Their activity involved the retail trade in meat, meat products, poultry, game and associated produces through

reception of material benefits by MHM administration employees from store managers." This data was confirmed by inspections carried out in two stores by the Inspectorate for Battle against Fraud in the Meat Economy (Inspektorat do Walki z Nadużyciami w Gospodarce Mięsnej) in Warsaw. As a result of these arrangements, several investigations were initiated at the end of 1963. This latter information is confirmed by the minutes of the meeting of the Executive Committee of the Warsaw PZPR on 20 April 1964, where Tadeusz Kozłowski, the Commander of the Warsaw MO, spoke about actions that had been taken.[171]

The fact that the detection of fraud could be credited to the operational work of the Warsaw MO was also mentioned by one of the participants of the staff (mentioned in the introduction above) called forth by the Minister of Internal Affairs to investigate fraud in the meat economy. Already in May 1964, the Warsaw MO was dealing with 14 operational matters in this regard, which involved 9 secret collaborators, 120 so-called personal information sources and 27 operational employees.[172]

---

a subordinate chain of stores. General supervision was exercised by the Ministry of Internal Trade, and directly by the Presidium of the Warsaw National Council [Prezydium stołecznej Rady Narodowej] through the Metropolitan Trade Board [Stołecznego Zarządu Handlu] (as of 1959 – the Department of Trade and Capital City Association of Trade in Food Products [Wydziału Handlu i Stołecznego Zjednoczenia Handlu Artykułami Spożywczymi]). In 1960, the MHM Warszawa – Zachód and Warszawa – Północ merged and the territorial scope of the store chain operation subordinated to MHM enterprises was changed. In December 1963, the Presidium of the Warsaw National Council decided to merge MHM – Warsaw – Praga – Południe and Warsaw – Praga – Północ into MHM Warsaw – Praga. As of 1 February 1964, MHM Warsaw – Śródmieście and MHM Warszawa Południe were merged. As a result of these transformations, there remained on 1 February: Warszawa – Północ, MHM Warszawa – Południe i MHM Warszawa – Praga. See Archiwum Sądu Okręgowego w Warszawie (hereafter cited as ASO), IV K 155/64, vol. III, Uzasadnienie aktu oskarżenia.

171 APW, Komitet Warszawski PZPR (hereafter as: KW PZPR), 30/IV-85, Protokół nr 7/64 z posiedzenia Egzekutywy Komitetu Warszawskiego PZPR w dniu 20 kwietnia 1964, p. 64. Inspectorates to fight abuse in the meat economy were set up under ordinance no. 178 by the Prime Minister of 1 October 1959. See Aleksander Kochański, *Polska 1944–1991. Informator historyczny*, vol. II, 180.

172 For more detail on the subject of individuals tied to the SB, see Tadeusz Ruzikowski, "Tajni współpracownicy pionów operacyjnych aparatu bezpieczeństwa 1950–1984," *Pamięć i Sprawiedliwość* 1 (2003): 109–113; Kamiński, "Lingua securitatis," *Pamięć i Sprawiedliwość* 1 (2003): 209–216.

Advanced cases of a similar nature were under investigation in other Polish cities.[173]

According to information from the prosecutor at the General Prosecutor's Office, Kazimierz Kukawka, dated 21 April 1964 and intended for the KC PZPR, detection of fraud in the meat trade was the result of the disclosure of criminal links between meat shop managers and MO functionaries at the Inspectorate for Battle against Fraud in the Meat Economy at the MO Provincial Headquarters in Warsaw.[174]

This material also indicates that complaints about fraud in institutions dealing in meat management in Warsaw were submitted to voivodeship officials and central party and state authorities. Jerzy Jagiełło, a member of the KG MO staff, stated on 4 March 1959 that identical anonymous letters had arrived "at certain state organs [. . .] whose author signaled that a director at MHM, Stanisław Wawrzecki, is taking bribes from subordinate shop managers."[175] According to information prepared in May 1964 by the Administrative Department of the PZPR Warsaw Committee, a total of 12 letters (including anonymous ones) had arrived there since 1961 regarding the situation in the meat trade and the meat processing industry, letters which came from people dismissed from their positions at the MHM not only complaining that they had been dismissed unfairly but also suggesting that "bad things are happening" in this organization, and that "bribery and cronyism are prevalent."[176]

Between May 1963 and May 1964, four "signals about fraud in the meat trade" had arrived, the importance of which varied in terms of their significance for activities related to the meat affair.

The first anonymous letter indicated signaled "meat schemes" being carried out at MHM Warszawa Północ. The allegations contained in the letter were clarified by a commission established in the District Committee (Komitet Dzielnicowy, KD) of the PZPR Warsaw-Wola, which found no fraud. The anonymous letter

173 IPN BU, KG MO, 1550/1782, Protokół nr 3 z posiedzenia Sztabu powołanego zarządzeniem nr 057/64 MSW odbytego w dniu 29 maja 1964 r., pp. 33–36.

174 AAN, KC PZPR, 2224 (mikrofilm 3381), Załącznik. Informacja w sprawie nadużyć w gospodarce mięsnej na terenie m. st. Warszawy K. Kukawki, Prokuratora Generalnej Prokuratury, Warszawa 21 kwietnia 1964, pp. 407–412.

175 Jerzy Jagiełło, "Przestępczość w przemyśle i handlu mięsem w świetle warszawskiej afery mięsnej," *Problemy Kryminalistyki* 53 (1965): 11.

176 AAN, KC PZPR, 237/VII-5264, Notatka dotycząca sygnałów o nadużyciach w handlu i przetwórstwie mięsnym w Warszawie Wydziału Administracyjnego KW PZPR z 23 V 1964, pp. 50–52.

was passed to MO offices, which, after examining the information contained in the letter, could also not confirm the allegations.

In June 1963, the next anonymous letter arrived, accusing the director of MHM Śródmieście of a "lack of collective work and the use of illegal methods of working with people." In this case, a party organization meeting was held at MHM attended by members of the Party Control Committee and the Organization Department (Wydział Organizacyjny) of the PZPR Provincial Committee (Komitet Wojewódzki, KW). Over the course of discussions, the allegations were confirmed, though none of the participants mentioned fraud or bribes involving the MHM director.

In September 1963, a worker reported to the Wojewódzka Komisja Kontroli Partyjnej (Party Control WK, WKKP) indicating thefts at the Meat Plant in Służewiec. "But he said that he does not want to personally provide these facts to law enforcement authorities, because he has no confidence in MO officers from the Mokotów district." The KW PZPR forwarded this information directly to Lt. Col. M. Janicki, deputy commander of the Warsaw MO.

In November 1963, the next anonymous letter arrived at Warsaw party organization offices about fraud at MHM as headed by Wawrzecki. It was forwarded to the Inspection and Audit Inspectorate (Inspektorat Kontrolno-Rewizyjny), which proceeded as normal. As a result, officials detected irregularities amounting to approx. PLZ 1.5 million.[177]

Similar correspondence also reached the KC PZPR, which is evidenced by a letter signed by "Malinowski Andrzej" (with no address but dated 29 May 1964), addressed to Władysław Gomułka and informing him that at the meat plant on Taśmowa St. in Warsaw ("Służewiec") "thefts continue. [...] If any of the employees do not want to steal meat, they are fired for being inefficient. The managers themselves steal and force workers to steal [...]." Militiamen from the police station at Wita Stwosza St., the author of the letter wrote later, found positions for their wives in meat plants as auditors and they are the ones who organized all thefts, while "their husbands [...] guard the employees with meat to calmly go home."[178] The facts offered in this complaint were checked by the Warsaw MO body and were largely confirmed.[179] On 12 February 1964, a

177 APW, KW PZPR, 30/IV-85, Informacja złożona na Egzekutywie KW PZPR w dniu 9 V 1964 r. w sprawie ujawnionych nadużyć w handlu mięsem, pp. 100–103.

178 AAN, KC PZPR, 237/XIV-306, Do Władysława Gomułki, Warszawa 29 maja 1964, pp. 9 ff.

179 AAN, KC PZPR, 237/XIV-306, Komenda Główna MO do Ministra Spraw Wewnętrznych Władysława Wichy, Warszawa 26 czerwca 1964, p. 6.

former blue-collar worker at these plants, the wife of a Special Battalion officer at the Ministry of National Defense, in a conversation held at the Warsaw MO Headquarters, informed investigators that two workers walked out with about 10 kilograms of cold cuts per day.[180]

Based on the above documents, it appears that as early as 1963, both the Warsaw MO and party organization authorities obtained information on fraud in Warsaw's meat economy, which did not necessarily mean that they would be subject to further investigative and judicial proceedings. The fact that this happened was undoubtedly the effect of a political decision made by the highest party authorities. However, before we explain how this happened, let us try to answer the question of what these instances of fraud were.

3.2.2. Fraud in Meat Plants

An analysis of methods employed in fraud discovered during the Warsaw meat affair was the subject of several reports prepared by both justice institutions and party organs. The meticulous oversight of the case carried out by the KC PZPR created a situation in which documents of various types describing the progress of the investigation were preserved in the party files.

According to these findings, meat theft occured in plants dealing with meat processing (meat plants, cold stores, processing plants). Industrial meat plants provided opportunities for fraud because the raw material processed there was heterogeneous and could quickly change its weight. Thus, it was not possible in the processing regulations to apply strict standards of slaughter and production; it was difficult to accurately predict meat weight loss in the individual phases of processing as a result of drying, leaking of liquids and grinding. The situation was additionally complicated by the uneven quality of slaughtered livestock (various types, classes, feeding and fattening methods, etc.). Relevant standards and indicators in this area allowed for certain weight variations, which provided the opportunity to "generate" surpluses, which were the object of speculation.[181] Artificial weight gain of cured meats could also be obtained by adding excessive amounts of water, salt and fat during processing. In the case of meat, the artificial inflation of weight occurred when it was subjected to such technological processes as, for example, curing. Opportunities for fraud arose in meat plants

180 AAN, KC PZPR, 237/XIV-306, Plan operacyjno-dochodzeniowych przedsięwzięć, Warszawa 12 czerwca 1964, pp. 11 ff.

181 AAN, KC PZPR, 237/XIV-307, Analiza i wnioski dotyczące nadużyć w przemyśle mięsnym, p. 14.

during the meat cutting process (adding lower quality meats to meats that were labeled high quality).[182]

Thefts also took place in a less complicated way. During transport, entire parts of meat weighing several metric tons disappeared.[183]

Official documents detail the nature of fraud in specific plants around Warsaw.

In the case of Warsaw Meat Plant at 14 Owsiana St., the meat and fats that were the object of the theft were "produced" in the manner described above (through broken norms that guided meat cutting, production, efficiency and losses, and – with pork fat – through excessive salting). The stolen raw material was transported using personal automobiles or vehicles that belonged to the Meat Industry Transport Works (Przedsiębiorstwo Transportowe Przemysłu Mięsnego). It was thereby delivered to the owners of private meat processing plants as well as state and cooperative stores in the Warsaw Voivodeship. Persons involved in this procedure (foremen and warehouse attendants) transferred part of the money obtained in this way to the management and employees of the plant administration. Similar mechanisms were at work in other Warsaw meat plants.

In the case of the City Slaughterhouse, the management and employees accepted bribes, primarily for selling meat outside the distributor. According to the findings of the investigation, almost all employees there had some links to corruption.

In the case of Meat Plant in Rembertów near Warsaw, the investigation led to the detection of a separate criminal group composed of drivers of Meat Industry Transport Works and deliverers in various commercial enterprises. Some of them searched for buyers and stole meat themselves from loaded vehicles, hiding shortages through the use of salting and watering or counting them as losses (caused in the drying process) in transport, which in reality did not happen. There were also cases of theft of imported meat, facilitated by the fact that it had not been weighed before loading; it was possible to remove the meat from sealed vehicles by removing the door from its hinges. A separate group in these plants,

---

182 AAN, KC PZPR, 237/XIV-306, Notatka o stanie śledztwa w sprawie przestępstw w gospodarce mięsnej w m. st. Warszawie i innych ośrodkach kraju, Warszawa, 8 września 1964, pp. 59 ff; Jagiełło, "Przestępczość w przemyśle i handlu mięsem w świetle warszawskiej afery mięsnej," 17–24.

183 AAN, KC PZPR, 237/XIV-306, Informacja w sprawie nadużyć w gospodarce mięsnej na terenie m. st. Warszawy prokuratora Prokuratury Generalnej K. Kukawki, Warszawa 21 kwietnia 1964 r., p. 22.

consisting mainly of directors and dispatchers, took "tribute" from drivers for establishing "lucrative routes" that allowed for theft and fraud.[184]

3.2.3. Fraud in the Meat Trade

The next link in the chain of fraud in the Warsaw meat affair involved trade.

Stolen meat went to certain stores (mainly those administered by MHM) and to private producers of cold cuts.

In the first case, goods received and sold were the subject of further schemes, the most common of which involved instances of fraud regarding weight, price and quality. Detailed and reliable information on this subject can be found, among other places, in the case files of the meat affair.

This type of fraud was facilitated by the fact that most shops received meat for sale in the form of carcasses, half-carcasses or quarters; only very small quantities of meat came in so-called culinary elements (divided by type: ham, ribs, bacon, shoulders, etc.)., which provided opportunities to obtain additional material benefits through incorrectly produced cuts of meat that worked to the detriment of consumers.[185] As one interrogated shop manager explained, fraudulently produced cuts of meat "may result in additional savings based on the fact that half carcasses, carcasses and quarters are counted according to single price for a given half carcass, carcass or quarters. When cutting, however, various elements are created, like pork loin, pork fat, bacon and others. At various prices. So if someone is dishonest in the process of cutting down half-carcass pork fat by adding a layer of bacon, then he has already made an additional profit because while bacon costs PLZ 26/kg, pork fat costs PLZ 33/kg. It is similar when cutting pork and shoulder where one can add a layer of fat which is cheaper than the pork and shoulder."[186]

In addition to this method of consumer deception, another one involved natural losses caused by the drying of meat and sausages over the course of the sale

---

184 AAN, KC PZPR, 237/XIV-306, Informacja o wynikach ustaleń śledczych w tzw. "warszawskiej sprawie mięsnej" Komendanta Głównego Milicji Obywatelskiej gen. R. Dobieszaka, pp. 96–100.

185 ASO, IV K 155/64, vol. VIII, Sprawozdanie do protokołu nr 050761 z przeprowadzonej inspekcji w dyrekcji Miejskiego Handlu Mięsem Warszawa Północ. See also: Jagiełło, "Przestępczość w przemyśle i handlu mięsem w świetle warszawskiej afery mięsnej," 31–32.

186 ASO, IV K 155/64, vol. XVII, Protokół przesłuchania świadka Jana Wasilewskiego dnia 16 IX 1964 r. w Warszawie przez podprokuratora Prokuratury Powiatowej Dzielnicy Ochota T. Kuszewskiego, p. 179.

process. From the actual weight of the products sold, shop managers could deduct the previously established norms regarding these losses without fear of being suspected of fraud. During his interrogation in June 1964, an MHM director talked about the behind-the-scenes reality of this commonly used procedure:

> At the time when I was working in the management of MHM Warszawa Zachód, natural losses were set by MHW and amounted to about 0.9 %. Due to the high rotation of meat and sausage products, these losses were not used by store managers as intended. There was even a lack of meat and cold cuts on the market, therefore the meat and sausages delivered to the shops were usually sold quickly, so the goods did not dry out, and thus did not lose weight; proceeds from the sale of meat in this way were appropriated store managers. In later years, it seems to me that in 1957–1958, the percentage of natural losses was increased to 1.5 % in relation to turnover. Based on the reports from the oversight of shops delivered to me [. . .], I realized that shop managers, or rather the shop staff, are cheating on weight.[187]

This opinion is basically confirmed by testimony related to this case given by one witness in September 1964:

> Regarding the rate of turnover of goods in the store, it can be generally stated that in all the stores where I worked the goods were sold out immediately. There were some deviations from this principle tied to the assortment. Namely, the most popular were pork sausages, common sausages and hams. These went on sale from the moment of delivery until they were gone – that is, these types of meat were sold on the day of delivery. There were cases when some cold cuts remained on the second day. But such facts were related to the delivery, namely in cases when these goods were delivered too late and they did not manage to see the delivered products by closing time – that is, by 19.00. Some types of cold cuts, such as beef cold cuts and cervelat sausages, did not have such success and they remained in the shop for several days."[188]

In this way, the "recovery" of surplus cash was often accomplished by the use in stores of so-called "silent remanents."

Store personnel participated in yet another illegal (according to regulations at the time) practice, one that resulted from the "mass meat policy" – as one defendant called it – being pursued in Warsaw at the time. It was tied to the fact that

---

187 ASO, IV K 155/64, vol. XIV, Protokół przesłuchania podejrzanego 27 VI 1964 r. w Warszawie przez podprokuratora Prokuratury Powiatowej dla Dzielnicy Warszawa Śródmieście Tadeusza Zaborskiego, p. 131. Opportunities for abuse in this respect were also caused by the fact that MHM directors established specific loss limits in individual stores, within the framework of general regulations.

188 ASO, IV K 155/64, vol. XXII, Protokół przesłuchania świadka Warszawa 17 IX 1964 por. [Włochalski] z KMMO, p. 111. See również: J. Jagiełło, 30–31.

in summer the distribution of beef for broth beef was withheld in the summer, when customers did not want to buy it in such quantities, and roasting meat was withheld in winter, when the former was in demand. As a result, stores had enormous remanents of pork fat and pork shoulder in one period, and shortages in another period. Store managers were thus forced to add salt to this pork fat to prevent spoilage (stores rarely had freezers and cold stores at their disposal). For the same purpose, at the back of the shops, they processed the meat they had in their possession for cold cuts or white sausage and thereby obtained additional profits. They passed such "unsellable" meat, with no documentation, to the owners of private craft workshops producing sausage, who in turn provided the shops with cold cuts of equivalent value.[189]

This practice of "mutual services" between private producers of cold cuts and state-owned stores was much more extensive. Trade in products from private meat establishments in state-owned stores, often made from meat previously conveyed by the managers of these stores, was referred to – using the sales jargon at the time – as selling "under-the-counter."[190] The reason for such a practice was explained by one of the interrogated suspects in May 1964: "And so the period since 1961 has been a period when [. . .] we were limited with regard to the allocation of raw material [meat], wanting to prosper and pay the necessary bribes to employees of various institutions, I was forced to buy raw material of illegal origin." Illegal meat purchases were carried out not only with stores but also with various processing plants. In addition, "I was forced to buy pork shoulder from almost all of the MHM store managers with whom I traded, and along with that various post-cut pieces [. . .] so-called slaughterhouse samples (samples intended for medical examinations) and other pieces – raw meat which the consumer did not purchase, and which, if not resold, could lead to the meat being spoiled.[191]

Another reason for such behavior came about as a result of the established economic policy at the time, according to which private meat shops were strictly

189 ASO IV K 155/64, vol. XXII, Protokół przesłuchania podejrzanego Henryka Gradowskiego Warszawa 17 VIII 1964 przez kpt. Tadeusza Ciołkowskiego z KG MO, p. 157.

190 AAN, PG 1/29, Notatka (nr 4) o przebiegu procesu w sprawie Stanisława Wawrzeckiego i innych, p. 129; ASO, IV K 155/64, vol. XXII, Ciąg dalszy przesłuchania Henryka Gradowskiego przerwanego w dniu 5 IX 1964, Warszawa 7 IX 1964, przesłuchujący podprok. Zdzisław Kwela, p. 175.

191 ASO, IV K 155/64, vol. XVIII, Protokół przesłuchania podejrzanego Antoniego Zawadzkiego przez mjr Stanisława Bornsteina z KG MO w dniu 12 maja 1964, p. 42.

licensed and limited in their functions to a supplement to the state trade network. This policy had deep ideological roots and had been implemented with varying consequences since 1944. As indicated by a document on this subject from 1957 preserved in the files of the Sejm Chancellery (Kancelaria Sejmu), meat processing development in the postwar period reached its apogee at the end of 1949, when there were 4,476 craft workshops, including 112 producing horse meat products. As a result of the socialization of meat processing and the trade in livestock and meat products, the number of private workshops began to decline at a rapid pace (to 107 by 31 December 1955, not counting 34 engaged in the processing of horse meat). Starting from the second half of 1956, they gradually increased in number: if on 31 December 1955 there were 107 of them in Poland (and 34 horse meat processing shops), on 31 December 1956 there were 263 of them. No clear guidelines defining the framework for the development of meat processing, along with the liberal policy followed by local administrative authorities, resulted in a rapid increase in processed meat workshops in 1957. The relevant offices in many voivodeships allowed the creation of meat workshops without major objections, and without considering what it would take to supply them with the necessary raw material: meat. Craftsmen, having the right to carry out meat processing, applied for bank loans, which were quite generously provided. From the state's perspective, it meant reprehensible chaos and encouraged a lack of restraint. In order to control this situation, the MPSiS and the Ministry of Small and Craft Industries (Ministerstwo Przemysłu Drobnego i Rzemiosła) issued orders on 23 January 1957 regarding the activity of these workshops, which would be allowed to function in cases where socialized processing plants lacked capacity to fully supply meat products to the market. These orders defined the forms in which finished product from workshops could be sold, and they established socialized meat wholesale establishment as the only source of raw material supply. Prices for slaughtered livestock allocated to meat processing workshops were set slightly higher than prices that applied to socialized industry.

In June 1957, workshop production of meat-related goods amounted to 575.6 tons of meat, 781.6 tons of cured meats, and 618.8 tons of cold cut products – i.e. 4.3 % of total production. In the case of Warsaw, this share was 8.4 %, and the Warsaw Voivodeship – 19.2 %, the largest in the country. In this situation, the capital city's susceptibility to fraud could have been – and was – particularly large.

Estimates were that, due to the low allocation of raw material, the production capacity of craft workshops was exploited in 1957 in various regions of the country at levels ranging from 25 % to 70 %. According to the above-cited orders from 23 January 1957, meat products from craft production could be sold from a craftsman's own shop, or – if the production was carried out on behalf of a socialized retail enterprise – through the network of socialized stores. According to data from 1 September 1957, of a total of 1,155 meat processing workshops, 179 produced for trade with socialized outlets, and 976 distributed products through their own chain of stores. Craft workshops producing meat produces were supplied with raw material from socialized wholesale companies in the form of meat or livestock. The amount of raw material designated for this purpose was specified in special supply lists and – as stated above – was far from fulfilling the production capacity of private processing establishments. This reality created a natural tendency to bypass the rules, which resulted in the application of procedures that were illegal as viewed from the law in force at the time.[192] This tendency does not seem to have been stopped after 1957 – especially since the private sector, although limited, had become a permanent part of meat processing in Poland. In 1963, private butcheries and delicatessens produced 2,511 tons of sausages and smoked meat (0.7 % of domestic production) and 8,379 tons (7.7 %) of cold cut products from offal. On 30 June 1964, there were 620 cold cut establishments employing 1,475 people, including 5 exporting plants.[193]

In order for the fraudulent mechanism described above to function well, it was also necessary to incorporate oversight institutions into its structure. In the light of the investigation's findings, employees of state and social oversight apparatus systematically took bribes, mainly from store managers and craft workshop owners for tolerating production which was inconsistent with production recipes and the rules of hygiene,[194] in return for which

192 AAN, Kancelaria Sejmu (hereafter cited as Kanc.S), 110, Ocena działalności rzemieślniczych (prywatnych) warsztatów wędliniarskich, p. 585–592.

193 AAN, KC PZPR, 237/X-156, Analiza przestępczości w gospodarce mięsnej w świetle afery mięsnej w Warszawie, Warszawa 7 listopada 1964, p. 2. The same document – AAN, KC PZPR, 237/XIV-307, pp. 6 ff.

194 The fact that non-hygienic conditions prevailed not only in craft workshops but also state-owned factories, can be demonstrated by, for example, a letter sent to Polish Radio by an employee of Wytwórnia Mięsna in Czarnków from 1957, which contained the following passage: "At the end of July this year, there were about 5 tons of animals heads which were spoiled due to poor warehouse storage (warehouse attendants not being professionals). So in this case, it was necessary to remedy the evil. After a short consultation with the factory collective, they came up with a great idea. The engineer relied on the law of physics that fat always floats on water. At night, the first batch of heads was placed where the pigs were scalding and flooded it with water. In the morning, without exaggeration, about a 2 cm thickness of worms was floating on the

they "closed their eyes" to financial and other crimes to the detriment of the consumer.[195]

Core corruption ties existed between store managers and the directors of the MHM network, which mainly concerned the procedures used to assign meat shops to "appropriate" managers. And the fact that these stores were "valued" differently is evidenced by testimonies given by witnesses and suspects in the meat affair. One MHM store manager claimed that while self-service outlets with high staff numbers were the most lucrative, the least lucrative were small single-person outlets with low turnover: "For example: when I was running a [single-person] shop on Wawelska St., I received around PLZ 1,100 monthly, and on Popularna [St.] in a four-person shop, I received about PLZ 1,700 a month. In addition, different rates applied in self-service shops and salaries reached several thousand zlotys."[196] This was confirmed by another witness, an MHM employee since 1952, who had been transferred often for the fact that – as she claimed – she was "too honest." She was called a "troublemaker" for her behavior:

> The whole secret lies in the fact that shop managers do not want to employ honest salespeople, because then they would not have the opportunity to earn the cash surpluses they need to pay bribes, "tribute" to directors, deliverers, trade department employees and inspectors. It was a public secret in the MHM that the store managers [. . .] made "payoffs" to the directors for the stores, as a result of which they treated the stores as their own [. . .]. These managers always had high-volume stores with the best supply and were treated well by the directors, and I even noticed that they had good personal

surface, and the second such layer flowed out after stirring. At the mere sight of this, people were disgusted that meat products could come from this. There were even those who refused to take these heads apart, for example citizen Paliwoda Bogusław, who was threatened with dismissal if he did not take up this job, and even though he had to vomit it, he had to do it and now he is hated for it." The person in charge of technical oversight could have been drunk on that day, because "it happens quite often, but it cannot be that she was drunk for four days, which is how long this swimming lesson took." This "commodity" was sent for processing to Obornicki Meat Plant and cold cuts from Oborniki were delivered, among other places, to Warsaw. See Archiwum Ośrodka Dokumentacji i Zbiorów Programowych TVP S. A. (hereafter cited as: AODiZP), 1050/19, Biuletyn Biura Listów Komitetu do Spraw Radiofonii "Polskie Radio," nr 66, 7 października 1957.

195 AAN, KC PZPR, 237/XIV-306, Informacja o wynikach ustaleń śledczych w tzw. "warszawskiej sprawie mięsnej". . ., pp. 104–106.

196 ASO, IV K 155/64, vol. XIX, Protokół przesłuchania świadka Warszawa 1 IX 1964 przez kpt. Tadeusza Ciołkowskiego z KG MO, p. 140.

relations with the directors, because they spoke with one another using the [informal] "you."[197]

The existence of these procedures was confirmed by a former deputy director for commercial affairs at Warsaw's Union of Industries in Trade of Foodstuffs (Zjednoczenie Przedsiębiorstw Handlu Artykułami Spożywczymi):

> This subject was widely discussed, as was the fact that some stores have to be "bought." I talked to the director about this topic. [. . .] but he told me [. . .] that I could lose my job because MHM directors and other employees of meat factories "have each other's backs." Such "backing" resulted from their shared drunkenness and contacts with influential people." These people are said to be high-ranking officers of the Warsaw National Council, the Warsaw Committee and the PZPR District Committees.[198]

The investigation files indicate that the corruption of the managerial staff in meat trade institutions by the store managers was routine, an "adaptation strategy" tied to the realities of everyday life. One person interrogated in the investigation described this procedure in the following way:

> I gave N money when there was a need for it. It was connected with the issue of supplying the store with a mass of goods. In times when I saw that the store's supply began to decrease, which threatened the plan's failure, I had to intervene with director N. At each visit I handed him between PLZ 500 to 1000. The amount I gave N. depended on the frequency of my visits to him, as well as the extent of the surplus from natural losses and the cut half-carcasses. I handed N money not only when it involved better store supply but also when I was forced to intervene with him in the matter of stopping the supply of a non-salable meat assortment, which created reserves in the store, and which threatened its spoiling. [. . .] I always handed money to N. in his office, directly into his hands, without wrapping it or putting it in an envelope. After each such delivery of money, I felt his assistance in the form of better supply of goods to the store, or stopping the delivery of nonsalable meat or meat products.

In 1961, a new director appeared in the company who was responsible for the interrogated shop. The two soon met in the corridor near the director's office" the management:

> He asked me if I would "stop by today." Because I had nothing to do directly with director X, I understood his invitation as an indication that the new director was already aware of the material benefits from the store managers. Based on my experience with

197 ASO, IV K 155/64, vol. XIX, Protokół przesłuchania świadka, Warszawa 4 września 1964 r. przez kpt. Tadeusza Ciołkowskiego z KG MO w Warszawie, 134–136.

198 ASO, IV K 155/64, vol. XIX, Protokół przesłuchania świadka 28 IX 1964 w Warszawie przez podprokuratora Andrzeja Jarzynę, pp. 141–143.

> previous directors, I was convinced that X wanted to make contact with me in order to receive money from me. For this reason, I was forced to go to X. [. . .] I took out PLZ 1000. from my pocket [. . .] and handed it directly into the hand of X, mentioning that I would come to him again one day. X replied: "I know," and he therefore made it very clear that you had to give money not just once, but often. [. . .] Through 1961 to March 1964, I gave director X money a dozen or more times in totals from between a thousand to PLZ 2,000.[199]

One MHM director in the investigation described the manner by which a manager of a store on Grójecka St. delivered bribes: in March or April 1964:

> [. . .] in the process of supervising the store, at the back, Z. put PLZ 500 in my pocket in support of the store, saying that he was giving me the money to buy shoes. I took the money out of my pocket several times and put it on Z's table, but he kept putting it back in my pocket every time. After a long at attempt by him to persuade me, I accepted the money, and I agreed with him that this fact would only remain between us, we both promised that, should some investigation develop, neither of us would reveal it, I was particularly concerned that his colleagues and my employees not know about this fact.[200]

This practice of "breaking in" officials involved in meat trade encouraged the implementation of improper staff policy, including the employment of people previously convicted for committing crimes. The affair also revealed that quite often the owners of private butchers and meat shop managers under MHM management were related to one another.[201]

Participants in these illegal transactions created their own rationales and explanations designed to "sooth their consciences" and justify bribery. Important components of this psychological self-lie were: the belief that they earned too little, the belief that "everyone is doing it," a fear they would be harassed if the "broke away" from the illegality. Corruption was facilitated by the conviction that it was simply part of the tradition of working in the meat industry "from time immemorial," and that those involved in the process were "untouchable" because they held high positions and have their patrons in the structures of local authorities.

Elements of this reasoning are found in the testimony of one of the main defendants, who complained about his low salary as, first of all, director of MHM

---

199 ASO, IV K 155/64, vol. XXI, Protokół przesłuchania podejrzanego Edwarda Składanowskiego, Warszawa 28 IX 1964 przez Józefa Ulatowskiego, p. 7.

200 ASO, IV K 155/64, vol. XIV, Protokół przesłuchania podejrzanego w dniu 25 VI 1964 w Warszawie przez podprokuratora Prokuratury Powiatowej dla Dzielnicy Warszawa-Śródmieście Tadeusza Zaborskiego, p. 123.

201 AAN, KC PZPR, 237/XIV-306, Informacja o ustaleniach śledztwa. . ., p. 90.

Warszawa Zachód (PLZ 3,000 per month), and then as the director of MHM Północ (PLZ 3,500). He claimed that:

> [...] it was very difficult for us [i.e. for him and his unemployed wife]. [...] I started accepting money from store managers because I earned little or not much, and besides that, when I was invited by my superiors or colleagues to restaurants, I sometimes wanted to add a smaller sums of money to the bill, but they laughed at that and said that I should put my money away, for the time will come when I will pay myself. With these directors I saw larger sums of money among their superiors, who were also in the restaurants, to which they did not react; rather they exploited it. I also wanted to be in possession of larger sums of money in order to be able to please my superiors, to be able to host them, and I hoped that I would gain their support, and it was clear from the behavior of these people that you could have additional sources of income and that they would not oppose it. In the first period of my work, managers of various shops approached me, proposing that I accept money from them. I rejected that at first, afraid, even though other directors enjoyed larger sums of money precisely from these sources. I was afraid even though my superiors tolerated such facts. Managers told me that for as long as they work, they would always provide directors with remuneration and that these directors would take money from them. They also told me not to be afraid, because they have been providing such benefits for several years now, even to many directors who are already in senior positions.[202]

The untouchable nature of the perpetrators of fraud from the "director group" was also a result of the fact that they were came largely from the party apparatus, in which they still had friends. It was thanks to this party experience that they were appointed to positions in trade, even though they often lacked any professional qualifications. As one of the suspects (a director at Warsaw's Union of Industries in Trade of Foodstuffs) testified during interviews conducted with him:

> [...] they mentioned the names of people high up in the party apparatus, and when I was invited by them to sumptuous parties related to some celebration, I was saw that these people really they took part in such parties and they used the [informal] "you" with their directors. There were several such parties and I honestly felt honored that I could establish contacts with such high-ranking people. At these namedays celebrations and other parties, I got to know or met, for example, [...] the head of the Trade Department, [...] the secretary of the District Committee of the PZPR, the prosecutor [...] the head of the personal department the Warsaw MO, whose name I forget, [...] and others. It is understandable, then, that I tried to maintain good relations with the directors mentioned at the beginning. [...] Therefore, I was forced to plan the personnel policy in filling directors' positions so that none of the directors mentioned would be unhappy

202 ASO, IV K 155/64, vol. XXII, Ciąg dalszy przesłuchania Henryka Gradowskiego..., pp. 174 ff.

> and often found myself in a very difficult situation, in particular when the number of directors was reduced as a result of mergers. In summary, I must say that not all of my actions related to these people were in line with my personal views, because I was often in a somewhat forced situation."[203]

The investigation findings confirmed the existence of these links.[204]

Finally, thanks to the fact that they were tied up in this corruption mechanism, its participants could lead a lifestyle that is unavailable to "average" Poles. Among other things, they dined at the best Warsaw restaurants. One witness, and soon a defendant, testified in the investigation that, to his surprise, a dinner had been organized after a July 1962 conference at the Sala Kongresowa at the Palace of Culture and Science in Warsaw, attended by directors in the meat trade, managers and deputy managers of all meat shops in Warsaw, representatives of the PZPR District Committees, of district councils, and of the MO, a dinner organized:

> [. . .] by Wawrzecki and other directors at "Trojka" [one of the best restaurants in Warsaw at the time] attended not only by MHM directors but also other people who had not taken part in the conference and who had been told by telephone of the event by directors, including Wawrzecki, who "played the first violin." I drew the conclusion that a number of people were aware of irregularities in the meat trade, that they treated the conference as a pure formality, that they agree with the state of affairs in which MHM directors are storing thousands of zlotys of known origin.

Wawrzecki organized such dinners "almost every day and for some of them he brought me in." This witness claimed that he initially took part in them, but from May 1961 he refused because he did not feel "strong enough health-wise to participate in them because of the amount alcohol that accompanied them."[205] One element of this lifestyle that was available to some owners of private sausage workshops and high officials of Warsaw's trade administration involved foreign trips, not only to Yugoslavia or Paris but also to the Canary Islands![206]

---

203 ASO, IV K 155/64, vol. XV, Protokół przesłuchania podejrzanego Tadeusza Skowrońskiego z dnia 3 IX 1964 w Warszawie przez podprokuratora Prokuratury Powiatowej w Warszawie – Żoliborz, pp. 70 ff.

204 AAN, KC PZPR, 237/XIV-306, Informacja o przestępczości w gospodarce mięsnej, Warszawa, grudzień 1964, pp. 127 ff.

205 ASO, IV K 155/64, vol. XIX, Protokół przesłuchania świadka 28 IX 1964 w Warszawie przez podprokuratora Andrzeja Jarzynę, pp. 141–143.

206 ASO, IV K 155/64, vol. XIX, Protokół przesłuchania świadka dnia 15 września 1964 r. w Warszawie przez podprokuratora Prokuratury Wojewódzkiej dla m. st. Warszawy, p. 119.

The investigation files indicate that pathological phenomena in the business of meat processing and the meat trade were common. We can even speak about the existence of a "culture of corruption." Deviations from the rules that guided this corruption could be punished, and following those rules was rewarded. In order to discover how large these "gratuities" were and to strengthen our hypothesis about the universality of corrupt practices, let us attempt to take a closer look at the investigation's findings in this matter.

3.3. The Investigation's Findings

The disclosure and publicizing of the meat affair, which came as a result of decision taken at the highest level of political power (we write more about this later in this work) meant that not only a significant number of prosecutors were assigned to the matter but also that special organizational structures were created. To this end, a special operational and investigative group was set up at Warsaw MO Headquarters. The most important, however, was the already mentioned "staff" intended to "direct operational and investigative activities into crimes in meat processing and marketing," established by order no. 057/64 issue by the Interior Minister, Władysław Wichy, on 8 May 1964. At the head of the staff was Colonel Bogusław Łamacz, head of the KG MO Investigation Department. Certain invited guests also participated in staff meetings. Alongside the staff, under the same order, a working group was set up in the KG MO, to which officers from Department III of the Ministry of Internal Affairs were delegated. The Interior Minister also ordered that the KG MO "delegate" to this group "10 experienced officers from investigative units of the KW MO," and that it appropriate the "necessary funds for the staff's technical needs."

The staff's tasks were defined in the following way:

a) determining the proper directions of operational and investigative activities in the scope of all circumstances disclosed in the case, with particular emphasis on criminal activities and criminal associations;
b) in the meat trade and meat processing;
c) in enterprises and institutions cooperating in the processing, distribution and marketing of meat and meat products;
d) in the administrative apparatus of this economic activity and in other established departments of economic and state administration;
e) the supervision over the proper functioning of the operational-investigative group at MO Headquarters in Warsaw and KG MO;

f) the initiation of proper and necessary projects for the development of the case in other voivodeships.[207]

At a meeting on 13 May 1964, the staff approved a program of major undertakings in the investigation of meat fraud in the economy, which was presented by Colonel B. Łamacz, and which included six thematic threads, including: MHM store managers, owners of cold cut factories, trade administrative apparatus, meat industry plants, people employed in various institutions and state and economic administration organs, and the "foreign exchange trade." The basic direction of the investigation was also established: "from MHM directors to the managers of meat shops, and from the latter – the theft of meat in production." It was at this time that the decision was made to promptly arrest a group of MHM directors.[208] The number of threads increased as the investigation progressed.

In addition to KG MO staff and the above-mentioned operational and investigative group at MO Headquarters in Warsaw, the prosecutor's office created separate structures for conducting operations related to the meat affair. Department II of the General Prosecutor's Office created a team headed up by Director K. Kukawka, with the participation of high-ranking prosecutors. Members of the team gained full access to the investigation files, and they were to discuss with head prosecutors issues regarding of regular procedure of hearings, to develop proper categories by which to legally qualify actions, etc. A team representative participated in staff meetings at KG MO, where he commented on further directions investigation might take.[209]

The first arrests of persons in the case involving fraud in the meat economy took place on 6 and 7 February 1964 and included seven employees of the Warsaw Meat Plant "Służewiec."

The creation of the Ministry of Interior Staff to oversee this case resulted in increased investigative activities. Out of 82 arrested by 17 June 1964, only 27 did not plead guilty. In the latter group, the least "talkative" meat shop managers (of 29 arrested, 16 "remained silent") and employees of Meat Plant "Służewiec" (of

207 IPN BU, KG MO, 1550/1782, Zarządzenie nr 057/64 Ministra Spraw Wewnętrznych z 8 maja 1964 r. w sprawie powołania sztabu kierującego działalnością operacyjno-dochodzeniową w sprawie o przestępstwa w przetwórstwie i obrocie mięsem, pp. 2–5.

208 IPN BU, KG MO, 1550/1782, Protokół nr 1 z posiedzenia Sztabu powołanego zarządzeniem nr 057/64 MSW odbytego w dniu 13 maja 1964, pp. 7–14.

209 AAN, PG 1/29, Zarządzenie [brudnopis] z lipca 1964 w sprawie objęcia nadzorem śledztw o nadużycia w gospodarce mięsnej, p. 307.

22 arrested, 7 refused to testify).[210] On 24 July 1964, 111 people were under investigation, including 106 arrested, 74 of whom had submitted testimonies.[211] By 4 September 1964, allegations were brought against 310 persons, of whom 249 were arrested, including 217 store managers. Among the latter, 151 remained in custody and 66 had been set free; testimonies given by 82 of them were considered "positive."[212]

Detailed information on the progress of the investigation as of 8 September 1964 is included in Table 9.

According to the data presented in the Warsaw investigation, evidence was obtained on the criminal activity of 914 people, of which 326 were charged and 246 were arrested.

Chronologically later and comprehensive data on the results of this investigation concern its status as of 1 December 1964 (Tables 10 and 11).

Referral of the first indictment in this case to the court and the trial of the principle defendants (which ended on 2 February 1965) slowed down the investigation in its other aspects, which did not mean that such work was not pursued. In connection with the Warsaw meat affair from the beginning of 1964 to 1 July 1965, the investigation involved 780 suspects and 503 people temporarily arrested. By that time, the courts had recognized 11 sets of indictments against 88 people. A further 22 sets of indictments against 240 people were waiting for consideration. Two cases were recognized in summary proceedings. On 1 July 1965, there were 372 people under investigation, and 250 people were in custody.[213]

The investigation files show that in November 1964, MHM directors and other people received bribes from 436 meat shop managers in Warsaw from a total of 467 (i.e. 93 % of them gave bribes!).[214] In September 1964, presenting the results of the investigation at the meeting of the MO Staff, Colonel Jagiełło stated

---

210 IPN BU, KG MO, 1550/1782, Protokół nr 5 z posiedzenia Sztabu powołanego zarządzeniem nr 057/64 MSW odbytego w dniu 17 czerwca 1964 r., p. 50.

211 IPN BU, KG MO, 1550/1782, Protokół nr 9 z posiedzenia Sztabu powołanego zarządzeniem nr 057/64 MSW odbytego w dniu 24 lipca 1964, p. 69.

212 IPN BU, KG MO, 1550/1782, Protokół nr 12 z posiedzenia Sztabu powołanego zarządzeniem nr 057/64 MSW odbytego w dniu 4 września 1964 r., p. 84.

213 AAN, PG, 1/29, Notatka informacyjna ujmująca syntetycznie zakres ścigania przestępstw w gospodarce mięsnej według stanu na dzień 1 lipca 1965 r., pp. 318 ff.

214 AAN, PG, 1/29, Notatka E. Kostro dotycząca niektórych głównych danych o wynikach śledztwa w sprawie nadużyć w gospodarce mięsnej na terenie m. st. Warszawy, Warszawa 11 listopada 1964, p. 260.

Table 9. State of the investigation into the so-called Warsaw meat affair as of 8 September 1964

Place of employment	People interogated	People charged in the investigation		Potentially charged in the investigation
		Total	Those arrested	
Meat industry administrative apparatus	146	42	36	104
Meat trade and its administration	360	231	162	129
Trade and its administration	84	6	6	78
The meat transport industry	30	12	11	18
The administrative apparatus of the Warsaw national council	25	3	3	22
Oversight institutions	23	2	2	21
Owners of private meat plants	68	26	24	42
Various people	53	4	2	49
Unidentified people	125	-	-	125
Total	914	326	246	588

Source: AAN, KC PZPR, 237/XIV-306, Notatka o stanie śledztwa w sprawie przestępstw w gospodarce mięsnej w m. st. Warszawie i innych ośrodkach kraju, Warszawa, 8 September 1964, pp. 59 ff.

that "all private producers are engulfed in the trial."[215] Corruption in the Warsaw meat trade was a common phenomenon.

The increasing number of arrested people also caused problems with the question of where to put them. On 5 June 1964, the KG MO staff decided to place some of the arrested meat shop managers who were in the custody of the Warsaw

215 IPN BU, KG MO, 1550/1782, Protokół nr 14 z posiedzenia Sztabu powołanego zarządzeniem nr 057/64 MSW odbytego w dniu 18 września 1964 r., p. 97.

Table 10. The number of people against whom evidence had been gathered that would allow for a charge of committing a crime in the so-called Warsaw meat affair, as of 1 December 1964

Place of employment	No. of people
Meat Ttrade (MHM)	518
Trade in food products	103
Meat industry	235
Other food industries	108
Private sector	85
Transport enterprises	50
Economic administration	37
State admnistration	36
Oversight apparatus	28
Persons from other meat industry plants located in other voivodeships	25
People with unidentified place of employment	202
TOTAL	1,427

Source: IPN BU, KG MO 35/2554, Informacja o wynikach ustaleń śledczych w tzw. warszawskiej sprawie mięsnej, Warszawa, 2 grudnia 1964, p. 95.

Table 11. The number of people arrested in the so-called Warsaw meat affair, as of 1 December 1964

Professional position	No. of people
Directors and their deputies, heads of departments in industrial plants (sections in institutions)	64
Auxiliary administrative staff	22
Auxiliary production personnel (warehouse attendants, weighers, blue collar workers)	19
Store managers	163
deliverers and drivers	29
Workshop owners	28
Others	14
TOTAL	339

Source: Former CAMSWiA, KG MO 35/2554, Informacja o wynikach ustaleń śledczych w tzw. warszawskiej sprawie mięsnej, Warszawa, 2 grudnia 1964, p. 96.

Metropolitan Police in a prison in Białołęka being built at the time; those was supposed to relieve the "burdensome housing situation."[216]

What was the scale of detected fraud and theft? Estimates made by the MO and prosecutor's offices varied depending on the stage of the investigation and the ongoing detentions and arrests of suspects. According to the situation on 11 November 1964, officials had established that, over the course of the investigation in Warsaw, over PLZ 17 million of meat and other raw materials had been misappropriated. In addition, by that time, 106 store managers (out of a total of 467) had pleaded guilty and confirmed that bribes had been given and taken in the amount PLZ 3 million. Regarding the owners of private meat and delicatessen workshops, officials found that they overproduced and then sold ("under the counter"), in socialized establishments, product worth a total of PLZ 22,280,000. Workshop owners were said to have given bribes to officials in the trade, industry, and oversight administration and other persons bribes in totaling approx. PLZ 7,600,000.[217]

Statements regarding property in the possession of certain people holding important jobs within institutions dealing with meat management testify to their corrupt practices.

As early as 5 June 1964, according to information presented at a meeting of the KG MO staff, non-real estate items valued at PLZ 4 million were "secured," along with 14 villas and homes not yet valued. In addition, it was established that people not yet arrested but suspected of fraud possessed, among other things, 94 houses and villas, 66 automobiles, 24 motorcycles, 15 farms, 13 cooperative apartments, 5 PKO account books with deposits made over PLZ 5,000, and 200 TV sets.[218]

As the investigation proceeded, the amount of seized property increased (Table 12).

The data contained in Table 12 illustrates the size of the seized property as of 7 September 1964. Over the course of further proceedings, estimates continued to increase, as evidenced by a note prepared in the Department for Combating Economic Crimes in the Production and Trade of Commodities in Warsaw, dated 14 June 1966, which shows that "over the course of the meat scandals"

216 IPN BU, KG MO, 1550/1782, Protokół nr 4 z posiedzenia Sztabu powołanego zarządzeniem nr 057/64 MSW odbytego w dniu 5 czerwca 1964 r., p. 43.

217 AAN, PG, 1/29, Notatka E. Kostro dotycząca niektórych głównych danych o wynikach śledztwa w sprawie nadużyć w gospodarce mięsnej na terenie m. st. Warszawy, Warszawa 11 listopada 1964, p. 260.

218 IPN BU, KG MO, 1550/1782, Protokół nr 4 z posiedzenia sztabu powołanego zarządzeniem nr 057/64 MSW odbytego w dniu 5 czerwca 1964, pp. 41 ff.

Table 12. List of seized property (valued in PLZ) and suspects as of 7 September 1964 in the Warsaw meat affair

Group name	**Cash and movable property (including automobiles)**	**Real Estate (including houses, villas, and building sites)**	**Foreign instruments (gold, currencies)**	**No. of suspects**
Group "Służewiec"	Property: 1,017,500 Cash: 126,000	1,379,000 (including 6 houses and 1 building site)	31,170	43, including 39 arrested
Goup of stores managers	Property: 5,446,482 Cash: 1,840,958	13,953,790 (56 houses and 8 building sites)	630,819	223, including 155 arrested
Group of directors	Property: 545,100 Cash: 503,000	800,000 (2 villas)	1,694,297	15, including 14 arrrested
Group of private producers	Property: 3,370,768 Cash: 2,987,265	2,100,000 (including 7 houses and 2 building sites)	2,528,225 (plus 3 kg of gold)	26, including 24 arrested
Others: a. slauherhouses b. MO	 Property: 289,000 Cash: 140,000	-	-	13, including 11 arrested
Total	Property: 10,668,850 Cash: 5,597,223 (including 42 automobiles, 18 trucks, 15 motorcycles and mopeds)	18,232,790 (including 71 houses-villas and 11 lots of land)	4,884,511 (plus 3 kg of gold)	320, including 243 arrested

Source: AAN, PG, 1/29, Wykaz mienia zabezpieczonego i osób podejrzanych wg stanu na dzień 7 September 1964 r. w sprawie "mięsnej," p. 113.

in 1963–1966, "property sanctions were quite widely applied, in which various kinds of property of 498 accused were secured." According to initial estimates, the value of this property was over PLZ 51 million (Table 13).

The property valuation presented does not include parts of houses and lots belonging to the defendants, whose value was initially estimated at almost PLZ

Table 13. Initial value of property seized and valued in the so-called meat scandals in Warsaw from 1963 through June 1966, PLZ values in thousands

Kind of property	No.	Value in PLZ	% of the total value of property
Houses and villas	80	19305,2	37.8
Buliding sites, land	33	1824,0	3.6
automobiles	98	5332,1	10.4
Motorcycles and mopeds	30	239,0	0.5
Cash and PKO deposits	211 people	7294,6	14.3
Foreign currencies in gold	37 people	3907,1	7.7
Foreign currencies in banknotes	60 people	1589,6	3.1
Jewelry, watches, etc.	98 people	1482,5	2.9
Movable property, various	475 people	10055,1	19.7
TOTAL		51029,2	100.0

Source: IPN BU, 1550/2633, Informacja ogólna w sprawie afery mięsnej w Warszawie, Warszawa, 14 czerwca 1966, p. 6.

29,973,700. In the end, the total value of secured property amounted to at least PLZ 60 million, of which about 50 % was real estate.

A detailed analysis of the property belonging to individual defendants showed that 23.7 % of them owned 77.3 % of the property, and 2.8 % (14) of them owned 26.4 % of secured property. These people were mainly MHM directors and owners of private meat processing plants.[219]

This conclusion is confirmed even by Wawrzecki's preliminary testimony. At the end of April 1964, he admitted to possessing, among other things, 96 pieces of twenty-dollar coins, 2 twenty-dollar gold pieces, PLZ 7 gold coins, 14 gold bars with a total weight of 1.4 kg, 9 gold bracelets, one gold watch, 26 rings including a few with diamonds, 4 gold chains, 4 gold medallions, 5 gold rings, 2 gold crosses, 2 pairs of gold clips, PLZ 135,000 in "circulation cash," and PKO booklets with deposits totaling PLZ 100,000. In addition, the investigation revealed that Wawrzecki possessed of a villa worth around PLZ 500,000 in

219 IPN BU, KG MO, 1550/2633, Informacja ogólna w sprawie afery mięsnej w Warszawie, Warszawa 14 VI 1966, p. 5.

Michałowice near Warsaw registered in the name of his wife's aunt.[220] For these reasons, Wawrzecki was particularly suited to the stereotype of the criminal, or even "enemy of the people," who had stolen social property.

3.4. The Wawrzecki Trial

The enormity of the fraud revealed by the investigations caused the first meat affair trial to be carefully prepared, both from the propaganda and legal perspective. Understanding its course is not possible without at least general knowledge of the PRL legislation involving attempts to combat so-called economic crime, including the theft of social property (because that is the crime of which persons involved in the meat affair were accused). Due to the complexity of these regulations and their evolution, we will focus only on necessary information, emphasizing the general evolution of legal provisions and focusing on legal documents used to convict the accused.

At the beginning, it is worth noting that the very definition of economic crime was not unambiguous among lawyers dealing with this issue.[221] Oktawia Górniok applies that term to "all penalized manifestations of pathology in economic activity – both socialized and unsocialized."[222] Igor Andreyev recognizes economic crimes as those that "undermine the order of economic relations in the state."[223] Tadeusz Cyprian defines them as "an act violating the economic order of the state either directly by an attack on the correct course of economic life, or indirectly through an attack on social property."[224] According to Cyrian, this category included such groups of crime as: attacks against the state economic system, crimes against social property, economic labor crimes, offenses in production and trade, financial crimes, currency and customs crimes, and offenses against certain economic interests.[225] In connection with the particular matter discussed below, going forward we will include bribery alongside the crimes listed above, which is usually classified as a clerical crime.

---

220 AAN, KC PZPR, 237/XIV-306, Notatka uzupełniająca wyniki śledztwa w sprawie ujawnionych nadużyć w gospodarce mięsnej na terenie m. st. Warszawy według stanu na dzień 26 kwietnia 1964 r., p. 17.

221 See, among others, I. Majchrzak, *Pracownicze przestępstwo gospodarcze*.

222 Oktawia Górniok, *Przestępczość gospodarcza (Wybrane przejawy i uwarunkowania)* (Katowice: Uniwersytet Śląski, 1986), 10.

223 Igor Andrejew, *Polskie prawo karne w zarysie* (Warszawa: PWN, 1980), 417.

224 Tadeusz Cyprian, Przestępstwa gospodarcze (Warszawa: PWN, 1960), 43.

225 Ibid., 44–45.

3.4.1. Legal context: Combating Pathology in Economic Life through PRL Legislation

The operation of the communist justice system in general, including in criminal matters, underwent changes whose rhythm was determined by political changes. When the foundations were being laid for the ruling system and Stalinization, which came to an end in the years 1955–1956, changes in criminal law were often made outside the framework of the binding penal code (p.c.) of 1932, by issuing numerous special acts. Reform of penal procedures was carried out in 1949 and supplemented in 1950 by, among other things, abolishing the institution of the examining magistrate (or the investigating judge). The entire preparatory proceedings came under the control of the prosecutor. In place of the previous two institutions where verdicts from first instance courts (cassation and appeals) could be appealed, there was the single institution of the appeals (*rewizja*) court. The prosecutor's control over the investigation conducted by public security bodies 10 (political police) became weaker. The rights of the suspect in the pre-trial proceedings were limited mainly by reducing a defense attorney's room for maneuver at this stage of a criminal trial. The grounds for pre-trial detention, which in many cases were mandatory, were laid out too broadly. In addition, the court's control over the prosecutor's use of detention was completely eliminated.[226]

The gradual political liberalization starting in 1955 was also reflected in changes in criminal law and criminal procedure. The amendment to the Code of Criminal Procedure (C.C.P.) of 21 December 1955 (Dz. U. No. 46, Item 309) restored the investigation as a preliminary phase of the pre-trial investigation, seriously expanded and strengthened the prosecutor's supervision role, and reformed provisions regarding the use of pre-trial detention (its obligatory use was abolished and the courts enjoyed greater room for maneuver in its application). Matters tied to pre-deadline dismissal and certain criminal acts (including fiscal/financial laws regarding the protection of social property, combating speculation, etc.) were liberalized. The use of the death penalty was also restricted.[227]

Postwar legislation in Poland contained many solutions that served to protect so-called social property. The battle against economic crime shortly after the war took place on the basis of a decree issued by Stalin's PKWN on 30 October 1944

226 Andrzej Murzynowski and Jan Rezler, *Wymiar sprawiedliwości w Polsce w latach 1944–1970. Ustawodawstwo, organizacja i działalność* (Warszawa: Wydawnictwo Uniwersytetu Warszawskiego, 1972), 57–70.

227 Ibid., 71–92.

(Dz. U. No. 10, Item 50), which established the criminality of acts that came under the name of sabotage. This decree called for imprisonment from 6 months to 15 years of anyone who damaged or made useless objects or devices serving the purpose of defending the State or the Armed Forces (Art. 1, par. 1). If such an act caused great damage to the military defense of the State or was committed during war, the perpetrator was subject to life imprisonment or the death penalty (Art. 1, par. 2). Imprisonment from five months to six years or arrest from one week to five years was the potential punishment for anyone who hindered or prevented the proper operation of plants producing weapons or other military material (Art. 2). Article 5 of the decree referred to sabotage, which was usually treated as an economic crime. According to this article, a prison sentence or the death penalty was the potential punishment for various types of sabotage committed "during war" (the end of the state of war in Poland took place pursuant to the decree of 16 November 1945), including: a) damaging or destroying objects or devices for general use or the defense of the Polish State or Allied States; b) preventing or hindering the proper functioning of state or local government offices, manufacturing plants or public utilities; c) the production of objects completely or largely unfit for general or military use.

Regulations regarding certain categories of economic crimes were also included in the PKWN decree "on combating war speculation" dated 25 October 1944, which set forth provisions to "prevent speculation and usury," imposing arrests and/or fines for demanding or charging higher-than-official prices and for consciously registering false or incomplete data in commercial documents (invoices, etc.) and statements (Art. 10). One who "consciously" demanded "obviously excessive" prices or benefits could also face long prison sentences, and one who perpetrated "dishonest machinations" that raised prices or maintained high prices for everyday goods faced imprisonment (from six months to ten years) and a fine of up to PLZ five million. If that person caused particularly severe damage to public interests during war or under exceptional circumstances caused by war, or disturbed public peace – he/she was subject to a life imprisonment or death penalty (Art. 14, par. 2). On 20 November 1944, the above-cited decree was further strengthened.

With the end of the state of war (17 December 1945), the decree on state protection was no longer valid, and the decree on particularly dangerous crimes came into force during the reconstruction of the State on 16 November 1945 (Dz. U. No. 53, Item 300). This new legal act also provided for strict criminal liability for offenses against the economic interests of the state and clerical crimes.

Economic crimes were still subject to severe penalty in subsequent legal acts that were in force in Polish legislation after 1944. In this context, we must point first of all to the decree entitled "On particularly dangerous crimes during state reconstruction" (O przestępstwach szczególnie niebezpiecznych w okresie odbudowy państwa) dated 13 June 1946, which was the so-called small penal code: Dz. U. 1946, No. 30, Item 192, which replaced the previously mentioned decree of the same name from 16 November 1945.

The crime that was treated as an economic crime and was subject to particularly severe penalties was still that of sabotage, for which one could be imprisoned for no less than three years and up to life, or could be given death penalty. According to Art. 3 point 1, an object of sabotage could be factories and public utilities, public communication or installations serving the defense of the Polish State or an allied State, regardless of whether the property was state, social or private. Even the destruction of a perpetrator's own property, if it involved a public matter or served the defense of the state – could be considered as such a crime.[228] In the light of guidelines dated 19 December 1952 and issued by the Assembly of Judges of the Supreme Military Court (Zgr. Og. 111/52), sabotage was a counter-revolutionary crime.

Chapter III of the decree ("Crimes against the Economic Interests of the State") left unchanged provisions of the decree of 1945, which provided for prison sentences (from six months to fifteen years) for damaging production (so-called economic damage – Art. 39) and fraud during the distribution of goods. The decree also provided for penalties (imprisonment of up to three years and fines) for other economic crimes characteristic of the postwar period – i.e. looting, defined as the export of movable property from the Recovered Territories.[229]

The act not only maintained the requirement that a convicted person's property be confiscated in the event of a death sentence (an unknown p.c. from 1932, introduced to Polish postwar legislation for the first time by the decree of 30 October 1944 on protection of the state) but also extended that requirement

228 Dekret z dnia 13 czerwca o przestępstwach szczególnie niebezpiecznych w okresie odbudowy Państwa, Art. 3 pkt. 1. See Jerzy Bafia, Leo Hochberg, Mieczysław Siewierski, *Ustawy karne PRL. Komentarz* (Warszawa: Wydawnictwo Prawnicze, 1965), 10.

229 The Recovered Territories are parts of the pre-war territory of Germany that were transferred to Poland after the Second World War as a result of decisions made at the Big Three conferences at Yalta and Potsdam. Bafia, Hochberg, Siewierski, *Ustawy karne PRL*, 74.

to apply (as an additional penalty) to sentences of life imprisonment and to sentences tied to convictions for certain other offenses (Art. 49, par. 1).[230]

Legal regulations concerning economic crime were significantly influenced by changes in the Polish economic system tied to Stalinization.

For this reason, on 2 June 1947, in the context of the above-mentioned "battle over trade," the previously described decree on combating war speculation was replaced by an act combating high prices and excessive profits in trade (Dz. U. No. 43 Item 218). It forbade the demand for, or collection of, prices in "sales enterprises" (stores) higher than the purchase cost plus the gross profit established for a given commodity or higher than the maximum prices set by the Minister of Industry and Trade. It also prohibited the refusal to sell goods in stock if the buyer offered the price disclosed in the price list and the amount of goods he wanted to buy was justified under normal demand.

The act provided for the possibility of the introduction by the Minister of Industry and Trade, in consultation with the Minister of Provisions, a list of priority food items for which maximum wholesale and retail prices could be set. The Minister of Industry and Trade, in consultation with other ministers, could set maximum wholesale and retail prices for goods manufactured by state-owned enterprises or under public administration (Art. 5, par. 6). It was also his duty to establish, by way of directives, rate card commissions (Art. 6, par. 1 and 2), which primarily set and announced prices for priority food items. These new solutions led to the actual liquidation of private and cooperative trade, which was replaced by the state. In this way, what remained of the free market and private enterprise was deliberately destroyed for ideological and political reasons.

The announcement of a further tightening of the legislation relating to crimes against the economic interests of the State involved a decree of 4 March 1953 designed to intensify the battle against poor quality production (Dz. U. No. 16, Item 63). This decree defined punishments for acts defined as the conscious introduction, sale or commissioning of poor-quality industrial products or of products unsuitable for their intended use.

The decree of 4 March 1953 on the protection of the interests of buyers in trade (Dz. U. No. 16, Item 64) headed in the same direction. Among other things, it introduced severe sanctions for speculation crimes and for fraud related to the sale of goods (up to five years in prison). In accordance with the ideological line

230 "Wytyczne wymiaru sprawiedliwości i praktyki sądowej w sprawie niektórych zagadnień w procesach o niedobory (K.O. 145/52)," Bafia, Hochberg, Siewierski, *Ustawy karne PRL*, 55–56.

in force at the time, the decree treated particularly harshly perpetrators of crime who were involved in private enterprise, against whom the court could adjudicate additional penalties in the form forfeiture of goods tied to the crime, forfeiture of the company's assets, which would cause the enterprise to close, deprive the perpetrator of commercial and industrial rights, deprive him of the right to occupy commercial premises, and – in some cases – prohibit the perpetrator from entering an area specified by the court for a period from two to five years.

In the same direction he headed a decree of 4 March 1953 on the protection of the interests of buyers in the course of trade (Dz. U. No. 16, Item 64). It introduced, among others severe sanctions for speculation offenses and for fraud related to the sale of goods (up to 5 years in prison). In accordance with the ideological line in force, the decree treated in a particularly severe manner the perpetrator of the offense of a private enterprise, against which the court could adjudicate a further additional penalty in the form of: forfeiture of goods whose offense concerned, forfeiture of the enterprise's facilities, which would cause the enterprise to close and deprive the perpetrator of commercial and industrial rights, deprive him of the right to occupy commercial premises, and in some cases – the ban on the perpetrator's stay at the area specified by the court for the period from two to five years.

The specific "concern" about social property already appearing in the previously discussed legal acts found its expression in the so-called March decrees (which were, in fact, special acts) – i.e. in a decree dated 4 March 1953 on increasing the protection of social property (Dz. U. No. 17, Item 68, amending Dz. U., 1954, No,. 57, Item 283), called the large March decree, and the decree of 4 March 1953 protecting the social property against minor thefts (Dz. U. No. 17, Item 69, amending Dz. U., 1954, No. 57, Item 283), called the small March decree. Together, they created a new basis for the prosecution of crimes against social property, defined in the large decree as the foundation for the PRL system. They were characterized by the introduction of new concepts such as the theft of social assets, definitions the crime's character, and the determination of what constituted the petty theft of social property. The tightened criminal policy that found expression in these acts was to raise the lower limit of the statutory penalty compared to penalties found in the regulations of the p.c.[231]

The provisions of both cited legal acts were liberalized in 1954.[232]

231 Bafia, *Odpowiedzialność karna za przestępstwa przeciw własności społecznej. Z problematyki zmian wprowadzonych przez ustawę z 18 czerwca 1959* (Warszawa: Wydawnictwo Prawnicze: 1960), 7.

232 Ibid., 9.

An expression of attempts to specify criminal liability related to various forms of speculation as economic crimes was the replacement of the 4 March 1953 decree to protect buyers' trade interests by the act of 13 July 1957 to combat speculation and protect the trade interests of buyers and agricultural producers. According to this act, persons employed in a socialized enterprise who misappropriated goods not intended for direct sale to consumers not entitled to resell at a profit (Art. 1, par. 1) were subject to imprisonment (from six months to ten years) and fines. Imprisonment from six months to five years and a fine could be imposed on a buyer whose purpose was to further resell such a good for profit (Art., par. 2). Anyone who sold the goods acquired in such a way for profit (Art. 1, par. 2) face the same penalties. Perpetrators of offenses specified in Art. 1, par. 1 and 2 were subject to imprisonment from six months to five years and fines or imprisonment from one week to five years and fines. The commission of the above crimes on a large scale carried the possibility of imprisonment from six months to ten years and fines.

But from the point of view of the trial of Wawrzecki and nine other defendants in the meat affair, the two acts that were the basis for their conviction are of particular importance: one dated 21 January 1958 on increasing the protection of social property against damage resulting from crime (Dz. U. No. 4 Item 11), and the other dated 18 June 1959 on criminal liability for crimes against social property (Dz. U. No. 36, Item 228). A new element in both of these normative acts, compared to the March decrees, was the increase in the potential criminal punishment, and especially economic punishment, and the introduction of measures to compensate, over the course of criminal proceedings, for damage caused to social property.

The act dated 21 January 1958 introduced a varied set of sanctions for crimes involving social property based on the amount of damage caused. If it amounted to between PLZ 50,000 and 100,000, the perpetrator was subject to imprisonment for a period not shorter than five years. And if it exceeded PLZ 100,000 – for a period not shorter than eight years and possibly life imprisonment. It also regulated situations in which persons colluded in crime, with sentences based on the total amount of damage (Art 2, par. 2). It also introduced changes in the scope of property forfeiture as an additional penalty. In contrast to the decree of 4 March on increasing the protection of social property, which provided for the optional possibility of add an additional penalty in the form of forfeiture of the offender's property in whole or in part only in cases strictly specified in the act, the new regulation imposed on the court an obligatory requirement when damage to social property exceeded PLZ 50,000 (Art. 2, par. 1). There was an option here only if the damage to social property did not exceed 50,000. PLZ

(Art. 2, par. 2). In all cases in which a criminal act caused damage to social property, the prosecutor could, over the course of the investigation, issue a decision to secure claims for its remedy and also to secure the suspected loss of property or impose a fine (Art. 3, par. 1).

The second of the above-mentioned acts (of 18 June 1959 on criminal liability for crimes against social property) replaced the above-mentioned March decrees of 1953 and the decree of 23 December 1954 by changing certain provisions on the protection of social property. It dealt with intentional crimes of theft, misappropriation, and fraud involving social property. And in this case, as in the act of 21 January 1958, higher or lower penalties depended on the value of social property stolen by the perpetrator. In the case of theft, extortion or other kinds of theft of social property, the perpetrator was subject to a prison sentence of up to five years and a fine (Art. 1, par. 1). The fine was introduced as a mandatory basic penalty imposed next to the deprivation of liberty for any crime against social property. If the value of stolen property did not exceed PLZ 300, the court could apply extraordinary and lighter imprison sentences (Art. 1, par. 2). In cases in which social property was stolen by a perpetrator whose job it was to protect and maintain that property, such a perpetrator was subject to a prison term between two and ten years plus a fine. Such penalties could be reduced (to under two years imprisonment plus a fine) when the value of property stolen did not exceed 2,000 PLZ. The provisions of the act (Art. 4, par. 2 and Art. 7, par. 2) also introduced a special, stricter punishments for fenced social property valued at more than PLZ 50,000 (a prison term of at least five years and a fine not lower than PLZ 30,000).[233]

The act of 18 June 1959, which repealed the March decrees, retained the notion of an organized criminal group (Art. 2, par. 2, a) which appeared in the so-called a large March decree (Art. 1, par. 3, b). In the act of 18 June 1959, theft of social assets as a result of activities conducted by such a group was punishable by imprisonment from two years to ten years and a fine. In the light of the guidelines for judiciary and court practice regarding the correct application of the provisions of the act of 18 June 1959 and the act of 21 January 1958, which increased the protection of social property against damage resulting from crime for an act committed by an organized criminal group (pursuant to the act of 18 June 1959), such an act was considered to have been committed as a result of the collusion of at least three perpetrators and if there was an element of organization within the group involving a division of roles and ensuring coordination

233 “Wytyczne wymiaru sprawiedliwości.”

by participants in the crime. In particular, this matter revolved around the organization of activities that made it possible or easier to commit a crime or made it more difficult to detect. That having been said, it was not necessary that all participants in the group knew each other and set up arrangements together; it was enough for each of them to have realized that he was active in an organized criminal group.

The act maintained the current concept of the enhanced protection of social property that had been introduced by the so-called March decrees.

The indicated regulations do not, of course, cover all the Polish legislation from that period tied to economic crime broadly understood. Some aspects of that legislation, for example on obligatory supplies of agricultural products, involve peasant attitudes and behavior and will be discussed later in this work. For now, we will limit ourselves to the argument that Polish criminal law in the years 1944–1965 provided for the severe punishment of perpetrators of the largest economic affairs.

This was not an exception in the criminal legislation of other Eastern bloc countries. One expert in these matters, Igor Andreyev, stated that in the penal systems of these countries, large economic scandals that caused a significant damage to the state or social organization, resulted in high sentences of imprisonment along with the confiscation of property.[234] In the 1960s, increased penalties for these acts often came as the result of the fact that Eastern bloc countries adopted solutions found in Soviet legislation. In contrast to the "Podstaw ustawodawstwa karnego ZSRR i republik związkowych" from 25 December 1958, which was passed during the Khrushchev thaw, the decree published on 5 May 1961 by the Presidium of the Supreme Soviet of the USSR to intensify the fight against particularly dangerous crimes provided for the death penalty for, among other things, "creating, for the purpose of circulating or having circulated counterfeit money and fake securities, done professionally," and "for theft of state or social assets in particularly large amounts."[235] On 20 February 1962, a decree of the Presidium was issued that stipulated severe penalties, up to and including the death penalty, for bribery.[236]

234 Ibid., 113.

235 *Kodeks karny RSFRR. Kodeks procesowy RSFRR. Ustawa o ustroju sądów RFSRR* (Warszawa: Wydawnictwo Prawnicze, 1961), 129–130.

236 Evgenija Evielson, *Sudebnyje prociessy po ekonomiceskim dielam w SSSR* (London: Overseas publ. Interchange: 1986), 62–63.

In our continuing discussion of the trial of those accused in the Warsaw meat affair, it seems relevant to analyze not only the evolution of legal norms regarding economic crime but also regulations governing summary proceedings. It was the application of these regulations that led to the death penalty being pronounced against Wawrzecki.

Officials made use of provisions in place since 1945. On 17 December of that year, the decree "On summary proceedings" (O postępowaniu doraźnym) dated 16 November 1945 (Dz. U. No. 53, Item 301) entered into force. According to this decreed, included under the category of economic crimes was theft (Art. 257 p.c., par. 1) and misappropriation (property of others and entrusted property Art. 262, par. 1 and 2 p.c.), if the perpetrator committed an act to the detriment of the State, local government, public law institutions, a state-owned enterprises, local governmental enterprise, whether they were under state administration, a public organization of national significance, or if the perpetrator committed an act in relation to property that was tied to transport by public means of communication or located in rooms or facilities connected with the movement of these means of communication. He was also subject to laws regarding venality (łapownictwo; Art. 290 p.c.).

The decree of 1945 stipulated that summary proceedings take place without an investigation (i.e. excluding the investigating judge) (Art. 10, par. 1). The investigation was conducted by the prosecutor in person or through MO. He could turn to investigating magistrates or local judges to perform individual court actions. The investigation could also be carried out by public security bodies (after the case was handed over to the public prosecutor); the prosecutor was to supervise the investigation conducted by MBP officers (Art. 11, par. 1 and 2), but the decree did not further specify procedures. The use of pre-trial detention in the course of the entire proceedings was mandatory and was managed by the prosecutor (Art. 9, par. 1 and 2). summary proceedings typically involved shortened deadlines. The indictment was to be lodged within 30 days and was to include a motion to hear the case in summary proceedings (Art. 14, par. 1 and 2). The summary trial would be conducted before a court composed of one professional judge and two lay judges. At the main hearing, the accused was required to have a lawyer (Art. 16, par. 1). Regardless of the statutory threat for a given crime, the following penalties could be imposed in summary proceedings: the death penalty, life imprisonment or prison for not less than one year and a fine. The court could not impose a penalty lower than the minimum provided for in the act for a given offense (Art. 2, par. 2). According to Art. 17, par. 1–4, after proceeds had been completed, the court had to immediately issue a verdict; postponement of the announcement of sentence was unacceptable. The judgment was to be justified in writing within 24 hours after its announcement. The death penalty could only be imposed in the event of unanimity as to both guilt and punishment. In 1945, the summary procedure was introduced as a single instance; judgment was not subject to appeal. In the event of resumption of proceedings, the case could not be re-tried in summary proceedings. The appeal court passed decision on the resumption of the proceedings (Art. 19, par. 1 and 2).

An amendment to the act on summary proceedings dated 13 June 1946 (Dz. U. No. 30, Item 193) extended the scope of summary proceeding to encompass the theft of movable property deprived of proper protection in connection with war (looting) or as a result of some other extraordinary event (Art. 43, par. 1 p.c.). Summary proceedings in cases concerning acts listed in the 1945 decree and the 1946 amendment were obligatory, and the lowest penalty that could be applied was three years.[237] The wording of Article 9 of the decree of 16 November 1945 was also changed. Temporary arrest in cases subject to summary proceedings not only remained compulsory, but it was applied if the allegation of committing a crime under summary proceedings was considered credible (Art. 9, par. 1). As in the decree of 16 November 1945, except in certain cases, it was the prosecutor who managed the temporary arrest. The prosecutor's decision on the application of the pre-trial detention was subject to complaint at the district court (Art. 9, par. 3). Article 17 of the decree of 16 November 1945 was amended and supplemented 17 of the decree of 16 November 1945. According to par. 3 of that article, a judgment with its justification was to be served immediately to both the prosecutor and the accused. Art. 17 (2), par. 1 and 2 regulated the issue of appeals against the judgment of the regional court, which could be brought only by the prosecutor (both for the benefit and against the accused), and the time of its submission (3 days from the date of the prosecutor's delivery of a copy of the judgment with justification). Art. 17 (4) regulated proceedings in the court of appeal. Art. 17 (4) stated that the regional and appellate courts could impose the death penalty only if there was unanimity regarding both guilt and the use of the death penalty. Verdicts handed down by the appellate court and decisions made by the regional and appellate courts were not subject to appeal (Art. 17 (5)).

Strengthened penalties in the area of economic crime were also the result of a second set of changes made to the act on summary proceedings implemented through the decree of 27 April 1949 (Dz. U. No. 32, Item 239). Among other

237 Decree of 13 June 1946 in Art. 2, par. 3 pkt c read as follows: "c) imprisonment for a period not shorter than 3 years and [. . .]."

things, this move allowed the court to withdraw from hearing a case in summary proceedings. The 1949 amendment widened the scope of crimes covered by such proceedings.[238] In the act of 27 April 1949, a provision was introduced which recognized both deliberate and unintentional crimes to the detriment of the State Treasury, local government, public law institutions, cooperatives, enterprises owned by or under the management of the State, local government, public law institutions or cooperatives, and other crimes, if the economic interests of the PRL were exposed to significant damage. The 1949 amendment maintained the following basic penalties: death penalty or life imprisonment, or imprisonment for a period not shorter than three years (which was an extended period compared to the decree of 16 November 1945). It also introduced the possibility (in some cases) of imposing a supplementary penalty in the form of forfeiture of the accused person's property in whole or in part. The unanimity requirement was preserved when applying the death penalty.

According to the amendment from 1949, temporary detention in cases concerning crimes subject to summary proceedings was obligatory. Temporary arrest was applied if the allegation regarding a suspected crime subject to summary proceedings was considered credible. It was matter for the prosecutor to handle. If the detainee's transfer to the prosecutor was burdened by extraordinary difficulties, it was the magistrate who would order the detention.

After the amendments to the Code of Criminal Procedure (k.p.k.) in 1949, provisions regarding the possibility of lodging a complaint against a decision on pre-trial detention to the district court were terminated (this had been provided for in the decree of 13 June 1946). A complaint against a detention order was recognized on general principles specified in the k.p.k. (an appeal court composed of three professional judges, and as of 1950 a senior prosecutor, added that to the amendment of 1950). The appeal, judgments, and court decisions not subject to appeal were abolished (only an extraordinary search was allowed).

The amendment also repealed the provision of the decree of 16 November 1945 stating that the indictment should be lodged within 30 days from the date the accused was detained (article 14 dated 16 November 1945); henceforth there was no time limit to prosecute. From 1949, one arbitral tribunal of the appellate court

238 The decree of 27 April 1949 extended the scope of application of the decree on summary proceedings to include persons guilty of committing deliberate offenses under Chapter XXXIII of the Criminal Code of 1932 (before the change, it concerned only the crimes from this chapter). The decree on summary proceedings was subject to the preparation of (Art. 218), and entering into an agreement concerning (Art. 219), crimes under articles 215, 216, 217 and two new articles – 221 and 222.

and two lay judges heard cases in summary proceedings. After the amendment of the k.p.k. of 1949, in matters falling within the jurisdiction of a regional or appellate court, the president of the relevant court could order the hearing of a case composed of three professional judges. The same regulation regarding the voivodeship court was in the k.p.k. after the 1950 amendment. Thus, from 1949, it was possible in summary proceedings to adjudicate a case with three professional judges.

These necessary general historical and legal remarks having been made, we can take a closer look at the Wawrzecki trial.

3.4.2. The Course of the Trial

On 24 October 1964, the provincial prosecutor for Warsaw, Władysław Komorniczak, filed an application with the Provincial Court for Warsaw to take up a case against 10 persons in a summary proceeding. According to the act of indictment,[239] bearing the date 24 October 1964, S. Wawrzecki, arrested on 18 April 1964, was accused of the following: "[...] from 1957 to March 1964 in Warsaw, as the director of State Enterprises MHM Warszawa – Północ, Warszawa – Śródmieście and Warszawa Praga, acting jointly and in consultation with the managers of the following MHM stores: Adam Stokłosiński, Aleksander Woźnica, Władysław Walendziuk and others covered by separate criminal proceedings, stole over PLZ 3,500,000, to the detriment of the said enterprises, based on a surplus of goods and money generated in these stores." He was alleged to have done this by allowing stores to build up illegal surpluses, through dishonest meat cutting procedures and by cheating customers on the weight, price and quality of goods sold to them. In addition, he was accused of concealing known facts of abuse from oversight and law enforcement authorities, and of hiding the fact that he had "tolerated other forms of criminal activity aimed at achieving unregistered surpluses of goods and money, and then he participated in their division by accepting a total of PLZ 3,500,000. from MHM store managers." These actions were punishable under Art. 2, par. 1[240] of the act of 18 June 1959 on criminal liability for crimes against social property in connection with

239 ASO, IVK 155/64, vol. III.

240 "Whoever steals social property over which he has management authority, or for whose protection, preservation or security he is responsible in connection with his position or function, is liable to imprisonment for 2 to 10 years plus fines."

Art. 1, par. 1, b[241] of the act of 21 January 1958 on increasing the protection of social property.

Henryk Marian Gradowski, arrested on 27 March 1964, was accused – in the period from August 1960 to March 1964 as the director of the Warszawa – Zachód, and later Warszawa – Północ – of acting jointly and in consultation with the subordinate shop managers to steal PLZ 2,300,000. to the detriment of these enterprises based on goods and money surpluses generated in them. The sum of bribes exchanged in these crimes was estimated at PLZ 1,500,000. The legal qualification of these acts was the same as in the Wawrzecki case. The crimes on which Kazimierz Witowski was arrested, on 15 May 1964, were classified in the same way. He was – in the period from 1954 to April 1964 as the director of the MHM Warszawa – Zachód, then Warszawa – Praga – Północ and Warszawa – South – acting jointly and in consultation with Ludwik Balczarek and other managers of MHM stores, to steal PLZ 1,500,000 to the detriment of these enterprises, much like Wawrzecki and Gradowski did. The amount of bribes exchanged with shop managers was estimated at PLZ 1,500,000.

Tadeusz Skowroński, arrested on May 30, 1964, was accused – in the period from October 1959 to the end of 1963 as director of Warsaw's Union of Industries in Trade of Foodstuffs, of assisting the MHM directors Wawrzecki and Witowski and subordinate store managers: Adam Stokłosiński, Aleksander Woźnica, Władysław Walendziuk, Ludwik Balczarek and others – in the "production of goods and money surpluses" by not organizing due control, and by tolerating fraud and irregularities. As a result, they were able to steal these surpluses in the total amount of PLZ 3 million and accept cash and objects of a total value of PLZ 340,000.

These actions were qualified as provided in Art. 27, p.c.[242] and Art. 2, par. 1 of the act of 18 June 1959 in connection with Art. 1, par. 1, b of the act of 21 January 1958.

Mieczysław Fabisiak, arrested on 1 June 1964, was accused – in the period from 1957 to spring 1964 as the head of inspection of trade in meat products in the Warsaw State Trade Inspectorate – of having enabled S. Wawrzecki, K. Witowski, H. Gradowski, A. Stokłosiński, A. Woźnica, W. Walendziuk, and

241 "Whoever, in an effort to make profit, in a the crime provided for by the provisions of the penal code or other laws, inflicting damage on social property, is subject to the following basic penalty: [...] b) if the damage is over PLZ 100,000 – imprisonment for a period of time not shorter than 8 years or life imprisonment."

242 "Assistance is given by someone who assisted, in word or deed, in the commission of a crime is allowed to commit a crime or deed to an offense."

others to produce goods and money surpluses by tolerating fraud, and was alleged to have given them assistance in the theft of social property worth PLZ 1.677,000 and accepted from them about PLZ 227,000. These actions were qualified in the same way as those for which Skowroński was accused.

For committing offenses provided for in Art. 2, par. 1 of the act of 18 June 1959 in connection with Art. 1, par. 1, b of the act of 21 January 1958, the following managers of MHM stores were also accused: Adam Stokłosiński (arrested on 27 July 1964), Aleksandra Woźnica (arrested on 5 June 1964), Władysław Walendziuk and Ludwik Balczarek (both arrested on 5 May 1964). The owner of a private butcher workshop at 104 Tykocińska Street in Warsaw, Antoni Zawadzki, was alleged to have been responsible for acts covered in Art. 1 par. 1 of the act of 18 June 1959[243] and Art. 1 par. 1 of the act of 21 January 1959. He was accused of accepting from employees of meat industry plants (meat plants, cold stores, processing plants, slaughterhouses, and meat transport companies) bacon, pork fat, intestines, half-carcasses, and other such products worth PLZ 1,275,600.

The prosecutor's request to have the case heard in summary proceedings was accepted by the court and, on 26 October 1964, the team of judges (which, by virtue of the order of the president of the provincial court in Warsaw, Henryk Kempisty, was headed by Supreme Court judge Roman Kryże) issued an order determining the framework of the main hearing in the Wawrzecki case and other defendants.

Based on Art. 18, par. 1 k.p.k.[244] and Art. 3, par. 2 of the act of 20 July 1950[245] (as amended) on the amendment of provisions of criminal proceedings to hear the case against Wawrzecki and the above-mentioned defendants, the President of the Provincial Court in Warsaw, taking into consideration the particular complexity of the case, issued on 31 October 1964 the order to recognized the composition of the three judges panel. Based on Art. 24, par. 1 and 2 of the Rules of Court Activities (Dz. U. No. 44 of 1953, Item 216) that panel was to be made up of – apart from R. Kryże – the regional court judges: Faustyn Wołek and

243 "Whoever steals, misappropriates, extorts, or otherwise assumes social property, is punishable by imprisonment of up to 5 years and fines."

244 "The provincial court shall decide on the composition of one judge and two lay judges, unless a special regulation provides otherwise."

245 "The president of a local or provincial court may order the hearing of a case, belonging to the jurisdiction of a given court, as a first instance, composed of three judges, if he deems it advisable due to the particular complexity of the case."

Kazimierz Gerczak. The president appointed Eugeniusz Rymkiewicz as the substitute judge.[246]

Wawrzecki's lawyers in this case were seasoned lawyers: Antoni Szczygieł and Krzysztof Bieńkowski. Attorneys for other defendants included Andrzej Kozanecki, Czesław Łapiński, Zbigniew Adamczyk, Witold Abert, Jacek Wasilewski, Stanisław Dryjski, Marian Piesiewicz, Mieczysław Ulatowski, Wanda Barciszewska, Janusz Odrobiński, Ireneusz Jechanowski, Witold Bayer. Wincenty Witkowski, Tadeusz de Virion and Stanisław Janusz.[247]

Even before the trial started, on 6 November 1964, Wawrzecki's lawyers filed a motion with the Provincial Court in Warsaw (Department IV Criminal) to change (abolish) the summary proceedings. Justifying their position on this matter, both lawyers pointed to views in the legal literature, including the opinion of eminent specialists in the field of penal and constitutional law (professors: Stefan Kalinowski and Stefan Rozmaryn), who in their works indicated (contrary to the existing legislation) the need for judicial review of the legitimacy of the prosecutor's request to employ the summary proceeding and, based on constitutional provisions, the need for the court to be free to assess the legitimacy of the prosecutor's request in this matter. Citing Rozmaryn's view that the summary proceeding constituted a serious limitation of the citizen's right to defense and was in violation of constitutional provisions, they stressed the normative (and not declarative) nature of the acts and the obligation to use them alongside ordinary acts. They referred to earlier decisions of the Supreme Court Chamber of Military Affairs stating that instituting criminal proceedings by the prosecutor in private and fiscal matters in the name of the "social interest" does not absolve the court from the obligation to consider whether the prosecutor's decision is correct, or whether court proceedings in such cases are expedient, or whether the social interest requires it. In their view, the reasoning cited in this ruling spoke in favor of the argument that the court has the right and the duty to consider whether the "circumstances of the case" referred to in Art. 1, par. 3 of the decree on summary proceedings[248] justified the prosecutor's request. They claimed that "one cannot, after all, assume that only the prosecutor, not the court,

246 ASO, IVK, 155/64, vol. II, Zarządzenie prezesa sądu wojewódzkiego w Warszawie H. Kempistego w sprawie wyznaczenia składu sędziowskiego w procesie Wawrzeckiego i innych, Warszawa 31 X 1964 r.

247 Ibid., Prokuratura Wojewódzka dla m. st. Warszawy, Wykaz osób [których wezwania zażądał oskarżyciel] oraz adwokatów i pełnomocników oskarżonych, pp. 168–176.

248 "Summary proceedings shall be applied if the appellate court's prosecutor, due to the circumstances of the case, submits an application for its recognition in this manner."

has legal and material responsibility with regard to the citizen and that only the prosecutor is responsible for restricting the citizen's right to defense, without any influence on the matter by independent judges." According to their arguments, Art. 46, par. 1[249] of the Constitution did not allow "the court to have tied hands in such a fundamental matter, especially since the quoted decree says nothing about the binding force of the prosecutor's request. Regardless of whether this interpretation is correct, the defense's proposal aims at persuading the provincial prosecutor of the inadequacy of the decision made." While interpreting the provisions in force, they also referred to an opinion contained in commentary on the k.p.k. that "not particularly complicated cases were not suitable," and they pointed out the inadequacy of the exclusion from the case of lay judges and the appointment to the court professional judges. It was also impossible for them to consider, for example due to the complexity and breadth of the matter, the implementation of the underlying legislation in establishing the summary proceeding and speed of repression.[250] "From crime through investigation and hearing, everything in this matter has been slow and taken many months or years," defenders wrote in their application. "Only the sentence must be quick, because according to Art. 13 of the cited decree, the court shall immediately give judgment and must justify it

249 "The administration of justice in the Polish People's Republic is exercised by: the Supreme Court, provincial courts, local courts and special courts."

250 ASO, IV K 155/64, vol. II, Wniosek K. Bieńkowskiego i A. Szczygła o zmianę (uchylenie) trybu doraźnego, p. 209. "Defenders opposing the principle of speedy proceedings in a summary manner in the abovementioned case referred in particular to the following arguments: [..]

a) the offense for which the defendant is accused continued for almost seven years before it was detected;
b) the investigation into this case has continued since the end of 1963 (p. 14, the indictment);
c) the hearing is scheduled for an entire month but, according to the general opinion of lawyers, it will take much longer;
d) there are 35 volumes of documents tied to the case;
e) the indictment represents a volume of 155 pages of dense typescript;

in this case there are 10 defendants, about 20 defenders, 186 witnesses and 4 experts. 237 protocols of further witnesses and 271 documents, sometimes very extensive ones, are to be read. In a word: the complete opposite of all haste, as that word is understood in the language of lawyers and non-practitioners throughout the entire civilized world."

within 24 hours."[251] When examining a "particularly intricate" case, the court not only had a statutory prohibition against taking its time in consideration of the case, it also had "to write a large book of many pages (see the indictment) in one day! This is, of course, physically impossible. Logic, therefore, indicates that this matter does not fall within the framework of the summary proceeding. This was a clear violation of Art. 53, par. 2 of the Constitution[252] because the defendant's right to defense boiled down to mere fiction. Why? Because of the fact that, in a particularly convoluted matter – and one that is therefore particularly suitable for oversight review – the Court is endowed with the trait of infallibility and finality, which are the religious properties that only divine beings have." The lawyers also pointed to their limited right to defend the accused, claiming that in a summary (single-instance) proceeding, the role of defense and the defendant's last word is irrelevant, since the justification of the sentence must necessarily be written not after its announcement (as the law demands), but before the parties vote. The speed of the proceedings (the scheduled hearing date was 20 November), in their opinion, made it impossible in such a short period (3 weeks) to thoroughly familiarize themselves with the extensive (36-volume) trials material.

Furthermore, the defenders referred to the inadequacy of the decree on summary proceedings with regard to the need to adjudicate "an affair that has lasted seven years and whose roots should be contained in a peaceful, normal court procedure, provided with all guarantees which the law provides (including the right to defense) so that the verdict should be as close as possible to the material truth." The defenders pointed out that the sanctions contained in the act of 18 June 1959 on liability for crimes against social property, including the act on Enhancing Protection of Social Property from 21 January 1958, were so severe that they did not justify entering into the summary proceeding. Anticipating that the prosecutor would demand the death penalty for the defendants, lawyers wrote: "the defense indignantly rejects the rumor that the artificial summary proceeding in this came about as the result of the intention to demand capital punishment in the present case. According to the defenders, the death penalty in

251 Dekret z dnia 16 listopada 1945 r. o postępowaniu doraźnym (Dz. U., No. 33, Item 244), Art. 13: "§ 1. After the hearing, the court will issue a verdict without delay; postponement of the announcement of sentence is unacceptable. § 2. The judgment shall be justified in writing within 24 hours after its announcement. § 3. The court shall impose the death penalty only if unanimity as to both guilt and the applicability of the death penalty. § 4. Judgments and court decisions are not subject to appeal."

252 "The defendant is guaranteed the right to defense. The accused may have a defender of choice or office."

this trial is out of the question." The Sejm, "as the highest exponent of the will of the working people of cities and villages" and "the highest organ of state power" (Art. 15 of the Constitution), during the discussion on the law in the relevant commissions, clearly rejected the death penalty for the theft of property in great size and would introduce it only according to its Art. 3 for cases of highway robbery. Therefore, they concluded, the death penalty could not be applied based on the decree of 1945, since the Sejm rejected this penalty in 1959. It would be a circumvention of the explicit will of the "supreme organ of state power." Thus, the "final argument for conducting this matter in a summary proceeding" was eliminated.

The defenders also filed a motion to change the trial composition. They based it on the following premises:

1. the Court did not include any of the judges from the 4th Criminal Division, normally called upon to hear such a case;
2. the provision of Art. 3, par. 2 of the act amending k.p.k. dated 20 July 1950, to which the President of the Provincial Court referred when designating the adjudication panel in this case, was not applicable in this case. They spoke about matters falling within the jurisdiction of the regional court "as a court of first instance," not as the sole and final instance – as was the case in summary proceedings. Moreover, they claimed, matters that are particularly complicated do not qualify at all for such a proceeding.
3. referring to the greater "educational power" of the judgments handed down by lay judges, defenders justified the participation of the latter in the adjudicating group as "a constitutional principle." "The only exception involves the professional composition of the judges. This exception must be applied as little as possible, they wrote, because the participation of people's lay judges in a court is – as the doctrine says – one of the forms by which "working people of cities and villages" exercise power (Art. 1, par. 2 of the Constitution). According to their justification, the provision of Art. 3, par. 1 of the act of 20 July 1950[253] gave excellent opportunity to avoid a professional composition in this case, because it provided for the recognition of two professional judges (which offered professionalism) and three lay judges, who should be heard in this case. For this reason, the defense submitted a request that this article

253 "The president of the provincial court may order the recognition of a case covered by the death penalty through the composition of two judges and three lay judges if he deems it advisable due to the nature of the case. In this case, the justification of the judgment is signed by the full court."

> be applied, stressing that such a request would be rendered unnecessary if the summary proceeding were withdrawn and the "threat of a death penalty" removed. The defenders also referred to the act on the advocate, which included a will to cooperate "in protecting and strengthening the legal order of the People's Republic of Poland." Due to the fact that the issues raised in the request went beyond the confines of the case and related to the basic principles of justice and, moreover, the interpretation of the PRL Constitution, a copy of their letter was also sent to the Presidium of the Council of State.

The President of the Provincial Court in Warsaw, based on an order which he issued, decided to remain, without taking into account the requests of Wawrzecki's lawyers to change the composition of the judicial team in this matter. He thus acknowledged that the order of 31 October 1964, designating the composition of three judges, was in full compliance with the applicable procedural rules and common practice by the courts. In the opinion of the President, there was no justification for the view that criminal cases of special complexity could not be taken up in summary procedures. This latter circumstance should itself provide evidence of the correctness of appointing three professional judges in this case.[254] On 19 November, this order was handed to attorney K. Bieńkowski.

The trial began before the Provincial Court in Warsaw on 20 November 1964. Because we did not manage to get to these files, we have reconstructed the scene based on notes kept in two sets of sources. The first is the archives of the General Prosecutor's Office of the PRL, in which we found notes on the course of the trial. They were prepared by the deputy prosecutor of the Provincial Prosecutor's Office in Warsaw, E. Kostro, and were intended for several persons dealing with this matter in the party and state leadership, among whom were secretaries of the Central Committee: Ryszard Strzelecki and Władysław Wicha (until December 1964 also the Minister of the Interior) and the head of the Administrative Department of the Central Committee Kazimierz Witaszewski. "Secret special information" from the trial was also preserved in the files of the PZPR Warsaw Committee; we were not able to determine the author. The importance of this source lies in the fact that it also contains various comments about the behavior of the accused outside the hearing room, and about the public mood. Realizing that this type of documentation cannot replace the main trial files, we will nonetheless attempt to describe the course of the process on this basis.

---

254 ASO, IV K 155/64, vol. II, Zarządzenie prezesa Sądu Wojewódzkiego dla miasta stołecznego Warszawy z dnia 18 XI 1964 r., pp. 241–243.

"Just before the beginning of the trial," we read in information provided by the PZPR Warsaw Committee, "we received information that the defendants will want to defend themselves by charging high-ranking people whom the MHM directors are said to have provided meat and meat products." However, the course of the trial's first day did not confirm these fears.[255] The court then responded to defense requests concerning the change of procedure, the change in the court composition (by admitting lay judges) and the participation of experts in the trial.

According to the position taken by the prosecutors, the Court did not consider the first two applications. As for the experts, it decided to allow them to participate in the interrogation of defendants and certain witnesses.[256]

On the following day, Wawrzecki put forward his explanation. He did not plead guilty to the theft of social property, but confirmed that he had accepted "material benefits" from his subordinate store managers, the total amount of which was estimated at between PLZ 1,600,000 and 1,700,000 (not the approx. 3,600,000 that was reported in the investigation). According to Wawrzecki, the money received came from the illegal ("silent") processing of non-salable meat assortments (especially shoulder, pork fat, and also bacon) for white sausage, smoked ham, and convenience products, and from the "material resources" of some store managers. He knew about the illegal processing, because store managers informed him about it. He claimed that he tolerated this activity, because it prevented losses that the company would have suffered as a result of the deterioration of less salable meat types. Some store managers, especially self-service stores, collected high salaries (PLZ 3–4,000) and it was possible for them to divert some of their earnings to bribes.

While reading the explanations given during the investigation, Wawrzecki essentially confirmed the fact that he had accepted money, "though he reduced the amount of certain totals and avoided specifying the sums accepted from individual store managers. Regarding the seven shop managers previously reported, he stated that he did not receive money from them." According to the accused, E. Kostro reported, "there was no way to achieve surpluses from the limit of natural losses, because this limit did not cover even the actual losses.

255 APW, KW PZPR, 30/VII-43, vol. 27, Tajna informacja specjalna nr 1 Sektora Informacji Wydziału Organizacyjnego KW PZPR dot. przebiegu procesu mięsnego, Warszawa 25 XI 964, p. 408.

256 AAN, PG 1/29, Notatka (nr 1) dot. przebiegu rozprawy głównej w sprawie Stanisława Wawrzeckiego i in. (26 XI 1964, E. Kostro), p. 118.

The cuts of raw meat were carried out correctly, and the value increase achieved in relation to the [...] slaughter in carcasses was on average consistent with the established margin. Any fact of committing fraud to the detriment of the consumer was severely punished." Of the accepted money, about PLZ 700,000 was supposed to have been spent on the purchase of foreign currency, and PLZ 600,000–700,000 for bribes. He gave bribes to, among others, the employees of the Slaughterhouse – approx. PLZ 430,000; the deputy director of Warsaw's Union of Industries in Trade of Foodstuffs – approx. PLZ 100,000; directors of this Union (objects worth PLZ 35,000), and other people – about PLZ 15,000. "In the course of the investigation, Wawrzecki's explanation about the amount of the benefits he had received was only a temporary estimate, and their rectification was to be based on the confrontation with the testimonies of the store managers and the explanations of other suspects."[257] During the submission of explanations, Wawrzecki reportedly showed remorse (he cried).[258]

Giving testimony on 23 November, Gradowski admitted to having received from the store managers a total of PLZ 1,600,000 – 1,800,000 (not the 2,300,000 that was reported during the investigation). He pointed out that the money came not from the social property but from illegal processing carried out by store managers. He explained that he was informed by store managers about their profits from unused natural losses. "This information," E. Kostro reported, "is currently assessed as untrue, because it concludes that relatively small limits to cover the shortages did not give rise to surpluses. Gradowski claimed that some small part of the amounts he received could actually come from the theft of social property." Gradowski also admitted to giving bribes. "Gradowski remarked that in the MHM enterprises there was an atmosphere of bribery and this circumstance influenced his behavior. In further explanations, the accused expressed remorse. He mentioned that he had handed illegally obtained property (foreign exchange assets) over to law enforcement agencies voluntarily and entirely."

In his explanation submitted the next day, Kazimierz Witowski admitted to accepting from store managers between PLZ 500,000–700,000 in bribes (and not the around 1,500,000 he claimed during the investigation). The money was supposed to have come from the production of their own store managers, who gave him money to ensure his favor. Witkowski also gave bribes of totaling around PLZ 300,000. As he maintained, "during the investigation, under the influence of interrogators' suggestions, he gave higher than actual amounts of property

257 Ibid., p. 104.
258 APW, KW PZPR, 30/VII-43, vol. 27, p. 408.

benefits, both accepted and given. He offered no special privileges to store managers from whom he received money."

All of the accused former MHM directors pointed out some common circumstances related to fraud. They claimed that meat distributors provided only about 80 % of the turnover planned for the company. Additional weight came as a result of the necessity to undertake procedures that were not always legal, because, for example, the employees of the Slaughterhouse conditioned the release of meat on the reception of bribes. They confirmed that the commercial enterprises they directed were interested in receiving meat in carcasses, because it offered particularly large possibilities for fraud during the cutting process. In MHM enterprises, the problem of managing non-salable meat species was not solved, which led to illegal processing or sales to owners of private butcher workshops. Finally, staffing difficulties did not allow for the consistent application of rules for removing from their positions in trade those who had been punished for fraud.[259]

On 25 November, the court heard Tadeusz Skowroński, former director of Warsaw's Union of Industries in Trade of Foodstuffs. He admitted to having accepted from Witowski about PLZ 120–130,000, and from Wawrzecki a gold watch, a golden signet, photo camera and clothing vouchers worth about PLZ 31,000. In his explanations, Skowroński stressed that he did not know about the fraud committed by MHM directors and did not believe he had assisted them in their theft of social property. Witowski had assured investigators that the money he had given them did not come from the enterprise he managed, and that he treated the items given by Wawrzecki as name-day gifts, purchased jointly by the employees of the MHM management. Witowski claimed that all MHM companies achieved good or even very good economic results and that this circumstance ought to influence the "disappearance of suspicions." All the MHM directors had a very broad network of acquaintances and dealt with various issues at the Trade Department of the National Council of Ministers and the Ministry of Internal Commerce (MHW), which made it difficult to supervise them.

On the same day, the court began hearing the explanations of M. Fabisiak, who admitted to receiving from the store managers MHM directors about PLZ 70–75,000. (during the investigation he talked of about PLZ 227,000). At the same time, he changed the explanations he had previously submitted regarding bribes received. He excused the changes by citing poor health and suggestions investigators had given him during the investigation. Fabisiak also changed his

259 AAN, PG 1/29, Notatka (nr 1)…, pp. 118 ff.

previous testimony, in which he had identified the sources of illegal profits taken by store managers and MHM directors (losses, surpluses from cutting, fraud against consumers).[260]

A KW PZPR informant, commenting on this initial period of the trial, wrote that "all the defendants are afraid of high sentences. Gradowski said that if he had to spend even a dozen years in prison, he could be released after 4–5 years." Zygmunt Woźniak – head of the Trade Department of the Warsaw National Council [. . .], who was to testify as a witness, allegedly feared that he could harm the defendants by revealing unknown aggravating facts. "He says he will attempt to escape [punishment] by faking mental illness and even suicide." Gradowski talked badly about Woźniak; he claimed that he had received bribes of several million zlotys from meat industry workers and owners of bazaar and street booths.

Member of the public in the room, the informant continued, would definitely condemn the accused and say that "it would be no big deal if someone were sentenced to death." Woźniak's absence among the defendants raised doubts about whether he had been rightly excluded from the first trial. "Gradowski said at the beginning that Woźniak must have "backing" of some kind since he is not being tried with the others in a summary manner." Many people in the room were taking notes. "As explained, these are delegates from individual institutions who are there with an obligation to inform management."[261]

On 27 November, butcher shop managers Woźnica and Walendziuk submitted their explanations. The former did not admit to the crimes alleged against him, but stated that he had given bribes to the accused MHM directors because of the harassment he had faced. He also denied that he had been engaged in the so-called side-deal production of sausages in the store they ran, because it was allegedly technologically impossible.[262] Walendziuk, in turn, partially admitted to having given bribes. He claimed that the money for this purpose was derived from his salary and partly from the unused natural losses. At the hearing, he emphasized that he was not aware of the obligation to pay surplus assets to the enterprise. He referred to official statements at the meetings, when – in connection with discussing the matter of low earnings enjoyed by trade employees – he declared: "what are you complaining about, you have losses."[263] He also

260 Ibid., p. 106.

261 APW, KW PZPR, 30/VII-43, vol. 27, pp. 408 ff.

262 AAN, PG, 1/29, Notatka (nr 3) z przebiegu procesu w sprawie Stanisława Wawrzeckiego i innych (Warszawa 28 XI 1964, E. Kostro), p. 126.

263 AAN, PG, 1/29, Notatka (nr 3). . ., p. 126.

explained that "the court and prosecutor's office were supplied in his shop and they were satisfied with it (a wave of laughter passed through the room)." "During the lunch break," we read further in the party document, "Gradowski and Wawrzecki recalled 'dinners' eaten in the private restaurant 'Baszta' in Pyras. [. . .]. At lunches, they played the game 'oczko', in which the directors 'lost' a significant sum of money to the other people."[264]

With his explanation submitted on 30 November, store manager Balczarek admitted only to giving bribes.[265] Characterizing the relations prevailing in the MHM, he pointed to the incompetence of MHM directors in the meat industry, who "therefore had no authority among store managers."[266]

On 1 December, the court interrogated A. Zawadzki, a private supplier of cold cuts, who claimed that he had not participated in the theft of social property and did not know about the existence of a criminal group. He confessed to fencing approx. 37 tons of stolen meat and pork fat, for which he had paid approx. PLZ 900,000. He pointed out that as a result of the transformation in 1961 of some butchers workshops into meat production facilities, the supply of raw materials for private butcher workshops significantly deteriorated, which forced them to search out raw materials of illegal origin. The increase in production due to the processing of meat and fats was not registered in the workshop sales books, and products were sold outside the register (so-called under-the-counter) in socialized stores. He added that throughout the entire period of mass production, he gave bribes to slaughterhouse employees, to MHM employees, and to other officials.[267]

As reported by the party informer during the breaks in the hearing: "(outside the courtroom) there is clearly nervousness among the defendants. The accused are angry at each other in connection with their complex explanations. For instance, Fabisiak screamed at Balczarek and was on the verge of striking him, similarly Stokłosiński accused Balczarek of unnecessarily implicating Witowski.

---

264 APW, KW PZPR, 30/VII-43, vol. 27, Tajna informacja specjalna nr 3 dot. procesu przeciwko Wawrzeckiemu i innym, Warszawa 28 XI 1964, pp. 413 ff.

265 APW, KW PZPR, 30/VII-43, vol. 27, Tajna informacja specjalna nr 4 dot. ósmego dnia procesu przeciwko Wawrzeckiemu i innym, Warszawa 1 XII 1964, p. 415.

266 AAN, PG, 1/29, Notatka (nr 4) o przebiegu procesu w Sprawie Stanisława Wawrzeckiego i innych, p. 129.

267 AAN, PG, 1/29, Notatka (nr 5) o przebiegu procesu Stanisława Wawrzeckiego i innych, p. 132.

The accused are preparing questions for witnesses, e.g. Skowroński, on issues involving the current situation in the meat sector."[268]

It is characteristic that the accused rejected the accusation that they had stolen social property but admitted to accepting material benefits that were being – one should presume – deliberately underestimated. After all, the first category of acts under examination here allowed for the application of the decree on summary proceedings and – in accordance with its Art. 2 – for a death penalty sentence. Acceptance of material benefits, however, was treated as a clerical crime and under applicable law could not be subject to such proceedings with all their consequences.

As of 3 December, witnesses and experts gave their testimonies. By 12 January 1965, when a break in the trial was announced a break (until January 20), a total of 320 witnesses were questioned, including 135 requested by the defense, and four experts. A large part of them, including those who had been taken into custody, confirmed that the accused MHM directors had received bribes and that there was widespread corruption in the meat industry. Store managers talked about having given bribes in order to retain their position, for additional product assignments, for "no oversight checks," for turning a blind eye to illegal trade.

Reports for the KW PZPR from the trial also include opinions offered by the accused and some witnesses outside the hearing room. Gradowski reported said "that the Ministry of Internal Trade is responsible for the meat scandal, because it set higher plans than supplies could handle, and this led to abuse. Gradowski said that he was counting on pardon by the Council of State because he has friends there. Zawadzki – the owner of the plant, is indignant at the other accused directors because they do not know the meat industry and do not care about the companies and were just waiting around for bribes."[269] At the end of the hearing on 8 December 1964, there was reportedly an exchange was to be held between the accused Balczarek and Fabisiak on the testimony given by one of the witnesses: "Fabisiak explained to Balczarek that detailed questioning of witnesses by defendants may reveal hitherto unknown crimes to law enforcement agencies. During the break the accused Gradowski expressed fears that if a fine

268 APW, KW PZPR, 30/VII-43, vol. 27, Tajna informacja specjalna nr 5 dot. procesu przeciwko Wawrzeckiemu i innym, Warszawa 2 XII 1964, p. 416.

269 APW, KW PZPR, 30/VII-43, t.27, Tajna informacja specjalna nr 7 dot. procesu przeciwko Wawrzeckiemu i innym, Warszawa, 9 XII 1964, p. 420.

were imposed, he would not be able to pay it, while Witowski had a villa in Leśna Podkowa (registered under another name), and considerable property transferred to the family."[270] Among the defendants, there was concern about the fact that they had admitted to accepting larger amounts than indicated in the witness testimonies. The ex-MHM employees arrested for the next trials hoped that "the largest sentences comedown in the current trial, while the next ones will be small or the accused will even go unpunished."[271]

The court announced its verdict on 2 February 1965, on the forty-first day of the trial.[272] In his sentence, it was stated that the defendants S. Wawrzecki, H.M. Gradowski and K. Witowski were found guilty because, as MHM directors acting in collusion with many store managers, they misappropriated, to the detriment of the companies they worked for, multimillions in goods-money surpluses created in these stores. Wawrzecki reportedly received PLZ 3,500,000 from these sums, Gradowski – PLZ 2,300,000, and Witowski – PLZ 1,500,000. For this reason, in line with the accusations as adopted in indictment, on the basis of Art. 2, par. 1 of the decree on summary proceedings, the court sentenced Wawrzecki to death and Gradowski and Witowski to life imprisonment. In addition, pursuant to Art. 2, par. 3 of the cited decree, the court ruled that their property was to be forfeited in full, and on the basis of the relevant provisions of the p.c. (Art. 47, par. 1 pt. a in connection with Art. 52 par. 2) – loss of public and civic rights forever. In addition, Gradowski and Witowski were charged with a fine of PLZ 150,000.

T. Skowroński and M. Fabisiak were found guilty of acts in accordance with the qualifications as adopted in the indictment, and on the basis of the abovementioned decree on summary proceedings, they were sentenced to life imprisonment, the forfeiture of property in full, the loss of public and civic rights forever, and fines amounting to PLZ 100,000. The other defendants were sentenced to the following penalties: A. Stokłosiński – for 9 years; A. Woźnica, W. Walendziuk – 10 years; L. Balczarek – a total of 11 years; and A. Zawadzki – 12 years in prison. In addition, all of their property was forfeited in full, fines were imposed, and they lost public rights.

---

270 APW, KW PZPR, 30/VII-43, t.27, Tajna informacja specjalna dot. procesu przeciwko Wawrzeckiemu i innym, Warszawa, 14 XII 1964, p. 422.

271 APW, KW PZPR, 30/VII-43, vol. 27, Tajna informacja specjalna nr 9 dot. procesu przeciwko Wawrzeckiemu i innym, Warszawa 17 XII 1964, p. 424.

272 ASO, IV K 155/64, vol. III, Sentencja wyroku, 2 lutego 1965.

The severity of the verdict, which was in line with the prevailing tendency among the party's leadership under Gomułka (we write more about this below), and especially the death sentence imposed on Wawrzecki encouraged lawyers to battle further to save his life struggle. On 4 February 1965, they sent the Warsaw Provincial Court an application for the delivery of a copy of the grounds for judgment in order to establish a review. Contrary to the view of the adjudication panel, they claimed that such a move was possible because the judgment in question had not been issued in a summary manner, but in an ordinary manner, and therefore a remedy in this regard was available. They claimed that the break in the break in the court session that had taken place during the trial was tantamount to postponing the announcement of the judgment sentence. According to the defense, the adjournment of the adjudication of a summary court judgment (regardless of the pretext, whether announced in ordinary session or even due to just cause), rendered the verdict pronounced in ordinary session and thus provided the accused a normal remedy. Therefore, defenders asked for a decision to be delivered to them for appeal to the Supreme Court if that decision were negative.[273]

By an order dated 16 February 1965, signed by the Chairman of the 4th Department of the Provincial Court in Warsaw, the complaint put forward Wawrzecki's lawyers in this matter was set aside.[274] The lawyers responded to the order with a complaint addressed to the Criminal Chamber of the Supreme Court, which decided on 17 February in a closed session to disregard it altogether. According to the judges, from the minutes of the main hearing of 1 February, the court adjourned at 10.28 am, announcing that the verdict would not be announced earlier than 6 pm. The very same day at 21.15, due to the late hour and fatigue of the judges' panel, a break of deliberation over the verdict was ordered lasting till 2 February, and it was announced at the same time that the verdict would not be delivered before 4 pm. In their opinion, the accused's defenders based their conclusions on the provision of Art. 13 of act 1 of the decree of 16 December 1945 on summary proceedings, commenting on this provision contrary to its clear wording. According to this provision, the Court in summary proceedings, after the hearing, should immediately pass judgment; any

273 ASO, IV K 155/64, vol. III, Adwokaci K. Bieńkowski i A. Szczygieł, obrońcy St. Wawrzeckiego, Warszawa do Sądu Wojewódzkiego dla m. st. Warszawy, 4 lutego 1965 r., p. 406.

274 ASO, IV K 155/64, vol. III, Zarządzenie z 16 lutego 1965 r.

postponement of the judgement sentence was unacceptable. In a given case, the Court did not postpone the issuance of the sentence, but only interrupted the council over the verdict, which – in terms of the late hour and fatigue on the part of members of the Court – was in the interests of the accused and was not prohibited by the provisions of the Criminal Code. It was also stated that the issue of stopping the hearing over the verdict recognized in summary proceedings was already the subject of deliberations at the Supreme Court, which spoke on this matter in its ruling of 21 July 1962 (OSN No. 6/63, Item 111).[275]

Wawrzecki's situation became even more dramatic when, on 18 March 1965, the Council of State refused his request for mercy.[276] The next day he was hanged.[277]

Court records show that the remaining convicts, in spite of individual requests, were usually denied any reprieve. It was not until 1970 that, after the new penal court went into force, Gradowski, Fabisiak, Skowroński and Witowski had their life sentences reduced to 25 years imprisonment.[278] On 28 May 1965, A. Stokłosiński died of a heart attack while serving his sentence. On 9 March 1971, L. Balczarek died, who in September of the previous year was released from prison based on his state of health. On 7 January 1971, W. Walendziuk was given a conditional early release. On 19 March 1971, Aleksander Woźnica left the Correctional Institution in Strzelce Opolskie. On 14 May 1973, A. Zawadzki was given a conditional early release. On 15 September 1977, Mieczysław Fabisiak died in the prison hospital at Barczewo.[279]

3.4.3. *The Warsaw Meat Affair: Launching an Avalanche*

Wawrzecki's trial, and especially the severe sentence, echoed not only in legal circles but also in circles not related to the administration of justice (which we

---

275 ASO, IV K 155/64, vol. III, Postanowienie Sądu Najwyższego z 17 lutego 1965, sygn. akt I. KZ. 9/65, p. 412.

276 ASO, IV K 155/64, vol. III, Decyzja Rady Państwa z 18 marca 1965 w stosunku do S. Wawrzeckiego, p. 425.

277 ASO, IV K 155/64, vol. III, Zawiadomienie o śmierci więźnia, Warszawa 19 marca 1965, p. 457.

278 ASO, IV K 155/64, vol. IV, Postanowienie z dnia 7 lutego 1970 r., p. 813; Ibid., Postanowienia z dnia 6 czerwca 1970 r., pp. 824–826.

279 ASO, IV K 155/64, vol. V, Notatka dotycząca wykonania kar w sprawie Sądu Wojewódzkiego dla m. st. Warszawy (IV. K. 155/64) przeciwko Stanisławowi Wawrzeckiemu i innym, Warszawa październik 1976.

write about below). However, it is worth remembering that severe penalties for perpetrators of fraud in the meat economy were handed down not only in Warsaw but throughout Poland. Outside the capital, in 39 so-called meat cases supervised by the General Prosecutor's Office, the number of suspects at the beginning of April 1965 amounted to over 370.[280] By 1 July 1965, law enforcement agencies outside the Warsaw Voivodeship had jointly conducted 137 investigations into cases against 809 people concerning irregularities in the meat economy. A total of 74 indictments against 440 people had been sent to court, including a request to review cases in a summary manner – 3 cases brought against 29 persons. By 1 July, the courts had recognized a total of 34 cases against 171 defendants, with the remaining two, involving 28 people, in the final stage of examination in summary proceedings.[281]

Information "on the results of criminal prosecution in cases of the most serious fraud in the meat economy," prepared by the General Prosecutor's Office and covering all of Poland, shows that in the period from 1964 to 31 December 1969, fraud of considerable size (involving over PLZ 200,000) were revealed in in 88 socialized facilities, including 29 meat factories, 24 cooperative farms, 8 retail trade enterprises, 7 enterprises involved animal slaughter, 2 voivodeship meat industry unions and 18 other establishments. Among employees of 84 enterprises and cooperative facilities, 167 indictments were issued covering a total of 2,067 people.[282]

The most important information about the extent of the investigations and their results on a nationwide scale is provided in Tables 14–18.

---

280 AAN, PG, 4/34, Informacja o ściganiu przestępstw w gospodarce mięsnej Departamentu Nadzoru nad Śledztwem i Dochodzeniem Generalnej Prokuratury, p. 48.

281 AAN, PG, 1/29, Notatka informacyjna ujmująca syntetycznie zakres ścigania przestępstw w gospodarce mięsnej według stanu na dzień 1 lipca 1965 r., p. 318.

282 AAN, PG, 1/43, Informacja o wynikach ścigania karnego w sprawach o najpoważniejsze nadużycia w gospodarce mięsnej, prowadzonych w latach 1963–1969 sporządzone przez wiceprokuratora Prokuratury Generalnej B. Jodelisa, Warszawa 5 stycznia 1970, p. 116.

Table 14. Summary of the results of preparatory proceedings in "meat" cases which concluded in an indictment*

Year	Value of stolen property in PLZ	Value of bribes in PLZ
1964	10,475,595	-
1965	42,263,301	4,672,803
1966	41,335,488	1,422,500
1967	28,682,359	1,854,450
1968	42,905,203	1,976,200
1969	31,413,783	1,096,040
Total	197,075,729	11,021,993

*** involving cases of fraud of considerable size (>200,000 PLZ)**

Source: AAN, PG, 1/43, Informacja o wynikach ścigania karnego w sprawach o najpoważniejsze nadużycia w gospodarce mięsnej, prowadzonych w latach 1963–1969 sporządzone przez wiceprokuratora Prokuratury Generalnej B. Jodelisa, Warszawa, 5 stycznia 1970, p. 125.

Table 15. The results of criminal prosecution in "meat cases"* in the years 1964–1969, according to voivodeship

Voivodeship	Value of stolen property in PLZ	Value of bribes in PLZ
Białystok	486,650	-
Bydgoszcz	621,080	324,720
Gdańsk	1,096,108	449,700
Katowice	25,000,205	245,000
Kielce	3,084,081	-
Koszalin	417,600	-
Kraków	5,530,622	84,000
Lublin	8,355,000	381,283
Łódź – city**	21,263,508	133,200
Łódź – voivodeship	-	-
Olsztyn	-	-
Opole	5,888,400	200,000
Poznań	6,941,163	1,078,540
Rzeszów	1,088,449	307,300
Szczecin	842,290	-
Warszawa – city**	50,027,410	5,273,850
Warszawa – voivodeship	48,531,517	1,866,400
Wrocław	15,581,682	518,000
Zielona Góra	2,319,964	160,000
TOTAL	197,075,729	11,021,993

*** involving cases of fraud of considerable size (>200,000 PLZ)**
**** separated city, urban voivodeship**

Source: AAN, PG, 1/43, Informacja o wynikach ścigania. . ., p. 127.

Table 16. Number of indictments and of those accused and arrested in cases of fraud in the meat economy in 1964–1969*

Year	No. of indictments	No. of accused	No. of arrested
1964	4	31	30
1965	52	631	501
1966	32	379	311
1967	22	306	248
1968	34	384	272
1969	23	336	280
Total	167	2,067	1,642

* **involving cases of fraud of considerable size (>200,000 PLZ)**

Source: AAN, PG, 1/43, Informacja o wynikach ścigania. . ., p. 125.

Table 17. Accused in cases of meat fraud in the years 1964 – 1969*

Year	No. of accused	Managerial positions	Sector			Employment area			
			state	cooperative	private	Processing	Trade	Purchase	other
1964	31	8	12	16	3	4	20	3	4
1965	631	35	538	62	31	212	324	17	78
1966	379	31	233	132	14	175	148	16	40
1967	306	11	220	82	4	125	104	11	66
1968	384	15	230	114	40	97	65	167	55
1969	336	12	257	58	21	165	46	42	83
Total	2067	112	1490	464	113	778	707	256	326

* **involving cases of fraud of considerable size (>200,000 PLZ)**

Source: AAN, PG, 1/43, Informacja o wynikach ścigania. . ., p. 126.

Table 18. Arrested and accused in cases of fraud in the meat economy in Poland in the years 1964–1969 according to voivodeship*

Voivodeship	No. of accused	No. of arrested
Białystok	24	17
Bydgoszcz	24	22
Gdańsk	41	31
Katowice	208	175
Kielce	17	17
Koszalin	15	8
Kraków	47	41
Lublin	42	41
Łódź - city**	156	148
Łódź - voivodeship	-	-
Olsztyn	-	-
Opole	140	100
Poznań	89	64
Rzeszów	43	27
Szczecin	52	25
Warszawa - city**	582	450
Warszawa - voivodeship	318	262
Wrocław	213	173
Zielona Góra	56	41
TOTAL	2067	1642

*** involving cases of fraud of considerable size (>200,000 PLZ)**
**** separated city, urban voivodeship**
Source: AAN, PG, 1/43, Informacja o wynikach ścigania, p. 127.

Jurisprudence in these matters was considered strict, even by the General Prosecutor's Office. In 1963–1969, the courts sentenced 1,767 defendants to prison and more, and only 38 (2.1 %) were acquitted. Cases against four people were ended due to their deaths. One of the accused (S. Wawrzecki) was given the death penalty, and in the case of 10 people the sentence was life imprisonment. Sentences for terms punishment are presented in Table 19.

Table 19. Penalties imposed by courts in cases of fraud in the meat economy in the years 1963–1969*

Scope of prison sentence	Numbers of sentenced
15 years	25
Above 12 to 14 years	58
Above 10 to 12 years	141
Above 8 to 10 years	344
Above 6 to 8 years	145
Above 4 to 6 years	297
Above 2 to 4 years	504
Above 1 year to 2 years	226
Less than 1 year	16

*** involving cases of fraud of considerable size (>200,000 PLZ)**
Source: AAN, PG, 1/43, Informacja o wynikach ścigania. . ., p. 117.

Of the prisoners sentenced to life imprisonment, four had committed fraud to the amount of millions while holding positions as meat factory directors, two as directors of MHM, and one as director of trade union, two as a warehouse attendant and a meat factory foreman, and one as head of the PIH. Persons sentenced to 15 years in prison committed affair crimes in connection with the employment of the director of a meat factory (4), as director of trade union (1), director of a convenience store (1), director of an animal-purchasing company (1), director of a trading company (1), manager of a cooperative butcher (3), head of the animal procurement section (1), chief accountant (1), transport dispatcher of the Meat Plant (1), manager of the MHM meat shop (1), and a warehouse attendant and foreman (10).[283]

Investigations and trials in cases concerning fraud in the meat economy revealed not only the mass character of corrupt practices but also the fact that they were common – i.e. included people occupying very different positions in all sectors of the economy. Allegations were even made against one of the judges of the Supreme Court, several high-ranking militia officers (in the KW MO Warsaw because they had dismissed two heads of departments and deputy commander of the provincial MO),[284] employees of oversight bodies, high party officials, etc.

283 AAN, PG, 1/43, Informacja o wynikach ścigania. . ., p. 117–125.

284 AAN, KC PZPR, 237/XIV-334, Protokół z posiedzenia Komisji Wymiaru Sprawiedliwości, Bezpieczeństwa i Porządku Publicznego w dniu 18 grudnia 1965, p. 62.

Viewed in this context, Wawrzecki's trial appears, on the one hand, as exceptional because of the sentence the court handed down, but on the other hand as "normal" from the point of view of the prosecution and court practices at the time. It is clear that what happened in Warsaw stimulated law enforcement agencies throughout Poland to take similar actions.

3.5. Affairs after the Affair

Draconian sentences in the Wawrzecki case did not result in any significant changes in the mechanisms of economic crime involving meat. Though it is true that the answer to the question about the scale of these abuses in subsequent years requires further research, undoubtedly meat scandals were, from time to time, of interest to various judicial authorities.

In 1971, there was evidence of abuse in meat processing in Piotrków Trybunalski. On 15 February – 23 March 1973, a criminal trial was held in front of the Provincial Court in Łódź against the first group of perpetrators of these crimes. A dozen or so people were sentenced, including the former head of one of the butcher's farms in Piotrków for a penalty of 25 years imprisonment, PLZ 600,000 fine, forfeiture of property in full and the loss of civic rights for 10 years.[285] That year, more than 100 investigations concerning the meat industry were carried out and continued from previous years, involving about 1,000 suspect, 700 of whom were arrested.[286]

In 1981–1982, Polish officials significantly sharpened methods for combating fraud related to the production and distribution of goods, including foodstuffs. On 10 August 1981, the Council of Ministers established, through resolution no. 156, national, provincial and local Extraordinary Commissions to Combat Speculation. On 25 September that year, the Sejm passed a law on combating speculation (amended on 9 October 1982), penalizing many acts that had hitherto gone unpunished, and introducing an expedited procedure in these matters. The establishment of the Central Commission to Combat Speculation (replacing the abovementioned Extraordinary Commissions) and its field counterparts made it easier to combat these crimes.[287] In 1982, the Council of Ministers adopted an

285 Jan Kierlik, *O przestępczości w przetwórstwie mięsnym* (Warszawa: Departament Szkolenia i Doskonalenia Zawodowego MSW, 1974), 7–19.

286 AAN, KC PZPR, 1763 (mikrofilm 2932), Stan porządku w kraju ze szczególnym uwzględnieniem zabezpieczenia zakładów przemysłowych i dyscypliny społeczno-produkcyjnej, Warszawa listopad 1972, W. Administracyjny KC PZPR i MSW, p. 391–402.

287 Kochanowski, "Zmagania ze smokiem…: działalność Centralnej Komisji do Walki ze Spekulacją (1981–1987)," *Przegląd Historyczny* 4 (2010), 611–640.

action program for the prevention and suppression of speculation. New elements were introduced by an act amending certain provisions of the criminal law and regarding particular types of criminal liability. While the MO and PIH were involved almost exclusively in the fight against speculation in the first half of 1981, a larger number of MO officers, Polish Army soldiers, and employees in state administration and professional oversight – as a result of party and government decisions in the second half of that year – were included in those activities. The "main blow" was directed at bazaars and marketplaces. It was not possible for us to determine what part of the speculation offenses revealed through investigations involved food products, including meat. According to MO information, the number of detected speculative offenses in 1981 was 6,646; in 1982 – 12,374; in 1983 – 10,860; in 1984 – 14,972, in 1985 (9 months) – 11,647. While in the early years, minor offenses were dominant, later the number of serious offenses, carried out in an organized manner or in which the value of commodities subject to speculation exceeded the minimum amounts (PLZ 300,000 according to the Criminal Code, and PLZ 200,000 according to the aforementioned act). The number of such crimes revealed in 1981 was 94; in 1982 – 471; in 1983 – 610; in 1984 – 1,633; and in 1985 (9 months) – 1,712. The most common categories of such crimes were:

- speculation in market goods in the area of socialized trade (article 221 of the p.c.); its share in relation to total cases in 1981–1985 ranged from 57 % to 24 % annually;
- extortion involving provisioning cards (Art. 4 of the act of 25 September 1981); in 1981, extortion accounted for 1.3 % of all detected offenses to the detriment of consumers; in subsequent years that number increased (up to 29.1 % in 1985);
- sale of goods directly from warehouses, during transport or in violation of regulations on rationing (Art. 1 of the act). In 1981 such sales constituted 6.75 % of all cases; in 1985 – 11.3 %;
- refusal to sell to, and hiding goods from, buyers (Art. 2 of the act); this type of crime showed a downward trend (24.8 % of all revealed speculative offenses in 1982; 6.9 % in 1985.[288]

According to the information from the Central Commission to Combat Speculation, in 1981–1985 MO authorities revealed almost 60,000 speculation crimes. At that time, district courts heard cases on almost 53,000 people for speculation offenses,

288 AAN, Urząd Rady Ministrów (hereafter cited as URM), 32/182, Informacja dotycząca zwalczania spekulacji w latach 1981–1985 oraz efektów uzyskanych przez Milicję Obywatelską, Warszawa 10 października 1985, p. 100 ff.

and sentenced nearly 46,000 of them. Seven thousand people were engaged in this work. In 1985, MO bodies initiated over 87,000 preparatory proceedings for these crimes. Particularly high numbers were indicated in crimes involving social property, the theft of property of considerable value, crimes of mismanagement, bribery of public officials, tax crimes and foreign currency smuggling.[289]

In the 1980s, as before, abuses in meat management were the cause behind many lawsuits. The rationing system was conducive to the emergence of new forms of fraud. It is worth pointing to fraud and theft detected in 1984 in Meat Factory in Jelenia Góra. In the course of the investigation, it was established that 70 kg to 120 kg of meat had been "saved" there illegally per month. In the ongoing trial in front of the Provincial Court, 14 people were sentenced to 1 to 4 years of imprisonment.[290]

Obviously, one must regard what was revealed in the course of trials focused on fraud in the meat industry as a small part of the "dark number" of crimes actually committed. What had a mass character was primarily the theft of social property (in this case, meat from processing plants and stores). Sociological research indicates that there was much greater consent surrounding meat them than surrounding, for example, theft of private property. Initial analysis of this phenomenon leads to a more general thesis that the slightest theft of social property (about which we will write more later) was a pathological, massively applied and largely socially tolerable adaptation strategy to a shortage economy, and the meat economy – because of the role it played in this economic system – was the area where such a strategy was employed especially often.

3.6. Punishment as a Political Act

3.6.1. Political Control of Justice: the Example of Economic Crime

The meat affair also prompts us to consider a completely different political angle that is not directly related to official actions to prevent food problems. Indeed, it seems that it is an excellent excuse to examine the essence of the relationship between the political authority and judicial institutions. As the introduction to such considerations, first of all, we must make some general remarks on this subject.

---

289 AAN, URM 1.5/43, Centralna Komisja do Walki ze Spekulacją przy Radzie Ministrów, Biuletyn z VI Krajowej Narady Antyspekulacyjnej odbytej w dniu 20 lutego 1986 r. w Urzędzie Rady Ministrów, pp. 289–291.

290 AAN, PG, 16/151, Odpis aktu oskarżenia skierowanego do sądu przez Prokuraturę Rejonową w Jeleniej Górze dotyczącego aferowego zagarnięcia masy mięsnej w Jeleniogórskich Zakładach Mięsnych w Jeleniej Górze, Jelenia Góra 1 lipca 1985, pp. 8–27.

In communist Poland, especially during the Stalinist period, in accordance with the ideological principles of Marxism-Leninism, the justice system and the rule of law were to be class based, which meant that in fact things they became instruments in the hands of the ruling party. The main idea was that – as Hilary Minc put it in 1951 – "the enemy in the people's state could not cause harm, he could not lift his head, and for every time he raised his head, he was punished."[291] With regard to the judiciary – according to Andrzej Rzepliński – the implementation of these ideas consisted in removing the separation of powers from the constitutional system, abolishing the monopoly of courts for resolving legal disputes, securing for the ruling communists the exclusive rights to appoint judges and to create a corps of judges. The principle of judicial independence was subordinated to the principle of the party's leading role.[292] The laws were to express the will of the "people" who were "building socialism." Crimes under Marxism-Leninism were acts that were aimed at the interests of the "ruling class." The definitions of these crimes were characterized by arbitrariness in determining the conditions for the criminal conduct of an act.

In the actual practice of justice, the implementation of these principles took various forms.

An important instrument in this regard was the so-called nomenklatura[293] which, in the context of the justice system, consisted in the fact that, to hold a managerial position in that system, one had to be accepted by various leadership structures of the communist party. In the draft list of nomenklatura positions from 1949, it was the KC PZPR's right to fill the positions of president, vice presidents, prosecutors, deputy prosecutors and Supreme Court justices, presidents and prosecutors of appellate and district courts. In a similar list from 1955, the Politburo reserved for itself the right to decide who would fill the position of PRL Prosecutor General and the president of the Supreme Court. The KC Secretariat's nomenklatura included, among others, the positions of the vice-presidents of the Supreme Court, and in the records and control of the departmental departments of the Central Committee – the positions of

291 Zdzisław A. Ziemba, *Prawo przeciwko społeczeństwu. Polskie prawo karne w latach 1944–1956* (Warszawa: Uniwersytet Warszawski, 1997), 30–31.

292 Andrzej Rzepliński, „„Przystosowanie ustroju sądownictwa do potrzeb państwa totalitarnego w Polsce w latach 1944–1956," in *Przestępstwa sędziów i prokuratorów w Polsce lat 1944–1956*, eds. Witold Kulesza and A. Rzepliński, Warszawa: Instytut Pamięci Narodowej, 2000, 15.

293 Nomenklatura – roughly, a counterpart of the western establishment.

provincial prosecutors and presidents of Provincial Courts. Similar solutions were in effect at later dates.[294]

There was also an emphasis on the broadly understood "partisan" nature of the judiciary. As a result of these activities, as early as in mid-1949, of the 3,090 judges and prosecutors in Poland, 852 belonged to the PZPR, and 828 belonged to the "allied parties" subordinate to the Communist party.[295]

During the Stalinist period, an important manifestation of the fact that the justice system subordinate to decisions made within the Communist Party and the system's instrumentalization in the battle against economic crime involved the origins and functioning of the above-mentioned KS. In official propaganda, its creation was the result of the "will of the people" as expressed in the resolution of the plenum of the Central Committee of Trade Unions (KCZZ) meeting on 31 August – 1 September 1945. Any real knowledge of the functioning of the power system in Poland at the time must be accompanied by a large degree of skepticism. Regardless of the "people's will," it is difficult to regard it as a coincidence that the decision in this case was made on 2 September 1945 at a meeting of the KC PZPR, where it was decided to put forward an initiative to establish a special commission to "prosecute bribery, theft of state property, fraud and corruption in the state, local government and economic apparatus."[296]

One should agree with the author of the historical and legal monograph on the Commission that the entire system of criminal repression used by that commission "played a significant modifying role – from the point of view of the authorities of that time – in the relationship between the codex and 'classic' punishments. Thanks to this system, Polish authorities gained a serious weapon in the fight against potential enemies, whose conviction on the 'normal' route would not have been possible or would not have provided what the government desired, namely – intensified criminal repression."[297] This procedure was marked

294 Andrzej Paczkowski, *System nomenklatury kadr w Polsce (1950–1970)* (Warszawa: Instytut Studiów Politycznych PAN, 2000), 49, 68–69, 76.

295 AAN, MS, 9, Krótkie sprawozdanie z działalności poszczególnych Departamentów Ministerstwa Sprawiedliwości za okres pierwszego pięciolecia Polski Ludowej, Warszawa 19 lipca 1949, p. 7.

296 Jarosz, Wolsza, „„Komisja Specjalna do Walki z Nadużyciami i Szkodnictwem Gospodarczym (1945–1954)," 9.

297 Piotr Fiedorczyk, *Komisja Specjalna do Walki z Nadużyciami i Szkodnictwem Gospodarczym 1945–1954. Studium historycznoprawne* (Białystok: Temida 2, 2002), 301.

by repression directed at specific persons, and not against the acts committed by them.

The "class" basis of the operation of this institution was most fully revealed in the context of the mass-scale action against speculation, which intensified after the adoption of the previously discussed act of 2 June on combating high prices and excessive profits in trade. Under the guise of the battle against corruption and economic fraud, what was in fact under attack was private trade, which was dysfunctional from the perspective of the adopted Stalinist economic model. Between June and December 1947, 90 % (and in 1948 – 89 %) of all penal protocols prepared by the Social Price Control Commissions, which had been established with the participation of KS employees, concerned private trading establishments.[298] As a result of these and other activities, the number of such establishments decreased from 184,000 in October 1947 to 98,000 in January 1949. It is also no accident that private buyers and entrepreneurs in 1946 and 1948 constituted as much as 27 % and 19 % of all persons whom the Commission's authorities sentenced to time in a labor camp.[299]

This subordination of the scale of repression to current political goals also serves perfectly as an example of how to deal with peasants who evaded compulsory supplies of agricultural produce. In 1951/52, special "KC PZPR Party instructions to party and state authorities on how to carry out the planned purchase and financial obligations in villages"[300] ordered local party and state officials to issues sanctions (mostly fines) provided for by the decree of 23 July 1951 regarding the so-called planned purchase of cereals on up to five persons obliged to deliver them in each municipality but who, despite two warnings, still missed the deadline and did not deliver cereals or delivered them in small quantities. Officials were allowed to initiate criminal and court proceedings on a few particularly "resistant" ones. They were to be "those rich ones who clearly refuse to supply grain, and who behave provocatively toward officials (by, for example, tearing up orders), or who try to persuade others not to supply grain." These sanctions were to be applied after exhausting other "awareness measures" such as: district meetings, individual talks, hanging public plaques with the names of "shirkers," mentioning their names in local programs, etc.

298 Jarosz, Wolsza, "Komisja Specjalna do Walki z Nadużyciami i Szkodnictwem Gospodarczym (1945–1954)," 23–24.

299 Ibid., 24.

300 AAN, KC PZPR, 237/XII-4, p. 78–82.

A KC PZPR telex document, dated 18 November 1951 and addressed to buying agents within the government, the KC, and the first secretaries of the KC PZPR, extended the scale of repression tied to grain purchases as envisioned in the instructions discussed above. In the "most difficult" municipalities and areas of the country, the number of fined persons could exceed five people for the commune and up to 10 farmers. It was also found that in some provinces, the amount of imposed fines was excessive, which could result in the farms being ruin. Hence, officials recommended that the courts soften these penalties. They also recommended that hearings in criminal and administrative matters be determined after seven days had passed since the accused was notified in order to give the defendant time to perform compulsory deliveries, which would serve as grounds for remitting or mitigating the sentence. The telex transcript contained a suggestion allowing for the application for punishment to be withdrawn if mandatory grain supplies were delivered.[301]

In January 1952, due to the successful completion of the "action to carry out village obligations," a KC telex document send to provincial committees ordered the abandonment, as of 31 January 1952, of the policy to calling "recalcitrant peasants" to district prosecutors and to bring criminal and administrative charges against them. Such charges were allowed only "in cases of exceptional resistance," but even then without the use of detention as a preventive measure.[302]

In the same year, the party's leadership detailed the scope of repression used in the purchase of milk and slaughter animals. Already at a meeting on 31 May 1952, Roman Zambrowski, the Politburo member responsible for the collectivization of agriculture, addressing the problem of administrative penalties for non-delivery of milk, said: "It is clear that first of all you have to say that we must determine, of course, without publicity, it should be treated confidentially [. . .] some kind of limit in this area. Let us say that at the beginning there are some three or five incidents in a locality, where it is at all advisable to take such steps [. . .] [incidents] which should be referred to criminal and administrative proceedings at the level of the National Council's Commune Council, which should decide who should be punished with a double fine, amounting to twice the sum of the milk that he did not provide."[303]

---

301 AAN, KC PZPR, 237/XII-6, Dalekopis nr 27 z 18 XI 1951 do Pełnomocnika Rządu i KC i I sekretarzy KW PZPR, pp. 90 ff.

302 AAN, KC PZPR, 237/XII-7, Dalekopis do Zespołu Wojewódzkiego i I sekretarza KW PZPR, 29 I 1952, pp. 4 ff.

303 AAN, KC PZPR, 237/V-28, Sytuacja i zadania na odcinku obowiązkowych dostaw mleka – referat R. Zambrowskiego z 31 V 1952, pp. 134–146.

Party instructions contained elements of "class"-based repression. Their victims were primarily "kulaks" and the "affluent average," who were treated as political enemies of the system in charge.[304] The central party structures determined the scale and social face of repression. These decisions were implemented by the justice system subordinated to PZPR officials. Appropriate recommendations and guidelines were issued during closed deliberations, often in the form of secret orders, circulars, letters, etc. This was the case, for example, at the Ministry of Justice. Minister Henryk Świątkowski issued detailed guidelines on the "policy of provisional penalties and detention" and on "the tasks of the courts in the area of compulsory supplies of agricultural products." Increased criminal repression for the "breaking of the kulak-speculative resistance" was recommended by guidelines given at the conference of the heads of Provincial Courts on 23 October 1953 and by the minister's order of 23 November this year, which ordered that sanctions be raised against kulaks, speculators and other people who, "succumbing to kulak – speculator pressure, maliciously shirk their responsibilities regarding mandatory supplies." Penalties imposed on kulaks were to range from two to three years, and in relation to other persons, not to exceed one year of imprisonment.[305]

The changes of October 1956 led to reduced terror and repression. This was also true in villages where the emphasis on the collectivization of agriculture and the destruction of large-scale farms was significantly eased. The size of compulsory deliveries was reduced and the peasants responsible for them were treated less strictly.

As we already stated, an important result of the liberalization of the economic system that followed was an increase in economic crime, especially at the intersection between state and private enterprises and institutions. This tendency, noticed in Warsaw ruling circles, prompted the government to develop new ways to combat fraud.

On 30 April 1957, the Politburo approved the draft special resolution "on the battle against speculation and trade fraud." It stated, among other things, that "alongside a shortage of attractive goods on the market, which favors the development of speculation, a convenient climate for the development of speculation and abuse in trade has also been created by a sense of impunity among

304 AAN, KC PZPR, 237/XII-9, Sekretariat KC do I sekretarzy KW i Pełnomocnika Rządu i KC, Warszawa 8 XII 1953, p. 115.

305 AAN, MS, 160, H. Świątkowski, Zadania sądów w dziedzinie obowiązkowych dostaw produktów rolnych, p. 1.

speculative elements, which has resulted from negligence on the part of the MHW, prosecutors, judiciaries and national councils regarding the protection of consumer interests." Among the many measures to improve the situation, it was recommended that the Ministry of Justice promptly put forward a legislative initiative and an appropriate interpretation of existing legislation to close all loopholes that foster the "currently existing paralysis in the investigation by prosecutors and the prosecution in courts of those guilty of theft of public property and speculative activities to the detriment of the people and the state."[306]

The promise of a harsher course to be taken against perpetrators of such crimes came in a speech by Władysław Gomułka delivered at the X plenum of the KC PZPR held on 24–28 October 1957. At this same time a resolution was passed that set the task for all party organs to purge the links between the state and economic administration and "corrupt and criminal elements." In November 1957, instructions were issued to the Secretariat of the KC PZPR "on the creation of teams to battle fraud and corruption." Among other things, it stated: "Previous experience in the battle against fraud indicates that its detection is largely the work of the control and inspection apparatus and the MO. Leadership within these institutions as well as within the basic party organizations in detecting crimes taking place in their institutions is still insufficient. At the root of this condition lies embedded liberalism and tolerance on the part of managers, and sometimes the existence of cliques, which makes it difficult to detect crime. Party agencies should direct the governing links of the state and economic apparatus toward revealing crimes and take up the decisive battle against corruption." The instructions pointed to the fact that members of the party had participated in criminal scandals. "In such cases, perpetrators must be excluded from the party and handed over to the competent authorities." It was also reported that the KC Secretariat had appointed a Central Team for the Battle against Fraud and Corruption. It was recommended that executives of provincial committees, in consultation with the Central Team, should form appropriate voivodeship teams, along with powiat, city and district committees – their own teams in agreement with the KW Executive. These teams included members of party organs, party members working in the prosecutor's office, the judiciary, state oversight, the

306 For the text of the resolution, see *Uchwały Komitetu Centralnego Polskiej Zjednoczonej Partii Robotniczej od II do III Zjazdu* (Warszawa: Książka i Wiedza, 1959), 487–490. See also "Protokół posiedzenia Biura Politycznego w dniu 30 kwietnia 1957 r." in *Centrum władzy. Protokoły posiedzeń kierownictwa PZPR. Wybór z lat 1949–1970,* eds. Antoni Dudek, Kochański, Krzysztof Persak (Warszawa: Instytut Studiów Politycznych PAN, 2000), 259–260.

MO, PIH, fiscal protection, workers' activists in the largest enterprises, party members among activists subordinated to the authorities in youth unions and trade unions. The chairman of the team was supposed to be one of the secretaries of a given party instance. In their work, the teams were to rely on materials held by state authorities regarding the criminal activities of party members, and were to draw conclusions about reports of abuse. Depending on the nature of the information, the latter were to be directed to the competent state authorities, whose decision it would be to launch an investigation. The teams had the power to adopt resolutions on party sanctions provided for in the statutes, but their decisions were subject to approval by executive groups. It was recommended that the teams focus their attention on party organizations that operated in places where the threat of fraud was particularly high – that is, "in trade organizations, in catering establishments, in the construction sector, in PGR, and in institutions and enterprises with wide contacts with the private initiatives." Those who were accused were entitled to appeal decisions in accordance with party statutes.[307]

Team findings indicated that there was significant corruption among party and state elites, especially in local communities. From November 1957 to the end of June 1958, the teams considered 12,738 cases, of which 2,337 were eliminated as unworthy of further investigation. In the remaining cases, penalties were imposed on 1,967 workers, 920 peasants, 7,353 white-collar workers (of whom 45 were in party management; 1,773 in the state-administrative apparatus; and 3,306 in the economic apparatus), and 101 "others." The reasons for imposed penalties were: abuse of power – 1,438; embezzlement and theft – 4,301; bribery – 557; speculation – 1,139; tolerance of crimes – 1,172; and others 1,734. The number of those found guilty who were thrown out of the party – 5,939. Party committees at various levels issued 3,720 requests that the guilty parties be removed from their positions.[308]

In July 1958, the teams' activities were completed. As for the reason behind this decision, authors of a letter from the Secretariat of the KC PZPR pointed out that the flow of cases had been significantly reduced and that the sanction powers that the party at the X plenum had granted the teams was only temporarily. From then on, all disciplinary matters were to be dealt with in a normal

307 "PZPR removes from its ranks so-called accidental elements. This action is the cause of social dissatisfaction. There were even demonstrations. In front of the Central Committee headquarters, a group of demonstrators spread a banner with the inscription: 'Do not clutter up the non-party ranks.'" See: *Nie tylko do śmiechu*, 44.

308 AAN, KC PZPR XI/281, Ankieta sprawozdawcza Centralnego Zespołu do Walki z Nadużyciami i Korupcją za okres od 1 VI do 30 VI 1958 r.

course by the Party Control Committee. The teams were supposed to perform only auxiliary functions at party committees, and their focus would now be "party inspiration and party supervision in the battle against fraud, carried out by appropriate administrative and social agents."[309]

As we see, the party teams' work proved that the scope of economic fraud involving party members was relatively large.

To be sure, this phenomenon did not disappear with the completion of the teams' work. In 1961 alone, 334 plant directors and 1,365 employees of the economic and administrative apparatus were expelled from the PZPR for bribery, fraud, and using one's position for business purposes. In 1962, the corresponding numbers were: 253 and 1,232. "Abuse of one's position for official purposes" was an important reason for dismissals within the party apparatus. In this aggregate category, one should look for allegations that could be classified as economic crimes. According to the findings, such transgressions were the second largest (after "drunkenness and demoralization") cause behind dismissals in the early 1960s. From the 50 KP, KM and KD secretaries removed in 1959, 15 (30 %) were removed from their positions because of economic crimes; in 1960, from the 48 removed – 14 (31.3 %); in 1961, from the 51 removed – 11 (21.6 %); and in 1962, from the 26 removed – 6 (23.1 %). The number of persons holding the position of secretary in these committees in 1959 was 1220; in 1960 – 1326; in 1961 – 1319; in 1962 – 1423. In 1959–1962, there were 13 incidents in which KP, KM and KD secretaries obtained, in exchange for various services in the form of loans, gifts, etc., obtained – from with the bureaucracy – privileges and concessions for private initiatives.[310]

The party teams' work showed the PZPR leadership that economic crime was a phenomenon of a relatively wide range. Thus, the search by central authorities in Warsaw for solutions aimed at increasing the effectiveness of the battle against this type of crime was constant. The aforementioned act on increasing the protection of social property against damage resulting from crime was passed on 21 January 1958.

For further changes in this respect, decisions taken at the meeting of the Politburo on 19 January 1959 were important. In attendance for this

309 AAN, KC PZPR, XI/281, List Sekretariatu KC PZPR w sprawie Zespołów do Walki z Nadużyciami i Korupcją, lipiec 1958, pp. 18 ff.

310 AAN, KC PZPR, VII/149, Załącznik nr 1 do Biuletynu nr 115 Biura Sekretariatu KC PZPR, 16 maja 1963. List Wydziału Organizacyjnego KC i CKKP do I sekretarzy KW, pp. 249–251.

meeting – alongside Politburo members – were Justice Minister Marian Rybicki, Deputy Justice Minister Stanisław Walczak, the PRL Prosecutor General Andrzej Burda, Deputy PRL Prosecutor General Jan Wasilewski, Minister of the Interior Władysław Wicha, Deputy Ministers of the Interior Ryszard Dobieszak, Mieczysław Moczar and Antoni Alster, First President of the Supreme Court Jan Wasilkowski, NIK President Konstanty Dąbrowski, and secretary of the KC Committee for Justice, Safety and Compliance, Jan Hessel.

Participants heard reports from Rybicki, Burda, Dobieszak, Wasilkowski, and Dąbrowski about the situation in the justice system. Politburo members, including Gomułka, took part in the discussion. The minutes of the meeting show that participants "pointed out sluggishness, liberalism and even a tolerant attitude on the part of some judges and prosecutors toward those guilty of economic crimes committed to the detriment of the state. It was found that serious economic crimes were not met with severe criminal repression and there is still a tendency to exert the lowest penalty and a significant increase in the rate of suspended sentences. The Politburo has recommended a series of measures to put an end to this situation."

The conclusions of the Ministry of Justice were adopted in terms of legislation, whose aim was to "increase the upper limit of punishment for recidivists, and at the same time to lower the lower limit of punishment for offenders who had caused less social harm (i.e. between PLZ 300 and 2000); the possibility of penalty suspension was retained only if reconsideration of the damage amount were ordered." BP recommended the development of proposals for the extension of MO powers regarding investigations and the methods for securing assets derived from theft.[311]

During the discussion, the General Prosecutor's Office received the recommendation to focus on rapid criminal prosecution in cases involving the most important economic frauds, to order summary proceedings for particularly serious crimes against social property, to secure claims for damages and the forfeiture of assets or fines, and to react quickly to criminal interference in economic life.

This course of action, aimed at tightening the criminal policy toward perpetrators of the most serious economic crimes, was confirmed by the Third Congress of the PZPR, which took place from 10 to 18 March 1959. In the document "On key tasks of political parties" we read, among other things: "The battle to establish socialist justice and the rule of law also requires vigorous overcoming

311 *Centrum władzy*, 321–325.

of unjustified liberalism, which is expressed when we disregard activities directed against the people's state, in the loss of class links to the judiciary, and in tolerant treatment of fraud and plunder of social property. The protection of social property requires more stringent measures. The party's constant struggle against the scourge of fraud, and its effort to create within public opinion an atmosphere of constant condemnation of corruption and thievery, is of great significance."[312]

The day-to-day political control over the implementation of these principles was exercised by the Administrative Department of the KC PZPR and its provincial counterparts. In his introduction to the second meeting of heads of Administrative Departments of the KW PZPR on 30 January 1961, KC Secretary Ryszard Strzelecki assessed the implementation of these guidelines by the Committee on Justice, Security and Public Order of the Central Committee, which showed that "the courts' repression for minor economic crimes, where losses do not exceed PLZ 300 is still rigid and severe and the most common penalties in these cases are the sentences of absolute imprisonment within one year. We are of the opinion," Strzelecki continued, "that there can be no leniency in these matters, if there is a crime there must be punishment, but the repression must be shifted to economic ailment, appropriately multiplied by the total losses [. . .] and suspend conditional short-term prison penalties, which will undoubtedly be educational. In a word, it should be punished so as not to push people unnecessarily to prison." Strzelecki also complained that the jurisprudence of courts in cases of serious economic crimes was liberal in nature, both in terms of imprisonment and fines and confiscation of property."[313]

Judicial authorities testified that they took great pains to implement the party's directives.

As written in the document submitted by the PRL Prosecutor General dated 8 December 1959, the overwhelming majority of inquiries in cases of economic fraud were carried out by voivodeship prosecutors, with the significant participation of MO officials, which was to guarantee insightful investigations, quicker completion and better preparation for legal proceedings. By 20 November of that year, the General Prosecutor's Office had special supervision over 289 cases, i.e. approx. 25 % of all investigations regarding economic crimes conducted by provincial prosecutors. In these cases (involving theft of property over PLZ

312 "Uchwała III Zjazdu o węzłowych zadaniach politycznych partii," *Nowe Drogi* 4 (1959): 656.

313 AAN, KC PZPR, 237/XIV-170, Protokół z II narady kierowników Wydziałów Administracyjnych KW PZPR odbytej w dniu 30 stycznia 1961 r., p. 33.

50,000), 1,068 persons (out of a total of 1268, i.e. 81.4 %) covered by the indictment were subject to pre-trial detention. From 1 January to 15 November 1959, as many as 26 cases (involving 59 persons) out of 38 directed to the courts with requests for summary consideration, concerned economic crimes. Among them were: 14 cases of fraud, 8 for robbery attacks on socialized entities, 4 for breaking and entering into socialized economy entities. Of these, by the beginning of December, the courts recognized 25 cases against 57 persons, of whom five persons were sentenced to life imprisonment; 15 persons to 15 years in prison; 14 persons to 10–15 years in prison; 8 persons to 10 years in prison; 13 persons to 5–10 years in prison; 1 person to 4 years in prison; and 1 person acquitted. In addition, 18 convicted persons were fined, and 23 lost their rights, and 12 lost half or all their property. During the first ten months of 1959, the prosecutor's office issued 1,303 decisions to secure claims for damages and fines as envisaged under the act of 21 January 1958 on increasing protection of social property against damage resulting from crime. The value of secured movable property, real estate and cash was estimated at PLZ 48,350,462 excluding certain amounts of "foreign valuables." The "sharpness of law enforcement" caused by "difficulties on the meat market" was also increased.

While in September 1959 six-hundred investigations of this kind were initiated, in October there were already 2,160, and from 1 to 15 November – 1,445. In September, indictments were filed against 289 people; in October – 799; from 1 to 15 November – 468 (data did not refer to cases addressed in the criminal-administrative mode).[314]

BP directives were also implemented through legislative changes. The result of these activities were, first and foremost, specific solutions contained in the laws of 18 June 1959, discussed earlier, on criminal liability for crimes against social property and changes in criminal proceedings. The latter increased the MO's powers to investigate and interrogate suspects and to seize movable property to secure claims for damages or to impose fines or the forfeiture of property.

The "promotion policy" was also adapted to the requirements surrounding the tightening of the penal policy toward economic crime. Until December 1959, ten district prosecutors were transferred to posts of district powiat prosecutors, and provincial prosecutors from Wrocław and Białystok who were not

314 AAN, KC PZPR, 237/XIV-215, Informacja Generalnej Prokuratury o wykonaniu dyrektyw Biura Politycznego KC PZPR z dnia 19 stycznia 1959, Warszawa 8 grudnia 1959, p. 1.

properly fulfilling their tasks were transferred to "smaller and easier-to-manage" prosecutors' offices in other provinces.[315]

As we can see, the party leadership under Gomułka, almost from the moment of taking power, pursued a policy of stricter repression in relation to perpetrators of more important economic crimes. This was the basic criterion for assessing court practices in the area of punishing crime against social property.

Such a conclusion can be drawn from information prepared by the Ministry of Justice in December 1960 on criminal policy in cases concerning economic crimes in the years 1957–1960. Officials judged court activities in this respect as being inadequate because courts were too mild in their "arrest policy" tied to theft of social property worth between PLZ 5,000 and 20,000. For similar reasons, courts were criticized for applying too few arrests in cash shortfall cases, although officials also noticed changes "for the better:" in 1959, out of a total of 4,075 people accused of causing cash shortages amounting to between PLZ 5,000 and 50,000, 556 were arrested (i.e. 13.5 %), but in the first half of 1960 this percentage increased to 19 %. The authors of this information claimed that in cases concerning cash shortfalls, the percentage of "unjustified" waivers from the application of temporary detention was too high. In voivodeship courts, for the most serious economic crimes (theft of social assets worth more than PLZ 50,000 – excluding fencing) in 1958, 1,538 people were sentenced, of which 3 (0.2 %) were given life sentences; 32 (2, 1 %) got over 8 years; and 124 (20.2 %) received suspended sentences. In 1959 those numbers, respectively, were: 2,203, 13 (0.6 %), 54 (2.5 %), and 210 (25.8 %). And in the first half of 1960 – 1,184, 1 (0.1 %), 108 (9.1 %), and 88 (20.2 %). In spite of legislative changes, which increased punishments in economic scandals, it was assessed that "criminal repression cannot yet be considered sufficient in this regard."

The rare use of the summary procedure also received criticism. In 1959 there were 48 such cases against 92 defendants; in the first half of 1960 – 36 against 89. About 63 % of these cases concerned economic crimes in which the minimum damage caused amounted to PLZ 150,000. In many cases the courts "did not appreciate" the possibilities offered by summary proceedings when it came to punishment. A significant part of the penalties imposed in summary proceedings was around the average, and sometimes the lowest, possible penal sanction provided for this type of crime in the laws of 21 January 1958 and 18 June 1959. In none of these cases did the sentences involve the death penalty. "Practice

315 AAN, KC PZPR, 237/V/453, Informacja Generalnej Prokuratury o wykonaniu dyrektyw Biura Politycznego KC PZPR z dnia 19 stycznia 1959 r., pp. 51 ff.

shows that in many instances these cases could have been handled using the ordinary course of action. This kind of situation is already blunting the edge of the summary mode." "It should be emphasized," we read further in the cited document, "that in the judges' environment there is some resistance to the application of the highest penalty even in cases involving crimes that are extremely large and dangerous to the national economy. It is therefore appropriate to intensify political work among these personnel accordingly."[316]

It is worth noting here that the severity of punishment applied to perpetrators of the largest economic crimes provoked resistance even among the highest party and state officials. This matter requires further research, but our research uncovered a few indications confirming this thesis.

The first indication concerns the previously mentioned so-called leather affair, or more precisely Bolesław Dedo, convicted on 21 December 1960 by the Provincial Court in Kielce and given the death penalty for economic fraud in the leathers trade. As Krzysztof Madej established,[317] decisions as to how to conduct Dedo's trial and death sentences were made during internal deliberations held at the Administrative Department of the KC PZPR. A preserved note from one of those deliberations, held on 6 October 1960, indicates that an advocate of severe punishment in cases of fraud was the head of this Department, Kazimierz Witaszewski. The record also indicates that despite political pressure, the highest penalty was not imposed on those previously tried for abuses in the leather industry, namely E. Galicki and M. Nowik (the aforementioned affair in the Warsaw Tanneries). General Prosecutor A. Burda, his deputy Kazimierz Kosztirko and Minister of Justice M. Rybicki, who took part in discussions, did not object to the argument that it was necessary to pronounce the death penalty for B. Dedo, an idea being promoted in central committee bodies. Rybicki also argued that the "mere" life sentence given to Galicki was the result of the fact that, in the last 10 days of the trial, the President of the Warsaw Voivodeship Court, Michał Kulczycki, had "broken down." In agreement with the Administrative Department of the Central Committee, the adjudication panel and the prosecutors were chosen so that a similar "mistake" would not be repeated. The death penalty was to be pronounced not only against Dedo

316 AAN, MS, 419, Polityka karna organów wymiaru sprawiedliwości w sprawach o przestępstwa gospodarcze w latach 1957–1960, Warszawa, 14 grudnia 1960 r., pp. 104–120.

317 Krzysztof Madej, "Kara śmierci za mięso," *Biuletyn Instytutu Pamięci Narodowej* 11 (2002): 55–60.

but also against the previously convicted prisoner in the Galicki case, M. Nowik, who was to be tried again.

In the light of the above, the attitude of Judge M. Kulczycki seems to be mysterious. He resisted the party's orders to impose the death penalty on Galicki.[318] According to a letter from Minister Rybicki addressed to KR secretary R. Strzelecki dated 3 December 1960, two committees were appointed in this case, regardless of the fact that the judge was the Central Committee for Party Control (CKKP). Their applications sought to dismiss him from the position of president of the Provincial Court in Warsaw.[319] In another document we read that "as the president of the Provincial Court (and therefore not only the judge but also the head of the court administratively subordinate to the minister) he found himself under the pressure of the legal and especially the lawyers' environment, creating an atmosphere marked by sentences allegedly predetermined sentences, etc. [. ..] Comrade Kulczycki, well aware of this mood and atmosphere, tried in an exaggerated and unjust manner to emphasize his 'objectivity, by among other things not reacting or reacting too weakly to the defense's excesses."[320] As a result of these accusations, he lost his position.[321]

---

318 In this case, a fragment from *Dzienniki polityczne 1958–1962* by Mieczysław F. Rakowski (Warszawa: Iskry, 1998, 250–251), an influential editor-in-chief of the most important socio-political weekly in Poland, *Polityka*, seems to be particularly interesting. Under the date 11 December 1960, Rakowski describes a social event attended by an attorney for one of the defendants in the Kielce trial. According to Rakowski, "they wanted to move [Kulczycki] to Zielona Góra" because he was resisting pressure to apply the death penalty. In fact, Kulczycki was removed from the Warsaw Provincial Court in April 1961 and sent to take up the position as vice-president of the Social Insurance Tribunal. In August 1962, he returned as a judge in the Warsaw Voivodeship Court and he continued work there as a judge until its liquidation in connection with the administrative reorganization of 1975. Then he was delegated to the Ministry of Justice and asked to be transferred to the Provincial Court in Siedlce. In 1978 he returned to the Provincial Court in Warsaw. He died on 10 April 1984. See Jerzy Zduńczyk, "Sędzia," *Tu i Teraz* 27 (1984). Wiesław Chrzanowski claims in his memoirs that Kulczycki opposed the death sentence to save his social position: "For this social position he would have risked even his career". See Wiesław Chrzanowski, *Pół wieku polityki, czyli rzecz o obronie czynnej. Z Wiesławem Chrzanowskim rozmawiali Piotr Mierecki i Bogusław Kiernicki* (Warszawa: Ad Astra, 1997), 296.

319 AAN, MS, 1/389, M. Rybicki do R. Strzeleckiego, 3 grudnia 1960, pp. 58–60.

320 AAN, MS, 1/389, Notatka dla K. Witaszewskiego, kierownika Wydziału Administracyjnego KC PZPR, Warszawa 2 listopada 1960, pp. 62 ff.

321 The documents concerning the Galicki trial and others that we were able to find indicate that the atmosphere during the trial was tense not only because of the pressure

As in the case of Kulczycki, it is difficult to determine the motives of the attitude taken by A. Burda, who as a public prosecutor on 17 March 1961, asked the Council of State to issue a pardon for B. Dedo, who had been sentenced to death. This request was taken into consideration on 31 March 1961; Dedo's sentence was changed to life sentence.[322]

The fact that the General Prosecutor's attitude aroused dissatisfaction in the highest party authorities is confirmed by a note issued by the KC secretary R. Strzelecki addressed to W. Gomułka on 22 March 1961. In it, Strzelecki wrote that in January of that year the Provincial Court in Kielce issued a summary judgment convicting B. Dedo to death. The Minister of Justice and the President of the Supreme Court regarded the punishment to be a correct one. Also, the Voivodeship Court, while reviewing the verdict, considered all mitigating circumstances as insufficient to support the request for a pardon. "Comrade Burda," Strzelecki wrote, "until the verdict was announced represented a view that supported the highest possible penalty for the accused Dedo, and the General Prosecutor's Office proposed issuing two death sentences in this trial. On 11 March of this year, Comrade Burda, without agreeing with his deputies and without informing the Administrative Department about the change in his

---

applied by authorities in favor of a severe sentence but also because of the brave appearances of the defenders. Deputy PRL Prosecutor General K. Kosztirko, in a note prepared for the chairman of the Council of State, Aleksander Zawadzki, dated 19 October, presented excerpts from some speeches of defenders coming from working records of prosecutors working on this case. Attorney Mirski reportedly said: "You cannot appeal to the decree on summary proceedings from 1945, because this decree was issued in the period of anarchy. I think that our nation does not want to set the gallows on the road leading to socialism. [. . .] Three checks weigh on You, Citizen Judges: 1. control of your consciences; 2. Control of our country's and foreign public opinion; 3. historical control. [. . .] I do not want it to be said about us that we are following in the footsteps of Bulgaria and Romania. [. . .] The death penalty in this case can be understood to be a return to terror." Attorney Marecki made very transparent allusions to the Stalinist period: "In the speeches of public prosecutors, one can sense a return to these times, when efforts were made to create class conflict, when for this purpose a forester was introduced into the poor village." Finally, it is worth recalling the dramatic-sounding words of advocate Ołomucki: "When I start speaking, I am terribly afraid. I am intimidated. I hear the crunch of broken bones of the spine. Down with the death penalty, you must not push a man into nothingness, even if he is a thief of cowhide." See AAN, Kancelaria Rady Państwa, 45/30, K. Kosztirko do A. Zawadzkiego, Warszawa 19 października 1960 r., pp. 55–58; W. Chrzanowski, 296.

322 AAN, PG, 23/37, Decyzja Rady Państwa, Warszawa 31 marca 1961, p. 73.

previous position in this matter, asked that the Council of State change the death penalty to life imprisonment. This request, made despite the unprecedented scale of fraud and damage, long-term criminal activity and the seriousness of this type of crime in the country, Comrade Burda opposed based on:

a) the attitude of the accused, who allegedly assisted greatly in the disclosure of crimes, but which was inconsistent with reality, because Dedo pleaded guilty only after having been shown evidence;
b) a supposed slight deviation of the harmfulness of Dedo's deeds from the acts of other criminals in these trials, sentenced only to life imprisonment. It was not taken into account in this case that the damage resulting from Dedo's activities was much higher than the damage caused by other accused;
c) an unjustified statement that Dedo committed crimes on a cooperative property, which is allegedly of lesser importance to the national economy than damage to state property;
d) Dedo's positive contribution to the construction of the 'Przyszłość' cooperative by making high contributions to its creation and development. It was not taken into account that these contributions came from the theft of social property;
e) alleged sufficient warning to individuals who intend to steal property, only by issuing the death sentence without having to execute it."

Strzelecki regarded it as significant that Burda's deputies – Jan Wasilewski and K. Kosztirko – opposed this position, and the third deputy, Marian Mazur, supported them claiming that Dedo's personality had been shaped "in capitalist Poland, which explains the fraud." On 21 March, Burda ordered a meeting of the General Prosecutor's leadership in this case, but he did not attend the meeting and he did not explain the reasons for his absence. It was this decision, combined with others, with a much smaller significance, that justifies the final conclusion of the cited document: "In this state of affairs, I see no further possibility of proper operation of the General Prosecutor's Office under the direction of Comrade Burda, and on this basis I am asking for his immediate dismissal from his position and the entrustment of comrade Kosztirko with the temporary management of the General Prosecutor's Office."[323] This political decision was quickly made: on 24 May 1961, Burda was indeed dismissed, and K. Kosztirko took his place.

323 AAN, KC PZPR, 237/XIV-273, p. 2.

We know much less about other opponents of such severe punishment in economic matters. One of those opponents, according to a report drawn up by a high party official, Andrzej Werblan, was the chairman of the Council of State, Aleksander Zawadzki, who allegedly opposed the decision to apply the death penalty against one defendant in an economic fraud trial who had received such a sentence. Unfortunately, it has not been possible to determine who this defendant was.[324]

It is very difficult to answer the question about the judges' attitudes toward the use of the death penalty. One opinion on this subject is provided by a speech delivered by J. Wasilkowski at the meeting of the Committee on Justice, Security and Public Order of the KC PZPR Central Committee on 6 January 6, 1961. According to the record, Wasilkowski said:

> Judges – opponents of the death penalty, are in the minority. There is basically no resistance to the death penalty being imposed according to Art. 225, par. 1[325] and others. Resistance arises when economic crimes are tried on a summary basis, because there are no grounds in the act when the death penalty should be applied to these offenses. Many judges have such an opinion. The judges would like the legislator to say when to apply the death penalty. Calls are heard for the law to provide for the death penalty in cases tried on the ordinary basis. In the draft law of 1958 [about increasing the protection of social property against damage resulting from crime] was a government proposal in this regard, but it was not accepted. Another reason for resistance is the lack of second instance in the summary mode, where the death penalty may be imposed. In economic crimes, a case lasts for months, for criminal offenses like murder, etc. the case is short and the punishment is fixed in law."

As a big drawback of summary proceedings, Wasilkowski pointed to the unanimity requirement:

> Judges are afraid of judicial mistakes, they remember rehabilitation processes. He states that personally there are no brakes regarding the death penalty in particularly dangerous economic crimes, but the consideration of judges and the public requires that this punishment be included in the law. The current legal situation prevents the establishment

324 According to Werblan, regarding the proposal to "sign the death penalty" (probably involving the refusal to grant a pardon), Aleksander Zawadzki, chairman of the Council of State, reportedly told Gomułka – "And I will not sign it." A further exchange of views reportedly went like this: Gomułka – "If the [Polit]Buro so decides, you will sign it." Zawadzki – "No, I will not sign. If you want, make yourself head of the Council [of State], then you can sign." Gomułka ordered a break, after which he stated: "Well, then do as you please." See relacja Andrzeja Werblana z 24 stycznia 2003 r.

325 "Whoever kills another human being is subject to imprisonment for no less than 5 years, or life, or the death penalty."

of extraordinary inspections if the court does not impose the death penalty, and such a possibility is needed."[326]

It seems that Wasilkowski's opinion aptly points to some of the most important reasons that judges feared using the death penalty in cases of economic crimes adjudicated on a summary basis.

In the years that followed, political pressure to impose severe penalties for economic crimes, especially those tied to the "affairs," did not diminish.

The use of harsh repression against perpetrators of economic crime was approved by the Secretariat of the KC PZPR on 19 September 1961. At that time, the Secretariat accepted the assessment and conclusions of the KC Committee on Justice regarding criminal policy and instructed interested ministries to develop a detailed action plan by the end of 1961.[327]

In the Commission document sent to the Secretariat on 4 July 1961, the detection of economic crimes was considered "clearly insufficient and slow." As a result, "major economic and other serious crimes are often revealed only after many years." There were complaints about the excessive length of proceedings in these cases, insufficient supervision of the prosecutor's office over investigations, in particular those carried out by deeper-state MO officials. As a positive fact, officials took note of the increase in 1960 of the application of imprisonment over 8–15 years in cases of theft of social property. This correction, however, involved only cases tried under the act of January 1958. "On the other hand, in cases reviewed on the basis of earlier provisions, the judgments were, and sometimes still are, seriously on the low side."

The Commission considered it appropriate, and the KC Secretariat agreed, that the edge of criminal repression should be aimed at economic crimes and related sales, corruption and fencing. Concerned authorities were to also pay more attention to criminal waste, a lack of supervision and toleration of fraud. In such cases, they recommended increased use of "economic affliction" to "more widely and more effectively secure state claims on perpetrators' property related to the execution of fines and property forfeiture."

Officials called for the continued use of summary proceedings, "both in terms of its repressive and preventive character as well as the speed of the proceedings." When selecting cases to be recognized for summary handling, the following

326 AAN, KC PZPR, 237/XIV-205, Protokół z posiedzenia Komisji Sprawiedliwości, Bezpieczeństwa i Porządku Publicznego w dniu 6 stycznia 1961 r., pp. 89 ff.

327 AAN, KC PZPR, 2221 (mikrofilm 3378), Protokół nr 15 spraw załatwionych przez Sekretariat KC, p. 444.

criteria were recommended: "justified social interest, the amount of the damage caused by the crime, the personality of the offender, the specificity of the area and public opinion's degree of interest in the crime."

At the same time, leaders ordered and end to the tendency to "view imprisonment as almost the only means of repression for minor offenses," because this tendency results in "excessive penalization of social life and the filling of prison with inmates sentenced to short-term penalties." In matters of lesser importance – according to the Commission – other possibilities of influence and punishment were to be employed, such as economic penalties, business consequences, and conditional suspension of penalties tied to imprisonment.[328]

Viewing the implementation of these recommendations two years later, in September 1963, officials stated that as a result of concentration of forces and means to fight this crime, the Prosecutor's Office and Interior Ministry had detected a number of serious abuses carried out by organized criminal groups in certain branches of the national economy, including in the leather, textile, milling and trade industries. A number of serious smuggling and foreign exchange affairs were revealed. They evaluate judgments handed down by the Voivodeship courts positively, in which the "tendencies" toward severe punishment of perpetrators of economic crimes, bribery and corruption were deepened. Repressive policy in matters of cash shortages and mismanagement still raised concerns, and according to these political decision-makers summary proceedings were applied too rarely in cases of particularly dangerous social crimes.[329]

Court judgments in basic groups of economic crimes gradually adapted to the recommendations formulated by central party and state institutions. Nevertheless, some judges still handed down penalties within the lowers limits laid down by the legal system. The use of summary proceedings was also uncommon.[330]

In the logic used by those in power at the time, one guarantee of the effective implementation of criminal policy was the "ideological and political attitude"

328 AAN, KC PZPR 2221 (mikrofilm 3378), Ocena i wnioski w zakresie polityki karnej, czerwiec 1961, pp. 480–488.

329 AAN, MS, 1/369, Informacja o realizacji w latach 1962–1964 wniosków w zakresie polityki karnej zatwierdzonych przez Sekretariat KC w dniu 20 września 1961 r., pp. 21 ff, 25–27.

330 According to data from the PRL General Prosecutor's Office in 1965, 68 cases were filed for summary proceedings against 196 defendants, and in 1966 – 90 cases against 211 defendants. Among them, there 28 cases (against 129 people) and 14 cases (against 76 people) involving economic offenses.

taken by officials administering justice. In practice, this meant above all an emphasis on "judging" the judges (the number of PZPR members among judges rose from 32.5 % in 1960 to 34.9 % in 1962) and prosecutors (increase from 59.7 % to 64.3 %). At the time, over 70 % of MO officials were party members.

In 1962, several steps were taken to better understand the sources and dynamics of crime. To this end, teams of employees with higher education were established in KG MO and MO Voivodeship Commands for the systematic analysis of economic phenomena accompanied by possible economic abuses. Operational and investigative groups were set up for the coordinated processing of business scandals. Similar teams existed in the General Prosecutor's Office and provincial prosecutor's offices. Officials noted the "activation" of the Prosecutor's Office and MO officials in operations aimed at preventing crime.

In practice, this course also represented a blow against the bar. In 1962, criminal proceedings were pending against 134 lawyers, 62 of which were prosecuted and 23 of which were subject to pre-trial detention. 180 cases were pending against the courts, of which 117 ended in a final conviction (including 11 lawyers for paid protection). The same purpose was served by the separation, effective as of 1 January 1964, of the practice of legal defense from the legal services of state-owned enterprises. A date was set for separating the advocate's profession from the profession of legal counsel.[331]

To increase the effectiveness of the battle against economic crime, the PRL Prosecutor General in October 1961 appointed a Central Coordinating Team composed of the General Prosecutor's Office, NIK, the Ministry of Justice, the Ministry of Interior (KG MO) and the Inspection and Audit Inspectorate. At the same time, voivodeship prosecutors received the order to establish, by 1 November 1961, Provincial Coordination Teams comprised of the provincial prosecutor, the president of the provincial court, the head of the NIK regional office, the Voivodeship MO Commander, the head of the provincial Inspection and Audit Inspectorate.[332] By 15 February 1962, these teams were established in all voivodeships with the exception of Bydgoszcz.[333]

331 AAN, KC PZPR, 237/XIV-216, Informacja Wydziału Administracyjnego KC PZPR o realizacji uchwały Sekretariatu KC PZPR z dnia 20 września 1961 r. w przedmiocie polityki karnej, Warszawa wrzesień 1963, pp. 56–63.

332 AAN, PG, 1/25, Pismo okólne GP PRL Kazimierza Kosztirko nr 14/61 do Prokuratorów Wojewódzkich z 7 X 1961, pp. 510–512.

333 AAN, PG, 1/25, Notatka dotycząca działalności wojewódzkich zespołów koordynujących [1962] prokuratora Generalnej Prokuratury Leopolda Kielskiego, pp. 433–451.

The problem of combating economic crime played an important role in discussions on the amnesty decree, adopted on 20 July 1964. In this case, the most important decisions were made within central party bodies, as evidenced by the discussion in this regard at the session of the Committee on Justice, Security and Public Order of the KC PZPR on 19 May 1964. It was then that the justice minister was told to re-draft the text of the decree. And it is also no coincidence that the decision on its final version was to be made by the Politburo, and not by any other constitutional body.[334] According to the committee's report dated 21 October 1964, which contained an evaluation of the implementation of this decree, about 33,000 people covered by the amnesty had been let out of prison. Many more people benefited from the amnesty because pending proceedings were cancelled and punishments not yet implemented were mitigated. Overall, about 260,000 people benefited from the amnesty's provisions. Most numerous among them were small offenders who had committed crimes against social property and highway robbery. Provisions of Art. 8 of the decree provided for a reduction in the imposed penalty by half when an offense that was previously unknown to law enforcement authorities was voluntarily disclosed. As a result of the operation of this article, by 15 October, about 800 crimes were disclosed, of which 50 % were economic nature, and 15 % were clerical. Amnesty covered 100 % of tax bribes (about 45,000 people) and about 3,000 offenses based on breaking customs and foreign exchange regulations. The total value of the contested goods returned amounted to approx. PLZ 6.5 million.[335]

Finally, a very important issue from the point of view of combating economic crime was the shape of the new penal code and the Code of Criminal Procedure. And in this case, party supervision over work done on these legal acts was strict. The central party links "made certain" that the solutions adopted in them would secure the harsh punishment for perpetrators of crime against social property.

This line of action is evidenced by note on the draft criminal code, as viewed "in the light of public discussion," drawn up on 5 February 1964 by the deputy head of the Administrative Department of the KC PZPR and addressed to Minister of Justice M. Rybicki, a note which certainly did not express the position of just its author. One of the objections to the project was that it did not "properly regulate

334 AAN, KC PZPR, 237/XIV-334, Protokół nr 2 z posiedzenia Komisji Wymiaru Sprawiedliwości, Bezpieczeństwa i Porządku Publicznego odbytego w dniu 19 maja 1964.

335 AAN, Kanc.S, 592, Protokół z posiedzenia Komisji Wymiaru Sprawiedliwości w dniu 21 października 1964, pp. 233–236.

the protection of social property." A manifestation of this tendency was "the attitude of the project toward the act of 1958 increasing protections for social property against damage resulting from crime." The draft left this act out of its scope, proposing instead to keep it in force as a special law. "Such a solution," we read in the cited document, "should be rejected because it would effectively omit from the penal code affair-type crime, which is one of the basic areas of criminal repression. The fight against this category of crime cannot be effectively carried out on the margins of the penal code. This would be understood by the public as an expression of the legislator's view that increased criminal repression for serious crimes against social property is a temporary measure, which would increase the liberalist tendencies in the use of repression in this kind of crime."[336] The party's point of view won the day, since the act of January 1958 was repealed on 19 April 1969 – i.e. after the adoption of the new penal code.

In the discussions on the draft criminal code, the Committee for Justice, Security and Public Order of the KC PZPR had particularly important influence; it dealt with this matter, among other times, in February 1967. One of the controversial problems in this context involved the application of the death penalty in affair crimes. Officials decided "to recognize that it is advisable to maintain the provision of the project providing for the possibility of imposing the death penalty on a person who organized or managed an economic affair; mark in the note to the [PZPR] leadership that views are divided on the maintenance of the summary proceeding in criminal cases and that the issue will be the subject of further reflection [. . .]."[337]

The matter of maintaining in the new penal code the threat of death penalty for anyone accused of managing or organizing a great economic scandal became a subject of controversy within the Sejm's Justice Committee and its session of 18 and 19 April 1969. During the parliamentary debate, it turned out that the Committee received numerous critical remarks in this case. Its chairman, J. Wasilkowski, explained that in the discussed case, it was not just that it involved the theft of social assets; more importantly, the point was that it constituted a crime which undermined the very foundations of the economic system, one which "causes serious disruption in the functioning of the national economy."

336 AAN, MS, 565, Notatka o projekcie kodeksu karnego w świetle dyskusji publicznej zastępcy kierownika Wydziału Administracyjnego KC PZPR dla ministra sprawiedliwości Mariana Rybickiego, Warszawa 5 lutego 1964, p. 42 ff.

337 AAN, KC PZPR, 237/XIV-334, Protokół z posiedzenia Komisji Wymiaru Sprawiedliwości, Bezpieczeństwa i Porządku Publicznego w dniach 2, 3 i 6 lutego 1967, p. 134.

In addition, Wasilkowski stated that the draft criminal code did not provide for summary proceedings "in which the death penalty can now be imposed for the theft of social assets of great value."[338]

After these discussions, the penal code passed in 1969 (which was in force from 1 January 1970 to 31 August 1998) introduced in Art. 134 a provision enabling the use of the death penalty for the commission of economic crimes.[339] It can be found in a separate chapter XIX of the special penal code, entitled "Crimes against the basic political and economic interests of the PRL." The Code of Criminal Procedure, which went into force on 1 January 1970, repealed the above-mentioned decree of 1945 on summary proceedings.

In the light of the above findings, political control of justice in the area of economic crime was manifested primarily in:

1. the binding nature of decisions made by party leadership bodies (the Politburo, the Secretariat of the Central Committee, the Committee on Justice, Security and Public Order of the KC PZPR), decisions regarding proceedings in cases concerning economic crimes;
2. party initiative and control of legislation;
3. control of criminal policy in this area, including in particular penalization for particular categories of economic crimes;
4. supervision of specific criminal proceedings in cases related to economic crimes, including the provision of informal directives as to the level of punishment to be imposed.

The Wawrzecki case and the meat affair provide an interesting pretext for a more detailed presentation of what this political oversight consisted of. So let us attempt to make such a presentation.

3.6.2. Political Oversight of the Meat Affair

This oversight was manifested in a variety of activities undertaken both by the KC PZPR and the lower-level committees, in particular the Warsaw Committee.

---

338 AAN, Kanc.S, 627, Sprawozdanie stenograficzne z posiedzenia Sejmu PRL w dniach 18 i 19 kwietnia 1969 r., p. 419.

339 "§ 1. Whoever exploits the activity of a social economy system by, in consultation with other people, stealing property of great value to the detriment of this system, of buyers or suppliers, and thus causes serious disturbances in the functioning of the national economy, is subject to punishment by imprisonment for not less than 8 years and as much as 25 years; § 2. In cases whose criminal activity is referred to in § 1 and was organized or managed, the court may impose the death penalty."

They included not only subordinate party organs and party members but also state institutions dealing with such a matter at central and local levels.

We begin our analysis with a reconstruction of the activities undertaken by the party organization in Warsaw, where the greatest abuses in the meat economy were detected.

3.6.2.1. Activities of the Warsaw Party Organization

The Executive Committee of the KW PZPR, chaired by its First Secretary, Walenty Titkow, addressed the issue of abuse in the meat trade in Warsaw on 20 April 1964, and as mentioned above, it was at this meeting where the Commander of the Warsaw MO, Tadeusz Kozłowski, submitted the information relevant to the matter.

Then, Zdzisław Żandarowski, KW secretary, presented the case of Apolinary Maciejewski – the First Secretary of the KD PZPR Warsaw-Wola and member of the KW PZPR Executive. The latter, Żandarowski claimed, having been "warned by MO Commander comrade T. Kozłowski about the abuses committed by H[enryk] Gradowski [director of MHM-DJ, MP], got involved in his defense after Gradowski's arrest, allowing the collection signatures (from managers MHM stores) of those who intended to testify to Gradowski's innocence, and declaring to the MHM Union delegation readiness to refer the case to a lawyer." According to him, Maciejewski "recently" took several loans from H. Gradowski totaling, as he himself said, PLZ 23,000, and "despite detecting Gradowski's participation in the affair, he did not cut himself off from the whole case." He continued: "Comrade A. Maciejewski reluctantly accepted the correct political assessment of his behavior in this matter." Żandarowski stated that talks were held with Maciejewski several times by members of the KW PZPR leadership. A meeting of KD Wola Executive was also held. Maciejewski turned to the KW Executive with a statement announcing his resignation from the position of the first KD secretary and member of the KW PZPR Executive.

The KW Executive assessed Maciejewski's proceedings critically and decided to remove him from his position as First Secretary of KD PZPR Wola and to appear at the next meeting of the KW Plenum, the subject being to remove him from the KW Executive. At the same time, Jerzy Łukaszewicz – head of the PZPR Propaganda Department – was recommended for this position.

It was also decided to set up a commission to deal with matters arising from the information provided and to examine the activities of party members arrested and involved in abuse. Alojzy Karkoszka headed up this commission. The body's program of activities envisaged producing a "detailed analysis of the causes underlying the discovered offenses." It was decided to establish the party affiliation of those involved in the affair in order to bring sanctions against them. The commission was also intended to deliver an analysis of the managerial staff at MHM, Warsaw's Union of Industries in Trade of Foodstuffs, the Trade Department of the Warsaw National Council, PIH and the Inspection and Audit Inspectorate. Given that officials presumed that similar abuses were taking place outside of the meat trade, similar assessments were to be carried out in gastronomy, the fruit and vegetable trade, the bakery sector, and foreign trade (by 15 May). The commission was to collect all letters describing abuse and "various instances of cronyism" flowing into party organs and institutions to determine who was guilty of crimes. Until 15 June 1964, the Command of the Warsaw MO was to carry out a thorough examination of the asses the members of management employed in Warsaw trade.

Among the activities defined as political work, it was recommended to organize meetings with members of the executives of meat handling enterprises to provide information on crimes in this industry. Party organizations were to also meet and discuss this topic.

A special commission of the Presidium of the Warsaw National Council was to be set up to efficiently supply the market with meat products.[340]

The first meeting of the KW Executive Committee looking into meat affair took place on 23 April 1964. At that time, it was decided to analyze management practices throughout the entire Warsaw trade sector, especially in industries involving meat, delicatessen, gastronomy, vegetable sales and baked goods. First of all, it was to cover persons employed in meat trade from the Trade Department of the PRN in Warsaw all the way down to store managers. For the next committee meeting, it was decided to prepare the first group of "personnel requests for the lack of supervision," and to set up a special team in the Party Control KW to expand party sanctions against those involved in the scandal. Individuals were also appointed who would be responsible for drawing conclusions and preparing assessments regarding meat plant management in Służewiec.[341]

The committee met for the second time on 28 April 1964 and decided to dismiss 9 high-ranking officials from the management of meat trading institutions in Warsaw. In addition, it was decided to remove four other officials from

340 AAN, KC PZPR, 237/X-156, Program działania Komisji powołanej przez Egzekutywę KW PZPR ds. Walki z nadużyciami w handlu [kwiecień 1964], pp. 74–77.

341 AAN, KC PZPR, 237/VII-5264, Protokół posiedzenia Komisji KW PZPR w dniu 23 kwietnia b.r. [1964], Warszawa, 25 IV 1964, p. 83.

their positions in the supervision and human resources departments MHM Warszawa-Północ, MHM Warszawa-Praga and MHM Warszawa-Południe. The cases of a further 12 people suspected of participating in the affair were to be examined by 5 May 1964.[342]

On 9 May 1964, the Executive heard information regarding the meat affair and familiarized itself with the draft action program submitted by the Warsaw Committee in the battle against fraud in trade. Then W. Titkow took the floor to present the position of the KW Secretariat regarding A. Maciejewski, Stefan Harasimowski (a member of the Executive and KW secretary), and Bogusław Antas (deputy chairman of the Presidium of the Warsaw National Council). Maciejewski, in accordance with the position taken by the KW Executive on 20 April was dismissed from his position as first secretary of KD PZPR Wola and, as a result of decision taken during a meeting of a committee plenum, was removed from this group. Further motions in his case were to be presented to the KW Executive at the next meeting. According to the Executive's protocol, the "WKKP should demand from Comrade Maciejewski a statement containing an assessment of his conduct and the damage that this conduct caused to the party and the district organization. Comrade Maciejewski should take up work not in an independent position – treating this as an opportunity for rehabilitation. The Secretariat attaches great importance to the idea that Comrade A. Maciejewski will take up such work as one that corresponds to a sense of social justice."

Having considered the Harasimowski case, officials judged that he had had no connection with the meat trade case in question. He not only knew Gradowski but also had maintained social relations with him, had attended "meetings with alcohol in public premises," and had used his services before leaving for East Germany, asking one night to provide cold cuts and vodka totaling PLZ 400, for which he paid." After the affair was revealed, Harasimowski informed the Secretariat about his relations with Gradowski and put himself at the party's disposal, "reasoning that his contacts with Gradowski – about which a great deal was known – are objectively harmful and prevent him from properly fulfilling his function as KW Secretary." The Secretariat concluded that Harasimowski's resignation from his party functions should be accepted; his transition to another job outside the party apparatus was approved by the KC Secretariat.

B. Antas submitted a statement to the KW Secretariat in which he wrote that he had maintained social relations with Gradowski that were "nothing

342 AAN, KC PZPR, 237/VII-5264, Protokół nr 2 Komisji Egzekutywy KW PZPR z dnia 28 IV 1964 r., pp. 84–87.

outside the normal framework." He had used Gradowski's services several times, acquiring cold cuts, mainly ham, for payment. After reviewing his statement, the KW Secretariat found no grounds to draw up organizational and business allegations against him.

The Executive also decided that Zygmunt Woźniak – Director of the Trade Department of the Warsaw National Council – was responsible for the supervision of trade in Warsaw, and in the light of certain evidence "tied to a MO investigation," it also decided to suspend him in his activities as head of the Department until final decisions had been made dependent on MO findings.

The Executive also approved the KW's action program to combat fraud in trade. It emphasized the need to quickly fix the situation in the meat trade "while creating the right work climate for tens of thousands of honest Warsaw trade-sector employees," and to oppose tendencies on the part of "hostile elements" to exploit the affair to defame the party and party organs parties. And it decided to look into the policy behind issuing concessions to owners of private butcheries and to the meat trade.

A particularly important part of the program was the announcement of a "thorough verification of the staff employed in meat trade and meat processing." This verification process was to cover the entire meat trade division from the Trade Department of the Presidium of the Warsaw National Council up to and including store managers. The criteria were to be: "professional suitability, improvement of qualifications, moral and political attitude, the discharge of duties over recent years, active attitude toward fraud, image of the employee outside work and his lifestyle." First of all, the management of meat trade was to be subjected to this procedure, followed by other commodity trading industries (especially the baked goods sector, gastronomy, vegetable growing, committees and cooperatives dealing in the purchase and sale of products of foreign origin). It was agreed that in order to establish verification in trade, a commission should be established headed up by the chairman of the Warsaw National Council. From now on, meat shop manager positions were to be filled by the directorates, but at the recommendation of social personnel committees composed of: representatives of the directorate, of the trade union organization, and the trade commission of the District National Council (Dzielnicowa Rada Narodowa, DRN) in the area in which the store operated. Control over staff policy was to be exercised by party organizations through periodic analysis of the composition of the staff.[343]

---

343 APW, KW PZPR, 30/IV-85, Protokół nr 9/64 z posiedzenia Egzekutywy Komitetu Warszawskiego PZPR w dniu 9 V 1964, pp. 91–94, 111–115.

On 4 July, this policy, focused on purging personnel, was intensified. The KW Executive, after hearing information about the commission's work to combat fraud in trade as presented by A. Karkoszka, decided to verify all employees in meat shops, and then employees in other industries. Officials decided to direct people from other economic sectors, university graduates and administrative employees to managerial positions in trade. It was decided to make personnel changes in the Provincial Union of Meat Industry Enterprises and its subordinate enterprises, and to submit a party action program in Warsaw's enterprises and trade outlets.[344]

Some personnel decisions made by the KW Executive clearly indicated a willingness to provide people involved in fraud a "soft landing" by employing them in institutions other than those tied to the meat trade to the point of not taking further measures in their regard. Thus, B. Antas was allowed to stay on as the deputy chairman of the Presidium of the Warsaw National Council, and Harasimowski was moved to the position of director of the Bureau of Radiotechnical Equipment Sales. Both the progress of the investigation and the position taken by the KC PZPR determined that this position would change quickly, which is evidenced by the minutes of the meeting of the Executive Committee of the Warsaw PZPR on 29 August 1964, during which a topic of debate was information on the CKKP's decision regarding St. Harasimowski, A. Maciejewski and B. Antas.

By this body's decision, Harasimowski was expelled from the party with the following justification: "[. . .] taking a responsible position in the leadership of the Warsaw Committee, he lost his sense of responsibility and vigilance in crucial matters, in managing his life within the party, in making decisions, and in overall social relations. He established and maintained friendly relations with the main schemer in the meat scandal, Gradowski, and with others. He participated with them in meetings that involved great amounts of alcohol. He took part in a gambling card games and made use of various services offered by Gradowski and other people. These facts damaged reputations, undermined authority and caused unpredictable damage to the Warsaw organization and to the party. Comrade Harasimowski bears responsibility for, among other things, the situation that emerged within the KD PZPR Wola, with which he cooperated and for whose activities on behalf of the KW he was responsible." At the same time, "ZO [Zespół Orzekający, or arbitration panel] CKKP decided to apply to the Warsaw Committee Executive for his dismissal from the position of the director of the

344 APW, KW PZPR, 30/IV-85, Protokół nr 13/64 z posiedzenia Egzekutywy KW PZPR w dniu 4 VII 1964, pp. 193 ff.

Bureau of Radiotechnical Equipment Sales and approval that he not be employed in responsible positions in professional work."

Based on a CKKP decision, A. Maciejewski was also expelled from the party, in the light of the fact that, as former secretary of the KD PZPR Warszawa – Wola, he had "maintained friendly relations with the main players in the meat case, particularly with Gradowski." He had made use of various "material and financial services," and had "participated in various social gatherings and drinking parties and gambled playing cards. He accepted various gifts and borrowed larger sums of money from speculators and schemers." He used his influence through his official position "to increase meat allocations for the gangs of swindlers at MHM Północ [. . .]. In the light of the above facts, and the stance taken toward them, Maciejewski deserved the highest punishment – expulsion from the party. At the same time, ZO CKKP decided to prohibit Maciejewski from holding responsible managerial positions."

B. Antas's expulsion from the party was justified by the fact that, as the deputy chairman of the Presidium of the Warsaw National Council, he did not show a party attitude in the entrusted position. He tolerated crony relationships, maintained friendly relations with Gradowski, he himself decided, based on cronyism, to increase meat allocations for MHM Północ, where a high-stakes scandal was revealed. As an activist on national councils, he did not show proper vigilance and ethics through his use of various services and gifts provided to him by Gradowski. Together with Gradowski and others involved in the meat affair, he participated in various events related to the opening of new stores. He also accepted mead from the Stołeczna Wytwórnia Win i Miodów (Capital City Winery and Honey Production Plant), free of charge. And using his position he ordered the production of 60 leather wallets at the sum of PLZ 3,600. The company was charged with the costs and the wallets were allocated to various people. In the absence of proper vigilance and of violation of ethical principles, ZO CKKP believes that Comrade Antas deserved the highest punishment – expulsion from the party. At the same time, ZO CKKP decided to apply to the KW Executive for Antas's dismissal from his post as deputy chairman of the Presidium of the Warsaw National Council and forbid him to hold responsible managerial positions." The KW executive took note of decisions made by the CKKP and decided to dismiss Antas from his post as deputy chairman of the Presidium of the Warsaw National Council, and to dismiss Harasimowski from his position as director of the Bureau of Radiotechnical Equipment Sales.[345]

345 APW, KW PZPR, 30/IV-86, Protokół nr 17/64 z posiedzenia Egzekutywy Komitetu Warszawskiego PZPR w dniu 29 VIII 1964, pp. 36–42. See również: AAN, KC

The investigation into the meat affair led to the discovery of other cases of fraud in which party officials in high positions were involved. At the end of 1964, the KW Executive dealt cases that included one involving high MHW officials: Stefan Kawecki, a department director in this institution, and Roman Malinowski, deputy director of the Department of Trade in Food Products.

The minutes of a meeting at the Branch Party Organization (Oddziałowa Organizacja Partyjna, OOP) at the MHW on 22 October 1964, which was attended by KW PZPR representatives and in which the above matters were discussed, indicate that Kawecki's wife had been a co-owner of a plastic products factory in Warsaw for several years, a fact which her husband hid from party and administrative authorities. This plant hired on average 5 employees. In 1963, Kawecki reported that his wife was not working, even though she had had the license to run this factory since 1959. As a result, he illegally received a family allowance, and his wife used the Ministry of Health's clinic (intended for high-ranking individuals). The Kawecki family also paid lower rent for a flat, contrary to applicable regulations. According to data from the Finance Department of the DRN Presidium, the annual turnover of the wife's firm was around PLZ 1,200,000, and derived annual income was estimated at about PLZ 160,000. Exploiting his position, Kawecki bought two Renault automobiles. Money for this purpose came from the income of his wife, who had previously been convicted of smuggling. Given that it had been proven earlier that Kawecki was not directly involved in his wife's criminal activities, the WKKP in 1960 issued him only a warning. When submitting explanations to the WKKP, Kawecki allegedly concealed the fact that his wife was running a private enterprise. Kawecki – OOP members learned – did not adequately appreciate the fact that the WKKP had cleared his record in 1962, "and through his conduct he showed that he is not worthy of being a party member."

Roman Malinowski was accused of holding a high position in the MHW supervising activities in the meat industry, which required exceptional "vigilance," while maintaining close social relations with people who led a "lavish lifestyle due to meat schemes," receiving expensive gifts (e.g. a gold watch) from these people "even though he knew that he could not properly pay them

PZPR, 237/VII-5264, Oświadczenie dla KW PZPR w sprawie moich stosunków z Gradowskim Stefana Harasimowskiego Warszawa maj 1964, p. 80; AAN, KC PZPR, 237/XIV-307, Analiza i wnioski dotyczące sytuacji kadrowej i pracy partyjnej, przesłana 3 grudnia 1964 r. dla uczestników posiedzenia Komisji KC do spraw Handlu i przemysłu mięsnego, Warszawa 7 grudnia 1964, pp. 23–33.

back, and drinking vodka with people over whose work he exercised indirect supervision," even with meat shop managers in their back rooms. Malinowski reportedly claimed that, among other things, he was forced to maintain relations with company directors and store managers "to allegedly create opportunities to purchase meat and canned ham for ministry employees and non-ministry employees." These purchases were made mainly in the pre-Christmas period for several dozen MHW employees. These matters were dealt with by the meat and fish department managed at the time by Malinowski. In May 1964, the Minister of Internal Trade banned this practice. The end effect was that both officials subject not only to punishment within the party but also to disciplinary dismissal from MHW.[346]

The act of "purging" the ranks of the Warsaw party organization of corrupt individuals and depriving them of positions in the administrative and economic apparatus also covered directors of meat-related enterprises who had already been arrested. On 8 May 1964, the KD Executive in Praga Północ approved the request to dismiss MHM Director S. Wawrzecki.[347] In June 1964, the KD Executive of the PZPR Warszawa-Mokotów decided to dismiss the director of the "Służewiec" Meat Plant, who had the reputation of being an honest man who was "surrounded by thieves."[348] In October 1964, the Secretariat of the KC PZPR approved the decision to dismiss the directors of the Provincial Union of Meat Industry Enterprises in Warsaw, including Władysław Rudnicki, who managed the organization, for "lack of supervision and bad personnel policy."[349]

Sometimes these activities were met with counter-actions on the part of high-ranking friends or colleagues, the most infamous of which was carried out by the MHM Zachód party organization, supported by the above-mentioned

346 APW, 238/I-15, KZ PZPR Ministerstwa Handlu Wewnętrznego, Protokół z zebrania POP przy MHW w dniu 22 X 1964 r., pp. 28–33. See również: APW, 238/I-15, KZ PZPR Ministerstwa Handlu Wewnętrznego Protokół nr 18 z posiedzenia egzekutywy POP przy MHW w dniu 5 X 1964. Obecni członkowie egzekutyw i przewodniczący WKKP Woźniak. Sprawy Kaweckiego i Malinowskiego, pp. 117–120.

347 APW, 33/IV-27, Protokół z posiedzenia Egzekutywy KD Praga Północ w dniu 8 V 1964, p. 32.

348 APW, 31/IV-44 KD PZPR Warszawa – Mokotów, Protokół z posiedzenia Egzekutywy KD w dniu 19 VI 1964, p. 209.

349 APW, KW PZPR, 30/V-t.3, Protokół nr 25/64 z posiedzenia Sekretariatu KW PZPR w dniu 22 X 1964, p. 323.

Secretary of KD PZPR Warsaw-Wola, Maciejewski, and involving the collection of the signatures of meat shop managers appealing for Gradowski's release.[350]

There was an increase in expulsions from the party and removal from management positions of people deemed to have been involved in the affair. The head of the commission investigating the affair, A. Karkoszka, informed the KW Executive on 4 July 1964 that by that time 104 persons had been detained in connection with the revealed fraud, including 28 party members, "more precisely – former party members, because after their detention, the Party Control Committee automatically considered the cases and expelled them from the organization." Among the detainees were: the head of the Trade Department of the Presidium of the Warsaw National Council, the entire management of Warsaw's Union of Industries in Trade of Foodstuffs, almost the entire management of the Meat Trade Enterprise with the exception of one person, many managers from meat processing plants, including the entire management of Meat Plants in Służewiec and the Warsaw Slaughterhouse (7 people). The main commission for verification of meat trade personnel started work. In total, 606 people were verified, i.e. 30 % of the staff employed in the meat division: in administration 65 %, and among store managers 100 % (462). 45 % of store managers and 30 % of administrative employees were set for dismissal. It was decided to continue these activities and to extend verification to entire shop crews. Similar verification measures were to take place every year. And it was decided to extend them to other branches of commerce (primarily gastronomy, the bakery sector, industrial goods).

Similarly alarming conclusions emerged from inspections carried out at the Provincial Union of Meat Industry Enterprises, where it was decided to make personnel changes starting from the managing director. Plans were set in motion to establish a main verification commission at the Union and the Warsaw National Council.

Officials also sought a remedy for fraud in the creation of shop social committees to supervise the regularity in trade (50 had been established by that time).

The prevalent view in the commission was to move toward liquidating private meat factories in Warsaw over the course of the year by "denying the supply of raw material and causing the takeover of this production by state industry."

350 APW, KW PZPR, 30/IV-86, Aktualne zadania organizacji i instancji partyjnych w kształtowaniu postaw członków partii, p. 201; AAN, KC PZPR 237/XIV-306, Notatka dotycząca b. sekretarza KD PZPR Wola ob. Maciejewskiego, pp. 241 ff.

Over the course of various discussions, the main problem involved the difficulty of replacing dismissed people. As reported, apart from 108 individuals under investigation – around 1,600 (including 501 from shop staff) were tied up in the investigation in one way or another. They were mainly butchers. One member of the investigation drew attention to public opinion: "In Warsaw, there is a characteristic lack of cold cuts, and the comment in Praga is that when there were thieves, there was meat."[351]

Other documents confirm the staffing difficulties caused by the meat affair. In meat processing plants alone subordinate to the Provincial Union of Meat Industry Enterprises in the period from the second half of 1964 through the first half of 1965, about 300 people were arrested and dismissed because of various abuses, including mostly employees in managerial and other white-collar positions (engineering and technical). Many people quit on their own because of the atmosphere created around the meat scandal. In September 1965, the KW PZPR anticipated that another 300 people would be replaced in connection with the verification of substantially responsible employees. Officials viewed the theoretical and practical preparation of employees then employed to perform professional duties as far from sufficient. Over 50 % of white-collar workers in engineering and technical positions had no secondary education. The management of Meat Plants was forced to accelerate the selection of new staff, which turned out to be random, and thus resulted in a large fluctuations.[352]

The policy of "purging party ranks" of people involved in the meat affair was implemented broadly in Warsaw. Beyond the information previously provided, this fact is evidenced by data contained in the WKKP reports, which show that out of 172 individuals expelled from the PZPR in 1962, 111 (64.5 %) were removed for economic fraud; in 1963, those numbers were 223 – 147 (65.9 %); and in 1964 – 345 – 226 (65.5 %). Among 226 people excluded from the Warsaw party organization for economic fraud in 1964, 161 (71 %) were white-collar workers, 53 were blue-collar workers, and 12 fell under the category "other."[353]

Progress in the "purge" of the party is also evidenced by reports on WKKP activities in the years 1965–1966. During this period, 704 members were expelled

351 APW, KW PZPR, 30/IV-85, Stenogram nr 13/64 z posiedzenia Egzekutywy KW PZPR w dniu 4 VII 1964, pp. 236–245.

352 APW, KW PZPR 30/V-t.7, Program usprawnienia organizacyjno-technicznego zaopatrzenia rynku warszawskiego w mięso i jego przetwory dyskutowany na posiedzeniu Sekretariatu KW 10 IX 1965, p. 74.

353 APW, KW PZPR, 30/IX-5, vol. 1, Sprawozdanie Warszawskiej Komisji Kontroli Partyjnej za rok 1964, Warszawa, styczeń 1965, pp. 123–136.

from the Warsaw party organization for various offenses, and that number was 3,234 when it includes candidates.

What is most important in the context of our topic here is the fact that among all those expelled, as many as 415 (58.9 %) were removed for involvement in economic crimes. Among them were 282 white-collar workers (including 33 directors), 125 blue-collar workers, and 8 people under the category "other." The largest number of expelled (218 people) were employed in industry and trade in goods (125 people).

In connection with the meat scandal, officials considered it necessary to verify party members and candidates in 14 Basic Party Organizations (Podstawowe Organizacje Partyjne, POP) operating in the meat trade, the meat industry and the WZG. Verification was carried out by the District Party Control Commissions under the leadership of the Executive of the KC PZPR. As a result of these verification activities, it was "necessary" to expel 98 party members and candidates out of 853 PZPR members and candidates of in these organizations. "The moral climate prevailing in verified POPs," as we read in the WKKP document, "is best reflected by the situation in POP Meat Processing Plant 'Służewiec.' In this establishment, only 9 members out of 124 members and candidates of the party were not registered as having been caught carrying off meat and sausages."

Similar results were obtained by the verification of employees conducted by the Provincial Union of Meat Industry Enterprises, in MHM Praga, Zachód and Południe, and at the National Delicatessen Enterprise. As a result of this verification process, 14.1 % of administrative employees, 45.6 % of store managers, and 4.9 % of sellers and journeymen were made redundant.[354]

In 1964–1965, 53 people were expelled from the party who had held directorships, 30 of whom for fraud, and 7 for using their official positions for personal purposes. In view of indications "showing the existence of the so-called carousel positions," the WKKP initiated the study of problems related to changes in managerial functions. According to the collected data 157 people were dismissed in 1964–65 from positions with the KD PZPR nomenklatura,[355] including 82 general directors and 74 deputies. Nearly 50 % of dismissals were for non-compliance, lack of supervision, and lack appropriate qualifications. It was shown that many of those dismissed had previously held managerial positions whose responsibilities they were not fulfilling. The negative assessment at the

---

354 APW, 30/IV-93, Protokół nr 6/66 z posiedzenia Egzekutywy KW w dniu 26 II 1966, pp. 344–346.

355 Oznaczało to, że pełnienie tych stanowisk wymagało akceptacji ze strony KD PZPR.

basis of a dismissal was not an obstacle to getting another, even higher position.[356] Managerial positions vacated by those involved in business scandals were occupied by other persons recommended by the KW and KD PZPR.

Among these personnel changes, made with significant (though certainly not always decisive) participation of the Warsaw party committees, there were a few changes that might or might not have been tied to the detection and disclosure of the economic scandals in Warsaw. We can only presume that there was a logical relationship here.

The first example concerns the person of the First Secretary KW PZPR, W. Titkow. At meeting of the KW Executive on 24 July 1964, Edward Ochab, on behalf of the KC PZPR, put forward a proposal to dismiss Titkow "due to work exhaustion," and to replace him with Stanisław Kociołek, who until then had been Secretary of KD Warsaw – Śródmieście. This proposal, previously approved by the Politburo on 9 September 1964, was accepted.[357] Titkow took the position of Undersecretary of State in the Ministry of Health and Social Welfare.

---

356 APW, KW PZPR, 30/IX-5, vol. 1, Sprawozdanie Warszawskiej Komisji Kontroli Partyjnej za lata 1965–1966, pp. 218–235. This phenomenon was obviously nothing new. It was known to the main authorities of the party, as evidenced by a note in the Bulletin of the Office of the Central Committee of the Secretariat of the KC PZPR on February 3, 1960 entitled "On inappropriate personnel policy inhibiting the battle against economic abuse." The note presents the results of the investigation undertaken by the Team at the Office of the Prime Minister for Combating Economic Abuse in 920 "organizational units," including 538 state-owned and 382 cooperative units. In 805 "operational units," registered losses as a result of abuse in 1958–1959 amounted to PLZ 413 million, and 4,721 employees were held criminally responsible. It was revealed that 1,845 fraudsters were still employed there, including 170 directors (presidents) and their deputies, 84 chief accountants, 348 department managers, 776 warehouse attendants and store managers, and 467 other employees. A total of 602 persons employed in management positions of the investigated entities were guilty directly or indirectly of fraud, and 254 individuals who held those positions had been nominated by higher authorities. The largest concentration of perpetrators of fraud were employed in state trade (11 % of enterprises covered by the investigation, in which as many as 24 % of the 1,845 persons guilty of fraud were employed). Among 1,845 perpetrators of crimes, 588 convicted of fraud by courts of final instance were in in managerial and materially responsible positions. See AAN, KC PZPR, 237/VII-145, Biuletyn Biura Sekretariatu KC PZPR, nr 80, 3 II 1960, p. 9.

357 APW, KW PZPR, 30/IV-85, Protokół nr 15/64 z posiedzenia Egzekutywy KW PZPR w dniu 24 VII 1964, p. 338; AAN, KC PZPR, 1732, Protokół nr 2 z posiedzenia Biura Politycznego KC PZPR w dniu 9 września 1964 r., p. 6v.

Could the allegations of inadequate supervision and the tolerance of fraud play an important role in the above decisions? We do not know.

Similar hypotheses are prompted by "personnel reshuffling" among those positions remaining in the PZPR nomenklatura at the Warsaw prosecutor's office and in the judiciary.

On 6 February 1965, the Executive of the KW PZPR complied with the request of Henryk Kempisty, President of the Warsaw Provincial Court, to be released from his duties.

A Supreme Court judge in the years 1954–1961, Kempisty was President of the Warsaw Provincial Court as of 1961. He was also the head of the Management Board of the Capital City Association of Polish Lawyers. "Despite his personal strengths and legal knowledge," we read in the minutes of the Executive meeting, "he has encountered difficulties in managing the Provincial Court, as he himself says in his resignation letter submitted to the Minister of Justice."[358]

On 5 March 1965, the Executive decided to fill the position vacated by Kempisty with Władysław Komorniczak, the then provincial prosecutor for the capital city of Warsaw. According to the official party opinion, he represented:

> [. . .] a high level of professional skills, has the ability to correctly apply the rules in practice, demonstrates great organizational skills, manages efficiently and resiliently the organization entrusted to him [. . .] Komorniczak is an ambitious and talented manager who is demanding of himself and resolutely enforces high expectations from the team of employees under him. [. . .] Based on his experience in managerial positions, his character traits as well as his lawyer's experience and knowledge, Comrade Komorniczak is a candidate who fully deserves to be entrusted with the position of President of the Warsaw Provincial Court.

For the new Warsaw Provincial Prosecutor, the Executive decided to recommend Edward Sanecki, deputy director of Department II of the General Prosecutor's Office. "Comrade Sanecki," according to the attached opinion, "has the ability to make correct decisions, is a good lawyer, shows a great deal of personal initiative and concern in improving the methods of combating crime, he is able to draw generalizing conclusions from ongoing investigations, especially investigations regarding *economic abuse*."[359]

---

358 APW, KW PZPR, 30/IV-88, Protokół nr 3/65 z posiedzenia Egzekutywy KW PZPR w dniu 6 II 1965, p. 98 i 177.

359 APW, KW PZPR, 30/IV-89, Protokół z posiedzenia Egzekutywy KW PZPR w dniu 5 III 1965, pp. 1–6.

To what extent were these promotions determined by the involvement of these individuals in the strict prosecution and court judgments in cases involving economic crimes? In the case of Sanecki, this motive is mentioned explicitly in the document cited above. It seems that this aspect could have been decisive also in the case of W. Komorniczak's transfer; Komorniczak was an outspoken supporter of severe punishment, on a summary basis, of perpetrators of such crimes. It was he who presented the proposal regarding the composition of the first group of defendants, which included Wawrzecki (more on this below).[360]

In addition to settling personnel matters, the KW PZPR dealt with the delicate problem of informing party members about fraud and creating a program to combat economic crime.

On 18 July the KW Executive approved a letter to the POP in this matter. The document recommended using only the names that had been made public by the press. Its content was to be consulted with the KC PZPR Secretary Witold Jarosiński.[361] The tendency to carefully dispense information is evidenced by the fragment which stated that "several party activists, demonstrating a lack of vigilance and resistance," participated in drinking sprees with a "criminal gang," remained on intimate relations with its members, "used their services, and thus caused the personal authority and the party organs in which they worked to be undermined." The reasons behind the criminal affair were: deficiencies in control and supervision, poor staffing policies, and formalized party work.[362]

On 30 September 1964, the KW Secretariat adopted a "program of action to protect social property and combat economic crime in the Capital City of Warsaw."

In the first part of the document, it was stated that in 1962–1963 and in the first half of 1964 more than 22,000 crimes had been discovered in Warsaw "to the detriment of the public interest," including 47 major economic scandals. Losses caused by the latter exceeded PLZ 100 million.

Reflecting on the ways to counteract these crimes, the document stated that responsibility for the protection of social property, and the main burden of the struggle for its proper protection against economic crime, rested in the hands of the managers of factories, their associated agencies, and supervising units. The

---

360 AAN, PG, 1/29, Prokurator Wojewódzki dla m. st. Warszawy Wł. Komorniczak do Prokuratora Generalnego PRL tow. Kazimierza Kosztirko, 23 IX 1964, pp. 227–231.

361 APW, KW PZPR, 30/IV-85, Protokół nr 14/64 z posiedzenia Egzekutywy KW PZPR w dniu 18 VII 1964, p. 305.

362 APW, KW PZPR, 30/IV-85, Projekt listu Egzekutywy KW PZPR [w sprawie afery mięsnej], lipiec 1964 r., p. 319.

argument was that a comprehensive control and supervision system had to be developed in all workplaces, one which would be accompanied by proper staffing of positions related to material liability. It was recommended to pay special attention to irregularities in the field of compliance with rules in the recording and documentation of materials management and production processes, in holding perpetrators of shortages materially responsible, and in making use of comments made by those in control organizations, law enforcement, and the justice authorities, as well as by public opinion. It was also recommended to strictly control the transactions of companies that did business with the private sector, to pay more attention to filling positions important for the protection of social property and to the reliability and correctness of performing commissioned works, paid expert opinions, and additional contracts with employees, which were often on the edge of legality. The management of workplaces – with the participation of party organization executives, factory councils and workers' councils – were to carry out analyses by 15 November 1964 and to take necessary precautionary measures. The argument was that a long-term program needed to be developed involving company administrations, party organizations, trade unions, and workers' councils. Branch associations, field unions and cooperative associations were obliged to evaluate these action programs and to present, by the end of 1964, their conclusions and control system to implement these programs. The Regional Boards of Trade Unions were to devote more space in their work plans to problems related to combating economic crime.

The detected abuses would become an excuse to strike at private entrepreneurship. The competent bodies of the Presidium of the Warsaw National Council were to present an analysis of the activities of the "non-socialized sector" in Warsaw, with particular emphasis on the role it plays in supplementing the activities of social economy, and on the usefulness of maintaining larger private factories focused on the production of finished products (including in the meat, printing, plastics, automotive and electrotechnical industries).

It was anticipated that, by 15 November, financial and oversight bodies of the Presidium of the Warsaw National Council would carry out analyses of individual branches of private enterprises, primarily in the areas of "tax issues, profits made in transactions with the socialized sector," legalities, and sources of materials and raw materials. All matters related to private sector activities were to be considered by the Presidium of the Warsaw National Council by the end of the year, and conclusions were to be presented to the Executive of the KW PZPR.

Authorities from the MO and the Prosecutor's Office were obliged to develop a program by 31 October 1964 aimed at increasing the detection of economic crimes, close cooperation with inspection bodies, and full use of information provided by the public, etc.[363]

Similar courses of action were described in a document delivered by KW First Secretary S. Kociołek at the plenary meeting of the KW PZPR on 16 October 1964. He argued that the financial departments of national councils must regularly and more thoroughly analyze the sources of income of persons "who, for example, purchase cars, purchase or build villas. [. . .] We cannot allow such situations in which, as is currently the fact in the financial departments of our national councils, there are as many as 7,000 pending cases regarding documentation of income." At the same time, he maintained that one had to oppose such opinions as: people steal because they earn too little. He admitted that living conditions are still difficult for many families, and some low-paid individuals are involved in criminal activities. But people who are well off are also involved in crime. In his opinion, the reasons for the crimes were different: "They are rooted in selfish tendencies in anti-social attitudes, in the pursuit of getting rich and a luxurious and easy life. One of the important social sources of this life philosophy is the anti-social attitude on the part of some involved private initiatives who try to circumvent laws and regulations, and exceed development directions and principles set by the party and the state." Without "creating a universal climate of condemnation of such actions directed against the social interest, a climate of actual joint responsibility for its protection, it will not be possible to effectively fight these phenomena." Kociołek recommended extending the activity of workers' courts in workplaces and the broader participation of party members in social control bodies appointed by the Central Council of Trade Unions (Centralna Rada Związków Zawodowych, CRZZ).[364]

This model of action adopted by the KW PZPR was reproduced by KD PZPR. They also set up their own commissions to investigate economic crime and made personnel decisions related to the affairs.[365]

The most important result of party activities undertaken in connection with the meat affair was the detection of abuses far beyond this industry, in which

---

363 APW, KW PZPR, 30/V-t.3 Program działania w zakresie ochrony mienia społecznego i walki z przestępczością gospodarczą w m.st. Warszawie, Warszawa październik 1964, pp. 341–345.

364 APW, KW PZPR, 30/II-49, Stenogram z posiedzenia Plenum Komitetu Warszawskiego PZPR w dniu 16 X 1964 (aktualne zadania instancji i organizacji partyjnych w kształtowaniu postaw członków partii), pp. 22 ff, 129 ff.

365 APW, KW PZPR, 31/IV-45, KD PZPR Warszawa Mokotów, Protokół z posiedzenia Egzekutywy KD w dniu 4 IX 1964, p. 125.

members of the PZPR holding managerial positions covered by the nomenklatura of the KW and KD PZPR actively participated. It turned out that belonging to the party did not guarantee honesty. In fact, it was just the opposite.

Information in connection with the meat scandal showed that crime of an economic nature, like cancer, was not contained within the meat industry. In the first half of 1964 alone, 155 theft investigations were initiated at 27 key Warsaw industrial plants. They involved primarily the theft of tools (totaling 50 % of all thefts in factories such as Huta "Warszawa" and the Zakłady Nowotki, Waryński, Kasprzak and Świerczewski) or products (Warsaw Motorcycle Factory, Passenger Car Factory, Kasprzak Television Factory, Confectionery Factory 22 July). To a large extent, they were carried out by groups of up to a dozen or so (Zakłady Przemysłu Tłuszczowego, „Uroda", FSO).[366] This feature of economic crime is characteristic of the socialist shortage economy. Given the deficit of goods, theft and resale on the "black market" was a fairly common strategy for perpetrators of such crimes.

In the face of the enormous scale of economic crime, members of the Warsaw party organization took the routine actions expected of them by their superiors. On the one hand, these involved personnel decisions (expulsions from the party and removal of people involved in scandals from their positions). And on the other hand, preventive measures of a highly diverse nature. However, their effectiveness was very limited. The systemic reasons behind the mass nature of economic crimes had not changed; their effective and lasting reduction thus proved impossible.

3.6.2.2. Activities of the Central Party Authorities

The issue of fraud in the meat economy was the subject of the first meeting of the Secretariat of the KC PZPR on 26 April 1964, in which W. Gomułka, Bolesław Jaszczuk, Z. Kliszko, E. Ochab, Artur Starewicz, R. Strzelecki took part, along with the head of the KC Organizational Department, Mieczysław Marzec, and the First Secretary of the Warsaw Committee, W. Titkow. According to the minutes of this meeting, one topic of discussion was the situation in the Warsaw party organization, including in connection with the Warsaw meat affair. It was decided to appoint a KC commission to investigate the activities of the relevant party and state organizations, especially those tied to trade in Warsaw and to personnel policy and organizational forms of work, and to submit proposals on

---

366 APW, KW PZPR, 30/IV-86, Aktualne zadania organizacji i instancji partyjnych w kształtowaniu postaw członków partii, pp. 189 ff.

the consequences to be paid by those responsible for the violations, as well as to improve the situation and help KW management to overcome the difficulties. The commission was also to prepare proposals for "healing party organizations" in workplaces, where abuses and "anti-party work of some party members" took place. The KC Secretary Witold Jarosiński was appointed head of the commission, which was composed of representatives of the Warsaw Committee and Central Committee Departments: Economic, Administrative and Organizational.[367]

The program of activities put forward on 5 May 1964 by the KC PZPR Commission looking into the meat affair in Warsaw provided for the establishment of a team to analyze the economic, organizational and legal conditions existing in meat production and marketing. It was headed by the deputy head of the KC Economics Department, Stanisław Kuziński.[368]

As a result of the commission's work, members of the party leadership received information regarding the scale of the offenses, the progress of the investigation, the number of those arrested, their personal details, etc.[369] The relevant organizational units of the KC PZPR were kept informed of actions, described above, taken by the Warsaw Committee in the area of personnel changes and removal from the party of persons caught up in the affair.

As in the case of the Warsaw Committee, one of the most important activities of party committees in all of Poland, undertaken on the initiative of the KC in connection with the meat scandal, was to get rid of the "black sheep" within party ranks. According to a CKKP report in 1964, 6,357 individuals were expelled from the PZPR, as were 2,791 members and candidates.

As in previous years, the most were removed for fraud, theft and bribery – that is, 2,824, or 44 %. Among them were 87 individuals who held managerial functions as plant and institution directors. The percentage of those expelled from the party in relation to the total number of party members was 0.4 % (in 1963 – 0.3 %); the largest expulsion rate was achieved in Warsaw (1.2 %) and the Warsaw Voivodeship (2.7 %). The most expulsions in relation to the total party members in individual sectors of the economy were recorded in the goods trade

---

367 AAN, KC PZPR, 2224, Protokół nr 30 z posiedzenia Sekretariatu KC PZPR w dniu 26 kwietnia 1964, pp. 372–375.

368 AAN, KC PZPR, 237/VII-5264, Program działania Komisji KC PZPR d/s afery mięsnej w Warszawie, 5 V 1964, pp. 6 ff.

369 See m. in. AAN, KC PZPR, 237/XIV-306, Informacja o przestępczości w gospodarce mięsnej, Warszawa grudzień 1964 r., pp. 1–7; ibid., Notatka uzupełniająca wyniki śledztwa w sprawie ujawnionych nadużyć w gospodarce mięsnej na terenie m. st. Warszawy według stanu na dzień 26 kwietnia 1964, pp. 17 ff.

(0.8 %), in construction (0.5 %), in transport and communications (0.5 %) and in industry (0.4 %). Punishment carried out by the party was used in 1964 much more often than in previous years.[370]

The KC Central PZPR strictly controlled the preparations for lawsuits directed against those guilty of fraud in the meat industry. According to the protocols of staff at the Ministry of the Interior who were in charge of operational and investigative activities regarding crimes in the processing and marketing of meat, its leaders were in constant contact with the head of the party commission, W. Jarosiński, who was presented with proposals regarding the arrest of suspects and their removal from posts. For example, at the staff meeting on 10 July 1964, Colonel Jerzy Jagiełło from the KG MO suggested that materials regarding two suspects should be sent to Comrade Jarosiński with a proposal to remove them from their positions.[371] During the meeting on 29 May 1964, it was proposed to arrest 10 managers of butcher shops "charged" with paying bribes and buying stolen meat. After discussion – according to the protocol – "the proposals were accepted: the date will be agreed after the conversation between Colonel Łamacz and Comrade Jarosiński."[372]

An important problem resolved by the KC PZPR with the participation of law enforcement and judicial authorities involved the composition of the first group of defendants and the type of charges that group would face.

Proposals in this matter were presented at a meeting in the Warsaw Provincial Prosecutor's Office on 29 July 1964, in which the director of Department II of the General Prosecutor's Office, K. Kukawka, participated. It was decided that the first indictment should include 22 suspects divided into groups: Meat Plant "Służewiec," MHM directors, butcher workshop owners, managers of MHM stores, employees of the Warsaw's Union of Industries in Trade of Foodstuffs, the Department of Trade in the Warsaw National Council and the head of the PIH Meat Department. In the group from Meat Plant "Służewiec," all suspects were to be charged with organized crime. In the following groups – store managers and MHM directors, officials considered most appropriate the accusation theft of social property. According to this view, directors would be held responsible for misappropriations committed along with all store managers (total amount),

370 AAN, KC PZPR, 237/V-548, Sprawozdanie CKKP za 1964 rok, Warszawa marzec 1965, pp. 2–27.

371 IPN BU 1550/1782, Protokół nr 8 z posiedzenia Sztabu powołanego zarządzeniem nr 057/64 MSW w dniu 10 VII 1964 r., p. 68.

372 IPN BU 1550/1782, KG MO, Protokół nr 3 z posiedzenia sztabu powołanego zarządzeniem nr 057/64 MSW w dniu 29 maja 1964, p. 36.

while store managers would be held responsible for misappropriations of property committed along with a given director up to the amount taken by each of the managers in a given store (part of the total amount). The adoption of such a concept was justified by the fact that only the director and a given store manager cooperated in committing abuses (2 people); the cooperation of some store managers with deliverers did not change the situation of MHM managers, given that they did not know of this circumstance.[373]

However, the original concept was quickly changed. In a note sent on 6 August 1964 by the PRL Prosecutor General, Kazimierz Świtała, to secretary of the KC PZPR Ryszard Strzelecki "in order to accelerate the investigation of the main suspects and bring the first indictment to the court in a speedier manner," it was proposed to separate a group of 22 defendants. In selecting them, Świtała claimed, "the demand for the quick punishment of the main perpetrators of abuse was to be taken into account." Officials did not anticipate the participation of persons who were in the process of submitting incriminating explanations and "a number of persons employed outside the apparatus of the meat industry and trade, because their explanations are necessary to pursue the investigation in this direction."[374]

However, this work to determine the list of accused was not final. W. Komorniczak, the Warsaw provincial prosecutor, also presented his ideas in this regard. The most important matter for prosecutors was not to determine who would find themselves in the first group of accused in the meat affair trial, but rather the classification of criminal acts and the potential that they could be proven. The attempt to quickly impose severe penalties influenced the selection of this group. Prosecutors were to find people with whom the collected evidence best justified severe punishment.

For this reason, K. Kosztirko, in a note addressed to the deputy head of the Administrative Department of the KC PZPR dated 29 September 1964, wrote:

> In connection with the telephone conversation, I inform you: on the matter of the first group of individuals to face charges brought up against them for fraud in the Warsaw meat trade, fundamental changes have occurred over the course of the investigation with regard to the original accusation concept. Evidence has been collected and is still

373 AAN, PG 1/29, Notatka z narady odbytej w dniu 29 lipca 1964 r. pod przewodnictwem Dyrektora Departamentu II K. Kukawki w sprawie konstrukcji pierwszego aktu oskarżenia w śledztwie o nadużycia w gospodarce mięsnej na terenie m. st. Warszawy, pp. 298–300.

374 AAN, KC PZPR 237/XIV-306, Prokurator Generalny PRL Kazimierz Świtała do sekretarza KC Ryszarda Strzeleckiego, Warszawa 6 VIII 1964 r., pp. 31–37.

> being gathered to justify the allegation that the suspects were collaborated in the theft. Although the evidence collected so far indicates that the amount of the theft was clearly lower than the amounts accepted as bribes, they nevertheless allow for the claim to be extended in terms of the amount of stolen property given the number of circumstances in the case. This approach to prosecution allows the case to be referred to the court on a summary basis, based on the 1945 decree on summary proceedings.[375]

It is no accident that W. Komorniczak, in a letter addressed to K. Kosztirko on 29 August presenting his indictment concept and including an indication of the specific persons to be included in that indictment, concluded:

> The version of the indictment presented has, of course, many disadvantages, not all proposed persons are connected with each other with clear causal relationships. Some circumstances require additional research. However, it seems to me that the presented concept also has its clear advantages, which include congruence with the actual nature of the crime, appropriate social eloquence, the possibility of completing the investigation within the set time limit and the possibility of examining the case on a summary basis without resorting to emergency measures.[376]

On 23 September, Komorniczak presented Kosztirko with subsequent versions of the list of persons and charges that were to be the subject of the indictment. "In my opinion," he concluded, "both the first and second versions can be examined by the Court in summary proceedings without the need to amend the decree."[377] The possibility of imposing more severe sentences was to be increased by changing the legal classification of the accusation. Initially, the accused were to be charged with taking bribes. As the trial approached, the charges were changed to complicity in the theft of property, which meant that they could be sentenced more severely.

This decision caused nervous reactions among some of the accused. As K. Kosztirko wrote to R. Strzelecki on 3 October 1964, "due to the change in charges from accepting bribes to complicity in the misappropriation of social property resulting from the findings of the investigation, the suspect Witowski showed an extremely violent reaction (nervous shock) and it was necessary to calm him down with force. The behavior of suspects in this phase of

375 AAN, PG 1/29, K. Kosztirko do zastępcy kierownika W. Administracyjnego KC Franciszka Ruska, 29 IX 1964, p. 183.

376 AAN, PG 1/29, Prokurator wojewódzki dla m. st. Warszawy Wł. Komorniczak do Prokuratora Generalnego PRL tow. K. Kosztirko, 29 VIII 1964, pp. 269 -273.

377 This involves a decree on summary proceedings from 1945. AAN, PG 1/29, Prokurator Wojewódzki dla m. st. Warszawy Wł. Komorniczak do Prokuratora Generalnego PRL tow. Kazimierza Kosztirko, 23 IX 1964, p. 231.

the investigation creates additional difficulties that also affect the difficulty of meeting the planned deadline."[378]

At the beginning of October 1964, talks continued between the General Prosecutor's Office and the KC PZPR regarding the matter of who would face the court first, as evidenced for example by a letter sent by K. Kosztirko to R. Strzelecki in which the former referred to the conversation of 5 October 1964 and raised concerns "as to the correctness of including in the first group of those accused of crimes in the meat trade the store managers Adam Stokłosiński and Władysław Walendziuk." The basic argument to be used to convince party authorities to accuse them was "to facilitate and strengthen the evidentiary side of the case;" their explanations incriminating Wawrzecki were to include "direct and full evidence against him, while store managers heard as witnesses have the right not to answer questions that could expose them to criminal liability [. . .] which weakens the value and power of such evidence." They were offered an accusation of complicity in the theft of social property with store managers by creating a system that enabled the theft of social property in stores by receiving part of the monetary equivalent of stolen property. "Stokłosiński and Walendziuk's explanations quite accurately explain how this system worked. By defending themselves at the trial, they will undoubtedly detail Wawrzecki's role in creating and exploiting this criminal system. Heard as witnesses – even if they do not refuse to testify – they will avoid detailed exposure of Wawrzecki's crimes. Thus, the inclusion of Stokłosiński and Walendziuk in the first group of defendants is not dictated by reasons tied to ensuring particularly severe criminal repression against them, but by specific evidence against Wawrzecki."[379]

Files produced by Colonel Łamacz's staff show that this group also had an important voice in completing the bench of the accused in the trial. On 9 October, 1964, at a staff meeting, Łamacz's boss said that the KC PZPR "has some reservations about the composition of the first group." In this connection, the staff presented Minister W. Wicha, in writing, the view that introducing any changes to its composition, although possible, would postpone the start of the trial. At the same time, criticism was directed at "the prosecutor's intention to go forth with accusations against private producers of foreign exchange offenses."[380]

378 AAN, PG 1/29, K. Kosztirko do zastępcy członka BP, sekretarza KC R. Strzeleckiego, 3 X 1964, p. 172.

379 AAN, PG 1/29, K. Kosztirko do zastępcy członka BP, sekretarza KC Ryszarda Strzeleckiego, 5 X 1964, p. 170.

380 IPN BU 1550/1782, Protokół nr 17 z posiedzenia Sztabu powołanego zarządzeniem nr 057/64 MSW w dniu 9 X 1964 r., p. 109.

The circumstances and reasons behind using summary proceedings in cases of fraud in meat management, as described based on documents cited above, was explained during our analysis of the Wawrzecki trial itself. What were amendments planned in 1964 about? In the files of the KC PZPR we find a draft amendment from August of that year, along with justification, which stated that:

> [. . .] bribery, corruption and clerical fraud committed out of a desire to make a profit, and committed in large proportions as indicated by a number of cases involving large-scale economic scandals carried out by entire criminal teams, not only represent a threat to legal order and public order, not only demoralize the state and the economic apparatus, and disorganize it, and delay its intended economic and social effects. They also condition and enable the commission of great crimes against social property and the interests of the working masses, and also cause widespread dissatisfaction and indignation.

In addition, the motive behind the amendment was the desire to more severely punish hooligan crimes. Its authors stated that:

> [. . .] statutory criminal threats against certain crimes of this type are insufficient, and the penalties applied for these crimes are within the average dimension of existing criminal sanctions. Furthermore, the blade of inadequate criminal penalties is increasingly dulled due to the length of the proceedings, which is largely a result of the two-stage trial eagerly used by the perpetrators. There is a need, therefore, to ensure conditions for more resilient prosecution, shortened criminal proceedings in offenses of this type, establishing statutory possibilities for the application of a penalty appropriate to the degree of the social danger.

What did this mean? In the proposed amendment, new categories of offenses not yet covered were intended to be subject to summary proceedings, such as: active bribery (Art. 134 and 135 of the p.c.), sale of office (Art. 290 or Art. 290 and 293 of the p.c.), disobeying authority and failure to fulfill an obligation committed by an official (Art. 286 par. 1 p.c.) "if the economic interests of the State or socialized economy units were exposed to significant damage or when there was a threat other socially dangerous effects on a significant scale." In addition, hooligan offenses were to be subject to these proceedings.

As if that were not enough, the project violated the principle of lex retro non agit, because it stated that the above-mentioned new categories of offenses (except hooliganism) "are subject to summary proceedings regardless of when they were committed."[381]

381 AAN, KC PZPR, 237/XIV-306, Dekret z sierpnia 1964 [projekt].

It is difficult to say why this novel idea was not adopted. Officials involved most likely recognized that it would be easier to obtain a harsh verdict before crime definitions were changed so that the accused could be tried in summary proceedings than it would be to make legislative changes in the decree that would face strong opposition.

The fact that such a project was considered clearly demonstrates that, at the center of power, there was a manifest will to strictly punish perpetrators of fraud to serve as an "example," which is evidenced above all by documents cited above, but also by statements made by members of the highest party leadership. This fact applies primarily to W. Gomułka himself. According to an unauthorized transcript of the 10th PZPR Electoral-Reporting Conference in Warsaw held on January 14 and 15, 1965, he reportedly stated during deliberations: "You know the meat affair, it's not worth talking about it, they will sit, people will answer, and a harsh judgment will be handed down."[382] The same attitude among party authorities was evidenced by W. Jarosiński's speech at the KC PZPR session on 19 November 1964. According to one of its participants, Mieczysław F. Rakowski, who at the time was the KC secretary: "We want the trial to take place on a summary basis."[383]

The above comments clearly show – in the context of the meat affair – how the PRL justice system functioned, along with how, in practice, that system was subordinate to political decisions made in the KC PZPR.

Perhaps an important effect of the meat scandal were the personnel shifts that took place in the PRL General Prosecutor's Office and the Ministry of Justice. In December 1965, K. Kukawka, former (since 1958) director of the Investigation and Investigation Supervision Department at the Prosecutor General's Office, became Deputy Prosecutor General. Kazimierz Świtała, who had previously held this position, become the Deputy Justice Minister. In June 1965, Stanisław Walczak took the place of M. Rybicki as Minister of Justice. That having been said, the motives behind these shifts are not entirely clear and the matter requires further research.

---

382 APW, KW PZPR, 30/I-23, Stenogram (nieautoryzowany) z obrad X warszawskiej Konferencji Sprawozdawczo-Wyborczej PZPR odbytej w dniach 14 i 15 I 1965, Warszawa, styczeń 1965, p. 321.

383 Rakowski, *Dzienniki polityczne 1963–1966* (Warszawa: Iskry, 1999), 233.

3.6.2.3. *The Meat Affair and Propaganda*

It was a routine activity among officials within the KC PZPR apparatus, in their relations with the press, radio and television, to interpret economic crime and related issues according to the dominant political line.

The implementation of this requirement was one of the important criteria for assessing their work, which concerned in particular journalism published in legal magazines. This opinion is confirmed, for example, by a characteristic note from the Secretariat of the KC Committee on Justice, Security and Public Order in October 1957, which contained an assessment of the political line followed by the weekly *Prawo i Życie* between April and September of that year. One of the basic charges against its editorial staff was marginal treatment of the issues of combating economic crime. Officials criticized them for the fact that though they had already published texts on this subject, they propagated the argument that the court and the prosecutor's office were playing a slim role in this regard, and that "everything depends on the economics."[384]

Among the many other pieces of evidence confirming that PRL authorities exercised strict political control over propaganda covering economic crime, it is worth pointing out the findings of the meeting on 20 June 1962, based the initiative taken by the KC PZPR Administrative Department and Press Office and devoted to the issues of justice as covered in journalism. It was also attended by representatives of the Ministry of Justice, Internal Affairs, the General Prosecutor's Office, the president of the Supreme Court, the president of NIK, and a group of editors and publicists. The adopted "Guidelines on education in the press, radio, and TV of issues related to justice and combating crime" stated, first of all, that those gathered "unanimously accepted the principle that the mainstream of journalism and press information should be fully subordinated to party policy tied to matters of justice, that it should widely promote the principles of this policy [...]."

The press's main task in this regard was to "mobilize society to cooperate in the battle against economic crime and sales and corruption tied to such crime." To that end, it was recommended to "properly inform the public through the press, radio and television" on combating crime against social property. One of the needs that this information policy was to satisfy was to provide the "deterrent and preventive effects that come with the facts of detecting crimes disclosed to the public and the punishment of the perpetrators." At the same time, however, it was stated that the cited goals of journalism could "be achieved only if

384 AAN, MS, 121, Uwagi o linii politycznej *Prawo i Życia*, p. 564–566.

the content of articles and press notes and their quantitative distribution in the press or on the radio and television would be primarily subordinated to these goals." This requirement was incompatible with "any kind of randomness in the selection of messages to be printed or broadcast, with a desire to mainly cause sensation, or a misunderstanding of the fact that too frequent reporting of fraud desensitizes people to this evil and does not mobilize them to fight it."

The excessive accumulation of articles on fraud sometimes received criticism because they "inclined" the reader "to believe in the banal slogan that 'everyone steals.'" Officials were also concerned that certain articles exaggerated the true nature of economic crime cases.

The guidelines established that decisions regarding publishing information on cases of fraud were to be taken only in consultation with the KC Administrative Department and the Minister of the Interior. Publications intended to be distributed throughout the entire country, in the capital city, or on radio and TV, were to be passed through the KC Press Office.

The adopted guidelines recommended caution when it came to press criticism of law enforcement agencies and the judiciary. Such criticism was not to lead to "harmful and false conclusions that the authorities are powerless or helpless in the fight against economic crime, that in Poland it is easy to steal with impunity, to take bribes, etc."[385]

According to these guidelines, the method by which the public would be informed about the meat affair was subject to detailed control. The press release about abuses in the meat economy in Warsaw was already subject to the approval of the highest party and state officials, including the KC PZPR, the PRL Prosecutor General and the MO Command.[386]

It was similar with Barbara Seidler's article on the subject written for the weekly *Życie Literackie*. Already on 1 July 1964, its text was the subject of a letter sent by Henryk Cieśluk, the Deputy Prosecutor General, to Prosecutor General K. Kosztirko, which shows that the author had received information about the affair from K. Kukawka, and that the text she wrote on this basis raised concerns. First, officials argued that the article could not be published before the communiqué on this matter prepared by the Polska Agencja Prasowa (Polish Press Agency, PAP). Second, Kukawka was to assess the article from the point of

385 Ibid., Wytyczne w sprawie oświetlania w prasie, radio, TV problematyki wymiaru sprawiedliwości i zwalczania przestępczości, Warszawa 23 lipca 1962, p. 211–217.
386 AAN, KC PZPR, 237/XIV-306, Plan operacyjno-dochodzeniowych przedsięwzięć, Warszawa 12 czerwca 1964 r., p. 15.

view of good investigation. After reading the text, Cieśluk shared his remarks that the article did not attempt to analyze the complex causes of the so-called meat affair, although it did not lack accurate observations by, for example, drawing attention to the mistaken staffing policy of employing in the meat industry large numbers of people from the so-called private initiative – former butchers and private meat dealers. "A positive note is the fact that young employees – vocational school graduates – did not succumb to corruption." There was, however, a problem requiring careful attention, namely analysis of the causes behind Wawrzecki and others having been "rolled into the bog" of work "in meat" by the Warsaw Committee of the PZPR. "In the absence of a broader analysis – the reader may get the impression that apart from the former private owners employed in butcher shops and butcheries, the initiators were party directors, guided to work by the Warsaw Committee. What is worse, one might get the impression that the causes of evil lie mainly here. That is why I think that the PAP communiqué is enough for now, and after a comprehensive analysis of the matter and assessment of certain phenomena by the Party Committee regarding the degree to which Party members participated in the affair – it will be possible to gradually discuss the issue in the press and journalism not from the perspective of who will first publish new unknown details, but for a deeper analysis of the phenomenon."[387] With this suggestion, the letter was sent to the KC PZPR Press Office.[388]

The aforementioned official PAP communiqué appeared in the *Trybuna Ludu* – the most important party newspaper in Poland – on 9 July 1964. It stated:

> According to the General Prosecutor's Office and MO Headquarters – as a result of the investigation into abuses in the meat economy, the facts of organized theft of significant amounts of meat and meat products to the detriment of meat factories in Warsaw have been established. It was also revealed that consumers were cheated on quality, price and weight in a number of Municipal Meat Trade stores. Stolen meat was sold to the owners of private butcher's shops or sold through certain socialized meat shops. Profits from criminal activities were shared among colluding store managers, certain individuals from the trade administration, and organizers of thefts in meat factories.

It then listed the names of nine selected persons who had been arrested over the course of the investigation, and it ended with the statement that prosecutors and

---

387 AAN, PG 1/29, Henryk Cieśluk do Prokuratora Gen. PRL Towarysza K. Kosztirko, 1 VII 1964, p. 313.

388 AAN, PG 1/29, Prokurator Generalny PRL K. Kosztirko do tow. Stefana Olszowskiego, Biuro Prasy KC PZPR, Warszawa 2 VII 1964, p. 312.

militia authorities seized and secured movable property in the form of cars, cash, foreign exchange and jewelry – valued at approx. PLZ 8 million, plus 20 villas and single-family homes."[389]

The publication of this communiqué marked the beginning of a press campaign on the meat affair. Many articles appeared in the press at that time attempting to analyze the affair's mechanism. A frequently recurring theme was the search for its causes in the socially conditioned mentality of those involved. Already at the beginning of August 1964, the above-mentioned B. Seidler wrote: "The vast majority of Warsaw meat shops were former private butchers. People with a specific morality, governed by their own laws, completely dominated by an overwhelming desire to get rich (most shop managers had newly built villas or single-family homes, as well as considerable wealth invested in foreign currencies), they created a powerful clique – well organized – which extended ruthless tentacles over every new director, every new controller [. . .] A bog made up of meat thieves stretched out its tentacles immediately . . . and almost without obstacles . . . and very quickly pulled them into the orbit of its interests."[390] A similar theme echoed throughout Tadeusz Strumff's article in the weekly *Współczesność* published after the Wawrzecki trial. According to Strumff, economic crimes were class-based. People from the meat scandal were mostly:

> [. . .] former owners or people from environments associated with greater private ownership. There were private butchers, cold cuts vendors, shopkeepers. The parents of one of the directors (he will be tried in the future) had a private pastry shop – a private butcher, and the later manager of an MHM shop, knew his later director from that pastry shop. For various reasons, especially many people in this category entered the meat trade. This class membership is not necessarily a bad thing. But it can be. It is worth remembering that a large group of people brings their specific mentality into the new environment. It brings a certain attitude to ownership, a certain style.

The author warned that "one should not generalize," because private trade and crafts are not "inherently" criminal or dishonest, but she explained further: "It is about other phenomena when we say that it should be taken into account that a group of people can under certain circumstances try their hand in new conditions: they will want to be the owners of a 'piece of People's Poland,' as they used to own their butcher shops."[391]

---

389 "Śledztwo w sprawie nadużyć w gospodarce mięsnej na terenie Warszawy," *Trybuna Ludu* 188 (1964).

390 Barbara Seidler, "Grzęzawisko," *Życie Literackie* 32 (1964).

391 Tadeusz Strumff, "Po procesie," *Współczesność* 5 (1965).

On the other hand, journalists at the time tried to cope with the fact that the main group of accused individuals – directors in meat industry enterprises – were "promoted people." However, Krystyna Świątecka claimed in *Wpółczesność* that they were characterized by their desire to achieve promotion in the pre-war sense of the word, when peasants sought to achieve the position held by the richest peasants, and the workers the position of private entrepreneur.

> Many of these concepts, attitudes and intentions have survived to this day. Changes in people's mentality are very slow. Young people were brought up among such attitudes. Many have rejected them without hesitation, finding in the new system others that suit them. They derived them from their families, from the environment in which they moved, or into which they entered through marriage. Anyway, the fact that these old attitudes and goals did not get completely contaminated, that they were the goals and designs of almost all "heroes" of these trials, is demonstrated, for example, by the way their apartments are arranged. By the way they spend their plundered money. [. . .] orgies in Zakopane, Sopot, Krynica, and in the most expensive Warsaw pubs. [. . .] This lifestyle has been accompanied by [. . .] hypocrisy at every step. It is striking in the testimony, in the lines of defense delivered in court. In recent attempts to justify themselves at the expense of our authority.[392]

This article presents another theme characterizing the accused in the Wawrzecki trial, one which highlights their sumptuous and raucous lifestyle.

A similar tone can be found in an article by Jerzy Zduńczyk in *Ławnik Ludowy*: "It is not poverty and trouble that pushes them to theft, but the desire for easy and pleasant life 'on a large scale' requiring minimal effort. The pursuit of the petty-bourgeois ideal of life is sometimes stronger than morality and integrity. Single-family homes, comfortably furnished, luxury cars, currency and jewelry confiscated from the 'heroes' of great scandals are more eloquent here than any verbal argument."[393] Reporting on the trial, Maria Osiadacz wrote that:

> [. . .] it is difficult to sympathize even when the accused weep – and this happens when the sums taken and given need to be explained. It is difficult to feel compassion when they are now talking about the shame they have brought to the family, about the difficult fate of these families. It is difficult to believe that, given such sums, families did not realize at least partially that the salaries of directors from month to month were increasing too rapidly. However, a person is overwhelmed with terror when he hears the defendants' explanations: "There was more and more money. I didn't know what to do with it anymore. There was nowhere to put it, I bought foreign currency and jewelry. But

392 Krystyna Świątecka, "Klimaty," *Współczesność* 6 (1965).

393 J. Zduńczyk, "W poszukiwaniu źródeł przestępczości aferowej," *Ławnik Ludowy* 9 (1964).

> it didn't go away. In the last year and a half I could not sleep anymore." Yes. The money was flooding in, strangling. It became the cause for neuroses and sleepless nights. The power of money obtained through dishonest ways is destructive. The explanations of the accused – certainly true in this respect – are a lesson whose significance is indisputable.[394]

The same journalist rejected the tendency contained in the explanations given during the trial that created the impression that "everyone steals," and she juxtaposed those staff members in butcher shops who were "eating off" the system (including with cooked dinners) with "John Does" who had no such opportunity: "We do not normal tear slices of bread from people's mouths. But in connection with Gradowski's explanations and testimonies of witnesses on this subject, the multitude of people going to work every day who eat every day in offices and factories their sandwich brought from home are reminded that those sandwiches are not always made with ham or other cold cuts. These people do claim no "privilege" to eat at the expense of their workplace and their clients. They manage their more or less modest budget as their life needs and possibilities require, without reaching for other people's property. These people recognize what the accused and witnesses are describing as outrageous and common thievery."[395]

In her next report, written after the trial sentence had been handed down, we find this conclusion: "Society is waiting for actions that would completely protect state-social property, as well as the interests of the average citizen. The penalties imposed on meat swindlers, very severe penalties, are an expression of the fact that there can be no indulgence for cynical thieves of social property and the property of thousands of consumers."[396]

The way Wawrzecki was treated undoubtedly had an impact on the abovementioned debate over the death penalty in the new penal code, a debate that had been conducted with varying intensity since 1956. Here it is worth recalling only that in 1956–1957 Polish legal experts – Stanisław Ehrlich, Władysław Wolter and Karol Koranyi – had spoken out against its use. Later, opinions set forth by the eminent sociologist Maria Ossowska were particularly significant.[397]

Not all of these statements passed the censor intact. In the files of the Main Office of Press, Publication and Performance Oversight (Główny Urząd Kontroli

394 Maria Osiadacz, "Na wokandzie: afera mięsna (II): Porządni ludzie," *Prawo i Życie* 25 (1964).

395 Osiadacz, "Na wokandzie: afera mięsna (3) Konfrontacje," *Prawo i Życie* 1 (1965).

396 Osiadacz, "Na wokandzie: afera mięsna (IV). Bilans dokonany," *Prawo i Życie* 4 (1965).

397 See Alicja Grześkowiak, *Kara śmierci w polskim prawie karnym* (Toruń: Uniwersytet Mikołaja Kopernika, 1982), 64–71.

Prasy, Publikacji i Widowisk, GUKPPiW), which dealt with, among other things, press censorship, we find the entire text of an article by Marian Cieślak entitled "Kara śmierci – problem wciąż aktualny" (the death penalty – a current problem), which was intended for publication in issue 11 (1965) of the professional legal magazine *Państwo i Prawo*, but which appeared (with significant changes) in the next issue. The author called for a discussion on this subject in connection with the preparation of a new penal code. He briefly presented the history of the struggle for abolishing this punishment, stating that repeated statistical surveys "in countries that abolished or restored the death penalty did not in the least confirm the hypothesis that abolition of the death penalty contributed to an increase in crime, and the introduction of this measure – to its decline. Quite the opposite: this data could even give rise to opposite conclusions." Cieślak stated that in the light of the impartial assessment of "a normal person, the death penalty appears to be a reaction of disproportionate (exaggerated) strength in relation to its cause, and for this reason alone one must raise fundamental reservations." In addition, it raises a "definitely negative assessment from the point of view of social culture requirements." Finally, as a fundamental argument, he used an extremely strong formulation: The death penalty is "a phenomenon of a different degree, but in the same category as what used to be called . . . cannibalism." All the wording cited above was changed or removed from the published text.[398]

The fact that it was not easy in Gomułka's Poland to find an objective explanation for problems surrounding the food supply and economic crime is confirmed by files preserved in the GUKPPiW on censorship interference in articles on this subject. It is worth referring to some of them in order to show what, from the point of view of political decision-makers, was inappropriate in press journalism on this topic.

For instance, an entire commentary entitled "Struktura towarowa" was rejected by censors, which had been intended for publication in the weekly *Polityka* (No. 25, 1965), and which criticized the production of "commodity assortments" that were more expensive at the cost of cheaper ones. The author wrote, among other things: "It is known that in some areas, the 'producer market' is maintained out of simple necessity. This is the case with, for example, meat in shortage. But this too small mass can be processed into ordinary sausage or *żuławska* sausage. The manufacturer has a natural tendency toward the more expensive *żuławska*

398 AAN, Główny Urząd Kontroli Prasy, Publikacji i Widowisk (hereafter cited as GUKPPiW), 133/8, M. Cieślak, Kara śmierci – problem wciąż aktualny.

variety, though at least a large percentage of customers would prefer the cheaper, ordinary variety. Practice proves that the producer's interest always wins."[399]

The censor also questioned an article by Mieczysław F. Rakowski, editor-in-chief of *Polityka*, entitled "Piękna nasza Polska cała" and intended for publication in issue 44 of this weekly on 30 October 1965 (finally, the text was not published). Particularly troublesome were the terms "permanently" when characterizing butcher shops that were empty "a few hours after their opening," and "unheard of" describing shortages in the assortment of cold cuts. Later in his text, Rakowski pointed out that "preparing meals consumes a huge amount of time and energy. Has anyone ever counted how much the national economy loses because of women having to jump out to the store 'for a minute' because something just 'came in'?' " In the original version of this text, the author's wording was sharper. The author wrote there that "queues constituting a permanent element of the Polish landscape are formed not in front of shops where they sell smoked salmon, but where they sell meat."[400] For similar reasons, a text describing queues for meat in some towns in Lower Silesia did not appear in *Polityka* in 1966.[401]

The way of presenting economic crime in press journalism was also subject to censorship, the best proof of which involves the 11 October 1964 (No. 41) issue of *Życie Gospodarcze*, which was devoted in full to economic crime. What was the censorship about? First of all, it was about details regarding the causes and characteristics of this crime. Concerns were raised by an interview with Doctor Jacek Marecki from SGPiS, in which it was stated that economic scandals "are very dangerous," and the battle against them is sometimes hampered by the "position taken by economic administration," which reluctantly counteracts them knowing that "this crime, although very harmful from a social point of view, is usually not directly reflected on the company's balance sheets." Censors also questioned the author's statement that "the percentage of people in senior management positions" who are part of organized criminal gangs "is increasing." For the same reason, part of an article by Supreme Court judge Tomasz Majewski was deleted in which the author stated that gangs are revealed and crushed, "even though they often have protectors in high places."

Censorship clamped down on a statement by Józef Barski, director of the Confectionery Factories (Zakłady Przemysłu Cukierniczego, ZPC) "22 July" and "Syrena," by deleting this wording: "The monthly salary of PLZ 1,200–1,900. Often

---

399 AAN, GUKPPiW, 133/9, Struktura towarowa.

400 AAN, GUKPPiW, 133/9, M.F. Rakowski, "Piękna nasza Polska cała. . ."

401 AAN, KC PZPR, 237/XIX/232, Problematyka ingerencji dokonanych w "Polityce" w 1966 r., p. 270.

encourages 'cooperation' with those who steal." The same happened to Stanisław Kuliński, vice president of the Association of Craft Chambers (Związek Izb Rzemieślniczych), who highlighted in his text "Przestępcy mimo woli" paradoxes in the treatment of craftsmen by economic authorities, jeopardizing those who tried to act in accordance with applicable law to charge economic crimes.

Passages from an article by Wacław Jarzębowski of the Institute of Internal Trade also aroused strong opposition from censors ("Przed ogłoszeniem 'pospolitego ruszenia'"). Among other things, he called for consistency in repressive measures, and that it not be limited to spectacular trials. "Do you know that some people call convicted employees of the bar 'Praha' martyrs of gastronomy because it was on these unfortunate ones that this phenomenon so commonly focused, so much so that it is known to film directors?"[402]

In November 1964, the GUKPPiW questioned in full the book *Ochrona interesów konsumenta i producenta rolnego* prepared for publication by Wydawnictwo Prawnicze. The main accusation against the book was formulated this way by the censors: "In the light of the materials used by the authors (surveys, direct sales reliability tests, assessments of over 1000 trial documents, PIH control materials and others), *the crimes we are talking about here are phenomenon on a mass scale*" [emphasis original]. According to these studies, we read later in the censorship review, "the average consumer – buyer is robbed every day – in a shop, restaurant, cafe, service outlets – and crimes against the consumer are carried out by a small group of dishonest employees, not just by large organized criminal gangs, but by the vast majority of people serving in the aforementioned fields of the economy." The book's authors cited the results of laboratory tests in five main groups of foodstuffs (about 15,000 samples) carried out in 1959–1962, which led to the questioning of 50 % of these articles in terms of their quality. The conclusion was that at least 30 % of the goods on the market showed deviations from the declared quality.[403]

What was most often "eradicated" from journalistic texts were arguments that individuals who had participated in crimes remained in managerial positions. In addition to the examples cited earlier, one can also point to an article by Krystyna Świątecka, written for the weekly *Współczesność* and entitled "Klimaty," which was questioned by the censors but eventually released. Characterizing the accused in the economic trials of that time, she wrote about their common features, including individuals "wandering around various institutions, offices, production plants, sometimes with extremely different production profiles." These trips were not for

402 AAN, GUKPPiW, 133/15, Szczotki "Życia gospodarczego" 41 (1964).
403 AAN, GUKPPiW, 686 [60/8], Recenzja A. Stempkowskiego, p. 25–26.

tourist purposes, "because although the names of the plants changed, the functions of these people did not change." They were always managers or directors.[404]

Some too "critical" satirical works on economic scandals were also subject to censorship. And it was for this reason that H. Wolski's "Era of scandals," which was to be printed in *Życie i Praca* in January 1965 was fully criticized. The accused text included, among other things, the following lines of verse:

Bo pomyślcie państwo, Cóż to za era, Wszędzie oszukaństwo I co krok afera, Piękna to era. [. . .] Skórzana, śledziowa, Mączna, celna, mięsna, Oh, Polsko Ludowa, Zhańbiona, nieszczęsna. [. . .] Posiedzi za czyny Swe w więzieniu bestia Na łono rodziny Zwolni go amnestia.[. . .] Na każdym towarze Klienta kantują, W sklepie, knajpie, barze Zdziercy egzystują. [. . .] Przeważnie traktują Cię jako natręta, Choć wille budują Kosztem konsumenta.[. . ..] Zakłady bez przerwy Buble wytwarzają, Wciąż ludziom na nerwy I kieszeń działają [. . .]	Because you wonder, What kind of era is this, Cheating everywhere At every step an affair, Beautiful is this era. [. . .] With leather, herring, Flour and meat, Oh, Polish People's Republic, Shamed, unfortunate. [. . .] Behind bars for his deeds is Your beast in prison In the bosom of the family Amnesty will release him. [. . .] For the customer's every good He swindles, In the shop, the pub, the bar Rip-offs exist. [. . .] They mostly treat You as pushy, Although villas they are building At the expense of the consumer. [. . ..] Placing bets without break Generating junk, Still getting on our nerves And digging in our pockets [. . .]

404 AAN, GUKPPiW, 133/15, Świątecka, "Klimaty," *Współczesność* 5 (1965), no. 5.

Na księżyc statkami Wkrótce polecimy A się żyletkami Golimy tępymi.[a]	To the moon by ship We will soon fly As we shave ourselves With dull blades.
[a] AAN, GUKPPiW, 133/15, H. Wolski, "Era afer," *Życie i Praca* (12 stycznia 1965).	

As we see, PRL authorities in the Gomułka period clearly excised those parts journalistic text which suggested that the theft of social property was common, indeed universal, and which viewed the sources of such theft as being inherent in the defects of the economic and socio-political system. Officials were particularly offended by "black" visions of Polish everyday life, with its queues and permanent shortages of basic goods. Above all, particular individuals guilty of "mistakes" and "distortions" were to be severely punished.

3.7. The Effects of the Meat Affair

In this analysis of selected elements of the meat affair, we have pointed to several serious effects. We wrote about purges in the party and the economic apparatus after suspects and those accused of stealing social property had been "gotten rid of." We speculated on the reasons behind promotions and demotions in the prosecutor's office and the judiciary, in which "zeal" or "tardiness" in combating economic crime, including within meat processing and the meat trade, could play an important role.

But this aspect of our considerations requires extension. First of all, it is worth mentioning that officials made many decisions to hinder abuses in trade and meat processing. On 29 August 1964 – that is, shortly after the public had been officially notified about the scandal, resolution 264 was issued by the Economic Committee of the Council of Ministers regarding the establishment of the Meat Inspection. The scope of its activity and organization were specified in detail in order no. 133 issued by the Minister of Food Industry and Purchase of 30 September 1964. Its tasks included the control of all matters related to industrial fattening, the purchase, slaughter, production, sale, storage, and transport of slaughter animals, meat, poultry and milk products. In particular, it was to deal with monitoring compliance with applicable laws, detecting fraud and circumstances facilitating its commission, checking technical devices and the correctness of technological processes, materials management, and supplies to retail trade enterprises. Units within the Ministerstwo Obrony Narodowej (Ministry of National Defense, MON) and the MSW were excluded from the scope of its authority. The institution was headed by the Chief Inspector appointed by the

Minister of Food Industry and Purchase. Regional inspectorates were established across the country.[405]

By the end of 1964, a detailed inventory of technical shortcomings in property security had been carried out in the meat industry. From now on, 100 % of pork and about 70 % of beef reached stores already separated into culinary elements, which was supposed to hinder trade fraud. The production of portioned ground meat also increased from around 50 tons at the beginning of 1964 to 550 tons at the end of that year. As of 1 November, new and more stringent defect standards were in force. Anti-fraud and waste programs had been developed in all meat industry companies along with internal control regulations. By then, trading enterprises had transferred 200 full-time jobs to meat factories with a payroll fund of nearly PLZ 2,300,000. "Vigilance" increased in the process by which people were brought into trade. While in the previous period, the MHW Central Registry received about 500 queries a day from enterprises reporting to national councils and trade cooperatives regarding applicants' previous employment, including any criminal record, then at the end of the year they received about 900 a day.[406]

In 1965, to prevent abuse in trade, a ban was introduced on grinding meat in stores. There was also a ban on employing relatives in stores in the meat industry and the obligation to prove the qualifications of candidates for managerial positions. In addition, the finances of trade employees were verified. Directorates of enterprises were obliged to fir those who could not document the legal origin of funds used for the purchase of certain assets during the period of employment in trade (cars, houses, etc.). They were also ordered to respond to signals indicating that their subordinates were pursuing "lavish lifestyles."

In the same year, the MHW also made decisions directed against fraud in gastronomy. Detailed rules were issued specifying the rules for paying waiters. In approx. 1,900 catering establishments (out of a total of approx. 4,000), a self-service form of sales was introduced, thus eliminating one possible abuse (the waiter). Vodka delivered to gastronomical outlets was marked with a special inscription ("gastronomic"). When dishonest employees found a way to circumvent this provision, an obligation to mark vodka with the special plant stamp was imposed to prevent alcohol from being illegally sold by staff. Meat to these plants was increasingly delivered in "culinary elements" (divided into individual

405 AAN, PG, 1/43, Organizacja i zakres działania niektórych organów kontroli w PRL, Warszawa, Prokuratura Generalna, Biuro Studiów Problematyki Przestępczości 1969, p. 177; Kochański, *Polska 1944–1991. Informator historyczny*, vol. II, 402.

406 AAN, 237/XIV-306, Informacja o przestępczości. . ., p. 135–137.

types), which limited the possibility of abuse in its subsequent cutting. The ministry defined the rules guiding internal controls, and in 1965 deputy directors in gastronomy outlets were appointed in branch unions. The purchase of foodstuffs from decentralized sources, often an area of fraud, was also limited.

In addition, PIH's quality control of food dishes and waiter service was increased. In 1965, it carried out 4,450 inspections, as a result of which 1,059 cases were referred to the courts and law enforcement agencies, 99 people were released, and 6,200 were punished. Finally, in the first half of 1965, a pay increase in gastronomy was introduced, a fact which created conditions for the recruitment more qualified staff.[407]

On 7 July 1965, the Politburo approved a proposal to regulate the wages of certain employees in the meat industry.[408]

In the atmosphere created by revelations surrounding the meat affair, in October 1964, the Council of Ministers and the CRZZ adopted a resolution that entrusted the Provincial Councils of Trade Unions (WRZZ) with organizing social control of trade, gastronomy and other services. With this plan in mind, WRZZ in Warsaw created a Social Control Team, which was joined by representatives of the Department of Trade, Industry and Services in the Warsaw National Council, the Warsaw Price Commission, PIH, NIK, the Provincial Prosecutor's Office in Warsaw, the MO Headquarters in Warsaw, and the Inspection and Audit Inspectorate. In the first period WKZZ appointed 500 and then 1670 controllers from 293 workplaces and institutions. About 50 % of the people selected to carry out oversight went through initial training organized through the Warsaw PIH Inspectorate and the Warsaw Price Commission. The first actions organized by WRZZ with the participation of social controllers took place in Warsaw in November and December 1964.

The inspections covered over 800 shops and service outlets, where, according to consumer information and complaints, various types of fraud and abuse had been committed. Their results, as a rule, confirmed the correctness of reported complaints. Deficiencies in the supply of basic items were discovered. In the meat shops, sought-after goods (pork, ham, bacon, smoked ham) lay hidden under the counter or in the back room reserved for relatives or friends of staff. It was a similar situation with certain types of cigarettes at all "Ruch" kiosks and with Christmas

407 AAN, MHW, 21/192, Analiza działalności uspołecznionego handlu wewnętrznego za rok 1965 (rozpatrzona na Kolegium MHW w dn. 6 maja 1966 r.), pp. 99 ff.

408 AAN, KC PZPR, V/79 (mikrofilm 2895), Protokół nr 17 posiedzenia Biura Politycznego w dniu 7 lipca 1965 r., p. 468.

trees at almost all points of sale, for which sellers often charged twice the value of the agreed price. As many as 60 out of the 100 trade outlets surveyed used non-legalized scales and damaged measurement weights. Half of the 64 stores inspected in November and December for compliance with the anti-alcohol act sold vodka on prohibited days. It was found that higher prices were being charged in grocery stores, phenomenon which was registered in 52 out of 61 stores controlled in the month of February. The differences ranged on average from PLZ 2 to 6. The underweight of packaged flour, groats, coffee, margarine and meat ranged from 1 to 3 dkg per package. Higher prices for fruit and vegetables were common. From November 1964 to September 1965, a survey of 755 service points was carried out in the following branches: hairdressing, laundry, dry cleaning, shoemaking, tailoring, as well as in cloakrooms of gastronomic establishments and theaters. In 60 % of the inspected points, no price lists and information about the category of the plant were visible, charging higher fees than applicable. As a result of these actions, taken in trade, service establishments and gastronomy, 494 applications were immediately submitted for disciplinary action.

Regardless, in 1964 the plan to establish Shop Committees was initiated, primarily in the meat industry. By the end of this year, more than 200 such committees were created.[409]

In Warsaw, an action was organized to clean up trade in the capital city. By March 1966, such enterprises as the following were liquidated: Miejski Handel Detaliczny (Municipal Retail Trade, MHD) Dairy – Baked Goods; two out of five MHM enterprises, MHD Textile Articles, MHD Perfume and Drugstore Articles, MHD – Komis and MHD – Miscellaneous.[410]

For their part, the structures within the Interior Ministry, in order to prevent the organization of criminal groups in trade, meat factories and processing plants, continued to carry out so-called confidential work. In June 1966 in Warsaw, the ministry had at its disposal 14 secret collaborators and 32 so-called personal sources of information.[411]

---

409 AAN, 237/XIV-306, Informacja o przestępczości. . ., p. 137.

410 APW, KW PZPR, 30/IV-96, Założenia programu rekonstrukcji handlu detalicznego, przemysłu gastronomicznego i transportu M. St. Warszawy, przygotowane przez Wydział Handlu [Prezydium Rady Narodowej] M.St. Warszawy, Warszawa, marzec 1966, p. 148.

411 This involves people cooperating with the SB – i.e. the political police. IPN BU, KG MO, 1550/2633, Informacja w sprawie wystąpień profilaktycznych oraz innych form przekazania wniosków i spostrzeżeń organów MO w warszawskiej sprawie mięsnej, Warszawa 14 czerwca 1966 r., p. 4.

Both the Warsaw affair and other scandals exposed during this period were even more painful for the party's center of power because they revealed the large-scale involvement in them of party apparatus employees. For this reason, in December 1966, the Secretariat of the KC PZPR sent a letter to the first secretaries of the KW, KP (KM, KD), which stated that in almost all voivodeships there were cases of criminal dismissal of employees in the party apparatus, "whose attitude and conduct deviated from the statutory norms and violated socialist principles of social coexistence. [. . .] A number of employees have been actually dismissed from positions for incorrect attitudes and various offenses, while other motives have also been given to justify an employee's dismissal – e.g. at their own request, poor health, etc." It was also confirmed that individuals were using their positions for material benefits, and even that employees of the party apparatus were directly participating in economic abuse. "Some employees in responsible positions – through close personal relationships, participation in receptions, purchase of discounted products, accepting occasional gifts, etc. – encouraged the creation of an atmosphere of tolerance of disorder in factories and institutions. Sometimes this behavior made it difficult for law enforcement agencies to detect crimes." Long-time party activists were also among those who relieved of their duties as a punishment. According to the Secretariat KC, the economic scandals showed that party organizations in factories and institutions did not take note of, or react to, this harmful activity. "A range of data indicates a lack of firm reaction on the part of certain party instances toward those who have committed offenses or undermine confidence in the party. [. . .] Those who were dismissed, or fired as a penalty, from responsible positions were often transferred to other no less responsible positions, which in the eyes of the public indicates indulgence toward acts unworthy of a party member and inconsistent with a civil attitude." Some employees of the party apparatus accepted additional and commissioned work, often without the consent even of their superiors, contrary to applicable regulations. "This practice is conducive to the emergence of an atmosphere of tolerance and indulgence, leads to abuse and the collection of state and social funds for unfinished work." In this regard, the KC Secretariat instructed the KW, KP and KD to periodically assess the "ideological and moral attitude of the party apparatus employees" and activists holding responsible positions in the state and economic apparatus (conducting warning talks with those violating these principles), to thoroughly investigate indications of violations of party statutory rules and party life standards, and to impose strict party sanctions for these irregularities, including removal from the party. It was suggested that candidates for the party apparatus and managerial positions in the state apparatus, economic apparatus and social organizations be selected more carefully, and that managerial positions not be allowed to be taken by apparatus employees and activists who were dismissed for violating the party's statutory rules. In the case of criminal dismissal, party instances were to set a period of time from 2 to 5 years in which these individuals could not be promoted to managerial positions. The KW was obligated to inform the KC Organizational Department and the CKKP about cases in which political employees had been criminally dismissed from the party apparatus.[412]

Did the measures taken by officials have an effect on the mechanisms of economic fraud in Poland?

It does not appear that they did. Despite the above-cited legal regulations, the employment of individuals in important positions with criminal backgrounds continued to be a significant problem. In 1966 and the first quarter of 1967, MO units of the following provinces – Białystok, Bydgoszcz, Gdańsk, Kielce, Kraków, Lublin, Łódź, Olsztyn, Opole and Poznań – carried out, in the course of preparatory proceedings and the surveillance of criminal element were able to carry out a fragmentary investigation and revealed that the management in many workplaces were not following the relevant recommendations on this matter. According to data gathered by the MO commands in these voivodeships, a total of 2,531 people were employed in these positions who had been convicted of economic crimes in the past. Among them were 290 directors, managers and presidents of factories, 445 department heads, etc. Many of them turned out to be co-organizers of criminal groups for a second time.[413]

Actions taken by the state authorities, in the atmosphere of combating major economic affairs, had the aim of tightening control of corruption-forming contact between the so-called socialized and non-socialized economy and the craft trades. But the effect of these activities was only partial. As indicated by the note from the deputy head of the KC Organizational Department Tadeusz Rudolf to KC Secretary Józef Tejchma in March 1966, according to estimates by the National Bank of Poland, the vast majority of private producers' turnover came from supplies, work and services provided for the socialized economy. 20 % of workshop production and service-production facilities were involved with socialized units at a level above 70 %, which indicated – according to the authors

412 APW, 30/XI-1, vol.1, Tajny list Sekretariatu KC do I sekretarzy KW, KP (KM, KD), grudzień 1966, pp. 148–155.

413 AAN, KC PZPR, 1738 (mikrofilm 2896), KG MO, Informacja nr 51/67, 16 czerwca 1967 dotycząca zatrudnienia osób karanych sądownie w jednostkach gospodarki uspołecznionej, p. 156.

of the note – a highly significant stratification within the crafts, along with the existence within it of a relatively small but financially strong group with high turnover. The main path to the commission of fraud in this industry involved the extraction of profit from social property by inflating prices for manufactured products and through criminal activities related to illegal supply, bribery, complicity in theft and robbery. Under the category of fraud connected to work and services performed within the social economy, what remained most frequent were abuses in the form of falsification of accounts (and thus the extraction of undue profits), the supply of products of a quality lower than officially stated, and payment for work not performed.[414]

The battle against fraud and corruption undertaken by the party leadership at the time, characterized by severe criminal repression against perpetrators of major economic scandals, proved to be only partially effective in combating these social pathologies. Their development was favored by such systemic features of real socialism as the expansion of the state's regulatory function, the shortage economy with its trade and exchange restrictions, and the quantity of goods and services produced. In this situation, the role played by people who were – as Stefan Wolle put it[415] – the "trustees of deficits" grew immeasurably, and theft of social property continued to play an important role in everyday life during the PRL.

414 AAN, KC PZPR, 237/VII-5247, Notatka dotycząca przestępczości występującej na tle kontaktów jednostek gospodarki uspołecznionej z podmiotami gospodarki nieuspołecznionej oraz nadużyć podatkowych w rzemiośle zastępcy kierownika Wydziału Organizacyjnego KC Tadeusza Rudolfa dla sekretarza KC Józefa Tejchmy, Warszawa marzec 1966, pp. 55–59.

415 Stefan Wolle, *Wspaniały świat dyktatury. Codzienność i władza w NRD 1971–1989* (Warszawa: Wiedza Powszechna, 2003), 307.

Part II: Meat as a Problem for Ordinary People

In our considerations so far, we have reflected on how PRL officials, broadly understood, reacted to the chronic lack of meat. We wrote about ideas for increasing its supply, reducing demand, and the criminal repression used against those who were found to be abusers in meat processing and distribution. All these actions on the part of the authorities were to at least "create an atmosphere of a fully saturated market," and came as the result of powerful social pressure. It often happened that the shortage of meat or changes in meat prices were a spark igniting the flame of rebellion against the government, whose goals went far beyond the requirements of food supply. It is therefore worth considering which social practices could have led to this sense of deprivation. Before presenting our findings on this subject, it seems necessary to answer questions regarding the provision of food to Polish families. Without this cultural and civilizational background, it is difficult to understand why meat, or rather the lack of it, prompted Poles to engage in behavior that was both important and fraught with political impact.

Chapter 1: Food (including Meat) in the Everyday Life of Polish Families

In research regarding a population's quality of life and material situation of the population, the level to which food requirements are satisfied is usually treated as an important indicator of poverty (wealth) of a society and its individual groups. Judgments on this subject are usually made using family budget analyses. In the case of Poland after the Second World War, such analyses can be used only to a limited extent, because in the years 1952–1955 the gathering of official statistics on this subject was discontinued.[416] Family budget surveys were not organized on a large scale again until 1957.

The first research on the family budgets of industrial workers in Poland came in 1947. It was carried out in November 1947 and covered 289 worker families, i.e. (according to the methodology applied at that time) 1,295 people in 26 Polish cities, and it shows that food expenditure consumed an average of 50.6 % of their budgets (between 68.1 % and 43.7 %, depending on family wealth). Their diet was based mainly on potatoes and bread, which accounted for 65 % (29.3 kg) of consumed products; "goods considered luxurious, such as meat and meat products, fats, sugar and sweets, were eaten sporadically."[417]

According to various estimates, expenditure on food in the household of manual workers in 1950 was 69.2 %, in 1957 – 50.9 % (miners) – 55.6 % (textile workers), in 1959 – 56.4 %, in households of white-collar workers in 1950 – about 50 %, and in 1959 – 53.2 %. In 1962, blue-collar family expenditures on food constituted 45.9 %, and among white-collar workers – 40.7 %, including meat, poultry and meat products, respectively 12.7 % and 10.6 %. Similar studies from the 1970s and 1980s indicate that in blue-collar households about 40 % of expenditures went for food. This indicator reached the relatively lowest value in the first half of the seventies (in 1974 41.3 %, of which 12.4 % went for meat and meat products). As the economic situation deteriorated, that value increased (45.8 % in 1980, 48.0 % in 1982, 45.8 % in 1989), especially in blue-collar

416 Andrzej Luszniewicz, *O metodach badania budżetów rodzinnych w Polsce w latach 1920–1957 (Szkic historyczny)* (Warszawa: Polskie Wydawnictwa Gospodarcze, 1959), 60–77.

417 Jędrzej Chumiński, *Ruch zawodowy w Polsce w warunkach kształtującego się systemu totalitarnego 1944–1956* (Wrocław: Wydawnictwo Akademii Ekonomicznej, 1999), 132–133.

households. In the latter, expenditures on food in 1982 consumed over 50 % of their budgets, and in 1983 – 48.4 % (in non-blue-collar households – 44.9 % and 42.6 % respectively).[418] However, the economic crisis of the 1980s affected pensioners' households the greatest. In 1982 and 1989 they spent over 58 % of their income on food (in 1980 – over 49 %, 1988 – 49.8 %).[419]

According to CSO data, the consumption of meat and cereal products in Poland in the period between 1938 and 1989 was subject to characteristic fluctuations (Table 20).

Scholars interpreting the development of consumption and living standards in Poland on this basis usually state that between 1945 and 1949/50 there was a quantitative increase in consumption. Growing income was primarily allocated to food and other basic needs. The real level of food prices continued to fall until 1949. The period between 1945 and 1949 was unique in this respect in PRL history, because with the highest average annual growth rate of food consumption in the history of the PRL (13 % in worker households), the share of food in overall consumption increased nonetheless. At the same time, it was a low level of meeting needs (large increases in consumption of potatoes and cereal products). This phase lasted much shorter in the households of white-collar workers. Starting "from zero" caused high consumption of industrial products (textiles, footwear).

In the area of food consumption, the period of particular deterioration came in the years 1952–1953 – i.e. the height of Stalinism and the militarization of the economy. If meat consumption is taken as a measure, then regression began after 1951, reaching the low-point in 1952; the level from 1951 was not exceeded until 1955. The years 1955–1958 represent a period of improvement, when food consumption was again on the rise, interrupted during the crisis of 1952–1954. Despite this "products for poor people" (potatoes, cereals) were being exchanged for "products of wealthy people" (meat, eggs, fats). The year 1958 is a fairly clear turning point; consumption of meat, butter, and animal fats reached its maximum, and consumption of cereals reached its minimum.

418 Jan Kordos, Agata Kubiczek, "Warunki bytu rodzin robotniczych w latach 1980–1983," in *Warunki bytu robotników*, ed. Przemysław Wójcik (Warszawa: IPPML, 1984), 149.

419 Maria Strzelecka, *Zmiany w konsumpcji gospodarstw domowych w latach 1980–1983* (Warszawa: IRWiK, 1984), 22, tab. 5; Bożena Gulbicka, *Zmiany w spożyciu żywności w grupach społeczno-ekonomicznych gospodarstw domowych w latach 1981–1990* (Warszawa: IERiGŻ, 1991), 8 – 10.

Table 20. Consumption of meat and cereal products in Poland in the years 1949–1989 per 1 person in kg[a]

Year	**1938**	**1949**	**1950**	**1951**	**1952**	**1953**	**1954**	**1955**	**1956**	**1957**	**1958**	**1959**	**1960**	**1961**	**1962**	**1963**	**1964**	**1965**	**1966**	**1967**	**1968**	**1969**	**1970**
Meat	26	28,0	36,5	36,7	32,7	35,2	36,2	37,7	41,0	43,9	45,3	44,1	42,5	45,2	45,8	46,3	47,1	49,2	51,0	52,3	52,2	52,6	52,6
Cereal Products		163	166	160	161	163	166	171	151	154	142	144	145	147	148	143	141	141	137	136	133	132	132

Year	1971	1972	1973	1974	1975	1976	1977	1978	1979	1980	1981	1982	1983	1985	1989
Meat	56,1	59,3	62,1	65,6	70,3	70,0	69,1	70,6	73,0	74,0	65,0	58,5	58,3	60,0	68,6
Cereal Products	128,0	127,0	125,0	123,0	120,0	122,0	121,0	120,0	120,0	127,0	121,0	119,0	122,0	118	

[a] The data presented is macroeconomic and estimated in nature, and is usually higher than the relevant information from household budget surveys. The first is particularly useful for characterizing changing trends and international comparisons. The second are irreplaceable when analyzing the diversity of consumption within a given country. See *Spożycie artykułów żywnościowych w gospodarstwach domowych w latach 1983–1986* (Warszawa: Zarząd Wydawnictw Statystycznych i Drukarni, 1987), 3.

Source: *Rocznik Statystyczny GUS 1967* (Warszawa: GUS, 1967), 46–47; Czesław Bywalec, *Wzrost gospodarczy a przemiany poziomu życia społeczeństwa polskiego w latach 1945–1980* (Kraków: Akademia Ekonomiczna, 1986), 119; Wojciech Życki, *Spożycie artykułów żywnościowych w Polsce. Przemiany w latach 1945–1966* (Warszawa: Wydawnictwa Naukowo-Techniczne, 1970), 39, tab. 17.

In 1959–1961, one can observe a halt in growth. Meat consumption fluctuated and in 1962 it was slightly above the 1958 level. At the same time, the consumption of low-value products (cereals) increased significantly.

The largest increases in meat consumption in the PRL took place in 1970–1975, when its consumption increased by over 17 kg per capita. This was the effect of the economic policy of the new government headed by Edward Gierek (1970–1980), which focused on an increase in consumption tied to significant levels of national debt. This trend broke briefly in 1976 and 1977 (69.1 kg and 70.6 kg). In 1980, the average Pole ate 21 kg more meat than in 1970. A more permanent break in this upward trend occurred as of 1981, reaching a level in 1983 similar to that of 1972. In 1981–1982, when Poland experienced first a period of political revival (the so-called "Solidarity carnival" from July/August 1980) and then martial law (as of 13 December 1981) and deepening signs of economic crisis, the nutritional and caloric consumption of food decreased to the level of the 1950s. However, the following year saw an improvement, and in the mid-1980s the level of food consumption returned to levels seen in the last years of the 1970s.[420]

Did meat consumption in Polish families differ significantly from such consumption in other countries in the analyzed period? The data contained in Tables 21 and 22 allow us to draw some conclusions in this regard.

It seems that meat consumption was determined not only by economic differences (level of economic development, supply, prices, income) between societies but also by a different diet, habits and civilizational and cultural norms, etc.[421] It is characteristic, however, that among countries located geographically close to one another, people in Czechoslovakia, East Germany and West Germany consumed much more meat than in Poland in the late 1960s. For both German countries, this increase was impressive given the low level of the late 1940s. Low meat consumption in Italy and Yugoslavia could have resulted – in addition to many other economic factors – from the different national cuisines of the Mediterranean region, in which meat did not play such a significant role as in the countries of Central Europe further north. In this respect, Poland was closest to Hungary, lagging far behind not only the USA and Australia but also Austria, France and Great Britain.

420 Bywalec, *Wzrost gospodarczy a poziom życia społeczeństwa polskiego*, 88–89.
421 For more, see Kos, Nowak, *Tendencje spożycia żywności w wybranych krajach RWPG i EWG*, 41–62, 94 - 115.

Data on the share of food expenditure in household expenditures shows the distance between Polish society and the Western world. In the richest countries in the years 1952–1958, such expenditures already oscillated around 30 % (Denmark, USA, Sweden, Belgium, Great Britain), while in Poland in the same period it fluctuated well over 40 %. The data found in papers containing the results of economic research on this subject indicate that, in this respect, Poland was not much different from the most economically developed countries of the Eastern Bloc. In 1955, expenditures on food in the budgets of Czechoslovak households consumed 46.6 %, in 1960 – 42.3 %, and in 1965 40.5 % of their real income. In Hungary, the corresponding indicator in 1960 was 40.6 %, in 1965 – 37.7 %.[422]

How did Poles view this level of food consumption? Opinion polls offer one way to answer this question.

In May 1959, the Public Opinion Research Center (Ośrodek Badania Opinii Publicznej, OBOP) conducted a survey on price policy in which 1,798 people took part, including 969 women. 38 % of surveyed inhabitants of towns (up to 10,000 inhabitants) and 27 % of cities (over 100,000 inhabitants) believed that their meat needs were insufficiently satisfied (17 % and 22 % respectively responded "well" satisfied). At the same time, 22 % of respondents said that with a 15 % increase in income they would increase food expenses, including majority of them (52.4 %) on meat.[423]

More detailed analyses of these issues were carried out in 1960 by Zygmunt Żekoński[424] on a sample of 1,430 respondents – residents of cities over 18 years of age. Survey participants were asked: "If you would earn 30–40 % more than now, on what would you spend the additional earnings?" Answers varied based on wealth. A total of 72 % of those surveyed would spend this extra income on better food. This research showed that in 1960 most Poles consumed meat 1–3

422 Bogdan Mieczkowski, *Personal and Social Consumption in Eastern Europe. Poland, Czechoslovakia, Hungary, and East Germany* (New York Washington London: Praeger Publishers, 1975), 210 and 234.

423 Archiwum Taylor Nelson Sofres Ośrodka Badania Opinii Publicznej (hereafter cited as ATNS OBOP), 9.098 B, I. Wiatr, *Opinie o zaspokojeniu potrzeb materialnych ludności miejskiej* (Warszawa: OBOP, listopad 1959); ibid., I. Wiatr, *Prognozy popytu i jego zasadniczych tendencji* (Warszawa: OBOP, listopad 1959).

424 ATNS OBOP 9.109, Zygmunt Żekoński, *Struktura żywienia ludności miast (Wyniki badań ankietowych)* (Warszawa: OBOP, 1961); ATNS OBOP 9.110, Żekoński, *Wstępne informacje o strukturze żywienia ludności miast* (Warszawa: OBOP, 1960).

Table 21. Meat consumption per capita in selected countries in the years 1948–1988, in kilograms

Country	Year	Consumption per capita	Country	Year	Consumption per capita
Poland	1950	37	Belgium	1948–1950	47
	1960	43		1960–1962	61
	1968	52		1966/67	65
	1970	53		1980	86
	1980	74			
	1982	59		1988	101
	1989	69			
Romania	1960–1962	36	Czechoslovakia	1950	45
	1963	31		1960	57
				1967	63
				1980	86
USA	1948–1950	82		1988	91
	1960–1962	95	Denmark	1948–1950	62
	1967	108		1960–1962	64
	1980	115		1967	41
	1988	117		1980	86
Hungary	1950	34		1988	101
	1960–1962	49	Yugoslavia	1952–1953	20
	1967	52		1960–1962	27
Great Britain	1948–1950	50		1966	28,7
	1960–1962	74	East Germany	1950	22
	1967/68	74		1960	55
	1970	76			
	1980	76		1968	63
Italy	1948–1950	15			
	1960–1962	31	USSR	1960	40
	1966/67	39		1968	48
Portugal	1960	18,7	Spain	1960/61	19,0
	1964	19,7		1964/65	25,5
	1968	28,1		1968/69	35,5
	1970	38		1980	71
	1980	46		1988	83

Sources: *Rocznik Statystyki Międzynarodowej GUS 1970* (Warszawa: GUS, 1970), 341–342, tab. 244(304); W.E. Komarov, U.G. Czierniavskij, *Dochody i potrieblienije nasielienija SSSR* (Moskwa, 1973), 113; *Statisticzieskij jeżegodnik stran-czlienow Sowieta Ekonomiczeskoj Wzaimopomoszczi 1976* (Moskwa 1976), 52, tab. 24; *Food Consumption Statistics 1955–1971* (Paris: OECD,1973); *Food Consumption Statistics 1960–1968* (Paris: OECD, 1970); Czesław Kos, Jan Nowak, *Tendencje spożycia żywności w wybranych krajach RWPG i EWG* (Warszawa: IRWiR PAN, 1988), 232–233; *Mały Rocznik Statystyczny GUS 1990* (Warszawa: GUS, 1990), 275, tab. 11(232).

times a week. At the same time, around 70 % of respondents thought that having to save on food was unjust.

Surveys from the 1970s confirm the thesis that this dissatisfaction with the shortage of food supplies affected a significant proportion of Poles even in the years of the Gierek consumer boom, although it undoubtedly manifested itself to a much lesser extent than before and after that period. In 1974, to the question: "What food would you eat in your home in greater amounts if income increased and the market supply was good," as many as 60.7 % of respondents said that this income would not be used for food. Among the 37.8 % who said that it would be used for food, as many as 42.3 % indicated meat as the object of their unmet consumer needs (next in line were cold cuts – 39.6 %, and southern fruit – 20.9 % next). At the same time, this research confirmed the tendency observed already in 1959 that one's view of the availability of meat and meat products depended on one's place of residence. The privileges enjoyed by residents of large cities with a population above 100,000 were particularly evident. In this way, the policy of redistributing meat supplies according to territorial criteria was reflected in social moods. In addition, a comparison of studies from 1969–1961 and those from 1974 shows that the level of dissatisfaction with shortages of meat and meat products had clearly decreased.[425]

Further studies on the frequency of meat consumption, although only partially comparable to those from 1960, were carried out in September 1977. They show a significant improvement in the quality of nutrition. As many as 69 % of respondents said that they consumed meat and meat products at least several times a week, including 15 % every day. The corresponding rates for poultry were 29 % and 2 %. More frequent meat consumption was characteristic for the urban population, and especially among higher-qualified socio-professional groups.[426]

Rates of meat and meat product consumption from 1977 were similar to those obtained by the Social Opinion Research Center (Centrum Badania Opinii Społecznej, CBOS) in July 1983 (Table 23).

Thus, sociological analyses indicate that since the end of the 1950s there was progress in the consumption of meat and meat products. At the same time, at least some analyses confirmed the argument that one of the most important barriers to this process involved income: in May 1959, as many as 41 % of respondents

425 Stefan Szostkiewicz, *Zaopatrzenie w żywność w opinii społecznej* (Warszawa: Wydawnictwa Radia i Telewizji, 1974), 30–31 and 39.

426 OBOP, Sposób odżywiania się społeczeństwa polskiego (wrzesień 1977).

Table 22. Structure of household expenditures on consumption (current prices) in % of total expenditure

Country	Year	Food a)	Clothing and footwear	Health
Denmark	1975	31,0	5,6	
	1980	25,2	5,9	1,8
	1987	22,6	5,8	1,8
France	1950–1954	37,2	14,1	
	1955–59	33,5	12,5	
	1965–1968	28,5	10,9	
	1975	24,0	8,0	11,2
	1980	21,3	7,3	7,7
	1987	19,9	7,0	8,8
Spain	1975	36,7	10,5	4,1
	1980	27,8	8,0	3,8
	1987	26,1	7,4	3,6
Italy	1950–1954	41,6	12,3	
	1960–1964	38,7	9,3	
	1965–1968	37,8	9,9	
	1975	36,8	8,6	8,6
	1980	28,0	11,2	4,5
	1987	23,3	9,8	5,9
USA	1975	17,8	7,3	10,8
	1980	15,7	6,8	11,9
	1987	13,4	6,5	14,8
Portugal	1980	36,9	10,5	4,3
	1987	37,1	10,3	4,5
Sweden	1975	28,6	7,3	4,1
	1980	25,4	7,7	2,2
	1987	23,0	7,6	2,6
Ireland	1980	41,7	7,4	2,1
	1986	41,8	7,4	2,7
West Germany b)	1950–1954	41,6		
	1960–1964	38,7		
	1965–1968	37,8		
	1980	24,7	9,8	10,4
	1987	22,6	8,9	10,0

a – in 1980 and 1987 – food along with drinks and tobacco; b – 1950–1954, 1960–1964, 1965–1968 – including drinks and tobacco

Source: *Rocznik Statystyki Międzynarodowej GUS 1991* (Warszawa: GUS, 1991), 96–97, tab. 1(65); *Rocznik Statystyki Międzynarodowej GUS 2003* (Warszawa: GUS, 2003), 409–410, tab. 6(286); *Rocznik Statystyki Międzynarodowej GUS 1977* (Warszawa: GUS, 1977), 296, tab. 5(287).

Table 23. Frequency of meat and cold cut consumption in families as examined by CBOS in July 1983

Social Category	Meat			Cold Cuts		
	Twice or less per week	3–4 times per week	5–7 times per week	2 times or less per week	3–4 times per week	5–7 times per week
All categories	46,0	41,6	12,4	44,1	37,3	18,6
Professionally active, including:	23,6	63,9	12,5	22,8	44,4	32,8
Intelligentsia and officials						
Workers	42,5	42,6	14,9	33,3	44,5	22,2
Mixed category	63,5	29,5	7,0	59,0	29,7	11,3
Farmers	58,6	24,6	16,8	75,4	15,8	8,8
Professionally inactive, including:	53,0	39,2	7,8	50,6	38,8	10,6
Pensioners						

Source: Lidia Beskid, "Sytuacja materialna i potrzeby robotników w 1983 r. (wyniki badania ankietowego)," in *Położenie klasy robotniczej w Polsce,* vol. 3 *Warunki bytu robotników* (Warszawa: IPPML, 1984), 287, tab. 8.

who were asked about methods of raising the standard of living reacted most favorably to a reduction in food prices, 35 % to an increase in wages, 6 % to a reduction in clothing prices, and only 5 % to a reduction in prices of durable goods.[427]

This apparently quite successful pursuit of greater consumption of meat and meat products was tied to dissatisfaction with the state of supply in stores, which is confirmed by the results of a OBOP survey conducted in May 1959 on price policy. Respondents were asked about supplies for various types of stores. It turned out that the percentage of people describing the supply at butcher shops as good was 18.4, and as insufficient – 37.9; respective indicators for dairy shops reached 48.5 and 9.6; for fruit and vegetable shops – 47.2 and 11.4; and other food shops 44 and 4.8. Respondents assesses the supply of meat products as particularly bad, and the distribution of these opinions among wealth groups showed no significant differences. Opinions were tied significantly to the fact that supplies differed depending on town/city size. The percentage of negative

427 ATNS OBOP, 9.098A, I. Wiatr, Opinie o metodach podnoszenia stopy życiowej 1959, OBOP listopad 1959.

responses about the supply of butcher shops in cities with up to 10,000 residents was 46; above 100,000 – 37. Positive responses – 15 and 18 respectively.[428]

These findings correspond to those obtained during a survey on purchases in Warsaw carried out in December 1961 on a sample of nearly 900 people. Respondents most often complained about the lack of goods in grocery stores (36.1 %), about poor service (31.4 %) and a lack of honesty (24.2 %), about the sale of products of an incorrect grade (15.2 %), and about filth, lack of hygiene and aesthetics (12.5 %). Indications regarding industrial shops were smaller. The most important demand made was to improve the supply of goods (46 %). Complaints most often concerned clothing, ready-made items of various industrial goods (18.9 % of respondents) as well as meat and sausages (17.3 %), followed by footwear (16 %), dairy products, milk and cheese (12 %), other food (9.9 %) and bread (9.7 %).[429]

More systematically conducted OBOP studies on food market assessments allow us to track changes in opinions on this topic since the mid-1970s. Interviewers asked, among other things, about the supply in grocery stores near respondents' place of residence (Table 24).

A comparison of research results from 1974–1988 indicates that the sense of satisfaction with the supply of grocery stores underwent characteristic changes. During this period it reached its apogee in early 1976 (30 % "good" and 34 % "bad"). A rapid collapse in this optimism occurred in September 1976, which should be associated with the circumstances surrounding the unsuccessful "price operation" (a price increase named euphemistically for propaganda purposes at the time) of June 1976. Public opinion on this topic reached a low point in the fourth quarter of 1980, which corresponds to the previously quoted indicators of meat and meat product consumption per capita. The state of relative satisfaction with grocery store supplies, characteristic of the beginning of 1976, did not recur in the next decade.

CBOS surveys can complement the OBOP research in this regard. In November 1987, in its survey of grocery store supply ratings, they obtained the following percentages: good – 21.4; neither good nor bad – 34.1; bad – 44.1; difficult to say – 0.2.[430]

---

428 ATNS OBOP 9.098 B, I. Wiatr.

429 ATNS OBOP 9.50, Roman Peretiatkowicz, Zakupy w Warszawie, Warszawa 1962.

430 AAN, KC PZPR, 2055 (mikrofilm 3224), Informacja o ocenach minionego roku w świetle wyników badań socjologicznych, p. 49.

Table 24. Distribution of answers (in %) to the question about supplies in grocery stores in place of residence; OBOP survey from 1976–1986

Supply	**Average for year 1974**	**Average for year 1975**	**January 1976**	**September 1976**	**September 1977**
Good	30	20	30	6	11
Average	31	31	34	16	26
Bad	36	48	34	73	62*
Difficult to say	3	1	2	2	1
Supply	September 1978	March 1979	IV quarter 1979	III quarter 1980	IV quarter 1980
Good	17	14	10	4	1
Average	32	33	29	18	7
Bad	50	52	59	77	91
Difficult to say	1	1	2	1	1
Supply	September 1981	May 1982	November 1982	November 1983	May 1984
Good	2	13	5	11	20
Average	7	37	36	38	47
Bad	90	47	57	48	31
Difficult to say	1	3	2	3	2
Supply	November 1984	May 1985	November 1985	November 1986	February 1988
Good	16	22	27	24	6
Average	44	47	44	43	22
Bad	38	29	28	31	70
Difficult to say	2	2	1	2	2

* according to other data – 59

Source: Komunikaty z badań OBOP z lat 1974–1986; AAN, KC PZPR, mikr. 3228 [d. sygn. 2959], Informacja o stanie nastrojów społecznych i działalności przeciwnika w pierwszym okresie II etapu reform, W. Propagandy KC PZPR, marzec 1988, p. 98.

Opinion polls also showed that in the early 1980s, the percentage of people declaring low satisfaction of food needs was 10,6, which was significantly lower than for culture (39,2), housing (24,4), clothing (22,4) and health care (14,4). Due to its basic importance, food was of particular concern for Polish families during economic crisis.[431]

431 Beskid, "Sytuacja materialna i potrzeby robotników w 1983 r.," 284–286.

What role did the lack of meat and meat products play in shaping social moods? More systematic research on these issues was the subject of OBOP analyses in the 1970s and 1980s.

Already in 1974, what was most often the object of complaint was the fact that meat and meat products were the kind of groceries that were lacking in stores located near one's place of residence.[432] Other studies from the end of 1974 confirmed that most Poles (84 %) considered meat and meat products as items whose supply should be increased so that "all citizens can eat in a healthy and rational way." At the same time, they pointed to the existence of widespread and very strong need for greater meat consumption, followed by fruit and vegetables, combined with a predominance of optimistic forecasts regarding the supply of food in 1975.[433] This optimism clearly collapsed in 1976,[434] which was undoubtedly an effect of, above all, the deepening food supply difficulties tied to the events of June 1976.

Indications of the availability of meat products, calculated by OBOP in relation to the total number of people declaring their views on the market supply for individual products, are contained in Table 25.

Both in the case of previously analyzed opinions on the supply of groceries to stores and in this case, the availability of individual types of meat and cold cuts was the lowest in the fourth quarter of 1980. The introduction of regulation of these articles increased the public sense of their availability.

Sociologists' findings complement studies done by economists. A survey conducted in September 1988 among the working population of the Wrocław region by academics from Wrocław's Akademia Ekonomiczna showed that only 18–22 % of households indicated that their needs for meat and meat products, as well as for fish and fish products, were being met satisfactorily. Between 35–40 % declared themselves to be more than 50 % satisfied.[435]

---

432 Szostkiewicz, *Zaopatrzenie w żywność w opinii społecznej*, 30–31 and 39.

433 OBOP, Komunikat z badań nr 2/43, styczeń 1975

434 OBOP, Komunikat z badań nr 23/105, październik 1976.

435 Krystyna Mazurek-Łopacińska, "Modelowanie konsumpcji żywności," in *Polski model konsumpcji, cz. 2. Problemowe modele konsumpcji lat osiemdziesiątych – wybrane techniki*, eds. Józefa Kramer, Zofia Kądzior (Katowice: Akademia Ekonomiczna Instytut Rynku i Konsumpcji, 1990), 38–39.

Table 25. Indications of the availability of meat products in the years 1977–1986* based on OBOP research

Article	**September 1977**	**September 1978**	**March 1979**	**December 1979**	**IV quarter 1980**
Beef with bone	12	12	9	7	4
Krakowska sausage	2	5	4	2	1
Pork meat	1	1	3	2	1
Beef without bone	3	2	3	2	0
Ham	-	-	-	1	0
Common sausage	24	18	27	16	7
Article	May 1981 **	September 1981**	November 1982**	April 1982**	May 1983**
Beef with bone	44	12	74	47	74
Krakowska sausage	25	6	25	26	37
Pork meat	32	6	21	36	30
Beef without bone	24	4	31	26	37
Ham	20	1	3	25	8
Common sausage	62	23	61	49	74
Article	November 1984**	November 1985**	May 1986**	November 1986**	
Beef with bone	69	69	66	66	
Krakowska sausage	22	26	32	35	
Pork meat	17	27	36	35	
Beef without bone	30	28	26	28	
Ham	4	5	12	9	
Common sausage	52	59	69	64	

* OBOP data from previous years are not comparable, as the availability rates were then calculated for all respondents, including those who had no opinion on the availability of goods.
** availability under the regulation system then in force

Source: see Table 24.

What conclusion can we draw from these findings? They show, firstl, that the supply of food in the everyday life of Polish families played an extremely important role; and second, that Poles spent a great deal on food, that they wanted to spend more on meat and meat products, and that they were critical of the food supply.

Chapter 2: Supplies, Food, Meat: Words

1. The Written Word

1.1. Letters to Authorities

Poles were dissatisfied with the lack of food supply, and they expressed their dissatisfaction with the written word, which is confirmed by letters – complaints written primarily to the country's highest-level authorities. Their importance for our analyses lies not only in the fact that they point to the role that food played in everyday life of the PRL. Reading them, we can also learn about what Poles thought about their leaders.[436]

The number of statements of this type usually increased in the wake of public or secret price changes (usually increases) applied to food and – less often – to industrial goods, energy, or public transport fares. All of price changes, according to the logic of the centrally planned economy, were determined and controlled by the state, not by the market. On 15 August 1957, the retail price of butter was increased and the retail prices of bacon, lard and margarine were reduced; on 20 June 1959 there was an increase in retail prices of beef; from September 1959, an increase in monthly train tickets; as of 17 October 1959, the retail prices of meat, pork fat, lard and meat products increased (by 25 % on average). From 31 July 1966, lard prices fell, and tobacco and fish prices increased. From

---

436 On the scale of this correspondence and its value for historical research and the subject matter – see Jarosz, "Akta Biura Listów i Inspekcji KC PZPR jako źródło do badań rzeczywistości społecznej w Polsce w latach 1950–1956," *Polska 1944/45–1989. Studia i materiały*, II (1997): 191–216; Jarosz, "Listy do centralnych instytucji państwa stalinowskiego jako źródło do badań życia codziennego w Polsce," *Kwartalnik Historii Kultury Materialnej* 3 (1996): 297–302; Anna Adamus, "Problemy wsi w Polsce w latach 1956–1980 w świetle listów do władz centralnych," *Dzieje Najnowsze* 1 (2017): 235–243; Adamus, *Problemy wsi w Polsce w latach 1956–1980 w świetle listów do władz centralnych* (Warszawa: Instytut Pamięci Narodowej, 2017).

1 April 1963, prices of coal, firewood, electricity and gas increased. The 10th plenum of the KC PZPR meeting in November 1967 decided to increase the prices of meat, animal products and meat products.[437] In November 1967, there was an increase in public transport fares, including new rules for the use of discounted monthly tickets.[438] All such regulations along with others, introduced "quietly," had a powerful impact on the deteriorating financial situation of the majority of PRL citizens and were reflected in letters sent to party and state institutions and in comments made during meetings or in private conversations. Sometimes, the reasons that led to these expressions of public opinion involved important events in internal politics or changes in the international situation.[439]

The vast majority of these comments were dominated by the belief that living conditions were gradually deteriorating, particularly when it came to the supply situation in Poland. In August 1956, in letters about the standard of living flowing into Polish Radio, you can find the following description: "I am hungry and my entire family and I have simply nothing to wear. I am a white-collar worker [. . .]. My average salary is PLZ 1,142.50 + PLZ 102.50 family allowance. My family consists of three people – I alone work because my wife has a lung disease and our child is only 5 years old. Imagine my life on my salary [. . .]. PLZ 915.75 for food, not to mention clothing, and the cost of coal and potatoes for the winter season. About PLZ 30 is left for daily maintenance. I still don't know what to do because I don't see any hope for the future. The last plenum of the KC PZPR guaranteed a 30 % increase in average wages in the 5-year plan [1956–1960], and I have nothing to wear and I'm hungry – and 5 years is a long time."[440] A similar sense of injury dominates another letter from this period: " 'Hunger and constant malnutrition of the broad masses are inherent features of capitalism' (a fragment from a Soviet cookbook). We lower-paid employees, i.e. those who do not have PLZ 1 thousand. A month, we warmly ask 'Fala 49' (a popular radio show) to intervene on our behalf, because living of PLZ 600 or 750 is very hard now and

---

437 AAN, KC PZPR, 1738 (mikrofilm 2896), Notatka Ministerstwa Przemysłu Spożywczego i Skupu i Państwowej Komisji Cen w sprawie cen detalicznych mięsa, artykułów zwierzęcych i przetworów mięsnych, Warszawa 20 października 1967, pp. 191– 202.

438 AODiZP, 1207/4, Biuletyn Wewnętrzny Komitetu do Spraw Radia i Telewizji "Polskie Radio i Telewizja" nr 375, listopad 1967. Statements and opinions related to price changes in public transport.

439 Zaremba, *Społeczeństwo polskie lat sześćdziesiątych*, 24–48.

440 AODiZP, 1050/17, Biuletyn Biura Listów Komitetu do Spraw Radiofonii "Polskie Radio," nr 51, 4 sierpnia 1956.

this salary is barely enough to provide food for a single person, let alone families who find themselves in the middle of a tragic financial situation. [...] We ask that you allow us to buy in convenient installments, that is if there can be no price reduction. We would also ask you to intervene to reduce prices, given that the availability of food, such as bread, butter, sugar and meat, is the basis of our lives."[441]

In these communications, the main reason for deteriorating material conditions was "their" government, party, and authority. "They" were accused primarily of cheating society. As one Polish Radio listener wrote, criticizing the hidden price increases of July 1958, "Human blood is flowing and one could go nuts looking at our order within the state. At the 11th Plenum of our party they said, we do not guarantee a raise for working people, but price stability is guaranteed. And as it really is, prices are growing like plants after rain, and our salaries are not. [...]. Yes, this people's state drains the worker at every turn. Why is it not said on the radio or in the press that such and such a thing has become more expensive, it is written that it is 5 % more expensive abroad. You see what's in the distance but not what's right under your nose."[442]

It was the authorities' fault that there were continuous prices increases on everyday goods and that adulterated butter, milk, fruit preserves and sausages were on the market: "The consumer is forced to accept what there is, because there is no other way, they hundreds of tons of fat and low-quality meat are going to rot, and 1 kg of pork bone costs PLZ 4, stocks of confections are rotting in warehouses around the country, the grain at PGR farms is overgrown with weeds."[443]

In highly impulsive opinions, citizens accused authorities of being simply incapable of governing, indeed incompetent. In 1958, a radio correspondent could not understand why there was no pork in the shops "if you overlook the homeopathic doses thrown here and there on the market, which one can gobble up only after standing an hour in line, among complaints, screams, curses! And when one finally gets it – very rarely! – a scrap of meat – and it is brought home, only to confirm once again that we were cheated on the weight, that it was again just an inedible abomination, that again the bone weight was at least 50 %. This

441 Ibid.

442 AODiZP, 1050/23, Biuletyn Biura Listów Komitetu do Spraw Radiofonii "Polskie Radio" nr 50, 25 lipca 1958.

443 AODiZP, 1050/26, Biuletyn Biura Listów Komitetu do Spraw Radiofonii "Polskie Radio" nr 73, 10 grudnia 1958.

all, of course, raises the price to such an extent that only a small number of people in Poland can afford to eat meat. Of course, there is no way to get any meat other than pork. Where is the rest left to rot? This is the secret of our notorious meat processing centers and their management. I am convinced that managers are probably mostly illiterate."[444]

PRL social and economic policy drew criticism primarily because it did not implement the officially proclaimed principles of justice and social equality. Commenting on statements that appeared among the workers of Łódź workplaces in the autumn of 1964, the party officials wrote that "many people think that what we have at our disposal should be fairly divided within society."[445] On other occasions, this feature of shared consciousness found expression in the following opinion: "You have little to give, but you should give it fairly and evenly."[446] This sense of injury was accompanied by a belief that people in power had an unjustified sense of privilege. A streetcar operator from Łódź – a participant in a strike in 1957 – expressed it as follows: "We cannot even support our family modestly from our salary, we often lack even enough for bread, and how do others live? They buy cars for tens of thousands, televisions, they drink constantly, families have places by the sea – and we can only look on. [. . .] Directors, ministers, earn several thousand, and we have different stomachs?"[447] In 1959, during a period of food supply difficulties, letter writers often formulated the opinion that "it is good in Poland only for the communist elite; honest people in this system must die of hunger."[448]

The same way of thinking was expressed in letters about price increases from the year 1967. At the beginning of 1968, a resident of the Żywiec area wrote to Polish Radio that "an alarming increase in the disparity in how citizens are living has been observed. A new bourgeoisie has been born, although it does not have its own means of production. The current uncompensated price increase is nothing more than a further step toward deepened disparities. [. . .] The promised [. . .]

444 AODiZP, 1050/24, Biuletyn Biura Listów Komitetu do Spraw Radiofonii "Polskie Radio" nr 40, 30 maja 1958.

445 AAN, KC PZPR, 237/VII-5217, Informacja nr 65/A/4023 z 3 października 1964. Trudności w zaopatrzeniu ludności w mięso, p. 139.

446 AODiZP, 1050/23.

447 AODiZP, 1050/19, Biuletyn Biura Listów Komitetu do Spraw Radiofonii "Polskie Radio" nr 62, 20 września 1957.

448 AODiZP, 1050/34, Notatka Biura Listów Komitetu do Spraw Radiofonii "Polskie Radio," 20 lutego 1959. Nastroje i postulaty w listach słuchaczy do Polskiego Radia z 1958 r.

compensation from the payroll fund will come to nothing, because again it will go first into the pockets of the wealthy. So meat taken from the mouths of the poor will fall in part to those who have already achieved prosperity and can afford anyway to buy meat despite the increase."[449]

This sense of social inequality, based on material differences, was not merely a criterion marking the division between leaders and society. In colloquial interpretations, it formed the basis for the expression of highly varied and often emotional opinions about individual social groups. A transport worker in Gorlice, living in the countryside in 1968, wrote to Polish Radio: "Why [. . .] is there such a glaring difference between the physically employed man and the white-collar worker, why does a worker have to wait 10 years for one month of rest; why is the family benefit available only after three months and the coal allowance after a year of work? The harder the work, the less it pays. [. . .] Today, the press, our radio and other means of propaganda deplore the fate of striking English and French workers, and the fate of American Negroes, paying no attention to their own Negroes."[450]

Awareness of the material difficulties of everyday life in Gomułka's Poland inclined "John Does" to comment critically on any information that could be interpreted as manifestations of lavish lifestyles being led by people in authority. Per Diem expenses were often the subject of irritation. In 1957, engineer Roman Lewandowski asked in his letter to Polish Radio: "We are a literally poor country, recovering from the ground up at every stage of life. Therefore, do we have the right, duty and resources to arrange expensive conventions, congresses, festivals etc. with parties at every opportunity, giving guests gifts?"[451] In 1966, an anonymous author stated: "All this foreign travel costs a lot, one can do without it and then not have to increase the cost of rent, medicine, bread and necessities."[452]

---

449 AODiZP, 1208/1, Biuletyn Wewnętrzny Komitetu do Spraw Radia i Telewizji "Polskie Radio i Telewizja" nr 394, luty 1968. Statements involving resolutions from the X Plenum of KC PZPR.

450 AODiZP, 1208/2, Biuletyn Wewnętrzny Biura Listów Komitetu do Spraw Radia i Telewizji "Polskie Radio i Telewizja" nr 457, wrzesień 1968. Letters about the earnings and household budget of working-class families.

451 AODiZP, 1050/19, Biuletyn Biura Listów Komitetu do Spraw Radiofonii "Polskie Radio" nr 62.

452 AODiZP, 1050/73, Biuletyn Wewnętrzny Biura Listów Komitetu do Spraw Radia i Telewizji „„Polskie Radio i Telewizja" nr 280, sierpień 1966. Letters on price changes for some industrial and food products and on wage increases.

In a situation in which Poland was struggling with food supply difficulties and Polish living standards were low, criticism increased about the legitimacy of importing luxury goods and luxury items from abroad. Here is a typical opinion expressed in 1957: "With today's modest wages, can our world of work (both physical and intellectual) afford to buy foreign perfumes, liqueurs, wines, fountain pens, motorcycles, scooters, passenger cars, footwear for PLZ 1,500, antique women's material, underwear, etc., which today fill our shop exhibitions with temptation? [. . .]. And at the same time we wear out our shoes chasing butter, meat, eggs, flour, etc."[453] In a letter from 1959, this anonymous author wrote in the same spirit: "Are we exporting meat to the West, taking it from the poorest, in order in return to give the rich of our country the ability to spend cash on imported luxury goods, like oranges, lemons, wines and liqueurs, cosmetics, luxury fabrics and home appliances? I am convinced [. . .] that if the import of these luxuries were to cease, there would be no need to apply such drastic measures as robbing the poorest people of a piece of lard to smear on their potatoes or cabbage, because the poor have already forgotten about spreading bread with butter."[454]

This sense of poverty also evoked criticism of the cost of Poland's participation in international politics, and it was not just about spending on foreign visits.

In 1966–1967, colloquial thinking often tied price increases in Poland with the Vietnam War and the need to help Arab countries. In 1966, an anonymous sender wrote a letter to the radio which included: "Instead of giving foreign currency to Vietnam, it is better to send them those refrigerators that have become cheaper to cool down the temperament of the warrior, and then send televisions so that they have time to meditate without robbing other nations. Let them work like us, and they will be fine because in capitalist countries it can be done without war [. . .]."[455]

Even later, the motif of product shortages, including foodstuffs and their prices, appeared as a constant subject of complaint addressed to central party and state institutions. In the second half of the 1970s, letters regarding agricultural production and food constituted as much as 15 % of the total correspondence flowing into KC PZPR offices. In the second half of 1976, the lack of meat

453 Ibid.

454 AODiZP, 1050/29, Biuletyn Biura Listów Komitetu do Spraw Radiofonii "„„Polskie Radio" nr 53, 26 października 1959.

455 AODiZP, 1050/73, Biuletyn Wewnętrzny Biura Listów Komitetu do Spraw Radia i Telewizji "Polskie Radio i Telewizja" nr 280, sierpień 1966.

and meat products, sugar, groats, pasta, butter, margarine and other fats, as well as many everyday industrial articles, were the subject of particular criticism. Against the background of these shortcomings, the problem of "silent" price increases was sometimes mentioned in very harsh terms. Senders cited examples of price increases on so-called new products after officials had simply changed the label, name or packaging. The withdrawal of cheaper products was the focus of criticism especially for lower-paid workers, for large families, and for single-parent women. Authors of correspondence criticized not only the lack of meat and meat products but also the deteriorating quality of cold cuts. They also gave examples of various types of speculation and abuse. Similar problems dominated letters addressed to the MHWiU.[456]

Complaints about speculation in food products, about their high prices and deficiencies were also a constant topic in correspondence flowing to the central offices in the 1980s.[457] Criticism was particularly passionate about the food supply in letters received by the KC PZPR at the end of 1980 and in 1981. Meat rationing introduced in April 1981 in conditions marked by permanent shortages strongly influenced the shaping of negative social attitudes toward Poland's leaders. It is no accident that in a letter from May of that year, anonymous "residents of Łódź" wrote:

> The Polish nation is tormented to such an extent that it is at the end of its rope. Ever longer food queues are driving us to despair. One has to queue for meat and sausage cards. To get a scrap of meat and cold cuts using a card you have to queue for several hours. [. . .]. One enters the store, there is only meat, and they bring in the sausages 12 or 1, and there is not always the kind of meat or cold cuts you can buy with cards. In a word, it is a huge mess, because there is no proper organization. [. . .] You comrades at high

456 AAN, KC PZPR, 1797 (mikrofilm 2909), Ocena listów oraz sposobu rozwiązywania spraw podnoszonych przez ludność w 1976 roku, Biuro Listów i Inspekcji, p. 245; AAN, KC PZPR, 1809 (mikrofilm 2978), Informacja o problemach wynikających z listów, skarg i interwencji do KC PZPR i instancji partyjnych w 1978 r., p. 77; AAN, KC PZPR, 1814 (mikrofilm B 2983), Informacja o problemach wynikających z listów, skarg i interwencji kierowanych do instancji partyjnych w 1979 r., p. 596; AAN, MHWiU, 15/1, Wykaz statystyczny wpływu i sposobu załatwiania skarg (wniosków) w okresie od dnia 1 stycznia 1970 do 31 grudnia 1970, p. 23; ibid., Wykaz statystyczny wpływu i sposobu załatwiania skarg (wniosków) w okresie od dnia 1 stycznia 1971 do 31 grudnia 1971, p. 113.

457 See, among others, AAN, KC PZPR, XI/1066, Informacja nr 39/XII/86 o treści listów kierowanych do Komitetu Centralnego PZPR, Biuro Listów i Inspekcji (hereafter cited as BliI) KC, Warszawa, styczeń 1987, p. 4; ibid., Informacja o treści listów dotyczących problematyki cen, BliI, Warszawa 19 stycznia 1987, p. 22.

> levels do not feel all this because you are not standing in queues. We are curious whether you Comrades in the Central Committee and in the Government also receive with cards the 400 grams of cold cuts and the 400 grams of meat that a worker receives?[458]

They were followed by Barbara Buchała from Bielsko-Biała:

> All our nerves are exhausted. How long will it last – this scarcity of food? [. . .] People walk blindly through empty stores. Meat cards were issued – which do not cover even 50 %. The first variety was allocated in such quantities that it was laughable. In contrast, the second variety was not delivered to the store for a week. Day after day I visit the store [. . .] to buy something – in vain. [. . .] A working person is forced to get up at 5 instead of resting in order to stand in a queue to get something to eat, to live somehow. We are not surprised that worker productivity is decreasing, I myself cannot work calmly. [. . .] All our hope was that if there were cards, there would finally be some order. We were disappointed again. [. . .] Let some minister or dignitary try to live in this pit where it is calculated how much one can eat and what! Is this democratic?[459]

As before, at the beginning of the 1980s, letter writers expressed views testifying to the intensification of social tensions between urban and rural residents as a result of food supply difficulties. In one letter from 1981, sent from a medium-sized city, the author ironically calls peasants "victims," asking: "why do they (peasants) tell us to pay a dozen times more for their products? Is it fair to force just any prices on the free market? Why is there this excess of food products on the free market, if working-class children in the city are starving? Is this just justice?"[460] In this correspondence one can also find information about a little-known form of these tensions, namely the spontaneous removal of farmers from queues in cities where they were trying to buy meat.[461]

The above-cited correspondence provides evidence for the argument that the WE-THEM division of the world co-existed with an awareness, often passionately declared, of internal social divisions.

458 AAN, KC PZPR, XI/1065, Wybór listów nr 71, Warszawa maj 1981 r., BliI KC PZPR. Tematyka: Wypowiedzi, uwagi, propozycje dotyczące zaopatrzenia rynku, reglamentacji artykułów spożywczych, p. 169.

459 Ibid., p. 169.

460 Ibid., Wybór listów nr 71, Warszawa maj 1981 r., p. 171.

461 AAN, KC PZPR, XI/1065, Informacja o głównych problemach występujących w listach do instancji partyjnych w 1980 roku, Warszawa luty 1981 r., p. 509.

1.2. Other Forms of Written Statements

Complaints addressed to party and state institutions were not the only forms of written expression in which we can find opinions about food supply difficulties in Poland.

In the Silesian Footwear Factories in Otmęt, during elections to worker councils in 1952, the following were written onto voting cards: "kiss our asses (in German)," "give us bread, meat, and then we will vote" (in German); "Give us more butter and meat" (in Polish). A swastika was drawn next to two names.[462]

The preserved files of cases considered by the KS contain information about leaflets (including their originals) that included critical comments regarding material conditions, including food shortages. The files of the case of Ludmiła K., accused of putting up leaflets in Kościan between December 1951 and July 1952 containing the following content: "We want meat and other food"; "Come to Poland, Eisenhower, but by bike because Stalin will take everything from us"; "We want meat, lard, sausage, milk butter, etc . . .!!!"[463]

Food supply difficulties found expression in "hostile inscriptions" that appeared with varying frequency usually on walls surrounding production plants or other public buildings. The word "meat" did not appear in them, in part because the symbol of demands in terms of improved material conditions in general was the demand for bread. It is probably impossible to determine the number of such inscriptions, but their systematic appearance is hard to doubt.

It is possible that the frequency of such symbolic and concise expressions of economic demands was significantly influenced by slogans formulated by the rebellious workers of Poznań in June 1956.[464] After all, nurse Stefania Goćwińska, hung banners on the PUWP Provincial Committee building in Poznan, after it was overrun by demonstrators on 28 June 1956, which read: "Freedom" and "Bread." On the same day, four banners were prepared for demonstrators, whose content was as follows: "We want to eat," "We demand bread," "Down with bloodsuckers,"

---

462 ARZ, CRZZ, Sekretariat Zygmunta Kratko 13, Notatka informacyjna dla Przewodniczącego CRZZ tow. W. Kłosiewicza, Warszawa 17 maja 1952, p. 39.

463 AAN, Komisja Specjalna do Walki z Nadużyciami i Szkodnictwem Gospodarczym (hereafter as: KS), 471, Akta sprawy Ludmiły Krysman.

464 On 28 June 1956 workers at Poznań's largest workplaces (including the Zakłady Przemysłu Metalowego H. Cegielski in Poznań, then called the Zakłady Metalowe im. Józefa Stalina w Poznaniu – ZISPO) struck and organized street demonstrations, bloodily suppressed by the army. Nearly 60 people died at the time or died later as a result of their wounds.

and "We demand wage increases, lower prices."[465] As Paweł Machcewicz pointed out, the sense of material misery, along with other factors, was rooted in the genesis of the decision to strike in "ZISPO." Already on 23 June 1956, one of the workers of this factory, referring to the Poznań International Fair that was taking place, expressed the following moods: "Let foreigners see that there is poverty in Poland and there is nothing to eat."[466]

From that moment, inscriptions and leaflets expressing protest against material conditions of being also appeared in other places. In Warsaw, already on 28 June 1956, an inscription appeared on the wall of the building of the Urząd of the Capital City of Warsaw: "We want bread, down with communism." A leaflet was found in the building of the Fireproofing Materials Factory in Świdnica on the night of 29–30 June: "Worker, what you spend through bloody sweat on a piece of bread, let those who feed on you hear your voice. Underground." On 4 July, an inscription appeared on the rettery building in Ełk: "Poznań workers demand bread, freedom and peace." On 21 July 1956, another slogan was found at the Potato Plant in Luboń: "Porridge in the morning, noodles in the evening, our Poland, but the Russian government."[467]

This type of inscriptions, both indicating dissatisfaction with both the material situation and expressing political demands, also appeared later. Here are some characteristic examples.

According to Interior Ministry files, a hand-printed inscription in capital letters was posted on January 6, 1958 inside one of the buildings at the Jeleniogórskie Zakłady Celulozy i Włókien Sztucznych ("Celwiskoza"), whose workers were preparing to strike. It said: "Attention, we employees of Celwiskozy want bread and demand a larger bonus, because if you don't give it to us blood will be in our plant [. . .]."[468]

On 16 November 1959, a photo ("cut out from a foreign newspaper") was posted at the entrance gate of the Lubańska Furniture Factory in Olsztyn in the Lubań Śląski powiat showing a group of people marching with a banner. Above the photo was the following text: "Because the blood of workers is on it" (a line from "The Internationale"), and below it: "We demand bread and freedom. We demand higher wages. We demand free elections." Security officers assumed that

465 *Poznański Czerwiec 1956*, eds. Jarosław Maciejewski, Zofia Trojanowiczowa (Poznań: Wydawnictwo Poznańskie, 1990), 74 and 79.

466 Paweł Machcewicz, *Polski rok 1956* (Warszawa: "Mówią Wieki," 1993), 81.

467 Ibid., 112–117.

468 IPN BU, 1585/982, KG MO, Telefonogram nr 578/58 do Dyrektora Gabinetu wiceministra i Departamentu III MSW, Wrocław 7 I 1958, p. 175.

this photo was taken by a foreign correspondent during the "Poznań incidents" of 1956.[469] A leaflet found on 30 November 1959 at 8:30 pm on a street in Jelenia Góra said: "Poles – the communist is our enemy. Work, salary increases and lower prices for industrial goods and food are required. Down with communism."[470]

On25 August 1966, Marian Pasieczny was detained on the premises of the Port Authority in Gdynia; he had painted the following on the walls of PKP (Polskie Koleje Państwowe, Polish State Railways) warehouses and train cars: "We demand a pay increase, we demand work and bread."[471] In 1967, the following demand appeared on coal carts in the "Wałbrzych" mine: "Give us meat because we are on strike."[472]

The authorities of that time treated leaflets distributed around Myślibórz on 1 May 1963 as a manifestation of enemy activity, one of which read: "Lenin clothed the naked, fed the hungry, and you what you do?"[473] In 1967 in Łódź, 35 leaflets were distributed saying: "Down with communist louts. Give us more meat and better wages."[474]

A lack of detailed research makes it difficult to answer questions about the scale of this phenomenon and how it changed over time. However, the examples presented above indicate that inscriptions and leaflets expressing dissatisfaction with the food supply situation were a permanent part of Polish everyday life.

2. The Spoken Word

2.1. Rumors . . .

The fact that food supply problems played an extremely important role in everyday thinking is also evidenced by the content of rumors that spread throughout Poland since the 1940s. Without going into theoretical considerations about their role in social life[475] and definitional disputes, we treat rumors

469 IPN BU, MSW II, 1585/2263, Biuletyn Informacyjny MSW nr 15/59, 1 XII 1959, p. 146.

470 IPN BU, MSW II, 1585/2263, Biuletyn Informacyjny MSW nr 16/59, 21 XII 1959 r., p. 171.

471 IPN BU, KG MO, 1078 (121/13), Depesza szyfrowa wchodząca nr 1824 z KW MO Gdańsk z 26 VIII 1966.

472 AAN, PG, 1/13, Notatka informacyjna, 22 XI 1967, p. 5.

473 AAN, KC PZPR, 237/VII-3971, Informacja nr 38/A/3887, 1 V 1963, p. 104.

474 AAN, PG, 1/13, p. 5.

475 See Jarosz, Maria Pasztor, *W krzywym zwierciadle. Polityka władz komunistycznych w Polsce w świetle plotek i pogłosek z lat 1949–1956* (Warszawa: Fakt, 1995), 3–19; Piotr Łukasiewicz, *Pogłoski i dowcip polityczny w PRL* (Warszawa: In Plus, 1987), 6–8.

in the below analysis as a certain "proposition to believe," usually spread from person to person, mainly (though not necessarily) through oral communication regarding events that are important to society or a particular group. This information is neither proven nor rejected. In our understanding, the rumor is a "lowercase rumor" and usually contains low-priority, trivial and malicious messages about other people's matters, often of a personal nature, usually spreading to a small audience. Truthfulness is imposed on the communicated news according to socially established criteria, and not over the course of evidentiary discourse.

The Polish People's Republic was a country which was particularly fertile ground for this type of message, for which there were several basic reasons.

First of all, throughout the years 1944/1945–1989, although to varying degrees, the public articulation of views different from those imposed by Poland's rulers faced systematic difficulties. Censorship and self-censorship, systematic harassment and repression – these are just the most important mechanisms and methods restricting freedom of speech. At the same time, official propaganda interpreted events of importance to society in a manner inconsistent with the feelings and attitudes of its recipients; it presented something of them only vaguely, or it omitted them. As we wrote in another publication:

> The divergence of the "world of performance" and reality meant that Poles treated the information broadcast from the center of authority suspiciously, they were taught to read it in a special way – translating the language of newspeak into a language understood concretely by the general public. People learned lessons not only from what was officially written but also from what official communications did not contain." In a situation where "spectacular and important events often cannot be exposed through normal informational channels, they become the subject of rumors.[476]

In reality of postwar Poland, rumors were often a kind of "spoken resistance" against authority. They are used in all closed societies; they filled the place taken up by credible news in open societies, helped to tone down emotions and tensions caused by a hunger for information, and gave the feeling that one was not completely manipulated.

A significant part of the rumors spread in postwar Poland expressed pessimism associated with the current and predicted material situation of large social groups. This manifest pessimism was particularly strong during the Stalinist period, which is associated with the economic development model that preferred heavy industry and the collectivization of agriculture. Very often, an additional

476 Jarosz, Pasztor, *W krzywym zwierciadle*, 12–13.

impulse for strengthened pessimism was periodically exacerbated deficiencies in the food market.

Already in 1945–1948, this aspect of deterioration in material living conditions, including food supplies, was also found in many colloquial statements related to internal and international events, both those that actually took place and those that were expected. Here are a few examples.

In October 1946, a rumor was spread around Warsaw saying that after the UNRRA suspended supplies, there would be terrible hunger in Poland and the government "will not be able to meet the tasks related to feeding the entire population."[477] In May 1947, in a village near Warsaw, peasants talked about the imminent outbreak of a Soviet-Turkish war, and "because Poland signed a mutual assistance agreement with the Soviet Union, so the grain stored by state institutions is being transferred to Soviet warehouses."[478] Near Warsaw, a commuter train commander claimed that the Polish government had signed a contract for the export of potatoes to the American occupation zone in Germany.[479]

It seems important, based on materials analyzed above, that already in this period certain thematic motifs appeared in the content of rumors, which in the following years were, in varying degrees, repeated and reproduced.

In particular, rumors emphasized the link between material shortages in Poland and Soviet domination. Such rumors took several forms. In May 1947, in various regions of the country, there was talk of the alleged purchase of grain by the Russians, which was supposed to prove that hunger existed in the USSR.[480] In 1946, the motif of the USSR's colonial exploitation of Poland appeared most frequently in this type of rumor, exploitation that involved the export of not only food, including grain, but also gifts received under UNRRA assistance – thread, vodka, salt, light bulbs, etc.[481]

---

477 *Biuletyny Informacyjne Ministerstwa Bezpieczeństwa Publicznego 1946,* eds. Wanda Chudzik, Irena Marczak, Marek Olkuśnik (Warszawa: Ministerstwo Spraw Wewnętrznych, 1996), 61.

478 *Biuletyny Informacyjne Ministerstwa Bezpieczeństwa Publicznego 1947*, vol. 1, eds. Bernadetta Grodek, Irena Marczak (Warszawa: Ministerstwo Spraw Wewnętrznych, 1993), 69.

479 Ibid., 192.

480 Ibid., 80.

481 Kamiński, "Plotka i pogłoska polityczna w Polsce w świetle akt Ministerstwa Informacji i Propagandy (1945–1947)," in *Wrocławskie studia z historii najnowszej*, ed. Wojciech Wrzesiński, IV (1997): 173.

The theme of Poles experiencing material harm was strongly embedded in various anti-Semitic rumors being spread at that time. The old motif of Jews using the blood of Christian children to produce matzo gained strengthened. In May 1947, information about gruesome rumors that Jews were committing murders arrived at the Ministry of Public Security, one of which claimed that in Chorzów "numerous murders on adults and babies have occurred. People are bloodthirsty and murder in order to meet their own needs and the needs of others." In Toruń – according to another rumor – "baby thieves walk around the city and steal children who are slaughtered for soap, canned food and sausages. The police have detected several such gangs. Recently a Jewish woman with two children was caught." In Wrocław, a slaughterhouse was reportedly discovered "where Jews killed children and sold their meat."[482] A similar message was noted by ministry officers in Rzeszów in July 1947: "A nine-year-old girl was killed again, the Jews certainly ate her and that is why they are fleeing Rzeszów."[483]

This anti-Semitism also found its way into less gruesome accounts of the alleged privileges that Jews enjoyed in the supply of everyday goods, including food.[484]

Rumors predicting food difficulties or even hunger were particularly widespread in connection with the decision to collectivize agriculture in the summer of 1948.[485] The threat that private peasant farms would be liquidated and replaced with production cooperatives, modeled on those operating in the USSR and considered synonymous in Poland with collective farms, triggered a wide array of negative associations. Poles repressed during the war and sent to Soviet labor camps (labor camps) repeated that, as in these camps, they would be forced in cooperatives to eat meals from a "common pot."[486] A farmer from the Sochaczew powiat claimed in the autumn of 1948: "In the kolkhoz half of the people work while the other half loafs around because they have no strength to work. For their work, they receive a bowl of soup and a piece of bread, one item of clothing per year, rag shoes ... because there are no leather shoes in the USSR."[487] In

482 *Biuletyny Informacyjne Ministerstwa Bezpieczeństwa Publicznego 1947*, 82.

483 Ibid., 135.

484 Ibid., 92.

485 Collectivization consisted primarily of the liquidation of private farms and the creation of collective farms (production cooperatives). This process took place in the face of manifest opposition by peasants. In Poland, unlike most other Eastern Bloc countries, after 1956 collectivization was not continued on a mass scale.

486 Jarosz, Pasztor, *W krzywym zwierciadle*, 45.

487 AAN, KC PPR, 295/IX-415, Ankieta MBP na temat stosunków na wsi, 23 IX 1948, p. 130.

this atmosphere, in September 1948, a rumor spread in one township that kolkhozes had already been organized in Poland in which Soviet commissars were working.[488]

Rumors in which the production cooperative (called by peasants a collective farm) was a symbol of hunger also appeared later.[489]

Due to the intensification of food supply difficulties in 1949, were spread in Olsztyn Voivodeship (in northern Poland) that there is hunger in Silesia, that "women are throwing themselves under cars to avoid starvation," and potatoes sent there from other provinces were highly sought after.[490] In 1951, in one of the production cooperatives, its members were concerned about information that there had been clashes in Szczecin due to lack of bread. In the same year, a worker from Łódź reportedly claimed that soon "potatoes would run out." A year earlier in the east of the country there was a rumor that the United States had stopped importing meat from Poland and because of that, rotten meat had been delivered to Kraków shops; as a result 700 people reportedly died there.

Some of these rumors had the macabre character described earlier. It is difficult to define as anything other than macabre information from one village in 1952 about the fact that the trial of nine people was about to being dealing with the sale of human meat. Another source from this year talked about the 12-month punishment in a labor camp given to a person who in Łódź (the second largest city in Poland) had allegedly disseminated "hostile propaganda" that "children were being kidnapped to Szczecin, where human flesh was fabricated into meat products." In this situation, it is not surprising that in a letter to the Polish Radio, one listener in 1954 asked: "Apparently in recent years it has happened that people killed for sausages, as it was discovered in Szczecin. Maybe it is still happening, because in Poland there is not enough meat, pork fat and sausage. I often hear that they are catching people for having killed, so I'd like to ask if it's true."

Among the reasons for food supply difficulties identified in this type of communication, what appeared most often was the motif of food exported to the USSR. In 1949, rumors claimed among other things that "Russia is taking everything from us to feed China, Indonesia, the workers of France and Italy."

488 Jarosz, "Relacja Artura Starewicza p nastrojach społecznych na wsi w sierpniu 1948 r.," *Dzieje Najnowsze* 2 (1993): 106.

489 Jarosz, Pasztor, *W krzywym zwierciadle*, 31.

490 Unless otherwise stated, all information about rumors from 1949–1956 comes from *W krzywym zwierciadle*, 81–92.

In another version, the Soviets were reportedly taking "everything from Poland [. . .] to Berlin." In 1950–1951, Polish food was allegedly being delivered to Korea in connection with the war. The credibility of this rumor was served by the rumor circulating in 1951 that "the Americans had detected meat of Polish origin in a Korean warehouse and had seized two meat wagons that were going to Korea."

The motif of Poland's deteriorating food situation was at the root of the rumors accompanying various events inside Poland. On the occasion of the National Census in December 1950, some peasants reportedly claimed that it was carried out to detect reserves, "because after the new year ration cards will be introduced for all items." According to other accounts, livestock was then recorded so that it could be picked up and sold at discounted prices.

From time to time, waves of rumors swept through Poland about imminent prices increases of basic foodstuffs, which usually resulted in the mass purchase of goods. For example, in March 1949 in Warsaw it was rumored that fat vouchers for families and children would be abolished and that the ration card for meat would be reduced to 7 dkg per week! Such standards were supposedly already in force in some Polish cities.

In this situation, it is understandable that actual price increases of foodstuffs or their regulation have "grown" into various, often fantastic messages. In March 1951, the introduction into circulation of high-quality, expensive sausages was often seen as a harbinger of price increases for meat products of all ranges. A partial rationing of these products in August 1951 resulted in speculation that ration cards were about to be introduced for all basic necessities, including butter, eggs, milk, etc. Similar reactions were caused by the regulation of trade in goods implemented on January 3, 1953 (abolition of ration cards, price and wage increases). Rumors predicted a massive increase in basic food prices, including bread prices that would be much higher than officially announced.

The pessimism contained in rumors about food supplies weakened slightly in 1953–1956, which should be associated with the progress of the political thaw that came in the wake of Stalin's death, as indicated mainly by comments made regarding the reduction of prices for certain food and industrial products as of November 1953. While some rumors anticipated rapid wage reductions, which caused another run on shops, other rumors anticipated in January 1954 a wage rise and a gradual reduction in food, footwear and clothing prices.

The October 1956 changes briefly strengthened hopes, expressed in rumors, that the material situation would improve. However, at least from the end of 1957, rumors predicting a deterioration in the Polish standard of living appear increasingly often. Already in October of that year, the Office of Letters of the Radio Broadcasting Committee received more and more correspondence containing requests to respond to "speculation circulating" about the cost of exchanging money and price increases (as 1 January 1958) for coal, gas, electricity, housing rent and train tickets.[491] Similar rumors were contained in letters as of the end of 1958.[492]

A large wave of correspondence on this topic reached Polish Radio at the end of 1959. Rumors were that sugar, meat and "everything in general" would be cheaper.[493] And people speculated that housing rents and bus and train ticket prices would rise, as would the cost of currency exchanges, while worker earnings would decrease and women would experience mass layoffs.[494]

In the 1960s, there were waves of rumors regarding food supplies. For example, in July 1960, rumors about a rise in bread, sugar and gasoline prices circulated in Szczecin. A large wave of colloquial messages swept through Poland in May 1963 referring to food price rises and the cost of exchanging money. Similar rumors were noted in many regions of Poland in 1967.[495]

As in the Stalinist period, people sought the causes behind unsatisfactory material conditions, and they found them in, among other places, the structures of the PRL's subordination to Moscow and the resulting international obligations. As early as 1959, letters sent to Polish Radio stated: "As for the price increase for meat, one hears that the Russians are taking meat from us."[496]

The lack of detailed research from the 1970s and the 1980s makes it difficult to point to the "food-related" contexts of rumors from those years. We know, however, that as market deficiencies grew during the collapse of the internal market in 1981, so did the public perception that the government was responsible for these deficiencies; government officials became the scapegoat. It was then that a rumor spread that state authorities were deliberately storing food in order to starve the nation. This view of society and government as two separate subjects

491 AODiZP, 1050/19, Biuletyn Biura Listów Komitetu do Spraw Radiofonii "Polskie Radio," nr 69, 23 października 1957.

492 AODiZP, 1050/26, Biuletyn Biura Listów Komitetu do Spraw Radiofonii "Polskie Radio" nr 73, 10 grudnia 1958.

493 AODiZP, 1050/29, Biuletyn Biura Listów Komitetu do Spraw Radiofonii "Polskie Radio" nr 50, 17 października 1959.

494 AODiZP 1050/29, Biuletyn Biura Listów Komitetu do Spraw Radiofonii "Polskie Radio" nr 60, 9 grudnia 1959.

495 Zaremba, *Społeczeństwo polskie lat sześćdziesiątych*, 31–48.

496 AODiZP 1050/29, Biuletyn Biura Listów Komitetu do Spraw Radiofonii "Polskie Radio" nr 53, 26 października 1959.

of social processes with different goals is characteristic – as has already been pointed out – of other kinds of colloquial messages, too.[497]

The content of rumors involving various aspects of the PRL's material situation indicates that such rumors were dominated by an ongoing fear that things would deteriorate. Poles usually anticipated that PRL officials, for both domestic and international reasons, were willing to increase prices on everyday articles, including meat and meat products.

2.2. . . . And More

The attitude held by various social groups toward food shortages in Poland was expressed not only in rumors but also during various meetings and conversations. Their content is partly known not only thanks to reports prepared by agents and informers of the political police but also by report materials produced by employees of other party and state institutions.

An important source of knowledge about such communications are the files of the abovementioned KS, which punished negative comments on Stalinist reality calling them enemy propaganda. Here are some typical examples.

A janitor in one of the NBP branches was sentenced in 1951 to several months in a labor camp for "for persistently [. . .] spreading false news. [. . .] In October 1951 [. . .], he said that there was no meat in Poland because it was being exported to the USSR, Korea and East Germany for propaganda, and we had nothing to eat here in Poland."[498] Similar information about the export of meat to the USSR and East Germany was disseminated at the same time by a musician at a "catering establishment" in Poznań called "Syrena." It cost him nine months in a labor camp.[499] In October 1951, the KS examined the case of a technician working at FSO in Warsaw, the accusation being that:

> [. . .] in the period from June to September 1951, at the factory in Warsaw [. . .], he spread false information that could cause significant damage to the interests of the Polish State, calling the battle against speculation a mere scam, [claiming that] in fact the lack of meat is caused by peasants having nothing to feed pigs because they [officials] have taken away excess grain, and what meat is produced is exported to Germany and Russia, and that the current governments will not last long.

497 Łukasiewicz, *Pogłoska i dowcip polityczny w PRL*, 17.

498 AAN, KS, 354, Rozpowszechnianie fałszywych wiadomości o gospodarce żywnościowej Polski przez robotnika w Pszczynie, p. 1.

499 AAN, KS, 377, Rozpowszechnianie fałszywych wiadomości o trudnościach aprowizacyjnych oraz zmianie ustroju w Polsce przez muzyka w Poznaniu, p. 2.

The author of these statements was sentenced to 18 months in a labor camp.[500] A similar verdict was handed down in 1953 in the case of a power plant worker in northern Poland. He reportedly claimed in private talks that "the current harsh conditions [. . .] arise from friendship with the USSR, that the worker is paid little, everything is taken from the farmer and delivered to the USSR, and it is difficult for Poles to survive in such a situation."[501]

Difficulties in the food supply significantly affected the conflict between urban workers and those who lived in the countryside (peasant-workers). In November 1951, the deputy head of one of the Warsaw factories claimed at a meeting of the PZPR cell that there was no meat because "there is no one to graze pigs since the shepherds had gone to the Polytechnic." In January 1953, one party cell meeting demanded that "peasants from the countryside not be allowed to work in the city, because farming was neglected and agricultural production was reduced."[502] Similar anti-peasant moods caused by food difficulties were recorded in 1959. In the Bierut Steal Works and the Częstochowianka textile factory in Częstochowa, workers came to the PZPR Factory Committee and pointed out peasants by name who owned farms and worked in the factory, throwing insults at them. Workers demand that the peasants leave the factory and take up farming."[503] Comments about the fact that "the party cares for and helps the peasant and that it cares for the worker less and less" were also noted at workplaces in the Bydgoszcz Voivodeship.[504] This type of explanation appeared often at meetings devoted to discussions of the new labor standards introduced in 1960. "Workers in conversations said that 'too much falls immediately on the shoulders of workers.' In addition to changing standards, they anticipated price increases for meat, an increase in vacation fees, and in rail travel. They said that peasants and officials do not bear such burdens."[505]

Sociologists came upon a similar manifestation of the conflict between urban and rural workers in 1960, when they studied the morality of work at the Ludwik Waryński Industrial Construction Plant in Warsaw: "In the factory,

500 AAN, KS, 388, Rozpowszechnianie fałszywych wiadomości o polityce żywnościowej w Polsce przez technika w Warszawie, p. 1.

501 AAN, KS, 404, Rozpowszechnianie fałszywych wiadomości o warunkach bytowych robotników i polityce żywnościowej Polski, p. 12.

502 Błażej Brzostek, *Robotnicy Warszawy. Konflikty codzienne (1950–1954)* (Warszawa: TRIO, 2002), 76.

503 AAN, KC PZPR, 237/VII-3967, Informacja nr 33/A/3614, 6 października 1959, p. 86.

504 AAN, KC PZPR, 237/VII-3967, Informacja nr 25/A/3606, 24 sierpnia 1959, p.. 70.

505 AAN, KC PZPR, 237/VII-3963, Informacja nr 13/1962 z 19 lutego 1960, p. 80.

workers coming from the countryside and having backup in the countryside are commonly called 'round ones' (they usually look good)." Opinions emerged from the interviews that "they are different from the rest of us by the way they dress. Nicely dressed, they have enough for everything, for vodka. This is not something we see with city workers. [. . .] The city worker [. . .] is indignant, aggressive, and the rural one does not resist, he is always quiet. [. . .] This is only competition for us – he doesn't demand anything and doesn't want anything, 1,500 zlotys is enough, because they give him food in the countryside, and when I don't have 2,000, I scream."[506] It happened that city workers often called colleagues from the village "boors."[507]

Workers were upset by price increases, especially for groceries. Such moods were expressed by, among others, workers in 1964 at the Nowotko Mechanical Plant in Warsaw. According to Interior Ministry informants, these workers supposedly said: "[. . .] so what that industrial and social investments are planned, and even lower prices for some industrial products, since they compensate for silent increases in food prices. As a result, the worker only loses twice as much. In the first years after liberation, although the country was destroyed – the working class was doing better than after twenty years of the PRL. It's getting worse and there are no prospects for improvement."[508]

A specific form of this type of message involved postulates and slogans chanted at various demonstrations, expressing protest against the material conditions of life (and about which we write more below).

Finally, it is worth mentioning a different kind of spoken word communicating a critical attitude toward food-related difficulties, including meat shortages, namely the political joke. Like a rumor, a political joke contains a message that circulates informally in social communication, but with less expressive genre features. By its nature, it deforms the image of reality, though is still

506 ATNS OBOP, 9.36, Danuta Markowska, Zbigniew Sufin, *Moralność pracy i zjawiska z nią związane w zakładzie przemysłowym (sprawozdanie z badań monograficznych w Zakładzie Budowy Urządzeń Przemysłowych im. Ludwika Waryńskiego w Warszawie).*

507 Grzegorz Miernik, "Dzień powszedni robotników w województwie kieleckim w okresie stalinowskim," in *Z przeszłości regionu świętokrzyskiego od XVI do XX wieku*, ed. Jacek Wijaczka (Kielce: Jard, 2003), 140.

508 IPN BU, KG MO, 1585/982, Komenda MO województwa warszawskiego do Dyrektora Departamentu III MSW, Warszawa 25 IV 1964, Informacja dotycząca nastrojów wśród załóg niektórych zakładów przemysłowych na terenie Warszawy, p. 139.

an interesting source of knowledge about the colloquial perception, atmosphere and climate of the era.[509]

Both in published anthologies of political jokes from the PRL and those found in archival sources, meat as a subject appears relatively often. The object of mockery was, of course, meat shortages. One of them, from the period between 1945 and 1956, was to read as follows: "Only pig heads were brought to the butcher's shop. Kowalska bought one such head. But after leaving the store, she began to punch the head. "What are you doing?" a passing policeman asked. "I am beating its head so that it tells me where its ass is."[510]

Both "systemic conditions" – meat shortages and the need to queue for meat – were the subject of ridicule in another political "joke" from before 1956, which went like this: "socialism, communism and capitalism arranged to meet. Capitalism and communism are waiting in the agreed place. Finally, socialism arrives and says:

- Sorry for the delay, but I was standing in line for meat.
- What is a line? – capitalism asked.
- And what is meat? – communism asked."[511]

Sometimes, jokes were given a more or less light "erotic coloration." In one of them, a prominent doctor agreed to treatment of a female patient provided that she give him one night. "Embarrassed, the patient agrees. [. . .] The doctor explains: – From the evening until seven in the morning you will stand in line for meat, and then my wife will relieve you . . ."[512]

Queuing for meat was the subject of many other jokes appearing throughout the PRL's entire existence. In 1963, one joke went like this: "What is a long, twisting, colorful, and lives mainly off dairy? . . . The line to a butcher shop."[513] In

---

509 Łukasiewicz, *Pogłoska i dowcip polityczny w PRL*, 27; Tomasz Szarota, "Śmiech zakazany – kawał (dowcip) polityczny jako informacja o postrzeganiu peerelowskiej rzeczywistości," *Polska 1944/45–1989. Studia i materiały* V (2001): 213; Norbert Wójtowicz, "Dowcip polityczny w Polsce Ludowej w latach 1944–1956," *Studia i materiały z dziejów opozycji i oporu społecznego*, ed. Kamiński, I (1998): 74–75.

510 *Dowcip surowo wzbroniony. Antologia polskiego dowcipu politycznego*, vol. 2 (Toruń: Comer, 1991), 12.

511 Ibid., 11.

512 Ibid., 22.

513 *Nie tylko do śmiechu*, 66.

another, the queue is "something long," at least 30 meters in length, which "has many legs and is carnivorous, but must be satisfied with potatoes."[514]

Malicious comments about Poland's eastern neighbor were often additional but important motifs in food-related political jokes. The hero of one of them was a poor man who, "wanting to show Bierut the 'prosperity' prevailing in the country, sat in front of party headquarters and ate hay. Fearing the scandal, Bierut sent one of his ministers to give the poor man PLZ 1,000. and sent him to a restaurant. Having seen such a turn of events, the poor man soon went to Moscow. He sat in front of the Kremlin walls and chewed hay. This time Stalin came to him and said: – Hey man! Keep hay for the winter, now it's summer, eat some grass."[515]

Beliefs about food shortages in the USSR survived the Stalinist period, since during Nikita Khrushchev's rule there appeared in Warsaw a joke with the "queue" leitmotiv: "What is 150 meters long and eats cabbage? – A meat line in the Soviet Union."[516]

In other jokes, the motif combining food supply difficulties in Poland with the export of foodstuffs to the USSR was clear.

Such was the message in the following joke: "what is the relationship between the butcher shop and the pig farm?" – "The Soviet Union."[517]

Another joke: "What does a Polish pig dream about on the way to the slaughterhouse? That at least its heart would remain in the country."[518]

Jokes often commented on price increases for food, gas and electricity. In 1963, in Warsaw, the ironic answer to the question: "why have no food cards been introduced?" was "to save paper."[519] The fundamental question of why there was no meat in Poland was answered with: because oxen work and rams govern.[520] This last joke dated back to the Stalinist period, when it was told in slightly different forms ("Why are there no fish? – To divert attention from the lack of meat . . . – And why is there lack of meat? – Because oxen are pulling the six-year plan and pigs are sitting in the party and government;"[521] "Why is

514 Adam Rosenbusch, *Śmiech zakazany. Antologia dowcipu politycznego Polski Ludowej* (Melbourne: Harold Press, 1987), 63.
515 *Dowcip surowo wzbroniony*, 15.
516 Jan Bigben, *Warszawski dowcip. Kawał Warszawy 1945–1968* (Toronto, 1980), 93
517 *Dowcip surowo wzbroniony*, 74.
518 Ibid., 74.
519 Bigben, *Warszawski dowcip*, 95.
520 Bigben, *Warszawski dowcip*, 95.
521 *Klapa bezpieczeństwa, czyli humor zakurtynowy*, ed. Aleksander Janta (Buffalo, 1953), 106.

there no meat in Poland? – Because pigs are at the troughs, cows in the Women's League [a mass women's organization in the PRL], and oxen – they work"[522]). In 1967, one witty comment on the meat price increase went like this: "Why is there more and more talk in Poland these days about UFOs? Because after the meat price increase, empty plates are appearing in a growing number of kitchens."[523] Food supply difficulties caused led to a growth in malicious comments about Władysław Gomułka, who at the end of his rule was called "the creator of the meatless age" in Poland.[524] The carcass of the "unsinkable" PRL Prime Minister Józef Cyrankiewicz encouraged a series of stinging jokes in which the food supply played a role. One of them, registered in 1965, asked: "What has the current system given the people? Skim milk, skim cheese and a fat prime minister."[525]

Jokes with food-related difficulties in the background were also spread after 1970. Children left unattended in Polish kindergartens had a rhyme for Edward Gierek, the first secretary of the KC PZPR in the years 1970–1980, with the following content: "There is no meat, there is no cheese – And this is Mr. Gierek's fault – One two three, and you will be Secretary!"[526] Another joke was set in a butcher's shop. An impatient customer standing in a long queue "speaks to the man standing in front of him – Please hold my place in line and I will pop over to the Central Committee [PZPR – referring to the Dom Partii, the Party House, in Warsaw] and I will give Gierek a piece of my mind. – Go, go. After a few minutes he returns. – Why did you come back so soon? asks the other man in line. – If you only saw the queue in front of the Central Committee, it's three times longer than this one."[527]

Gierek was also ridiculed because of Poland's export policy, which – it was widely believed – contributed to meat shortages. This is the sense of the following joke: "People accused Gierek of exporting 9/10 of meat with only 1/10 remaining in the country. Gierek tried to prove that just the opposite was the case: what stays in the country are four legs, a snout, the tail, lungs, the left ear, and the right ear, which means exactly 9/10 stays in the country."[528]

Finally, the combination of the "food motif" with Wojciech Jaruzelski (First Secretary of the KC PZPR in 1980–1989 and chairman of the Council of State 1985–1989) took the following form in 1982: "Do you know that a new sausage

522 Ibid., 129.
523 *Nie tylko do śmiechu*, 87.
524 Ibid., 104.
525 Ibid., 76.
526 Ibid., 130.
527 *Dowcip surowo wzbroniony*, 81.
528 Ibid., 82.

is coming out? – Which one? – It's called the Podjaruzelska. And do you know why it has not appeared yet? – No! – Because there is no one to kill this pig!"[529]

Food problems were also an important topic of anonymous political poetry and ballads, often sung to the tune of well-known songs.

Already in December 1970, in songs sung by striking workers on the Baltic Coast, one of the most important thematic threads was hunger, functioning – like bread – rather as a stylistic figure. The best example of such a song is a fragment from an anonymous song sung in Gdańsk at the time: "Gomułka has everything he wants – and who gives us poor folk bread – because we already know what hunger is." In a fragment of an anonymous workers' poem from that time, its author clearly indicates who starves the workers, namely Poland's rulers in the name of great slogans and socialist ideas: "Are the ideas of class not more important – than salceson, ham and sausage."[530]

During the strike in August 1980 at the Lenin shipyard workers sang a song that retained the style and rhythm of the famous Polish popular hit "Kolorowe jarmarki" with the words:

"Kiedy widzę przez szybę Puste haki na tle bieli, Myślę wtedy gdzie wędliny Czy je diabli wzięli? Gdzie zginęły przez te czasy? Balerony i kiełbasy Szynki schaby i rolady. Ale zawsze wam powiem, Że najbardziej mi żal: Pieczonego prosiaka Z przedświątecznej wystawy Bez kolejki schaboszczaka I prawdziwej kawy,	"When I look through the glass Empty hooks on a white background, I wonder then, where are the cold cuts Did the devils take them? Where did they die over time? Smoked hams and sausages Pork hams and roulades. But I'll always tell you What I most regret: Roast piglet From the pre-Christmas offering A cutlet with no queue And real coffee

529 Wojciech Łysiak, *Wielka kontestacja. Folklor polityczny w PRL* (Poznań: PSO, 1998), 146.

530 Anna Błaszkiewicz, "Prawda i konwencja. Analiza poezji robotniczej okresu napięć społecznych (grudzień 1970 i sierpień 1980)," *Studia nad ruchami społecznymi*, eds. Ewa Lewicka-Banaszak, Piotr Marciniak, Wojciech Modzelewski (Warszawa: Uniwersytet Warszawski, 1987), 210–211.

Rozłożonych na półkach W czekoladzie rodzynek, Ziemniaczanej mąki I bez dewiz szynek."[a]	Spread out on shelves A raisin in the chocolate, Potato flour And ham without foreign exchange."
[a] Ibid., 30.	

These and other elements of political folklore, omitted here because of a lack of space, offer further proof of the significance of food shortages in the lives of Polish workers.

Chapter 3: Supplies, Food, Meat: Actions

1. The Dispute about Poles' Behavior toward PRL Reality

Problems involving the material situation in Poland, including food-related difficulties, contributed in important ways to how Poles thought about their surrounding reality, especially about the governmental and state system. They revealed an important feature of Polish society's collective state of mind, consisting in the tendency to make critical judgments about the PRL as a particular institutional order and about people exercising authority within it. However, in order to better understand the importance of these issues for everyday life in the People's Republic, let us attempt to analyze their impact on social behavior.

Such an analysis is important primarily because the relationship between social consciousness and behavior in the system of real socialism was complicated. In this respect we find most inspiring comments by Polish sociologists based on research they conducted in the 1970s and the 1980s. Among them, the concepts of Andrzej Rychard deserve special mention. Referring to the realities of Poland in the second half of the 1980s, he claims that the scientific descriptions of relations between the institutional system of the PRL and society were dominated by concepts he called collectively "conflictive" and "adaptive." The former hinged on the assumption that it is possible to have a uniform interest within the structures of power, the essence of which is to subordinate the whole of social life, including the economy, in order to maintain the continuity of political power. In turn, they attributed to society a common interest in the form of an effort to free itself from total domination and ensure social subjectivity, resulting from attachment to tradition and culture. The most well-known expression of the tendency for such an analysis is the theory of the "new class" put forward by Milovan Djilas. According to such an interpretation, the main factors ensuring the stability of social order is, on the one hand, the possibility that rulers were able to use violence and, on the other hand, the fear characterizing society that violence could be used. In certain situations, when the level to which society's civic and material aspirations are satisfied fell below a certain minimum, the barrier of violence was not high enough and there was an outbreak of conflict, which was quite common in Poland's postwar history.

The "adaptive" concepts, which are closer to our way of thinking, hinge on the assumption that it is impossible to speak of a single interest within either the institutional system or society. The political and economic systems are internally diverse and their operation is determined by the constant interplay between various interest groups. The economy is not treated as fully dominated by the political system, it is credited with a certain autonomy and the managers of industrial enterprises are aware of their own interests, striving for autonomy with respect to political power and economic administration. Within these concepts, emphasis is placed on internal diversity within society, divided into various groups, often competing with each other. The extreme version of this concept assumes that the main conflict line does not separate "rulers" and "society," but that there is a multitude of dividing lines within the society itself. In this form, it gained a certain level of popularity among Polish communist elites in the 1980s, because it tried to legitimize the state's position not as a party to the conflict with society, but as an arbitrator in disputes between various groups. These concepts seem to reject the role of violence as the main stabilizing force and point to the role of motives and pragmatic interests in stabilizing the system.

They point to the inconsistency we see in empirical studies based on the simultaneous rejection and "consent" to the PRL's institutional system, the point being that while this system could be unacceptable on the axiological (value) layer, it was accepted through behavior in the sphere of "everyday interest." And the latter is important because on a mass scale it was decisive in the perception of reality in a "normal" state – i.e. one in which values do not have a regulatory function and are replaced by pragmatic interests. This situation can be considered a kind of social anomy, though it seems to have dominated Poland – in varying degrees – throughout the period from 1945 to 1989.

To describe this situation, Andrzej Rychard created his own concept of the so-called active adaptation. He maintains that among many possible mechanisms that ensure this adaptation as a way to reduce discrepancies between the system and society, the key role is played by those mechanism that ensure that individuals are able to fulfil their personal aspirations and interests (mainly those tied to everyday living). According to this concept, this is an active process "in the course of which not only the individual or group is transformed but also the 'system' itself, which is modified by the adaptors [...]. In the postwar period, through the two-way process of adaptation, both the system and society changed." From the beginning, change in the nature of the system, in principle, consisted in the acceptance of significant discrepancies from the ideological pattern, which essentially means that this change is basically a change not a result of historical transformation (e.g. attitudes toward the Church and private agriculture) but rather change in relation to this pattern. More dynamic changes are a matter of tolerance toward various informalities, illegal practices in the economy, etc.[531]

In the way of thinking presented above, the findings of Mirosława Marody are also relevant. On the basis of research from 1983–1984, she stated that rejection of the system was mainly in the symbolic sphere, i.e. the sphere of attitudes and judgments, which was not accompanied by actions aimed at changing or transforming that system. Conversely, in the sphere of individual actions, one could observe behaviors that – although they did not necessarily derive from acceptance of the system – certainly supported it or at least did not refute it. In Marody's opinion, the division between the sphere of symbols and the sphere of activities occurred not only in the specific, observable behavior of people but also at the level of consciousness. People who rejected the system in the sphere of values and attitudes were at the same time convinced that they would live in, and be active in, that system – willingly or otherwise.

The social values with which Polish society identified itself did not find – on a mass scale at least – their expression in the sphere of activities. Rejection of the system took place mainly in the symbolic sphere.[532] The same author, referring to the issue of the relationship between society and those in power throughout the entire PRL stated: "Nobody today questions the fact that the political model which for forty-five years created the institutional framework of social life in Poland was a foreign model, one that was introduced by force. Nevertheless [. . .] for a long time that framework enjoyed the support of significant sections of Polish society, which helped bring about social and civilization advancement. It is also true that Polish society has repeatedly and actively resisted at least certain actions taken by the authorities, and in so doing defended itself against pressure to adopt their decisions or fought for change. However, it was not struggle but adaptation that determined how individuals functioned on a daily basis."[533]

Finally, we cannot help but find the reflections of Winicjusz Narojek interesting here. He argues that adaptation to the prevailing order does not mean absolute subordination to the will of the public decision-maker. Narojek wrote:

---

531 Andrzej Rychard, "Konflikt i przystosowanie: dwie koncepcje ładu społecznego w Polsce," in *Rzeczywistość polska i sposoby radzenia sobie z nią*, eds. Mirosława Marody, Antoni Sułek (Warszawa: UW, 1987), 89–108.

532 Marody, *Warunki trwania i zmiany ładu społecznego w relacji do stanu świadomości społecznej* (Warszawa: Instytut Socjologii UW, 1986), 18–50.

533 Marody, "Przemiany postaw ideologicznych i przystosowanie w systemie komunistycznym," in *Komunizm. Ideologia, system, ludzie*, ed. Tomasz Szarota (Warszawa: Neriton, 2001), 137.

> By failing as a tool to realize social utopia, state power unleashes particular aspirations within the framework of the entangled interests created by its own organization. The real sense of totalitarianization of society is not about shaping personalities willing to blindly listen to official authorities through propaganda and repression – which has proved futile, especially in Poland – but to impose on people seeking to achieve personal prosperity the rules of the organizational game in state structures. This is a negative sense, which is not conducive to the creation of state-society's "moral and political unity," though it provides state structures with pragmatic legitimacy through the common social behavior of people.[534]

For our research, the most important conclusion that follows from these comments is recognition of the need to search for source messages that describe not only manifestations of resistance, caused by a sense of material shortage (strikes, appearances at various meetings, street demonstrations) but also various strategies used to adapt to the communist reality. Let us now try to point to some of these strategies, which in fact demonstrate behavioral diversity.

2. Food Shortage "Games" with Authorities

Food difficulties in postwar Poland were particularly acute in the years 1944/45 – 1956. It was at this time, in the face of the introduction of the aforementioned benefits in kind (from 1944) and then of compulsory deliveries, that various social practices were undertaken, as noted in the sources, which we treat as food-related "games" played with authorities, which in turn were to "save" as much of agricultural production as possible from being handed over (or sold at discounted prices) to the state.

As the results of earlier cited studies show, drastic restrictions on food consumption and the collapse of the upward trend in this respect occurred in the Stalinist period, all of which was the effect of the model of economic development adopted at the time marked by increasing collectivization pressure and accompanied by the introduction of the abovementioned obligatory deliveries of potatoes, milk, cereals and slaughter animals.

---

534 Winicjusz Narojek, *Perspektywy pluralizmu w upaństwowionym społeczeństwie* (Warszawa: ISP PAN, Toruń: Adam Marszałek, 1994), 91. See also Jarosz, "Citizens of communist Poland as "small individualists," *Acta Poloniae Historica* 105 (2012): 157–177; Jarosz, "POST-1989 historiography's distorted image of the relation between authorities and society in Poland during the period from 1944 to 1989," *Revue d'études comparatives Est-Ouest* 45 (2014); Jarosz, "Poles and the collapse of communism: in search of a new paradigm. Not only social resistance and political opposition," *Divinatio* 39–40 (2015).

Peasants resisted the execution of these measures, though their resistance was not absolute. It is true that the scale of repression in response to non-compliance with mandatory deliveries was enormous. In 1952–1955, nearly 600,000 people were punished (mainly with fines), and no doubt this data is evidence of social conflict in the countryside. But it also indicates that peasant resistance was in its own way rational.

Peasants tried to "tame" the Stalinist repression apparatus by playing a "game" with it. It is no accident that, having received the order for punishment, many farmers against whom they were directed ended up making deliveries (from 22 % in the case of livestock in 1954 to 42 % in the case of grain in 1955). Another "impulse" for delivery was punishment issued not by the courts but by the above-mentioned criminal and administrative councils. Only a small proportion of those punished were detained.[535] Subsequent stages of repressive measures meant that the next groups of peasants performed imposed deliveries. In a situation in which ruinous fines on farmers became ever more real, or – even worse – in which farms were deprived of their head farmers, farm owners rationally chose the "lesser evil" and – if possible – fulfilled outstanding deliveries. This delay game had other causes as well. Usually, the fact was that penalties actually executed were much smaller than those imposed.[536] If we add to the mix corrupt practices at the local authority level, thanks to which it was possible to apply relatively widely a relief system involving the notorious errors in supply and tax registers – then we get the image of peasants "quietly" but persistently battling, using various means, to defend their own farms.[537]

Another peasant strategy for adapting to Stalinist agricultural policy was the illegal slaughter of farm animals. In a situation where compulsory deliveries actually served as an additional tax and were compared with wartime quotas, peasants showed great inventiveness in finding ways to sell their products in a more profitable way. A relatively large income came from sales to private customers, the problem being that, in accordance with applicable regulations, such sales of products covered by compulsory deliveries were only possible after those

535 AAN, KC PZPR, 1678A (mikrofilm 2829), Informacja w sprawie wpływu orzecznictwa karno-administracyjnego na realizację planów dostaw obowiązkowych, 72–74.

536 AAN, KC PZPR, 237/XII-7, Dalekopis 7 VII 1952, 69.

537 Jarosz, "Oswajanie wrogiej rzeczywistości. Chłopi polscy a instytucje państwowe w latach 1948–1956," *Pamiętnik Instytutu Macieja Rataja* 3 (1996): 70–92; Jarosz, "Chłopskie oswajanie Polski Ludowej,", *Dzieje i przyszłość ruchu ludowego,* vol. 2: *Polska Ludowa (1944/45–1989)*, eds. Waldemar Paruch, Stefan Pastuszka, Romuald Turkowski (Warszawa: Ludowa Spółdzielnia Wydawnicza, 2002), 395–413.

deliveries had been completed. In the case of farm animals, their slaughter "for one's own needs" required the consent of the village leaders. In practice, however, this ban was circumvented in various ways, the most common of which was to "convince" local authorities through bribes. It was not uncommon for village leaders to agree to a slaughter on the pretext that the slaughtered animals were sick when in fact peasants slaughtered healthy animals and sold them secretly.[538]

In addition, they traded in meat with each other: "[...] a peasant receives permission to slaughter, resells half or quarter of a pig to his neighbor, who later returns it after killing his own animal."[539]

The difficult food supply situation in cities, involving especially the lack of meat and flour, led to the development of forms of trade that were illegal from the point of view of communist law. At roundups, collection points for slaughter animals, "speculators" – condemned by the authorities – would buy up some of the livestock brought in by peasants.[540] As reported in Department IV of the MBP in February 1949, the illegal meat trade and the storing of fat and pork fat by butchers became widespread throughout the country. Private traders persuaded farmers to sell slaughter animals to them.[541]

Free-market trade in grain and flour took place in a similar way. Farmers from around Kraków accused by KS in 1950 "bought grain in the commune where they live, milled it [...] in nearby mills and exported the finished product to Kraków, where they sold it for profit."[542] Sometimes railway men engaged in delivering agricultural products to cities. They reportedly made mass purchases

---

538 AAN, Centralny Urząd Skupu i Kontraktacji (hereafter cited as CUSiK), 7, Protokół z narady aktywu terenowego, 30 VIII 1952, pp. 16–18.

539 Archiwum Zakładu Historii Ruchu Ludowego (hereafter cited as AZHRL), Naczelny Komitet Zjednoczonego Stronnictwa Ludowego (hereafter cited as NK ZSL), II/101, Sprawozdanie dekadowe za czas od 6 do 17 V 1953, p. 108.

540 AAN, KS, 42, Sprawozdanie miesięczne opisowe z działalności Delegatury Komisji Specjalnej w Olsztynie w czerwcu 1954; AZHRL, NK ZSL, II/314, Informacja o realizacji skupu mleka i żywca za styczeń i luty 1955 r. w województwie krakowskim, Kraków 10 III 1955, p. 116.

541 IPN BU, MBP, 1572/1451, Sprawozdanie miesięczne Departamentu IV MBP za miesiąc luty 1949, pp. 48 ff.

542 AAN, KS, 1221, Akta sprawy Michała i Józefy Kurkiewiczów; see also: AZHRL, NK ZSL, II/28, Protokół z odprawy aktywu powiatowego ZSL w Świdnicy w dniu 28 II 1950, p. 62. For more on the Special Commission, see Tomasz Grosse, Jarosław Grużewski, Michał Kozak, Marcin Kula, Marcin Meller, Konrad Piasecki, Paweł Piskorski, Piotr Salak, Marcin Woźniak, Piotr Zalewski, "Szarzy ludzie zaplątani w codzienności komunizmu," *Przegląd Historyczny* 3 (1993): 335–350.

of meat from illegal slaughters in the villages, and then they brought them to cities using free tickets.[543]

In January 1949, an informational report from the Political-Educational Board of Military District II drew attention to mass trips taken by Szczecin residents to "less populated centers" in search of pork fat and meat.[544] Such information serves as testimony to the existence of a wider phenomenon, consisting in the creation of rural enters, especially near large cities, where people dealt in "illegal slaughter."[545]

Sometimes this trade took the form of an exchange of "goods for goods." In the absence of coal in the countryside, farmers interested in buying coal established direct contacts with miners. It was not uncommon for peasants to queue in front of warehouses where miners sold coal in return for cereal products.[546]

Sometimes the post office was used for similar purposes: in Łódź before Easter in 1949, there was a sudden increase in parcels, among which parcels containing meat constituted a significant part.[547] One butcher, accused by the Poznań delegation of the Special Commission in the period from 30 September 1947 to 14 April 1948, sent to Wrocław shipments of meat whose weight was estimated at about 7 tons.[548]

Most of the activities described above were dangerous to those participating in them, because in the legal system of that time they were punished as forms of speculation. In 1945–1954, it was the above-mentioned KS that dealt with the issuance of such punishment. We must remember that the KS had the authority to sentence a person found guilty of speculation for up to two years in a labor camp or (and) a fine.[549]

The way these penalties were handled within the framework of applicable legal acts changed. According to guidelines issued by the Director of the KS Executive Bureau on 1 October 1949, the main penalty for illegal slaughter and illicit meat trade was to be time in a labor camp, and only – in exceptional cases – a fine. The

543 Jarosz, Pasztor, *W krzywym zwierciadle*, 85.

544 Centralne Archiwum Wojskowe, Główny Zarząd Polityczno – Wychowawczy Wojska Polskiego, IV.502.1.218, Meldunek informacyjny z pracy polityczno -wychowawczej OW II za styczeń 1949 r., p. 60.

545 AAN, CUSiK, 7, p. 16.

546 AAN, KC PZPR, 237/VII-124, Meldunki z terenu nr 14/543, 24 I 1951, p. 81.

547 Kochanowski, "Do uboju," *Polityka* 33 (2002): 64.

548 AAN, KS, 1464, Delegatura w Poznaniu do Komisji Specjalnej w Warszawie, Poznań 26 października 1948, p. 2.

549 Dz. U. No. 43, Item 218.

lower limit of punishment, applied to those dealing professionally with illegal slaughter, was set at 12 months in a labor camp, and for "incidental persons" involved in slaughtered – 6 months. For professional traders, the lower limit of punishment was to be 6 months. "As for peasants exporting meat outside the borders of their group," as stated during the Executive Bureau meeting, "punishment should be up to 6 months in a camp."[550]

The new guidelines set by the Commission authorities of March 22, 1950 expanded the possibilities to hold peasants accountable for selling meat inside their village, which was reportedly a "widespread phenomenon." Officials adopted the policy that henceforth arrest would be obligatory as a preventive measure in "speculation" cases. What primarily applied to farmers were those parts of the guidelines that ordered punishment not only for those who purchased meat, sausages, and edible fats but also those who possessed and transported them for sale in an amount "exceeding one's own and family needs." An exception were peasants who possessed meat from slaughtering for their own needs.[551]

The battle against this "illegal trade" meant that trains and peasant carts heading toward cities were inspected for "smuggled" agricultural products. For example, on the night of 7/8 April 1949, officers in the Railway Protection Service (SOK) carried out an inspection throughout the District Directorate of State Railways in Lublin. Three tons of meat, pork fat and other meat products were examined and 23 people were detained. In this case, according to KS guidelines, meat not weighing less than 5–8 kg was usually not confiscated.[552] There were cases, however, in which the rules were "bent": in 1949, passengers getting off trains were searched in the Baltic cities of Gdynia, Sopot and Gdańsk. "In pursuit of meat and pork fat smugglers," briefcases and suitcases were searched and even 0.5 kg portions of sausage and bacon were confiscated.[553] On the other hand, the so-called suitcase trade developed on a large scale in Poznań Voivodeship: record holders reportedly transported up to 120 kg of meat in this way.[554] In October 1951, authorities in the Skolimów commune near Warsaw decided to not allow

550 AAN, KS, 9, Protokół z posiedzenia Biura Wykonawczego Komisji Specjalnej z 1 X 1949 r.

551 AAN, KS, 36, Sprawozdanie Delegatury Komisji Specjalnej w Katowicach za wrzesień 1951 r.

552 AAN, KS, 108, Sprawozdanie z dorywczej kontroli Wydziału d/s Przestępczości masowej Delegatury Komisji Specjalnej w Lublinie w dniu 11 IV 1949.

553 AAN, KC PZPR, 237/VII-184, A. Langer, Uwagi o "przegięciach" na Wybrzeżu, 1949, p. 24.

554 Jastrząb, *Puste półki,* 38.

carts to enter the capital at all. Police stopped them, and their owners were forced to sell transported products at "minimum prices."[555] In Kutno, at city toll gates, policemen equipped like "prison guards" checked peasant carts for hidden products.[556]

Interestingly enough, this illegal trade in meat and other goods extended beyond Poland's borders. On 21 December 1946, the KS Warsaw Delegation carried out an action in the capital in order to detain people engaged in trade in bacon and other food products, previously purchased at the Warsaw Fair and resold to service the transit train running on the Moscow – Berlin route (toward Berlin). As a result, many people were detained. The contested meat and sausages had come from illegal slaughter. In the files sent to the KS Headquarters in accordance with the "spirit of the era," officials stated that the Delegation "did not believe suspects' denials that they were engaged in unlawful trade, and that it regarded all of them not only as economic pests but also as disloyal citizens who were aware that by selling bacon and other foodstuffs and thus supplying the transit train [. . .] they were feeding the Germans on their way to Berlin, and by carrying out mass purchases in Warsaw markets they were causing a shortage and an increase in prices for necessities, especially for bacon and pork fats [. . .]."[557]

KS files do not contain data allowing us to answer the question how many people were punished for illegal slaughter or speculation in agricultural products. We know only that the number of Commission decisions regarding illegal slaughter that led to sentences in a labor camp in 1948 was 314 (6.1 % of all such decisions); in 1949 – 2,119 (23.1 %); 1951 – 2,094 (19.8 %); 1952 – 3,741 (16.7 %) and 1953 – 742 (3.9 %)[558] A fine as a basic penalty in cases involving secret slaughter was imposed in 1951 in 2,335 cases (7.7 %), and in 1952 – 8,200 cases (18.5 %).

After the Commission's work ended in December 1954, speculation cases were taken over by the courts. We do not have complete figures on those cases, but according to information regarding June, July, and August 1955, 1,400

555 APW, WKW PZPR, 60/XI-6, t.3, Protokół zespołu woj. warszawskiego z 16 X 1951.

556 AAN, KC PZPR, 237/V-25, Narada z 25 IX 1951, p. 179.

557 AAN, KS, 1226, Delegatura Warszawska do Komisji Specjalnej w Warszawie, 4 stycznia 1947, pp. 1–3.

558 *Komisja Specjalna do Walki z Nadużyciami i Szkodnictwem Gospodarczym 1945–1954. Wybór dokumentów*, 9, tab. 3.

investigations were initiated involving meat speculation in Poland, 413 people were arrested, 648 indictments were brought, and the courts heard 255 cases.[559]

After October 1956, when forced collectivization of agriculture came to an end and the level of compulsory deliveries was reduced (and, in the case of milk deliveries, abolished as of 1957), tensions in this context weakened considerably. Although documentation of these developments is far from complete, partial data seems to indicate such a tendency.

According to information contained in a document preserved in the files of the Office of the Secretariat of the KC PZPR in 1959, 47,586 motions for punishment (making up about 5 % of cases investigated) were submitted to councils adjudicating offenses regarding obligatory deliveries of livestock. The mechanism in the Polish countryside in the Stalinist period, described above, by which forced deliveries increased as repressive measures intensified, was also at work here.[560]

The size of illegal slaughter is difficult to estimate, but because of this phenomenon, it was possible to partially overcome regional differences in the food supply sector. It is symptomatic that calf slaughter increased in areas surrounding large cities (Warsaw, Kraków, Łódź, Katowice and the Tricity region of Gdańsk, Gdynia, and Sopot) and in the typically agricultural regions of Eastern Poland (Białystok, Lublin, Kielce, Rzeszów) – i.e. where such slaughter was the basic form of supply for rural and small-town populations.[561] In the vicinity of large urban areas, "meat and dairy facilities" flourished, supplying those cities with food, especially meat.[562]

In Polish popular culture, the image of the "old lady with veal" – a rural woman who systematically visits urban flats and offices to supply them (illegal) meat – established itself.[563]

---

559 AAN, KC PZPR, 237/XII-211, Notatka Wydziału Rolnego KC PZPR w sprawie stosowania sankcji karno-administracyjnych i karnych za niewykonanie dostaw obowiązkowych oraz w sprawie zwalczania nielegalnego obrotu zwierzętami rzeźnymi i spekulacji mięsem, Warszawa 17 X 1955, p. 21.

560 AAN, KC PZPR, VII/145, Biuletyn Biura Sekretariatu KC nr 81, 22 lutego 1960, Załącznik 4. Orzecznictwo karno-administracyjne w 1959 r. w sprawach o wykroczenia z dziedziny obowiązkowych dostaw żywca, gospodarki zwierzętami rzeźnymi, mięsem i jego przetworami.

561 Sławomir Dyka, Roman Urban, "Uboje gospodarcze i niezorganizowany rynek mięsa," *Badania Rynku Żywca i Mięsa* 2 (1964): 49–53.

562 Kochanowski, *Tylnymi drzwiami,* 192–193.

563 Ibid., 192–198.

In complaints directed at state institutions, peasants pointed to the notorious fraud carried out by people working in the purchasing apparatus. A typical example of these common practices was described in a letter to Polish Radio in November 1958. Its author wrote:

> Is there nothing on the thieves who rob us and our work during the roundups [...]? I will give one fact that I saw with my own eyes during a roundup: citizen O. brought [...] a hog to the roundup, it weighed 206 kg. The classifier [...] gave it a grade four. All the peasants shouted that it shouldn't be allowed to steal from a poor peasant in this way. Classifier Z. gave it this grade because citizen O. had slipped no one any money beforehand. The car with the pigs was about to leave for Kłodzko, when citizen O. removed his hog from the car and took it home, and on the next Monday he took it [...] to another gmina and got a grade one. So how can we breed pigs when people like Z. are robbing us? One purchase manager is O., who also takes money and has a company with weights and classifiers. From one of the roundups one animal is left for these officials, later this animal is supposed to be brought for sale and sold, and then they take the money. I saw [...] how the classifier [...] took bribes from peasants, then he gave a different grade to those peasants – which means a better grade. Receipts are fake so that it all can go into their pockets, they rob us and you mock stupid peasants as the dark masses.[564]

A similar picture emerges from other complaints contained in the above-cited document. For example, purchase managers, weight controllers and classifiers participated – for bribe – in the dishonest underestimation of the weight and class of slaughter animals. Farmers asked such embarrassing questions: how is it possible that a cattle and pig classifier at purchase can erect a brick house valued at PLZ 450,000 (in 1958) in a situation where his monthly salary comes to about PLZ 2,000 and he has a wife and three children to support?[565]

On the one hand, these "peasant laments" point to the corrupt practices within the purchasing apparatus, but on the other hand, they show that the common adaptation procedure to this situation involved farmers paying bribes.

3. The Queue

Queues in front of stores selling basic groceries, including meat, were a visible testimony to the food supply difficulties in Polish cities. This phenomenon took on a particularly dramatic character during the Stalinist period, strongly

564 AODiZP, 1050/26, Biuletyn Biura Listów Komitetu do Spraw Radiofonii "Polskie Radio" nr 72, 6 grudnia 1958; see also: AODiZP, 1050/29, Biuletyn Biura Listów Komitetu do Spraw Radiofonii "Polskie Radio" nr 54, 30 października 1959.

565 AODiZP, 1050/26, Biuletyn Biura Listów Komitetu do Spraw Radiofonii "Polskie Radio" nr 72, 6 grudnia 1958.

influencing workplace moods and behaviors, which was especially true of women, who were traditionally involved in supplying families with food.

The universality of queues, however, resulted not only from actual shortages of goods but also from behavior motivated by panic resulting from the kind of rumors we wrote about above. "Runs on shops," during which everything that could be found there, and the hoarding of goods – these were the most typical reactions to this kind of colloquial messages. Poles often intensified their shopping habits due to recurring rumors of coming war. Similar behavior on a mass scale was caused by actual or expected regulations of trade in goods, such as price increases, the introduction or withdrawal of rationing (the card system), etc.

Queuing was a time-consuming, nerve-racking and sometimes fruitless occupation. In the summer of 1951, in Warsaw people gathered in front of shops in the evening to wait for morning deliveries. Purchasing goods that could replace meat caused the disappearance of fish, cheese and eggs. The authorities' reaction to these difficulties was to send party activists to queues to explain the reasons for the shortages. They were exposed to the anger of those standing in line. In order to alleviate the mood of dissatisfaction, in August 1951 officials introduced supply vouchers in selected factories. However, this system, at least in the initial period of operation, did not lead to shortened queues. As we read in a report put together by a special committee appointed by the KC PZPR in September 1951, "the voucher system did not put an end to the queue, one could even say that it rather expanded it, because those who possess vouchers usually try to stock up on the free market, and the quantity [of meat] designated for the free market has thus gone down compared to the old days."[566] The introduction of vouchers often caused hostility; those standing in queues who possessed them were called "kacapskie folksdojcze" ("Katzap Volksdeutsches," a derogatory term; a Russian version of wartime racial elites who got special privileges). Cases of open destruction of vouchers were reported, because the principles of food rationing dividing entitled persons into different categories were considered unfair; after all, "everyone has the same stomachs." Another reaction to this regulation was the inflow of employees from factories that did not receive vouchers to factories covered by a card supply.[567] There were also more demonstrative behaviors: on

566 AAN, Państwowa Komisja Planowania Gospodarczego (hereafter cited as PKPG) 5478, Notatka Komisji powołanej przez Komitet Centralny PZPR dla spraw związanych z zaopatrzeniem bonowym w mięso i tłuszcze wieprzowe, złożona na ręce wicepremiera H. Minca w dniu 27 IX 1951 r., pp. 1 ff.

567 IPN BU, 1572/566, Biuletyn dzienny MBP nr 209/51, 8 IX 1951.

13 September 1951, 58 employees of a brickwork around Rybnik, including 25 women (who had initiated the protest), stopped work demanding that they be issued meat vouchers. After being ensured that they would receive meat, they returned to work and promised to make up for the losses.[568]

The lack of food supplies exposed women working at night to extreme fatigue, which was allowed by Polish law as of 1951.[569] In a letter to the First Secretary of the KC PZPE Edward Ochab in June 1956, weavers from Pabianice wrote: "We are coming forward with a great request to abolish night work. There is no time to sleep during the day because you have to queue to get some butter or some meat or pork fat. You don't know whether to send children to school, to queue or to sleep. In addition, cooking and washing. We, the workers of weaving company 'C', beg you, Comrade Ochab."[570] In turn, the workers of the steel mill in Ostrowiec Świętokrzyski in 1951 complained that wives "are queuing for meat at night."[571]

Queues were a permanent part of the urban landscape also after 1956. At the beginning of 1959, for the first time since the war, this phenomenon became the subject of public opinion research. In that year, 1,909 Warsaw residents responded to an OBOP survey on time spent on everyday shopping (Table 26).

These studies showed that over 70 % of women devoted from 1 to 2 hours to daily errands. People with a primary and secondary education spent much more time in queues than people with a higher education.[572]

However, the findings of the OBOP survey regarding Warsaw are not representative of the situation in other Polish cities. Warsaw, as the Polish capital, benefited from a privileged supply of food. The accumulation of central

---

568 IPN BU, 1572/566, Biuletyn dzienny MBP nr 215/51, 15 września 1951.

569 A ban on women's night work was introduced by the Bern Convention of 1906. Some extension of the possibility of such work occurred in the conventions of the International Labor Organization (ILO) No. 41 of 1934 and No. 89 of 1948. The Polish act of 1924 provided for a ban on the night employment of women. It was repealed in 1951 (act of 26 February 1951 amending the act of 2 July 1924 on work carried out by children and women, Dz. U. No. 12, Item 94). From that moment, women's night work was subject to the same restrictions as employing men at night (provided for in Art. 15 of the act of 18 December 1919 on working time in industry and trade – Dz. U. 1933 No. 94 Item 734, as amended).

570 AAN, KC PZPR, 237/XXV-18, Biuletyn nr 29/140, 22 VI 1956, 207.

571 Quote from Miernik, "Dzień powszedni robotników w województwie kieleckim w okresie stalinowskim," 159.

572 ATNS OBOP, 9.73, Zygmunt Skórzyński, *Podstawowe zajęcia mieszkańców Warszawy w codziennym budżecie czasu* (Warszawa: OBOP, 1962).

Table 26. Number of hours devoted to everyday shopping by Warsaw residents in 1959

No. of hours devoted	GENDER		Total
to shopping	Men	Women	
	762	1147	1909
Does not do shopping	62,5	12,5	32,5
Around a half hour	11,9	9,5	10,5
Around an hour	12,1	25,0	19,6
An hour-and-a-half	4,3	15,8	11,2
2 hours	3,1	19,2	12,8
More than 2 hours	1,5	12,3	8,0
No data	4,6	5,7	5,4

Source: ATNS OBOP 9.73, Zygmunt Skórzyński, *Podstawowe zajęcia mieszkańców Warszawy w codziennym budżecie czasu* (Warszawa: OBOP, 1962).

institutions and foreign diplomatic missions resulted in the functioning of various types of special systems for the supply of food goods (shops "behind the yellow curtains"). In the provinces, the situation was much more difficult because of disproportionately smaller supplies, as evidenced, for example, by an anonymous letter from Krasnystaw (a town in the eastern, agricultural part of Poland) of October 1968, in which the author wrote: "A lot of time is lost in queues. This is true, because in Krasnystaw there are queues day and night. If you want to buy a kilo of meat or meat bones, then you have to get in line at two in the morning, and Saturday and Friday at midnight, and stand until 7 am because at seven they open the store. After returning home from the queue, you have to make breakfast for the children to school and go to work – after a restless sleep all night." The situation in this respect seems to be slightly different than in the Stalinist period due to the wider supply possibilities on the free market, which, however, came with higher costs. The quoted correspondent wrote that "It cannot be said that there is no meat on the market. Yes, peasants come in three times a week and you can buy on the market, but not everyone is buying there, because not everyone can afford it. Pork chops cost PLZ 80, ham 90, bacon 50–60, so not everyone can afford it."[573] As we see, supply difficulties increased in some periods, decreased in

573 AODiZP, 1208/5, Biuletyn Wewnętrzny Biura Listów Komitetu do Spraw Radia i Telewizji "Polskie Radio i Telewizja" nr 476, grudzień 1968. Trudności w zaopatrzeniu w artykuły pierwszej potrzeby. In 1968, the average wage in the socialized economy

others, and capturing these "waves" in the light of the examined source materials is not always possible.

The first growth in such difficulties after October 1956 took place in 1959. Official party information from August 1959 indicates that in the Kraków Voivodeship the food supply situation was difficult, in particular with meat and sausages. Residents of Kraków, Nowa Huta, Jaworzno, Chrzanów and Oświęcim felt shortages most powerfully. According to the same source, people in Brzeszcze in the Oświęcim powiat were queuing throughout the night. Not only meat but also eggs, pasta, fish fillets, and especially hard and processed cheese and milk were unavailable. People blamed local authorities and their ineptitude or bad will. The situation in the Warsaw and Łódź Voivodeships was similarly described. In the latter, there were widespread complaints that after eight hours of work you had to stand in queues for several hours.[574]

Another growth in food supply difficulties occurred in 1963. It was then that people in many voivodeship cities had to line up even for milk from the early morning hours.[575]

The aggravation felt by "queuers" was aroused not only by the waste of time that came from having to stand in long lines for goods (which might be gone by the time a person got to the front of the line) but also the unclear and cronyistic rules of their sale.

The above is evidenced by, for example, complaints about trade within the MHD, Universal Food Cooperative (Powszechna Spółdzielnia Spożywców, PSS) and MHM chain stores that flowed into Polish Radio in three quarters of the year 1965 (Table 27).

It is characteristic that as many as 16 % of the correspondence involved current complaints from listeners about fraud committed by butcher shop staff. Propaganda around the "meat affair" clearly animated correspondence on this subject.

Complaints about shop staff expressed irritation at the way meat was sold. The author of one letter wrote:

---

was PLZ 2,108 gross. See *Rocznik Statystyczny GUS 1969* (Warszawa: GUS, 1969), 538, tab. 2 (838).

574 AAN, KC PZPR, 237/VII-3967, Informacja nr 24/A/3605, 21 sierpnia 1959, p. 67.

575 AAN, KC PZPR, 237/VII-3971, Informacja nr 7/A/3856, 16 stycznia 1963, p. 17.

Table 27. Complaints addressed to Polish Radio about the functioning of shops in three quarters of 1965

Kind of complaint	Origin of complaint			TOTAL
	Countryside and settlements	Cities	Voivodeship cities	
Fraud by shop personnel	24	30	11	65
Fraud in meat shops	4	19	6	29
Fraud and improper work by catering staff	6	19	8	33
Bad attitude of shop staff to customers	17	29	7	53
Total	51	97	32	180

Source: Archiwum Ośrodka Dokumentacji i Zbiorów Programowych TVP SA (hereafter as: AODiZP), 1050/64), "Biuletyn Wewnętrzny Komitetu do Spraw Radia i Telewizji "Polskie Radio i Telewizja" nr 214. Listy o nadużyciach i kulturze w handlu, listopad 1965.

> I live in Pasłęk in a small town where everyone knows each other and cronyism flourishes. I am now stigmatized for having dared to point out a butcher shop salesman. Well, Mr. L. is the uncrowned king of the butcher shop and Pasłęka. What an ordeal has to be gone through by those who want to buy a piece of meat and do not belong to Mr. L.'s mafia [...]. There is not much meat, and [...] the seller's favorites get some without queuing. In addition, keeping meat under the counter for friends and sausage is normal. On 24 August, when I was in the store, I noticed how L. was cutting off beef and bone for PLZ 26 and throwing it on a leg for PLZ 36. I asked the woman standing next to me if she saw it, she said that she had seen such things more than once. Since then, he has harassed me.[576]

Allegations of fraud and insulting treatment of buyers were made in another letter:

> In Radom at Miedzianowska Street 102, there is a butcher shop headed by Mrs. Antonina P. We want to ask if she is not allowed to add a piece of sausage weighing 2 dkg for every 10 dkg, and 17 dkg for each kg of meat. We are only working people and we don't have any side income, that's why we can't give P. a second salary. She values herself more than the minister himself, because she thinks that on such a periphery as Młodzianów there are ignorant people who can be cheated. If you notice that she adds nothing, she

576 AODiZP, 1050/64, Biuletyn Wewnętrzny Biura Listów Komitetu do Spraw Radia i Telewizji "Polskie Radio i Telewizja" nr 214. Listy o nadużyciach i kulturze w handlu, listopad 1965.

responds with vulgar words that would make you 'ears swell up.' Controllers can never catch Mrs. P. cheating because she knows regular customers and when a stranger comes in, she will never cheat him or use vulgar words.[577]

Queues were a place where not only verbal skirmishes occurred. In 1947, a reporter for the *Trybuna Dolnośląska* wrote, not by accident: a kilo of meat costs 4 broken teeth and a black eye."[578] In February 1951, in Skarżysko-Kamienna, the crowd in a queue demolished the shop and beat the staff over a lack of sugar.[579] In Ostrowiec Świętokrzyski, it even came to the death (probably by suffocation) of a woman standing in a queue for meat.[580] A resident of Świebodzice in October 1959 informed Polish Radio: "From 3 in the morning there are queues at butcher shops. At 12 o'clock they bring goat, mutton, horse meat. There is not enough meat for everyone. Pork or beef is a medicine. People quarrel in the queue. They stand all day and often return home without meat."[581] In 1967, in several Lublin shops, there was a struggle, with meat being snatched away.[582]

Similar scenes accompanied queuing at a later stage, especially in periods when food supply difficulties intensified, for instance when, during the purchase of the non-rationed portions of meat products (kaszanka, liver sausage, salceson) during martial law in 1982.[583] It was also at this time that women used holiday days to queue.[584]

The above-cited statements document a broader practice, one that is difficult to grasp in the analyzed source materials.

However, the queue was not only a "battlefield" but also a place to make comments unfavorable to authorities, and to spread rumors. The fact that we know about them on the basis of written sources also indicates another function: the

---

577 Ibid..

578 Quote from Chumiński, *Ruch zawodowy w Polsce,* 136.

579 IPN BU 1572/564, Biuletyn MBP z 9 lutego 1951 r.

580 R. Kwiecień, *Kielecka Delegatura Komisji Specjalnej do Walki z Nadużyciami i Szkodnictwem Gospodarczym (1946–1954)*, maszynopis pracy magisterskiej napisanej w Instytucie Historii Akademii Świętokrzyskiej w Kielcach (promotor D. Jarosz), Kielce 2003, 29.

581 AODiZP, 1050/29, Biuletyn Biura Listów Komitetu do Spraw Radiofonii "Polskie Radio" nr 50, 17 października 1959.

582 M. Zaremba, *Społeczeństwo polskie*, 46.

583 See also Tadeusz Ruzikowski, "Mazowsze, Warmia, Mazury," in *Stan wojenny w Polsce 1981–1983*, ed. Antoni Dudek (Rzeszów: Instytut Pamięci Narodowej, 2003), 343.

584 Jarosław Neja, "Górny Śląsk, Podbeskidzie, Ziemia Częstochowska," *Stan wojenny w Polsce*, 149.

queue was a "workplace" for many party informers and the security apparatus. In May 1959, according to party information from the Bydgoszcz Voivodeship, people standing in line ridiculed a press interview given by the Deputy Minister of Internal Trade Emil Kołodziej on the reasons for the food supply difficulties ("If he didn't eat a piece of meat or sausage for several days in a row, he would have a different opinion.").[585] In May 1963, Voivodeship Committees of the PZPR in Lublin and Łódź informed the Warsaw headquarters about shortages in the food market, as a result of increased purchases. Allocations of meat in the Lublin region were sought within half an hour. "In queues for bread, you can even hear voices saying that it has gotten worse with supplies than during the occupation, because then you could get bread using ration cards. [...] Due to the lack of meat and sausages in the city of Lublin, there is a rumor that in the near future meat shops will be open only 5 days a week."[586]

Food shortages in the Stalinist period had – as we have already mentioned – a significant impact on the escalation of conflict between residents of villages and cities. It not only took the form not only of opinions expressed on this subject, but it also triggered behaviors that can be reproduced, at least partially. Peasants were accused of "stripping" city shops, especially on market days. Against this background, there were countless disagreements and even fights. In 1952, such conflicts were recorded in many Polish cities.[587] "Self-defense" efforts put up by municipal authorities against these buyouts consisted of, among other things, closing shops on market days. In Wieluń in 1951, the local PRN agreed that city residents would be able to shop it until 12 o'clock, and only after that time could visitors from the village.[588] Such solutions (officially banned by the Presidium of the Government in August 1951[589]) were unable to eliminate the causes of these conflicts inherent in the Stalinist economic policy. We have not been able to determine whether such strategies were also used by city authorities later.

585 AAN, KC PZPR, 237/VII-3967, Informacja nr 25/A/3606, 24 sierpnia 1959, p. 70.

586 AAN, KC PZPR, 237/VII-3971, Informacja nr 41/A/3890, 8 maja 1963, p. 109.

587 AAN, KC PZPR, 237/VII-129, Meldunki z terenu nr 75/889, 11 IV 1952; AZHRL, NK ZSL, II/105, Protokół nr 10 z posiedzenia Prezydium WKW ZSL w Kielcach, 24 III 1952 r., 28.

588 AAN, KC PZPR, 237/V-25, Odprawa w dniu 25 IX 1951 – referat R. Zambrowskiego, p. 179.

589 Jastrząb, *Puste półki,* 61.

4. Food Supply Difficulties and Work Discipline

Food supply difficulties had a negative impact on the quality of work and on work discipline in Polish enterprises. In May 1951, reports from Łódź factories indicated increasing instances of workers arriving late, which workers explained by the need to stand in queues.[590] On 18 August 1951, the Provincial Office of Public Security in Łódź reported to headquarters in Warsaw that "workers are declaring that they will no longer work without meat." On the day before Christmas, people were dismissed from work to queue for meat.[591] Due to supply difficulties on 18 August 1951, workers in the rayon plant in Chodaków refused to work overtime (to which they had committed), stating that they had to go stand in line for meat. After talks, all but three of them started working.[592] In August 1951, in Warsaw, there were cases of trams coming to a halt because tram drivers had gone to queue for meat.[593] Behavior of this type must have been quite common, as evidenced by a memo found in the files of the CRZZ[594] which was based on discussions in factories throughout Poland at the beginning of 1952 in which students from the Central School of Trade Unions had participated. Having heard opinions expressed during meetings in 23 companies in the construction industry, the memo's authors stated, among other things, that due to numerous shortages of goods, "workers often leave work to stand in queues."[595]

It was sometimes the case at the time that workers fainted and were forced to take breaks at work because of malnutrition. Information about such cases in Łódź and the Łódź region is included in the daily bulletin of the Cabinet of the Minister of Public Security from 1951.[596] As Hanna Świda – Ziemba stated on the basis of her research in Łódź production plants in the years 1949–1950, it happened that "after working for twelve hours, there were cases of severe fainting, attacks of genuine hysteria among women, so that the company physician (who

590 IPN BU 1572/565, Biuletyn dzienny MBP nr 112, 16 maja 1951, p. 61.

591 IPN BU 1572/565, Biuletyn dzienny MBP nr 191/51, 18 VIII 1951, p. 359.

592 IPN BU 1572/565, Biuletyn dzienny MBP nr 192/51, 20 VIII 1951, p. 361.

593 B. Brzostek, 136, 142, 144, 157; Jastrząb, *Puste półki,* 163; IPN BU 1572/566, Biuletyn dzienny MBP nr 209/51, 8 września 1951.

594 In the years 1949–1980, CRZZ was the supreme organ of the Trade Union Association: the monopolistic central union controlled by communists.

595 ARZ, CRZZ Wydział Ekonomiczny 33/35/52, Notatka dla Sekretariatu CRZZ o przebiegu kampanii sprawozdawczo-wyborczej wg informacji słuchaczy Szkoły Centralnej Związków Zawodowych [luty 1952].

596 IPN BU 1572/565, Biuletyn dzienny MBP nr 197/51, 25 sierpnia 1951, p. 377.

was on alert when 'commitment time' was coming) had to intervene."[597] On 20 and 21 August 1951, several factories in Poland reported refusals to work motivated by weakness due to meat shortages. For this reason, workers did not want to work overtime and were unable to comply with certain standards.[598]

Supervisors of some Silesian hard coal mines also pointed to malnutrition as one of the most important reasons for the failure to implement production plans. An inspection of the Chorzów mine on 9 August 1949 showed "frightening" levels of absenteeism, which only on Sunday,[599] 7 August, reached the number of 513 work days (of which 171 were unexcused) among a crew of 1,359 people. The mine suffered from a lack of workers partly caused by the exodus of miners to other plants "to improve living conditions." This report wrote: "The crew is feeling the effects of a lack of meat, fats." Absenteeism was also reportedly caused by "excessive exhaustion experienced by people because they have to work with a reduced crew."[600] Similar moods were noted in the "Bielszowice" mine. Trade union officials who went underground heard from miners: "[. . .] give us more meat and fat, and we will do twice as much." Working hours were shortened due to frequent breaks and rests because of weakness. Miners showed an unwillingness to work on Sundays and holidays.[601] Such feelings had to be quite common since officials pointed to them as one of the most important reasons for the failure to implement plans in the entire mining industry in the summer of 1949.[602]

---

597 Hanna Świda – Ziemba, "Robotnicy lat pięćdziesiątych," in *Elity władzy w Polsce a struktura społeczna w latach 1956 – 1981*, ed. Przemysław Wójcik (Warszawa: Uniwersytet Warszawski, Polskie Towarzystwo Socjologiczne, 1994), 33.

598 IPN BU 1572/565, Biuletyn dzienny MBP nr 195/51, 23 sierpnia 1951, p. 370.

599 During this period, the authorities forced miners to work on Sundays to increase coal production, which was needed not only by Polish industry and individual recipients. It was the raw material that constituted the basis of foreign trade at the time. Conscripts from groups discriminated for political reasons also worked in the mines, were called into the army under the so-called substitute military service in the Military Mining Corps. See Edward J. Nalepa, "Wojskowe bataliony górnicze w Polsce w latach 1949–1959," *Przegląd Historyczny* 1–2 (1994): 123–133; *Skazani bez wyroku* (Warszawa: Krajowy Zarząd Związku Represjonowanych Żołnierzy Górników 1999).

600 ARZ, CRZZ Wydział Ekonomiczny 39, Sprawozdanie z lustracji w dniu 9 sierpnia 1949 r. w kopalni Chorzów.

601 ARZ, CRZZ Wydział Ekonomiczny 39, Sprawozdanie z lustracji kopalni "Bielszowice" w Bielszowicach [1949].

602 ARZ, CRZZ Wydział Ekonomiczny 39, Sprawozdanie z konferencji odbytej w dniu 8 sierpnia 1949 r. w Zarządu Głównego Związku Zawodowego Górników poświęconej zagadnieniom planu w górnictwie.

We also find information about the impact of food supply difficulties on work discipline later in PRL history. The authors of letters arriving at the KC PZPR in the 1970s complained about having to leave work in order to line up in front of butcher shops.[603] In 1977 a railway man from Wrocław wrote: "It is now common for workers to leave work and queue."[604] Another correspondent wrote at the time: "Things are going badly in our city Lubartów. A piece of meat can be gotten only by those who have connections with people in the shops and by various kinds of loafers wandering around the city looking for some scrap they throw out for sale. Workers must eat carbs and dairy products. And is it any surprise then that people get sick, that there is an increase in absence from workplaces, that time intended for production is devoted to 'hunting' for a piece of meat?"[605] A similar practice was noted in sources in 1982.[606] It seems that this was a part of Polish life in varying degrees until 1989.

5. Strikes and Demonstrations

The most spectacular kind of worker protest, characteristic of a workers' culture, were strikes. The strike movement in Poland after the Second World War has not yet been covered by an exhaustive monograph, which does not mean that interesting works on this topic have not been produced.[607] Researchers' findings on this issue show that in 1945 at least 231 strikes broke out; in 1946 – 565; in 1947 – 284; in 1948 – 140; in 1949 – 30; in 1950 – 53; in 1951 – 73; in 1952 – 68. As of 1949, sit-down strikes grew not only fewer in number but also shorter duration (from several minutes to several hours) and usually included only part of the worker crew. Relatively speaking, textile workers and miners were relatively the most susceptible to the strike.[608]

603 AAN, KC PZPR, mikrofilm 2978 [d. sygn. 1809], Informacja o problemach wynikających z listów, skarg i interwencji do KC PZPR i instancji partyjnych w 1978 r., p. 77.

604 AAN, KC PZPR XI/1063, Wybór listów nr 13 BliI KC PZPR, Warszawa wrzesień 1977, p. 255.

605 Ibid., p. 256.

606 See among others Ruzikowski, "Mazowsze, Warmia, Mazury," 343.

607 See Kamiński, "Strajki robotnicze w Polsce w latach 1945–1948" (Wrocław: Gajt, 1999); Wojciech Górecki, "Strajki robotnicze w Łodzi w latach 1948–1949," *Polska 1944/45–1989. Studia i materiały* IV (1999): 111–147.

608 Chumiński, "Formy obrony interesów pracowniczych w warunkach totalizacji życia społecznego (1949–1956)," *Studia Historyczne* 1 (1999): 99; Kamiński, "Strajki robotnicze w Polsce 1945–1948. Próba bilansu," *Dzieje Najnowsze* 4 (1997): 114–115.

The findings of Łukasz Kamiński regarding the years 1945–1948 show that the vast majority of strikes (84 %) at the time were, at their foundation, economic in nature. In 1945, among strikers' demands, those related to food supply were dominant. In the following years, workers more often demanded pay increases and payment on time.[609] The first strike wave caused by food supply difficulties erupted in the Łódź textile industry in May 1945.[610]

During the Stalinist period, the reduced strike movement came mainly as a result of intensified government repression of this form of protest. As of 1947, establishments with special susceptibility to anti-system behavior began to create Defense Units, cells within the political police apparatus dealing with the control of workers' behavior. In protests organized at that time, economic demands continued to dominate. Workers went on strike mainly to improve their difficult financial situation, although in Stalinist Poland it is difficult to draw a clear line between political and economic motives. What prompted usually short-lived strikes were: wage cuts most often due to increased quotas; the transition from piecework pay to day pay; a change in items produced; various forms of production "rationalization"; exhausting overtime work; the introduction of new collective agreements; food supply difficulties and shortages in coal allocations; the delayed payment of wages; poor working conditions (no protective clothing).

Lack of meat was one of the causes behind the great wave of strikes that swept through Poland in the summer of 1951. The center of workers' protests at the time was Żyrardów, where large textile factories existed since the nineteenth century. According to information intended for the MBP, on 16 and 17 August, workers in the flax spinning mill and weaving factory of the local Żyrardów Plant took several hours of "work breaks."[611] Five strikes took place in the Żyrardów factory between September 1950 and August 1951. The first broke out on 8 September 1950 in the sewing room, the second in the same department on 7 April 1951, the next in June 1951 in the cotton mill, the next on 12 July in the weaving mill. There were many causes. In the case of sewing room, the reason for the protest was standards introduced administratively without the knowledge of the workers. In June 1951, the strike was sparked by the crony-dominated distribution of coal receipts in the cotton spinning mill. In July 1951, workers protested the careless organization of the fuel supply by the Municipal National Council (Miejska Rada Narodowa, MRN). The strike that broke out

609 Kamiński, "Strajki robotnicze," 114–115.
610 Ibid., 7.
611 IPN BU, 1572/565, Biuletyn dzienny MBP nr 191/51, 18 sierpnia 1951, p. 359.

on 16 August 1951 at 8 am in the spinning mill reportedly involved about 750 people. On the second and third day, 1,950 and 546 workers protested, respectively, the reason behind this action also being a lack of meat, and bread and low pay. Some party members, especially women, were particularly aggressive in the strike. According to the findings of KC functionaries, of the seven mill workers who first stopped work, three were party members. As a result of the protest, food supply in the city improved.[612]

The August strikes also included other workplaces. Due to a lack of meat, short "breaks" took place on 20 August at the Warsaw Clothing Industry Factory, the Transport Union, and the National Cotton Industry Factory in Pabianice. In the latter, on 18 August about 100 employees of the spinning mill went to the head of the department demanding "clarification regarding meat." Reports on employee dissatisfaction tied to food supply difficulties were sent from Poznań to the MBP.[613] Strikes took place for the same reasons in workplaces in Warsaw and in the State Clothing Industry Plant in Pabianice.[614] We know from the same source that on 20 and 21 August, "in several factories in Poland," workers who refused to work were motivated by a shortage of meat.[615] Similar agitation, reinforced by news of the Żyrardów strike, continued several days later.[616]

What was the intensity of the strike movement after 1951? The information we have on this topic is sketchy and requires verification based on more detailed research. Documents preserved in the files of the Interior Ministry show that in the third quarter of 1956 there were 25 incidents involving "refusal to start work or to leave it," of which 20 were in industry and 5 were on state farms. In total, over 400 workers stopped work for one to several hours. The largest number of people refusing to work was 80, the smallest – 5. The most common reason for leaving work or not working was low wages. In addition, workers were on strike because of excessive norm, the goal being to accelerate the payment of a family

612 AAN, KC PZPR, 1646 (mikrofilm 2821/1), Notatka w sprawie strajku na Zakładach Żyrardowskich w dniach 16–18 sierpnia 1951 sporządzona przez grupę pracowników KC (załącznik do protokołu nr 114 posiedzenia Sekretariatu Biura Organizacyjnego KC PZPR w dniu 20 sierpnia 1951 r.). For more on the strike, see Małgorzata Fidelis, *Kobiety, komunizm i industrializacja w powojennej Polsce* (Warszawa: W.A.B., 2015); Fidelis, *Women, communism, and industrialization in postwar Poland* (Cambridge: Cambridge University Press, 2010).

613 IPN BU, 1572/565, Biuletyn dzienny MBP nr 193/51, 21 VIII 1951, p. 365.

614 Ibid.

615 IPN BU, 1572/565, Biuletyn dzienny MBP nr 195/51, 23 VIII 1951.

616 IPN BU, 1572/565, Biuletyn dzienny MBP nr 196/51, 24 VIII 1951, p. 375.

benefit, because they had not been upgraded to the appropriate salary group and because of difficulties in purchasing food products.[617]

According to the data requiring verification, presented by the SB, there were 66 "breaks from work" (of which 10 came in the fourth quarter) in Poland in 1963, in which 5,085 employees participated. In 1964, that number was 37 (of which 14 were the second quarter and 10 were in the fourth), with 2,087 participants. This same secret police institution judged that these actions had not been politically hostile in nature, but "were mainly the workers' protest against the soulless actions of the administration."[618] In 1966, the number of "breaks from work" was reportedly 33 (2,832 people participated), and from the beginning of January to 25 November 1967.[619]

Due to the lack of adequate research, an attempt to quantify the nature of strikes in Poland, especially after 1956, seems very difficult.[620] We base our analysis below on our own findings, resulting from reading the very incomplete archival materials made available to us by the IPN. We managed to find references to nearly 250 strikes in the years 1957–1967. These references provide the basis, above all, for making research hypotheses that will require verification in the course of further analysis.

What is most characteristic, from the perspective of our considerations here, is the fact that food supply demands appear in the materials relatively rarely. Does this mean that food problems ceased to play an important role in strikes in Poland? It seems that such a statement is doubtful for several basic reasons. First of all, our knowledge about the strikers' demands is far from complete. Second, there are many indications that their demands, including those related to food, were not always formulated *expressis verbis*. They appeared especially often in the years 1945–1946 and – as the Żyrardów example seems to show – in

617 IPN BU, Komitet do Spraw Bezpieczeństwa Publicznego (hereafter cited as KdSBP), 1583/289, Sprawozdanie kwartalne pionu Departamentu IV za III kwartał 1956 r., p. 161.

618 IPN BU, MSW II, 1585/4041, Tezy do narady krajowej. Analiza niektórych ważniejszych form wrogiej działalności w kraju i wynikające stąd zadania dla pionu III Służby Bezpieczeństwa na rok 1965, marzec 1965, pp. 220 ff. Similar conclusions: IPN BU, MSW II 1585/492, Informacja o pracy SB MSW za IV kwartał 1963, p. 10.

619 Zaremba, "Gdzie jest mięso," *Polityka* 8 (1988): 66.

620 Although Polish historiography now contains many serious monographs on these strikes, which had a significant impact on political changes in the PRL, we have no comprehensive quantitative analysis like that which was carried out on strikes in the immediate postwar period.

the summer of 1951. These were periods in which – for various reasons – food problems were extreme and malnutrition was something experienced by many Poles. They were not able to meet their food needs not only because they had no money but also (and perhaps, above all) because basic food was in very short supply. While in the mid-1940s this fact was mainly due to the economic effects of the war, in the early 1950s it was the result of the socio-economic model of development imposed on the country. In Gomułka's Poland, difficulties in the supply of foodstuffs intensified from time to time, but they were of a slightly different nature. Periodically there was a shortage of sausages and meat, but rarely cereal. In addition, food supply problems were partly relieved by an increased willingness on the part of authorities, compared to Stalinist times, to allow for a wider free market for food products (bazaars, "green [farmers'] markets," etc.).

In this situation, the basic problem was often the lack of cheaper types of meat or sausages in shops, but not a lack of all kinds of meat. For this reason, most likely, worker demands in this regard often appeared indirectly, camouflaged in the form of wage demands. Information we examined about 250 strikes from 1957–1967 indicates that wage demands appeared directly in at least 177 of them! This estimate should be increased by about 40 cases, in which the formal reason for the strike was formulated in a slightly different way, but in fact related to workers' remuneration. Above all, demands focused on work quotas. Therefore, it seems reasonable to conclude that the "economy nature" of the strike movement in Poland in 1945–1967 also involved dissatisfaction of its participants with daily difficulties tied to the food supply.

Demands for a reduction in food prices, along with an increase in wages, appeared directly as an important element of the strike in December 1970. It was then that the increase in food prices played an important and direct role in the social conflict that led to the tragic massacre of the workers on the Baltic Coast. Non-economic demands appeared much less frequently.[621]

The random and incomplete data contained in documents produced by the structures of the Interior Ministry and the PZPR indicate that in the years 1956–1970, as probably was the case previously, workers struck mainly for economic reasons, in particular wage and price problems. It was not only about low wages

621 Bogumiła Danowska, *Grudzień 1970 roku na Wybrzeżu Gdańskim* (Pelplin: Bernardinum, 2000), 114–120; *Postulaty 1970–71 i 1980. Materiały źródłowe do dziejów wystąpień pracowniczych w latach 1970–1971 i 1980 (Gdańsk i Szczecin)*, eds. Beata Chmiel, Elżbieta Kaczyńska (Warszawa: Niezależna Oficyna Wydawnicza "Nowa," Stowarzyszenie "Archiwum Solidarności," 1998), 24–86.

and price increases on everyday items but also about the delayed payment of wages and changes resulting from the introduction of new standards, product ranges, etc.

Do these conclusions also apply to a later period? The lack of in-depth research on the strike movement of the 1970s makes it difficult to answer this question, which does not mean, however, that we know nothing about it. The February 1971 strikes in Łódź are relatively well documented. It was then, under the influence of talks with striking textile workers, a new team of authorities led by Edward Gierek, who took power in December 1970, decided to withdraw the increase in food prices that had caused mass social protests. This development took place after high-tension talks between the newly appointed Prime Minister, Piotr Jaroszewicz, striking workers on 14 and 15 February 1971. It was then that workers from the Marchlewski Cotton Industry Factory, in emotional speeches, presented the misery of their situation. One of them, according to records of the event, said: "I take PLZ 100 to the butcher, I buy half a kilo of meat, kaszanka, and then there is no money (he starts crying, a number of workers in the hall are crying)." Another participant stated: "We are poor all the time." Another complained: "I paid the installment, the school, kindergarten and I do not even have money to buy candy for my child [. . .] and besides, what kind of food is available anyway, people are being poisoned, the cheapest sausage or kaszanka on the second day is not suitable to eat."[622]

We know, however, that the largest strike wave in this period was caused by the price operation of June 1976, which was based an increase in food prices. Estimates of the number of employees protesting at that time range between 55,000 and 71,000.[623]

Food supply difficulties also led to the strikes of July 1980. Their immediate impulse was the secret increase in meat prices initiated by the state authorities, which entitled the "shift" of certain types of meat and sausages from ordinary shops to so-called commercial shops and raising their prices in delicatessens, canteens and company buffets. According to researchers of this issue, these protests cannot be treated only as a simple reaction to a specific "price and wage measure." In the material layer, the strikes were caused by the very low material standard of living of numerous groups of employees. They point to yet another aspect of the strikes of July and the first half of August 1980, one which is

622 Krzysztof Lesiakowski, *Strajki robotnicze w Łodzi 1945–1976* (Łódź: IPN, 2008), 296–305.

623 *Czerwiec 1976 w materiałach archiwalnych*, ed. Jerzy Eisler (Warszawa: IPN, 2001), 51.

extremely important in the context of this book, namely that, in their opinion, the experience of the years 1970 and 1976 led to "strikes against meat price increases being, in a sense, validated by authorities. These were the only strikes in the recent history of the PRL that were publicly and officially recognized by the state as justified (irrespective of consistent unofficial repression). This undoubtedly had significance for the 1980 strikes – both at the moment of their outbreak and in terms of the strikers' demands. The realization that the strike against the meat price increase was 'legal' made it easier to overcome workers' fears, and helped them take the first step. On the other hand, this quasi legality forced authorities to limit their initial reactions and negotiate with the strikers."[624]

The strike demands of the summer of 1980 often focused on an improved food supply, including the liquidation of special stores and the so-called commercial stores.[625] This effect of these demands was a provision in the text of the agreements between the Inter-Enterprise Strike Committee (Międzyzakładowy Komitet Strajkowy, MKS) in the Gdańsk Shipyard and the Government Commission of 31 August 1980 that "the meat supply to the population will be improved by 31 December 1980, as a result of which the profitability of agricultural production will be increased, limiting to the necessary minimum export of meat and the additional import of meat." At the same time, a program to improve the supply of meat was to be presented, taking into account the possible introduction of a ration card system." The MKS requested the liquidation of commercial stores and the harmonization of the prices of meat and meat products at an average level.[626]

Strikes were the most important, but not only, form of active social resistance whose participants expressed their dissatisfaction with, among other things, food shortages.

Demands of this type also appeared as a part of street demonstrations that were a constant presence in PRL reality. According to Łukasz Kamiński, women in Ostrowiec demonstrated in March 1945 over a lack of food. Screams of "give us bread" could be heard from a crowd of women demonstrating in front of the local government headquarters in Wąbrzeźno on 16 May 1945. It was also women

624 Jerzy Drążkiewicz, Rychard, "Strajki w regionie warszawskim w lecie 1980 r.," in *Studia nad ruchami społecznymi*, ed. Jolanta Kulpińska (Warszawa: UW, PTS, 1990), 12.

625 Piotr Marciniak, "Horyzont programowy strajków w 1980 r." in *Studia nad ruchami społecznymi*, eds. Marciniak, Modzelewski, vol. II (Warszawa: UW, PTS, 1989), 160. Commercial stores sold goods at prices far above those that generally applied.

626 Fuszara, Iwona Jakubowska, Kurczewski, "Sprawiedliwość czasów reglamentacji," *Umowa o kartki*, 13.

who, during a demonstration in front of the City Council building in Kościerzyna on 18 September 1945, demanded that bread cards be issued.[627] Because of a lack of bread cards, women in Płock protested on 20 October 1945.[628] In Dobrzyń nad Wisłą (in the Bydgoszcz Voivodeship) on 1 September 1951, several dozen people (adults and children) went to the market and shouted: "Bread!" (of which there was none in local stores).[629] On 8 January 1949, in a Siemianowice mine, because of an insufficient meat supply through the local cooperative, there was "ferment" among the wives of workers demanding that the workers' council increase their allowances.[630] On 14 April 1949, in the "Bankowa" steelworks (Katowice), as a result of the failure to issue meat allowances, there was a demonstration of workers' wives at the main reception desk stating that they would not let their husbands go to work unless the sale of meat began. The conflict was resolved by its immediate sale.[631] In the morning hours of 24 August 1951 in Oborniki, a larger group of women arrived at the Central Meat Center shouting: "Sell us meat."[632] The slogans "We are hungry" and "We want bread" were chanted on the streets of Poznań on 28 June 1956, and demonstrators screamed the following through a Polish Radio transmission vehicle under their control: "Our goods are being exported without pause and our children have no bread."[633]

The transformation of October 1956 was accompanied by a wave of rallies at which various demands were posed to authorities, usually spontaneously. An analysis of statements from these rallies indicates that demands regarding an improvement in food conditions appeared relatively rarely. Why? It seems that developments in Poland after the VIII plenum of the KC PZPR encouraged the formulation of far more "bold" political demands. Rally participants demanded Poland's independence from Moscow, freedom of speech, an increased role for the Church in social life, limits on the terror and repression apparatus, etc. Demands regarding the food supply appeared rarely and, moreover, underwent a kind of politicization; they were usually formulated in such a way as to express a critical attitude toward the country's rulers, which is how we interpret demands

627 Kamiński, *Polacy wobec nowej rzeczywistości 1944–1948*, 36–37.

628 Zaremba, *Wielka trwoga*, 527.

629 IPN BU, 1772/566, Biuletyn dzienny Ministra Bezpieczeństwa Publicznego (hereafter cited as Biuletyn dzienny MBP) z 3 IX 1951.

630 IPN BU, 1572/558, Biuletyn dzienny MBP nr 6, 10 I 1949, p. 26.

631 IPN BU, 1572/559, Biuletyn dzienny MBP, nr 86, 15 IV 1949.

632 IPN BU, 1572/565, Biuletyn dzienny MBP, nr 200/51, 29 VIII 1951, [. 386.

633 Machcewicz, *Polski rok 1956*, 86.

appearing here and there regarding the liquidation of "privileged stores" ("behind the yellow curtains").[634]

Those who participated in street demonstrations, which were often (though not always) tied to strike actions, quite unequivocally expressed to the Polish leadership their dissatisfaction and sense of helplessness connected with the food supply. It is no accident that the crowd invading PZPR headquarters in Poznań on 28 June 1956 showed particular interest in the canteen. As one of the leaders of this rebellion, Stanisław Matyja, recalled years later: "A group of people entered the Provincial Committee – it is not known who it was – after a while the windows opened and they called out: 'Look how they live here!' Tableware and food dishes, ham and vodka and other delicacies were shown. This excited people because they were fighting for bread, fair standards, and decent human treatment, and here the people's authorities had everything."[635] Another account talks about how marching workers on 28 June "entered shops and shouted to sellers: 'Come with us, you also have nothing to eat.'"[636]

A similar scenario developed almost exactly twenty years later, on 25 June 1976 in Radom. One group of enraged demonstrators who entered the KW PZPR headquarters headed for the buffet, where they found a supply of canned ham and cold cuts, something "which no one in the city had seen for a long time. Showing this to the assembled people, they said: 'Look how these fatbellies live! And what about us?" One of the committee's employees, recalling this event twenty years later, also talked about how "young gap-toothed ladies" appeared from local meat plants with hideous expressions on their faces manifesting their rage by throwing rotten bones brought in containers.[637] In both cases, for those participating in these revolts, meat had ceased to be just a desirable item and had become an object of unsatisfied desire. It had become something even more – a symbol, an archetype of the injustice inflicted by the system, the quintessence of a polarized social world divided between "WE" and "THEM."

This spectrum of expressions of social dissatisfaction with the food supply situation would be incomplete if we did not mention another such expression,

634 Ibid., 157 and 167. In Poland at this time, special shops for party and administrative elites were called "shops behind yellow curtains." The military had the Wojskowa Centrala Handlowa (Military Trade Center) and the Ministry of Public Security the "Konsumy." Jastrząb, *Puste półki*, 285–326.

635 *Poznański Czerwiec 1956*, 239. See also *Poznański Czerwiec 1956 w dokumentach*, eds. Stanisław Jankowiak, Edmund Makowski (Poznań: IPN, 1995), 85.

636 *Poznański Czerwiec 1956*, 271.

637 *Czerwiec 1976 w materiałach archiwalnych*, 41–42.

which appeared on a mass scale in 1981,[638] namely hunger marches, which were provoked by the decision of the Minister of Trade in July that year to reduce ration card meat allocations, and which began that summer in many Polish cities.[639] The first of them took place in Kutno on 25 July 1981.[640] As early as 27 July, Solidarity in Łódź responded to the news of a reduction in ration card assignments. A cavalcade of a dozen or so banner-covered municipal transport cars moved toward the City Hall. The banners read: "We stand in line 24 hours," "Our children are hungry," "Our daily bread," "Hungry of all nations, unite," and "We will not agree to reduced food rations." A day later, in a demonstration on city's main street – Piotrkowska – demonstrators made use of vehicles from the State Automobile Transportation (Państwowa Komunikacja Samochodowa, PKS), and on 29 July – trucks and cisterns. However, the women's hunger march on 30 July was the most spectacular. At the head of the procession formed at the regional headquarters of the Independent Self-governing Trade Union (Niezależny Samorządny Związek Zawodowy, NSZZ) "Solidarity" were women with children in prams and in their arms. The banners had similar slogans as before ("Bread," "Eat," "We want to live," "Are hungry children the goal of socialism?" "How can we eat a card with a knife and a fork?"). Bishop Józef Rozwadowski and the head of the regional Solidarity, Andrzej Słowik, spoke to march participants, and together they sang Polish patriotic songs. In the following days similar marches, with similar slogans, took place in other cities. On 3 August, a procession of vehicles from capital transport companies were organized to block the city's main streets. The prospect of a worsening the meat supply also caused local strikes and prompted rallies.[641]

In the light of what we wrote above, we can offer the following hypothesis regarding mass social behavior caused by food-related difficulties: street strikes

---

638 In July 1980, a wave of strikes built in Poland, which led to the creation in September of the Independent Self-governing Trade Union (Niezależny Samorządny Związek Zawodowy, NSZZ) "Solidarity." A period marked by a kind of "dual authority" in Poland lasted until 13 December 1981, when martial law was introduced, "Solidarity" was dissolved, and its activists were arrested.

639 The hunger marches of 1981 were formally similar to the women demonstrations of 1945–1951, about which we wrote above. They differed primarily in scope and organization.

640 Dudek, Tomasz Marszałkowski, *Walki uliczne w PRL 1956–1989* (Kraków: Krakowska Oficyna Wydawnicza, 1992), 158.

641 See, among others, Małgorzata Bartyzel, "Na ulicach miast," *Tygodnik Solidarność* 19 (1981); "Obraz tygodnia," *Tygodnik Powszechny* 32 (1981).

and demonstrations were the most spectacular form of social resistance in the PRL used to force authorities to improve the material situation of workers. Their participants were exposed to repression and harassment, which meant that such strikes and demonstrations were quite rare. Every day, Poles expressed their attitude toward economic difficulties rather in the form of critical comments, which sometimes took the form of complaints addressed to authorities. Their fears and, less often, hopes related to the material situation were expressed in rumors. Food difficulties led them to stand in line and complain more than to strike.

Finally, it is worth noting that material difficulties, including food supply problems, were undoubtedly an important element influencing social attitudes, social behavior, and political conflicts with the authorities beyond Poland's borders, in other countries of the Eastern Bloc as well. Research on this subject is still progressing and does not allow us to draw far-reaching conclusions, but some of the events that testify to social tensions against this backdrop have become the subject of historical analysis. They show, for example, that strikes caused by the deterioration of material conditions erupted in Czechoslovakia (street demonstrations in Brno) in November 1951.[642]

Widespread protests took place in Czechoslovakia in 1953 in connection with the currency reform and the abolition of ration cards for food and industrial goods. On 1 June, the first anti-government protests took place in Pilzno: strikes and street demonstrations. The protest movement was gradually expanding; according to incomplete data, 129 factories in ten (out of nineteen) provinces (voivodeships) were on strike at the beginning of June; at least 32,000 workers participated in these strikes. The government soon put them down. However, in the political thaw, the "hard" behavior of the Czechoslovak authorities failed to gain Moscow's approval, which resulted in criticism of the behavior and – as early as the autumn of 1953 – the beginning of a "new course."[643]

Concerns of a similar nature were also noted in East Germany. Until 1958, there was a food control system in place; a daily ration of meat – depending on card category – from 35 to 45 grams. The food situation worsened particularly at the turn of 1952 and 1953 and was exacerbated by the increase in prices in April 1953, which was officially referred to as price "regulation." The straw that

642 Andrzej Małkiewicz, "Demonstracje robotnicze w Brnie w 1951 r." in *Studia i materiały z dziejów opozycji i oporu społecznego*, ed. Kamiński, II (1999): 23–35.

643 Paweł Piotrowski, "Reforma walutowa 1953 r. w Czechosłowacji i jej skutki społeczne," in *Studia i materiały z dziejów opozycji i oporu społecznego*, ed. Kamiński, III (2000): 20–32.

broke the camel's back came on 28 May 1953 with the government's decision to raise technical quotas by 10 %. It is true that on 9 June 1953, the East German Politburo adopted a resolution to follow "a new course," but it did not calm the mood. On 16 June, spontaneous protests by bricklayers took place in central Berlin. A day later, as a sign of solidarity with them, workers' demonstrations took place in more than 560 East German towns, despite the fact that the government withdrew its decision to raise quotas. About 500,000 people took part in the strikes, including about 418,000 in demonstrations. The rebellion was suppressed using Soviet tanks. While demands made by the protest participants were initially of an economic nature, political demands ("Freedom for political prisoners," "Free elections," "National unity") eventually began to prevail.[644]

The largest and most brutally repressed riots were caused by material misery felt in the "homeland of the proletariat," more precisely in Novocherkassk, Russia, in 1962. The immediate cause of the workers' rebellion in this city became public information on 1 June 1962, when news was released of the Soviet government's decision to increase prices of meat, meat products and butter. The response was a strike from workers at electric production factories (soon employees of other factories joined the original protesters). It was there that the first banner appeared with the words: "Meat, milk, and wage increases." The same slogan was chanted by the crowd demonstrating on the city's streets on 2 June. The demonstrators captured the headquarters of the municipal party committee. During the attack, one of the demonstrators brought two plates to the headquarters balcony – with cheese and sausage – and reportedly told the assembled demonstrators: "Look what they eat, and what we can't eat." As a result of battles with army and militia forces, on 1–3 June, twenty-three people were killed (none of the "security forces" was killed).[645]

The decision by Soviet authorities to raise prices caused the public mood to deteriorate, which is also expressed in colloquial opinions carefully noted by the KGB. It is characteristic that – as in Poland – dissatisfaction with deteriorating living conditions resulted primarily in criticism directed at authorities. Some of the comments noted were: "Our government sends gifts, feeds others, and now we have nothing to eat, so they are trying to solve the problem at our expense";

644 Erhard Cziomer, *Zarys historii Niemiec powojennych 1945–1995* (Warszawa – Kraków: Wydawnictwo Naukowe PWN, 1997), 144–145; Małkiewicz, Krzysztof Ruchniewicz, *Pierwszy znak solidarności. Polskie odgłosy powstania ludowego w NRD w 1953 r.* (Wrocław: Arboretum, 1998), 36–67.

645 V. A. Kozlov, *Massovyje besporiadki w SSSR pri Khrushchevie i Brezhnevie (1953 – naczalo 1980-ch gg.)* (Novosibirsk, 1999), 308–363.

"We won't die, but we should be ashamed of looking abroad. If only they stopped bragging that we are catching up to America."[646] "Anti-Soviet leaflets" found by security officers were similar in tone.[647]

The above-cited examples indicate that it was not only in Poland but also in other countries in communist Europe, that material difficulties, including food shortages, provoked spontaneous social protests, which took the form of strikes and street demonstrations, critical comments and leaflets. Polish society's reactions to these difficulties did not, in principle, deviate from this pattern. However, it seems that the trend involved a move from material, "existential" demands to political demands tied to civil liberties and various national slogans.

---

646 Vladislav Zubok, Konstantin Pleszakov, *Zimna wojna zza kulis Kremla. Od Stalina do Chruszczowa* (Warszawa: Książka i Wiedza, 1999), 320.

647 Kozlov, *Massowyje besporiadki,* 367.

Chapter 4: Poles and the Death Penalty "for Meat"

The issue of the food supply, in particular the meat supply, appears to have been one of the most important issues with which Poles had to contend during the period of communist rule. But the question remains: did expressions of dissatisfaction with food shortages, including meat shortages, mean that severe punishment should be applied to persons involved in meat production and distribution who had been convicted of fraud? What was the attitude of PRL citizens toward the Wawrzecki trial and the sentence passed against him?

The meat affair aroused keen interest. Opinions on this subject can be at least partially investigated thanks to preserved source materials of various kinds.

These materials indicate that this matter was already a topic of discussion in the run-up to the Fourth Congress of the PZPR (held on 15–20 June 1964). According to information from KW PZPR in Kraków, employees of the Nowotarski Leather Industry Factory expressed "great outrage at the meat scandal in Warsaw. According to many workers, this scandal discredits the highest state agencies in part because 'in the name of higher interests,' the public was not widely informed about it. In workers' communities of the Kraków voivodeship, criticism is increasingly heard about the scope of information on issues generally mentioned in our press (e.g. the meat affair) or infiltrating society through 'Free Europe' or through various rumors [. . .]."[648]

Assessments of a similar tone were made during and immediately after the congress at meetings with delegates. Information gathered by the Organizational Department of the KC PZPR on 17 June 1964, prepared on the basis of materials coming in from individual voivodeship party structures, indicated that there was still a great deal of talk "in society" about the Warsaw meat affair. "Against this background, demands are made for the party to curb thievery, bribery and speculation. There are questions why our press did not inform the public about this, and the exact news in this matter is provided by foreign radio. Among state administrators, teachers, and some workers (including railway men) in Olsztyn and Ostróda, there are various versions of gossip on the subject."[649]

648 AAN, KC PZPR, 237/VII-5217, Informacja nr 34/A/3992, 14 VI 1964 r., p. 73.
649 Ibid., Informacja nr 36/A/3994 z 17 VI 1964, p. 77.

Many comments were recorded particularly in the Warsaw Voivodeship. According to information provided by the Party on this subject on 20 June 1964:

> The most common questions are: – Who was the main organizer of the meat affair? Who took part in it? Why did our press not write more about it? It is supposed that people in high state and party positions were involved in the meat affair, and that is why the press did not respond to these problems. Awaiting public clarification of these matters. There are many rumors surrounding this scandal, such as those talking about the flight abroad of various personalities from leading state positions. Also at the Lenin Steelworks rumors are circulating among workers about the arrest of one of the ministers who allegedly has a private bank account at a Swiss bank. According to workers at the Lenin Steelworks in Warsaw a scandal has been revealed related to the import of 'Simca' cars and serious fraud at the Ministry of Health related to the import of medical equipment and medicines. A party activist is being questioned on this subject.[650]

In a post-congress discussion in the Bydgoszcz Voivodeship, questions were reportedly asked why the Congress had not responded to the meat affair in Warsaw. "It was also said that the Party devotes too little attention to fraud issues. Such voices are most common among workers who emphasize that a worker is punished for the slightest offense, while those in high economic positions responsible for crimes reaching millions of zlotys receive a small penalty – they are often defended and moved over to another equivalent position."[651]

Party materials indicate that the item published on 9 July 1964 in the *Trybuna Ludu* about the meat affair, containing names of those suspected of fraud and information about their arrest, evoked similar comments. Workers in the Praga district of Warsaw were reportedly convinced that further arrests of "people in positions," "fat cats," and not just the usual "little fish," were to be expected.[652]

Based on information flowing into the Warsaw Committee of the PZPR in July 1964, it appeared that "people are not fully convinced that all persons responsible for abuses were investigated." There were questions about how this could have happened, some of which concerned "the responsibility for lack of supervision on the part of MHW comrades (the name of Minister Lesz is often mentioned)" and other high-ranking party and state officials.

---

650 Ibid., Informacja nr 40/A/3998, 20 VI 1964, p. 90.

651 Ibid., Informacja nr 47/A/4005, 18 VII 1964, p. 101.

652 APW, KW PZPR, 30/VII-43, vol. 24, Informacja nr 8/VII/451 Sektora Informacji Wydziału Organizacyjnego KW PZPR, dotycząca pierwszych odgłosów na temat zamieszczonej w dzisiejszej "Trybunie Ludu" notatki o nadużyciach w handlu mięsem (opracowana na podstawie rozmów z Komitetami Dzielnicowymi i Zakładowymi), p. 264.

In this cited document, an important motif appeared, one that characterized colloquial thinking about perpetrators of economic crimes: "In many statements, comrades state that there is a need to tighten penalties for economic fraud. They quite often demand the death penalty for more serious abuse."[653] Moreover, workers at some Warsaw companies said that "criminals should be beaten senseless so that they cannot rob people anymore."[654]

It is worth noting here that the demand for strict punishment of perpetrators of crimes of this type, as in the meat scandal, was nothing new. As early as 1957, some of those writing to Polish Radio proposed as a deterrent even the death penalty for repeat offenders.[655] In 1962, the demand that the death penalty be applied to the perpetrators of crimes involving major fraud appeared (sporadically) among the surveyed employees of the Rychliński Wool Industry Plant in Bielsko Biała.[656] Mention of workers' severe attitudes toward racketeers can be found (though rarely) in memoirs.[657] To what extent did these voices reflect wider social moods, and to what extent were they isolated, a result of temporary irritation, or the effect of a consciously created propaganda campaign?

---

653 Ibid., Informacja nr 11/VII/454 Sektora Informacji Wydziału Organizacyjnego KW PZPR dotycząca dalszych odgłosów na temat zamieszczonej w dniu wczorajszym w "Trybunie Ludu" notatki o nadużyciach w handlu mięsem, pp. 269 ff.

654 Ibid., Informacja nr 9/VII/452 Sektora Informacji Wydziału Organizacyjnego KW PZPR, dotycząca dalszych odgłosów na temat zamieszczonej w dzisiejszej "Trybunie Ludu" notatki o nadużyciach w handlu mięsem, p. 266; AAN, KC PZPR, 237/VII-5219, Informacja nr 71/2373, 9 lipca 1964 r. Wyniki badań ankietowych na temat IV Zjazdu Partii. Wypowiedzi i stanowiska o Zjeździe Partii, pp. 18 ff.

655 AODiZP, 1050/21, Biuletyn Biura Listów Komitetu do Spraw Radiofonii "Polskie Radio," nr 49, 5 lipca 1957.

656 Agencja Robotnicza, Wyniki ankiety przeprowadzonej w Zakładach Przemysłu Wełnianego im. T. Rychlińskiego w Bielsku-Białej na temat stosunku do przestępczości gospodarczej i jej przyczynach, marzec 1962 (material in the authors' possession), 20.

657 This is how a lawyer under the pseudonym "Szarotka" in the late 1960s wrote about workers' attitudes in her memory: "You have to listen to the discussions among workers when the press reveals news of a great economic scandal, fraud in the amount of millions. How strong are their words of condemnation for perpetrators of fraud and those who participate in gangs. One feels their anger arising from the awareness that these are attacks on shared property. While the severe punishments imposed in many scandal trials have often raised reservations among the intelligentsia, I have not encountered these reservations in the workers' community [. . .]." See "Szarotka," "Bez retuszu," *Pamiętniki prawników. Wybór prac nadesłanych na konkurs pod nazwą „„Pamiętniki prawników. Wspomnienia z 25 lat Polski Ludowej"* (Warszawa: Wydawnictwo Prawnicze, 1969), 87.

A precise answer to this question seems extremely difficult. Reactions to sentences handed down in the fraud trial, in particular the death sentence imposed on S. Wawrzecki, seem to indicate that the opinions expressed in the above-cited documents were not dominant. From 15 February 1965 to the end of this month, the Office of Letters at Polish Radio received 41 statements on this subject, of which 37 objected to the judgment and only 4 supported it.[658] Opponents of the death penalty argued that it should be imposed only on murderers. Confiscation of property and imprisonment for many years was, in their opinion, a sufficiently severe punishment. Correspondents also pointed to the joint responsibility of control and supervising bodies. Some of them underestimated the gravity of the crime, which was reflected in the following opinions: " 'He robbed people, the state, but nobody got hurt', and 'for a few zlotys to take a man's life?' ". Other opinions stated: " 'they steal everywhere and you can't do it', 'no looter loots from another.' " One letter writer asked: "If you punish theft of money with death, then what punishment do you give murderers who took money and human life and health and orphaned the family. [. . .] where is justice, where is the law, where is a bit of humanity. Definitely no honest man will agree with this." An anonymous author stated: "You explain that it's the national treasure, the nation. No, no – no people want to punish with death. The nation is outraged by this punishment. In the streetcar, at the hairdresser's, in shops, it is said everywhere – this is a disgrace, a disgrace for the entire group of judges who approved this verdict. We demand that this sentence be revoked. We have the right to demand, because we are a part of this society that you refer to, not being careless with the death penalty." Another anonymous letter writer declared: "I am a widow, a pensioner, and for me every penny counts, but listening to the radio about the verdict of the meat affair, I can't stand the idea of taking human life because of meat. [. . .] I believe that the loss of freedom, loss of the good life, hard labor on public roads in a special uniform would be enough to humiliate [those convicted]." According to another assessment, the verdict "handed down in this case was for me – as probably for many normal people – a shock. It is a judgment that resembles medieval times, a judgment that causes worry. Against our will, it reminds us that Temida is portrayed with a sword in her hand and a blindfold: she strikes blindly. She cuts some of them with all her might, barely touches others." "For economic criminals who, after their venom runs dry, will be able to harm no one and cannot be redeemed, draconian laws shall apply. For a normal citizen, this

658 AODiZP, 1050/61, Biuletyn Biura Listów Komitetu do Spraw Radia i Telewizji "Polskie Radio i Telewizja" nr 134 z lutego 1965 r.

provides neither satisfaction nor a guarantee that henceforth no one will deceive him when purchasing the goods. On the contrary, we know from sad years of experience that 'they will not be them – they will be different.' I think they will only change the industry again, which is small consolation for us. We would prefer the detection of economic crimes in their early stage, and not the cruelty of punishments which in the normal social sense are thoughtless and lead to nothing."[659]

How do we explain this reluctance to punish the perpetrators of theft and fraud tied to the meat affair? Perhaps the answer to this question should be sought in sociological analyzes from the mid-1960s on the attitude of Poles toward the law, including economic crime in general.

In this context, the findings of Adam Podgórecki, the author of research carried out in 1964 on the prestige of law in Poland entitled *Surowość czy łagodność* (Severity or leniency) are interesting. They showed that 50 % of urban residents and 48.8 % of country folk were in favor of maintaining the death penalty (32.7 % and 31.8 %, respectively, were in favor of abolishing it). Support for the death penalty was observed especially among people with a sense of social threat, who were raised severely, were socially maladjusted and dissatisfied with life. Particularly interesting from Podgórecki's research seems to be the clear relationship between a tendency toward leniency and religiosity. It is tempting to hypothesize that Catholicism, as the worldview accepted by most Poles, might have led them to take a negative view of the death penalty as applied to economic crimes.[660] One may formulate the conclusion resulting from these findings in the following way: some Poles condemned the main perpetrators of fraud in the meat affair and demanded that they be severely punished, but they usually considered Wawrzecki's death penalty too high.

It is worth emphasizing that this tendency to severely punish the perpetrators of major economic scandals was associated with widespread indulgence of petty theft of social property. This issue, which was present in our above considerations, requires further reflection.

The problem of petty theft in workplaces began to increase just after the war. Workers whose income did not allow them to meet basic needs, demoralized as

---

659 AAN, PG, 1/29, Biuletyn nr 134 Komitetu do Spraw Radia i Telewizji „„Polskie Radio i Telewizja" Biuro Listów z lutego 1965 r. Temat: wypowiedzi o wyrokach w aferze mięsnej, pp. 11–27.

660 ATNS OBOP, *Prestiż prawa. Problematyka, zakres i metody badań* (Warszawa 1966), 9–28.

a result of the war experience, resorted to theft in workplaces and "understood" those who acted similarly. As Łódź workers openly admitted in 1945, "they are forced to steal, because the allocations of necessities for both working people and children and parents who are unable to work are very low, and with their earnings they cannot afford to buy these items on the free market because of very high prices."[661] Similar wording was used by one of the participants in the strike at the Łódź Postal Transport Office in September 1945: "Let the one who set our salaries give us an idea of what to buy and how to feed the family. Some of us steal. You can't be surprised, because they are hungry, they bring dry black bread as their daily food."[662] It was in the years 1945–1946 when strikes broke out demanding the return to work of workers thrown out for theft. Such was the case, for instance, with protests at "Ferrum" and Otto Hahn in Łódź in December 1945, ad at Gamp and Albrecht in January 1946.[663]

Admittedly, we lack information about such strikes in subsequent years, but the issue of social consent to petty thefts aroused interest, even if its sources were a part of a deliberate official propaganda campaign. This is evidenced by the response to the thematic programs of Polish Radio. After broadcasts on this issue, there were more than 240 letters received in May 1957 alone.[664] In the following years it was similar. From January to June 1959, 3,200 complaints were received on the radio about various types of embezzlement, which accounted for 5 % of all letters.[665] In 1963, there were 518 letters concerning fraud in industrial plants, of which 258 were anonymous; "according to people analyzing them, this is understandable when, after examining the complaint, we come to the conclusion that the author is often harassed for having shown 'courage' to write."[666] In three quarters of 1965, nearly 130 complaints to the radio involved fraud in trade (mainly with meat).[667]

---

661 Chumiński, *Ruch zawodowy w Polsce,* 139.

662 Górecki, "Strajki robotnicze w Łodzi w latach 1948–1949," 102.

663 Kamiński, "Strajki robotnicze," 22–23; Padraic Kenney, *Rebuilding Poland. Workers and Communists 1945–1950* (Ithaca and London: Cornell Univeristy Press, 1997), 93–94.

664 AODiZP, 1050/21, Biuletyn Biura Listów Komitetu do Spraw Radiofonii "Polskie Radio," nr 49, 5 lipca 1957.

665 AODiZP, 1050/30, Biuletyn Biura Listów Komitetu do Spraw Radiofonii "Polskie Radio" nr 4, 3 lutego 1960.

666 AODiZP, 1050/50, Biuletyn Wewnętrzny Biura Listów Komitetu do Spraw Radia i Telewizji "Polskie Radio i Telewizja" nr 83, lipiec 1964.

667 AODiZP, 1050/64, Biuletyn Wewnętrzny Biura Listów Komitetu do Spraw Radia i Telewizji "Polskie Radio i Telewizja" nr 214. Listy o nadużyciach i kulturze w handlu, listopad 1965.

Their authors criticized the imposition of mild sentences for fraud, which did not act as a deterrent, and of amnesty for economic criminals. At the same time they condemned the use of two measures: the investigation and punishment of petty criminals, and the avoidance of large-scale fraud investigation. "They repeat," authors of analysis of this correspondence in 1957 wrote, "complaining about the great difficulties that come with exposing thieves of social property, because the latter create strong cliques and mafias that unscrupulously destroy anyone who tries to point the finger at them. [...] With their Demand to take decisive and consistent action against the scourge of fraud, the authors drew various conclusions, among others: the imposition of higher sentences, the use of summary courts, the rejection of convicted persons for managerial positions and in the commercial apparatus, the repayment of stolen sums through work in prison, etc. Calls for educational programs are also interesting, which included "rallies at workplaces, programs condemning thieves, the establishment of a "League of the Honest" organization, and others."[668]

In subsequent years, the motif of criticism of "two measures of justice" repeated itself, which meant relatively painful and severe penalties for petty theft and leniency for perpetrators of major fraud.[669]

The belief was quite common that petty theft of social property and fraud were a "normal" phenomenon. They were widely used as a colloquial explanation for why Poles lived in poor material circumstances.

In popular opinion, it was not only functionaries at various levels who were the perpetrators of these acts classified as crimes. In some letters to the radio, Poles wrote that "the 'wise ones' [...] steal, they want to improve the state budget at our expense and therefore they raise the price for more 'salable' goods" (1958),[670] but in others they claimed that thefts and fraud were common practices in Polish social life in that period. The writer made this most clear in the comment: "A famous saying in Poland is that only eggs are not the object of scam."[671] The author of one letter to the radio after the price increase of 1957 expressed the belief that theft was a universal phenomenon: "How can a thief watch over the thief, because we all steal, and steal we will until the abominable communists

668 AODiZP, 1050/21, Biuletyn Biura Listów Komitetu do Spraw Radiofonii "Polskie Radio," nr 49, 5 lipca 1957.

669 AODiZP, 1050/30, Biuletyn Biura Listów Komitetu do Spraw Radiofonii "Polskie Radio" nr 4, 3 lutego 1960.

670 AODiZP, 1050/23, Biuletyn Biura Listów Komitetu do Spraw Radiofonii "Polskie Radio" nr 50, 25 lipca 1958.

671 AODiZP, 1050/31.

raise our wages. We will not last long in this Bolshevik misery. If we have to live like this, it is better to die for the glory of our homeland. I feel that all of Poland will soon be like Poznań. All workers curse this communist government. We lived to see paradise in Poland under the boots of communism."[672]

Poles most often blamed PRL officials for creating conditions conducive to the proliferation of theft and abuse. In 1957, a "devoted listener" wrote about this topic as follows:

> It is true that our society is depraved to the last limits, that it believes only in swindle and fraud as ways to get money. . . . And who created the soil that is susceptible to all kinds of dodgers and fraudsters? Who set the example for fraud and abuse? The Party and the Government. From the very beginning, the Party and the Government showed the people demoralized by war and occupation how to cheat, lie, steal and to survive through cunning. The Party and the Government carried out fraudulent elections, deceived the peasant by promising him land and then by pushing him to kolkhozes, and lied that it is good for us and better and cheaper, and issued decrees [. . .] only to later withdraw them, deceitfully. The Party and the Government robbed people, secretly exchanging money in the course of one night, took houses and villas in which to set themselves up. [. . .] The citizen had in front of his eyes yellow curtains, special sanatoriums, palaces, privileges to swindle, all covered with falsehood and propaganda. And what kind of man was to grow up in such a school? Could he believe in work and honesty?[673]

The problem of the universality of petty theft of social property was also the subject of scientific analysis.

Among others, sociologists Anna Pawełczyńska and Jan Malanowski wrote on this topic in a collective study from 1961, intended for party authorities and entitled "Attitudes toward Work and Social Property in Polish Society." There, the authors stated that according to research conducted in 1960, minor thefts in workplaces were absolutely condemned 56 % of respondents (including 51 % of unskilled workers, 55 % of trained workers, and 63 % of white-collar workers), as were non-repayment of private debts (85.4 %) and private property damage (92 %). Interestingly, there was a weak relationship between individual earnings and attitudes toward theft of social property. "The social good," the authors of this document concluded, "is an anonymous good, sometimes identified with the good of the state (or government), or with the 'common' good in the literal sense, which authorizes the independent use of this good. Violation of this

672 AODiZP, 1050/21, Biuletyn Biura Listów Komitetu do Spraw Radiofonii "Polskie Radio," nr 55, 9 sierpnia 1957.

673 AODiZP, 1050/20, Biuletyn Biura Listów Komitetu do Spraw Radiofonii "Polskie Radio," nr 32, 10 maja 1957.

good is not associated in the minds of a significant part of society with anyone's specific harm, which undoubtedly affects the fairly unambiguous assessment of theft of private goods." Private property was of a much higher rank than social property in the consciousness of the majority of society. In their opinion, the attitude to work and reliability in matters of obligations arising from it were valued much lower in Polish society than reliability in matter tied to family and friendship. According to workers, violation of discipline and an inappropriate attitude toward production tools and the work product occurred most often in the so-called peasant-workers.[674]

In their findings, the quoted sociologists depended primarily on the results of a study conducted by Andrzej Siciński in 1960 entitled "Attitudes toward Work and Property," in which he concluded that workers were convinced that they had little influence over the functioning of "their" workplace. Evidenced came in their answers to the question: "Do you think that an employee, practically speaking, has an impact on what is happening in the plant (regardless of the duties performed and the work assigned to him)? 35 % of respondents said that the worker "has no influence"; 32 % – that "it varies;" 28 % – that the worker "has an impact;" and 5 % said that they "do not know." It also turned out that workers did not identify with their workplace. As many as 52 % of respondents said that an employee should only be morally responsible for their work section, and only 36 % – for the entire plant (12 % did not have an opinion). In Siciński's studies, the percentage of people condemning the absolute failure to return private debts was 85; ruining someone else's borrowed goods and returning them without repair (washing machine, iron, vacuum cleaner) – 92; arranging personal matters during business hours 16; performing sidelines during work hours – 41. The higher the respondent's socio-professional position, the greater was the tendency to identify social goals with their own aspirations. The lower the respondent's income, the more that material pressures limited broader thinking. The survey also tied higher earnings with an increase in sensitivity to criminal acts directed against social property. A poor financial situation limited this sensitivity.[675]

The existence of similar attitudes was indicated by Podgórecki's above-cited study, which indicated that the opinion that if a theft was detected by a worker, the

674 ATNS OBOP, 9.46, Anna Pawełczyńska, Jan Malanowski, "Stosunek do pracy i własności społecznej w polskim społeczeństwie 1961." The authors of this study made use of research conducted by Andrzej Siciński entitled "Postawy wobec pracy i własności" (Attitudes toward work and property) carried out in the first quarter of 1960.

675 ATNS OBOP, 9.63, Siciński, "Postawy wobec pracy i własności," 1961.

manager should talk to that worker only in private was prevalent in both urban and rural populations (32.4 % of respondents among urban residents and 39.7 % among rural residents). Thus, an attitude of tolerance rather than strictness was dominant (a small number of respondents thought that a good punishment for perpetrators of fraud was mere dismissal). The tendency for greater tolerance was represented by women, white-collar workers, people with a significant range of social and religious affiliations. Qualified workers, people living under a sense of threat, those showing social isolation and psychosocial inhibitions, and those who were dogmatic and non-religious, were inclined to be stricter.[676]

Similar results were obtained from studies conducted in 1965 in one large (2,000 employees) Warsaw plant. The survey covered 100 manual workers. It turned out that for a large part of respondents did not associate taking (stealing) some small thing (e.g. screws, nails, a piece of metal sheet) as an act detrimental the plant (as in such a statement: "If I take a small thing needed at home – this plant will not be poor"). The act of petty theft was not equated with acting to the detriment of the plant. Only 16.7 % of respondents said that cases involving theft up to the amount of PLZ 1,000 should be taken to court, according to the law. A reprimand was enough in the eyes of 42.8 % of respondents, and dismissal in eyes of 13.5 %. A characteristic feature of the opinions expressed was the search for an explanation for theft in objective factors, mainly in the country's general economic situation, low wages and difficult material conditions (49.4 % of respondents). The lack of a sufficient number of goods on the market was the proper explanation for 36.3 % of respondents. 23 % of respondents believed that thefts were the result of organizational flaws in the company (poor material documentation, low standards, hence the possibility of savings that could not be accounted for, no systematic control at the front office, the connections some workers had with security guards, bad security with departments, etc.). As a reason for theft, 21.1 % of respondents gave a low level of social and moral education and a person's character (greed, recklessness), and 15.4 % attributed theft to mental disorders.[677]

Witold Świda, in a study published in 1960, compared crime in Kalisz – a medium-sized city in the center of Poland – in the periods 1933–1938 and 1948–1953. While in 1937 two thefts were committed in this area in industrial

676 ATNS OBOP, *Prestiż prawa*, 9–28.

677 APW, KW PZPR, 30/VII-43, vol. 27, Informacja nr 15/XI/842 z 20 listopada 1965 r. Sektora Informacji Wydziału Organizacyjnego KW PZPR dot. niektórych uwag na temat stosunku pracowników do własności społecznej i pracy.

plants (to the detriment of the manufacturer), in 1953 – as many as 56 were committed. Among the latter, minor thefts of raw materials dominated. Explaining the reasons for this, Świda claimed that the situation of the unemployed did not threaten the worker after the war, hence he did not have to fear losing his job. He concluded: "a very important barrier preventing the prewar worker from dishonesty in the workplace" fell away after the war.[678]

Quantifying the scale of petty theft in workplaces is very difficult.

Based on historical research, it is known that this phenomenon grew rapidly in the postwar period. At the end of 1945, according to statements from directors of a Łódź plant, between 10 % and 30 % of their production was stolen.[679] In 1947, the scale of these thefts in the textile industry alone was estimated at 17 % of production.[680] In May 1955, during an economic conference at the CRZZ, one participant stated: "There is an unhealthy phenomenon of theft of social property. One of the Łódź plants was missing 40,000 pair of stockings."[681]

Crimes of this type were committed – probably with varying degrees of intensity – in facilities under the control of several industrial ministries. For example, in 1957 widespread petty theft was found to have occurred in the metal industry and related industries. Small amounts of non-ferrous metals were stolen, as were spare parts in car, motorcycle and bicycle factories. Officials discovered mass theft of lamps and radio parts Kasprzak Radio Factory. As a result, nine employees were arrested, and as many as 12,000 radio lamps worth about PLZ 900,000 were confirmed missing.[682] As previously mentioned, petty theft was massive in light industry factories, often in collaboration with gatekeepers.[683] As early as 1946, representatives of Western charities operating in Poland complained about the plague of petty thefts at seaports of gifts imported from abroad. The application

678 Witold Świda, *Wpływ zmiany ustroju na przestępczość (w świetle przestępczości w Kaliszu i powiecie kaliskim)* (Wrocław: Zakład Narodowy im. Ossolińskich, 1960), 35–42.

679 Chumiński, *Ruch zawodowy w Polsce,* 139.

680 Kenney, *Rebuilding Poland,* 91–92.

681 ARZ, CRZZ, W. Ekonomiczny, 14, Protokół z narady ekonomicznej zorganizowanej dnia 10 V 1955 przez W. Ekonomiczny CRZZ z kierownikami Wydziałów Ekonomicznych i członkami Prezydiów ZG odpowiedzialnych za pracę ekonomiczną oraz kierownikami Wydziałów Ekonomicznych WRZZ.

682 IPN BU, KG MO, 4365, Notatka dotycząca sytuacji w państwowych przedsiębiorstwach przemysłu metalowego i pokrewnych, Warszawa luty 1958.

683 IPN BU, KG MO, 4365, Notatka dotycząca przestępstw na obiektach podległych Ministerstwu Przemysłu Lekkiego, wpływ 26 III 1958.

of penal sanctions did not improve the situation because – as we read in one report, "the reason for theft is low salaries and a lack of food and clothing among dock workers."

Combating petty crime was an important goal for judicial authorities. As mentioned earlier, the term "petty crime" underwent changes in legislation, which affected how petty crime was reported. We should recall that the decree of March 4, 1953 on the protection of social property against petty theft defined petty theft as a crime involving property up to PLZ 300, in which case it provided for a milder criminal sanction. The provisions of the act of 18 June 1959 on criminal liability for offenses against social property did not mention the concept of petty theft. A milder penalty was anticipated depending on the amount. For analytical purposes, prosecutors reported on theft of social property by distinguishing its value up to PLZ 300 and up to PLZ 5,000.

In the 1960s, the idea prevailed among party and state leaders (as we have already written) that minor thefts of social property should be penalized less by the use of an obligatory short-term prison sentence, and more by the application of suspended sentences. These decisions affected judicial practice. In 1960, sentences were suspended in approx. 40 % of cases, and in quarters 1 through 3 in 1966, 87 % of total cases.[684]

Perpetrators of these crimes were extremely resourceful, as evidenced by, for example, several letters cited above addressed to central party and state institutions. Some of them sent to the KC PZPR show that thefts were carried out not only by factory managers but also by workers. In 1956, the conduct of inspectors at the Tomaszów Wool Industry Factory, who performed gynecological (vaginal) examinations on women while removing yarn from the factory, caused great indignation. According to the KC's findings, the same methods were used not only by people employed in light industry but also – allegedly sporadically – by those employed at tobacco and pharmaceutical plants in Łódź. Inspections of this type, in search of high-quality thread at the Hanka Sawicka State Cotton Industry Factory in Łódź, where the doctor finally refused such tests, and women categorically opposed them.[685] In 1951, a clothing factory in Warsaw regularly stole needles, drums, lengths of material, and even fully made clothing. One employee "managed to carry out 3 windbreakers [jackets] in a briefcase."[686]

---

684 AAN, MS, 1/369, Orzecznictwo karne [1966], p. 150.

685 Jarosz, "Akta Biura Listów," 204.

686 Maciej Tymiński, "Malwersacje w przedsiębiorstwach socjalistycznych (1950–1970)," *Dzieje Najnowsze* 4 (2002), 102.

The mechanisms of petty theft in gastronomy were described in a "professional" way in a letter addressed to Polish Radio from Janusz Ch., a longtime manager of Warsaw restaurants, winner of a *Życie Warszawy* contest for best restaurateur in Warsaw. He wrote: "Do you know that a buffet pouring vodka in a 'natural' way brings in almost 100 grams per liter – that's over a dozen zlotys? And within an hour with heavy traffic, a rush, that comes to five liters. Does that not tempt you; does that not create opportunities for further abuse?" Cliques developed naturally:

> [...] a waiter who wants to "earn" something by handing out a dish "to the left" – and these are common cases – must enter into an agreement with the cashier. They can "work" together only for a certain time – until the chef figures it out. So then you have to bring the chef into the deal. It becomes so common that "arranging" the chef is the cashier's job – it is not the waiter's business. The chef and waiter don't know anything about each other. The chef does not interfere with the waiter because the cashiers are not interested in the further interests of the chef, who, after all, has to calculate. The chef is the calculator in this chain. Anyway, it has some possibilities on its own considering its natural defects. For understandable reasons, he doesn't take away raw meat, because when he is a good specialist, he can also make out of a kilo of veal 10 "de voillaes."[687] Of course, he must do it with a calculator who develops recipes and has supervision over losses. And the manager? The manager sees everything and knows nothing. He only requires that the final balance be in order, that the customer is served politely and cleanly, and that there are no primitive and gross edges in the bills. And at the end of the day, with absolute discretion, "settlement" occurs.[688]

As we have tried to show, petty theft by workers was a fairly common practice by which Poles adapted to PRL reality, more precisely to its economics, characterized by chronic shortages. The axiological belief that theft is evil was "softened" at the level of everyday life, which led to a search for excuses for this act by distinguishing theft of private property from theft of social property.

These "rationalization procedures" favored the creation of phenomena in workplaces which have sometimes been called a "cheating culture"[689] or a "climate of lawlessness."[690] One of its basic features was permission to commit fraud and to embezzle funds, which turned them into common practices. In such an

687 The name, spelled in Polish as *dewolaj*, stands for the Chiken Kiev dish.

688 AODiZP, 1050/52, Biuletyn Wewnętrzny Biura Listów Komitetu do Spraw Radia i Telewizji "Polskie Radio i Telewizja" Biura Listów nr 62, maj 1964.

689 A term used by Tymiński, "Malwersacje w przedsiębiorstwach socjalistycznych 1950–1970," 110.

690 Krystyna Daszkiewicz, "Klimaty bezprawia," *Prawo i Życie* 23 (1964).

atmosphere, opposing these pathologies, or even just a reluctance to participate in criminal practices, could mean (and often actually meant) exposure at least to various types of harassment.

Investigative materials collected in the meat affair confirm this thesis, and it is on their basis that we have written about the development of a particular culture of corruption in this industry. According to its rules, "being honest" required . . . courage. Even if we believe that not all the information obtained during the investigation was true and that it could have been used by those under interrogation to clear themselves, it is worth quoting from these materials even if only as an indication of the existence of this phenomenon. They are confirmed by, among others, a manager of a butcher shop who was allegedly threatened by a dishonest MHM director who lodged a complaint against him at PIH. As an act of revenge, she was branded a "penalized shop," after which the PIH was sent to investigate, as a result of which the manager was sentenced to one month in prison with a suspension of two years, all for having committed a "mistake" totaling PLZ 4.20 in the sale of smoked ham.[691]

This thesis seems to also be confirmed by the case in 1953 of B. B., an employee of the State Transportation Enterprise No. 1 in Warsaw. His opinions involved, among other things, the delivery of meat to MHM shops. For this reason – as he testified – "in addition to the basic monthly salary, I received from deliverers a kilo of meat and 20–30 zlotys. Meat and money came from the managers of individual butcher shops handed in the form of 'tips' for bringing meat to the store and hanging it on hooks." At the end of the 1950s he was dismissed from this job, which meant he was deprived of this additional income. From 1961, he worked at the City Slaughterhouse in Warsaw as a meat deliverer for shops. His "rebellion" against corrupt practices ended with him being "framed" in a meat theft scheme. B.B.'s next workplace was the Meat Plant "Służewiec," where he was asked to participate in the "liquefaction" of 3 tons of pork and offered additional income. Another person involved said: "If I'm scared, I'll join the infantry." The word "infantry" meant dismissal: "Because I had a similar situation in the City Slaughterhouse, I finally agreed [. . .]. My criminal activity in the Meat Plant 'Służewiec' dates back to that point." It consisted of delivering stolen meat to the appropriate shops.[692]

---

691 ASO, IV K 155/64, vol. XX, Protokół przesłuchania świadka Mieczysławy Włodarczyk przez kpt. Tadeusza Ciołkowskiego z KG MO w dniu 17 września 1964, p. 15.

692 ASO, IV K 155/64 vol. XXII, Protokół przesłuchania podejrzanego, Warszawa 19 marca1964 r. przez mjr. St. Klimiuka z KG MO, p. 7.

Similarly, it was difficult to be honest while at work in the Warsaw food industry, as evidenced by the above-cited letter by Janusz Ch. from Warsaw, manager of several Warsaw restaurants. The author had grown up in a family of "taverns," but had abandoned his profession despite all of his knowledge and his passion. Explaining the reasons for this decision, he wrote:

> Everyone who wants to run a food establishment has two options: either entangle oneself in a "clique" and thus put oneself in a situation that is at least ambiguous both legally and morally, or act in accordance with the law and one's own conscience, which in turn inevitably leads to conflict with the "clique." I am not a wizard, but it seems to me that unfortunately such situations are common. For example, my many years of observation make me suppose that about 80 % of the managers of Warsaw establishments extract their "share" from waiters and bartenders. Those who sit in this environment even know exactly what the average "tariff" is – these days a barmaid probably "kicks back" PLZ 100 a day to the manager.[693]

The author of these words chose the honest solution, which meant giving up his chosen profession. However, such a choice does not seem to have been universal. More often, less "heroic" procedures were followed to reconcile the "conscience" with "reality of life." And in the end this did not have to mean a "rigid" sticking to the letter of the law.

Such a lenient attitude toward the theft of social property and its proliferation was present not just in the PRL. Similar phenomena developed in other Eastern Bloc countries, with the USSR at the forefront. Theft of "socialized property" became daily routine in the Soviet Union; indeed, such behavior was not treated as deviant.[694] The universality of theft testified to the defeat of communist ideology, which failed to gain real influence over the value system of the citizens of countries over which it ruled.

693 AODiZP, 1050/52, Biuletyn Wewnętrzny Biura Listów Komitetu do Spraw Radia i Telewizji "Polskie Radio i Telewizja" nr 62, maj 1964.

694 Maria Łoś, *Communist Ideology, Law and Crime. A Comparative View of the USSR and Poland* (Houndmills, Basingstoke, Hampshire, London: Macmillan Press, 1988), 206–207.

Conclusion

Based on the above analyses, we can draw several general conclusions relating to the history of meat in the PRL.

1. The lack of meat in People's Poland came primarily as the result of the economic model tied to the ideological assumptions of communism. An immanent feature of the so-called centrally managed socialist economy was a chronic shortage of goods and services. Such shortages were a constant feature of Polish society in the years 1944–1989, though their intensity varied.
2. To address this shortfall, the authorities used several basic strategies. Milder methods used to increase supply focused on stimulating agricultural production, including through gradual abandonment of the system of obligatory deliveries of agricultural products, including livestock (as of 1972), periodic increases in purchase prices for pigs and cattle, and the import of the means of agricultural and meat production. The latter instrument was used particularly often in the 1970s. Polish officials also attempted to manage the "meat mass" as economically as possible, which meant, among other things, the production of items whose meat content was as low as possible and could be replaced with plant products. During the worst food shortages, drastic efforts were made to force supply (strict enforcement of compulsory supplies of agricultural production, including the slaughter of animals).

   In the face of constant meat shortages, in addition to methods used to increase supply, various methods were used to limit demand. In relatively good economy times, the gentlest method of achieving this goal was to stimulate the consumption of food with ingredients other than meat and its meat by-products. In the 1970s, an attractive alternative to spending money on meat involved saving for the purchase of a small car or for a contribution to a cooperative apartment. Replacing meat with other products with similar calories was a constant topic in cookbooks published since the 1940s. These "gentle" methods of reducing demand did not always result in a socially acceptable improvement in meat supply. For this reason, they were often implemented alongside, or replaced by, methods that we might call conventionally-restrictive. These included the so-called meatless days in catering establishments. A much more effective form of limiting demand was direct administrative regulation (the ration card system). Demand was also limited by price increases of meat and meat products, which, however, was a rather dangerous solution because it often initiated outbreaks of social dissatisfaction with far-reaching consequences, including political upheaval.

3. There was a belief among those who ruled People's Poland that the shortage of goods and services was severe not only because of insufficient production but also because of the theft of some of what was produced. The belief that the shortage of goods (including meat) in Polish shops was the result of theft on the part of those employed in their production and distribution created the temptation to severely punish the thieves. In the case of meat, this way of thinking among party/state leaders led to a show trial in which the main accused – Stanisław Wawrzecki, who managed the company involved in coordinating the meat trade in Warsaw – was sentenced to death (a sentence that was carried out in 1965).

   Wawrzecki's case was only one of many brought against suspects in the meat economy. In 1963–1969, 1,809 defendants were brought up on meat fraud charges, of which as many as 1,767 were sentenced to imprisonment and additional penalties; one of those convicted (Wawrzecki) was given the death penalty. The findings of law enforcement agencies and special party committees dealing with crime in the meat industry showed that many party and state officials were involved in criminal activity or tolerance of fraud, including those holding high positions in central power institutions. In 1965–1966, 704 members from the Warsaw party organization alone were removed for various offenses, of which as many as 415 (58.9 %) for involvement in economic crimes.

4. Wawrzecki's trial took place under the pressure applied by several party and state institutions on the court in order to condemn Wawrzecki to death. Already in 1964, legal definitions and procedures raised serious formal and legal doubts. Submission or resistance to the directives of political authorities supervising punishment both in the Wawrzecki case and in cases involving perpetrators of other economic crimes provided the reasons that people in medium and central level of judicial institutions were promoted or demoted. Archival materials have allowed us to analyze the mechanisms by which the prosecutor's office and the judiciary in the so-called affairs were subordinated to central party authorities, and to show how punishment became a political act. The KC PZPR made decisions regarding not only legislative changes, promotions and demotion in central judicial institutions, but even specific indictments and penalties to be imposed in the most important economic fraud cases. However, these decisions were implemented with some resistance. A symbol in this regard is the figure of Judge Michał Kulczycki, who in 1960 resisted political pressure to impose the death penalty on the main

accused in the leather "affair," Eugeniusz Galicki. There are many indications that Alexander Zawadzki, chairman of the Council of State, was an opponent of the death penalty in economic crime cases.

5. The mechanisms for controlling the administration of justice in communist Poland, as used in the economic affairs of the 1960s, had their systemic, historical determinants. An important element in existence since the 1940s was the so-called staff nomenklatura and the "politicization" of prosecutors and judges. During the Stalinist period, one manifestation of how the judicial system was subordinated to decisions made within the communist party was the way in which the Special Commission to Battle Fraud and Economic Sabotage was set up and operated, and the "distribution" of criminal repression, motivated by political requirements, against peasants evading compulsory supplies.
6. Our study also showed the role that food shortages played in the everyday life of Polish families. Between 1945 and 1949/50, there was a quantitative increase in food consumption. As a result of the war, including changes in social stratification, there was a significant leveling of differences in this respect. From 1950, the transition to the implementation of the so-called six-year plan and – soon after – to the militarization of the economy, caused a fundamental break in the development of consumption; over the next four years, its pace declined significantly. In terms of food consumption, the period of particular deterioration came in 1952–1953. If meat consumption is taken as a measure, the deterioration began after 1951, reaching a low point in 1952, and the level from 1951 was not exceeded until 1955. The years 1955–1958 were a period of improvement, when food consumption rose again. An upward trend could be observed in 1959–1961. Meat consumption fluctuated, and in 1962 it was slightly above the level of 1958. At the same time, the consumption of low-value products (cereals) increased significantly. At the beginning of the 1960s, Poles still spent over 40 % of their income on food and their needs in this area were not met. The largest increases in meat consumption in the PRL took place in 1970–1975, when its consumption increased by over 17 kg per capita, which was the effect of the economic policy of the new government headed by Edward Gierek (1970–1980), focused as it was on increased consumption accompanied by increased national debt. This trend broke down briefly in 1976 and 1977 (69.1 kg and 70.6 kg). In 1980, the average Pole ate around 21 kg of meat more than in 1970. A more permanent break in this upward trend occurred as of 1981. In 1983, the level of consumption was similar to that of 1972. In 1981–1982, when Poland first experienced a period of political revival (the so-called Solidarity carnival starting in July/August

1980) and then martial law (from 13 December 1981), and as signs of a deepening economic crisis were becoming clear, the nutritional and caloric value of food consumption decreased to 1950s levels. However, the following year there was an improvement, as a result of which food consumption levels in the mid-1980s returned to the level of the late 1970s.

7. The demand for better nutrition, commonly equated with an increased consumption of meat, took various forms. Food supply demands were one of the most important topics contained in letters addressed by PRL citizens to central state institutions. Their analysis prompts us to hypothesize that a common pattern took root in the popular thinking among Poles, according to which the most important (and almost only) reason behind their poor material condition was the country's rulers. In colloquial opinions, "they" were cheating society, and were both incompetent and deprived of honor. It was "they" who were unable to govern well, who falsified the quality of food and industrial products. It was "they" who did not implement officially proclaimed slogans of social justice and equality, despite the fact that "we have equal stomachs." Poles identified their incompetence to constant price increases. They regarded their rulers as having created a "new bourgeoisie" with unjustified privileges. Poles were upset by the expensive way by which Poland's leaders exercised power. They criticized the policy of importing luxury goods when the "average" PRL citizen had difficulties buying basic food items. Colloquially, Poles also believed that their material deprivation was the result of USSR's exploitation of Poland and the need to bear the burden for Vietnam, Arab countries (since 1967) and Cuba.

A critical assessment of the food supply situation can also be found in private letters, leaflets, inscriptions on walls, and other written forms, the so-called hostile propaganda. We see the same kind of messages in rumors spread throughout Poland in 1945–1989, in political jokes, and in other colloquial statements.

Food-related problems also affected PRL citizens in their behavior, caught as they were between resistance and adaptation to everyday reality. In the case of peasants, the subject of the "game" with the authorities in this area involved benefits in kind and the compulsory delivery of basic agricultural products, including slaughter animals. It took the form of "illegal" slaughter, the exchange of "goods for goods," delayed deliveries, corruption among local authorities in order to reduce delivery sizes, etc. In cities, queues in front of grocery stores were a visible sign of food shortages. Theses queues were not only a place for verbal skirmishes, in which comments unfavorable to the government, including rumors, were made, but also they were – in a literal sense – "the battlefield."

Food difficulties had an impact on work discipline. Because of the need to queue, some employees (mainly women) often arrived late to work or left the workplace early. It was also not uncommon to leave work during working hours. In the Stalinist period, work breaks often came as a result of employees fainting due to malnutrition. For this very reason workers often refused to work overtime. Food shortages were one of the most important reasons why production plans were not implemented.

In 1945–1948, the vast majority of strikes were economic. In 1945, food supply demands were dominant. Workers tended to engage in these usually brief protests for many reasons, including wage cuts often tied to raised quotes, the transition from piecework pay to daily pay, and the change in items produced, various forms of production "rationalization," food supply difficulties, exhausting overtime work, introduction of new collective agreements, shortages in coal allocations, delayed wages, and poor working conditions (no protective clothing). A lack of meat – among other reasons – was the cause of one of the largest wave of strikes that swept through Poland in the summer of 1951. The center of worker protest at the time was Żyrardów.

During the Gomułka period, food supply demands leading to strikes were rare, but it seems that this could have been because they were "camouflaged" in the form of wage demands. The "economism" of the strike movement in Poland in 1945–1967 was also the result of its participants' dissatisfaction with daily difficulties tied to the food supply.

Demands for a reduction in food prices, along with an increase in wages, were an important part of the strikes of December 1970. It was at that time when an increase in such prices was a direct cause of the social conflict that resulted in the tragic massacre of workers on the Baltic Coast. Non-economic demands appeared much less frequently.

The food shortage motif also emerged during the strikes of July/August 1980. In 1981, the most spectacular manifestation of dissatisfaction due to food shortages came with the women's hunger marches, which took place in many cities. These marches harkened back to the women's demonstrations of 1945–1951, although the two differed in both scope and organization.

8. Analyses of economic crime in the PRL indicate that Poles were quite willing to forgive people for the petty theft of social property; this willingness points to one of the most important mass strategies for adapting to the PRL social order. Poles created their own procedures to justify these strategies, which encouraged growth in the workplace of a "culture of corruption" or a "climate

of lawlessness." One of the PRL's basic features was permission to commit fraud and embezzle funds; thus, their universality. In such an atmosphere, opposition to these pathologies, or even just reluctance to participate in criminal practices, could mean (and often actually meant) exposure to at least various types of harassment.

Acronyms in Footnotes

AAN	Archiwum Akt Nowych
ADH PRL	Archiwum Dokumentacji Historycznej PRL
AODiZP	Archiwum Ośrodka Dokumentacji i Zbiorów Programowych TVP S.A.
APW	Archiwum Państwowe w Warszawie
ARZ	Archiwum Ruchu Zawodowego
ASO	Archiwum Sądu Okręgowego w Warszawie
ATNS OBOP	Archiwum Taylor Nelson Sofres Ośrodka Badania Opinii Publicznej
AZHRL	Archiwum Zakładu Historii Ruchu Ludowego
BKRP	Biuro Kontroli przy Radzie Państwa
BP KRN	Biuro Prezydialne Krajowej Rady Narodowej
CAMSWiA	Centralne Archiwum Ministerstwa Spraw Wewnętrznych i Administracji
CKKP	Centralna Komisja Kontroli Partyjnej
CRZZ	Centralna Rada Związków Zawodowych
GUS	Główny Urząd Statystyczny
IPN BU	Instytut Pamięci Narodowej Biuro Udostępniania
Kanc.S	Kancelaria Sejmu
KW PZPR	Komitet Warszawski Polskiej Zjednoczonej Partii Robotniczej
MA	Ministerstwo Aprowizacji
MHWiU	Ministerstwo Handlu Wewnętrznego i Usług
MHZ	Ministerstwo Handlu Zagranicznego
MKP	Ministerstwo Kontroli Państwowej
MPSiS	Ministerstwo Przemysłu Spożywczego i Skupu
MS	Ministerstwo Sprawiedliwości
NBP	Narodowy Bank Polski
NK	Naczelny Komitet
PDT	Państwowe Domy Towarowe
PG	Prokuratura Generalna
PKPG	Państwowa Komisja Planowania Gospodarczego
PKS	Państwowa Komunikacja Sacmochodowa
PTE	Polskie Towarzystwo Ekonomiczne
WKW	Warszawski Komitet Wojewódzki
PZPR	Polska Zjednoczona Partia Robotnicza
ZSL	Zjednoczone Stronnictwo Ludowe

Acronyms in Main Text

CAP	Centrala Artykułów Pozaprasowych "Ruch"
CBOS	Centrum Badania Opinii Społecznej
CHZ	Centrala Handlu Zagranicznego
CUSiK	Centralny Urząd Skupu i Kontraktacji
CZSP	Centralny Związek Spółdzielczości Pracy
DRN	Dzielnicowa Rada Narodowa
FSO	Fabryka Samochodów Osobowych
GUKPPiW	Główny Urząd Kontroli Prasy, Publikacji i Widowisk
GZG	Gdańskie Zakłady Gastronomiczne
KG MO	Komenda Główna Milicji Obywatelskiej
KC PZPR	Komitet Centralny Polskiej Zjednoczonej Partii Robotniczej
KCZZ	Komisja Centralna Związków Zawodowych
KD	Komitet Dzielnicowy
KM	Komitet Miejski
KP	Komitet Powiatowy
KRN	Krajowa Rada Narodowa
KS	Komisja Specjalna do Walki z Nadużyciami i Szkodnictwem Gospodarczym
MBP	Ministerstwo Bezpieczeństwa Publicznego
MHD	Miejski Handel Detaliczny
MHM	Miejski Handel Mięsem
MHW	Ministerstwo Handlu Wewnętrznego
MKS	Międzyzakładowy Komitet Strajkowy
MON	Ministerstwo Obrony Narodowej
MpiOS	Ministerstwo Pracy i Opieki Społecznej
MZO	Miejskie Zakłady Opałowe
NIK	Najwyższa Izba Kontroli
NSZZ	Niezależny Samorządny Związek Zawodowy
OOP	Oddziałowa Organizacja Partyjna
PAP	Polska Agencja Prasowa
p.c.	penal code
PGR	Państwowe Gospodarstwa Rolne
PIH	Państwowa Inspekcja Handlowa
PKO	Powszechna Kasa Oszczędności
PKWN	Polski Komitet Wyzwolenia Narodowego

POP	Podstawowa Organizacja Partyjna
PKP	Polskie Koleje Państwowe
p.o.	pełniący obowiązki
PRL	Polska Rzeczpospolita Ludowa
RNm.st.W	Rada Narodowa miasta stołecznego Warszawy
RZO	Radomskie Zakłady Obuwia
SB	Służba Bezpieczeństwa
SGPiS	Szkoła Główna Planowania i Statystyki
UNRRA	United Nations Relief and Rehabilitation Administration
WKKP	Wojewódzka Komisja Kontroli Partyjnej
WRZZ	Wojewódzka Rada Związków Zawodowych
WZG	Warszawskie Zakłady Gastronomiczne

Bibliography

1. Archives

Archiwum Akt Nowych w Warszawie

Biuro Kontroli przy Radzie Państwa

Biuro Prezydialne Krajowej Rady Narodowej

Centralny Urząd Planowania

Centralny Urząd Skupu i Kontraktacji

Główny Urząd Kontroli Prasy, Publikacji i Widowisk

Kancelaria Rady Państwa

Kancelaria Sejmu

Komitet Centralny Polskiej Zjednoczonej Partii Robotniczej

Komisja Specjalna do Walki z Nadużyciami i Szkodnictwem Gospodarczym

Ministerstwo Aprowizacji

Ministerstwo Handlu Wewnętrznego

Ministerstwo Handlu Wewnętrznego i Usług

Ministerstwo Kontroli Państwowej

Ministerstwo Przemysłu Spożywczego i Skupu

Ministerstwo Sprawiedliwości

Najwyższa Izba Kontroli

Państwowa Komisja Planowania Gospodarczego

Prokuratura Generalna

Urząd Rady Ministrów

Archiwum Dokumentacji Historycznej PRL

Biuletyny Informacyjne Biura Sekretariatu KC PZPR

Kolekcja Stefana Jędrychowskiego

Kolekcja Eugeniusza Szyra

Archiwum Państwowe w Warszawie

Komitet Warszawski Polskiej Zjednoczonej Partii Robotniczej

Warszawski Komitet Wojewódzki Polskiej Zjednoczonej Partii Robotniczej

Centralne Archiwum Wojskowe

Główny Zarząd Polityczno – Wychowawczy Wojska Polskiego

Archiwum Ośrodka Dokumentacji i Zbiorów Programowych TVP S.A.

Biuletyny Biura Listów Komitetu do Spraw Radiofonii "Polskie Radio" i Komitetu do Spraw Radia i Telewizji "Polskie Radio i Telewizja"

Archiwum Ruchu Zawodowego

Centralna Rada Związków Zawodowych

Archiwum Sądu Okręgowego w Warszawie

Akta sprawy IV K 155/64

Archiwum Zakładu Historii Ruchu Ludowego

Naczelny Komitet Zjednoczonego Stronnictwa Ludowego

Archiwum Instytutu Pamięci Narodowej

Komenda Główna Milicji Obywatelskiej

Ministerstwo Bezpieczeństwa Publicznego

Komitet do Spraw Bezpieczeństwa Publicznego

Ministerstwo Spraw Wewnętrznych

Archiwum Taylor Nelson Sofres Ośrodka Badania Opinii Publicznej:

9.36 D. Markowska, Z. Sufin, Moralność pracy i zjawiska z nią związane w zakładzie przemysłowym (sprawozdanie z badań monograficznych w Zakładzie Budowy Urządzeń Przemysłowych im. Ludwika Waryńskiego w Warszawie).

9.50 R. Peretiatkowicz, Zakupy w Warszawie, Warszawa 1962.

9.46 A. Pawełczyńska, J. Malanowski, Stosunek do pracy i własności społecznej w polskim społeczeństwie 1961.

Prestiż prawa. Problematyka, zakres i metody badań, Warszawa 1966.

9.63 A. Siciński, Postawy wobec pracy i własności 1961.

9.73 Z. Skórzyński, Podstawowe zajęcia mieszkańców Warszawy w codziennym budżecie czasu, Warszawa 1962.

9.098A I. Wiatr, Opinie o metodach podnoszenia stopy życiowej 1959, OBOP listopad 1959.

9.098B I. Wiatr, Opinie o zaspokojeniu potrzeb materialnych ludności miejskiej, Warszawa listopad 1959.

9.098B I. Wiatr, Prognozy popytu i jego zasadniczych tendencji, Warszawa listopad 1959.

9.105 K. Zagórski, Obraz poziomu stopy życiowej w badaniach OBOP-u, Warszawa 1964.

9.109 Z. Żekoński, Struktura żywienia ludności miast (Wyniki badań ankietowych), Warszawa 1961.

9.110 Z. Żekoński, Wstępne informacje o strukturze żywienia ludności miast, Warszawa 1960.

2. Periodicals

Biuletyn Instytutu Ekonomiki Rolnictwa, 1953

Economic Survey of Europe, 1967

Gazeta Prawnicza, 1981

Nowe Drogi, 1959

Ławnik Ludowy, 1964

Magazyn Rodzinny, 1982

Nowe Drogi, 1959

Prawo i Życie, 1964, 1965

Przyjaciółka, 1949, 1953, 1964

Współczesność, 1965

Wprost, 2002

Trybuna Ludu, 1956, 1964

Tu i Teraz, 1984

Tygodnik Powszechny 1981

Tygodnik Solidarność, 1981

Życie Gospodarcze, 1964

Życie Literackie, 1964

Życie Warszawy, 1956

3. Published Primary Sources

Atlas przestępczości w Polsce. Edited by Siemaszko, Andrzej. Warszawa: Oficyna Naukowa, 1994.

Bigben, Jan, *Warszawski dowcip. Kawał Warszawy 1945–1968*. Toronto, 1980.

Biuletyny dzienne Ministerstwa Bezpieczeństwa Publicznego 1949–1950. Edited by Kamiński, Łukasz. Warszawa: Instytut Pamięci Narodowej, 2004.

Biuletyny Informacyjne Ministerstwa Bezpieczeństwa Publicznego 1946. Edited by Chudzik, Wanda, Marczak, Irena, Olkuśnik, Marek. Warszawa: Ministerstwo Spraw Wewnętrznych, 1996.

Biuletyny Informacyjne Ministerstwa Bezpieczeństwa Publicznego 1947, vol. 1. Edited by Grodek, Bernadetta, Marczak, Irena. Warszawa: Ministerstwo Spraw Wewnętrznych, 1993.

Centrum władzy. Protokoły posiedzeń kierownictwa PZPR. Wybór z lat 1949–1970. Eds. Dudek, Antoni, Kochański, Aleksander, Persak, Krzysztof. Warszawa: Instytut Studiów Politycznych PAN, 2000.

Chrzanowski, Wiesław. *Pół wieku polityki czyli rzecz o obronie czynnej. Z Wiesławem Chrzanowskim rozmawiali Piotr Mierecki i Bogusław Kiernicki*. Warszawa: Ad Astra, 1997.

Czerwiec 1976 w materiałach archiwalnych. Ed. Jerzy Eisler. Warszawa: IPN, 2001.

Dowcip surowo wzbroniony. Antologia polskiego dowcipu politycznego, vol. 2. Toruń: Comer, 1991.

Dziennik Ustaw, 1944, 1945, 1946, 1947, 1949, 1951, 1952, 1953, 1958, 1959, 1963, 1969, 1971.

Food Consumption Statistics 1955–1971. Paris: OECD, 1973.

Food Consumption Statistics 1960–1968. Paris: OECD, 1970.

Katalog niektórych spraw: kryminalnych, gospodarczych, dewizowych i innych prowadzonych przez jednostki Milicji Obywatelskiej na terenie kraju. Warszawa: Wydawnictwo KG MO, Oddział Kontroli, Badań i Analiz, grudzień 1966.

Klapa bezpieczeństwa czyli humor zakurtynowy. Ed. Aleksander Janta. Buffalo: Sunrise Press, 1953.

Kochański, Aleksander. *Polska 1944–1991. Informator historyczny*. Vol. II. Warszawa: Wydawnictwo Sejmowe, 2000.

Kodeks karny RSFRR. Kodeks procesowy RSFRR. Ustawa o ustroju sądów RFSRR. Warszawa: Wydawnictwo Prawnicze, 1961.

Komisja Specjalna do Walki z Nadużyciami i Szkodnictwem Gospodarczym (1945–1954). Wybór źródeł. Ed. and intro. Dariusz Jarosz, Tadeusz Wolsza. Warszawa: Główna Komisja Badania Zbrodni przeciwko Narodowi Polskiemu Instytut Pamięci Narodowej, 1995.

Mały Rocznik Statystyczny GUS 1990. Warszawa: GUS, 1990.

Nie tylko do śmiechu. Dowcipy z czadów Peerelu 1948–1989. Z wieloletniej kolekcji Bronisława Sałudy. Warszawa: Omnipress, 1991.

Pamiętniki prawników. Wybór prac nadesłanych na konkurs pod nazwą "Pamiętniki prawników. Wspomnienia z 25 lat Polski Ludowej." Warszawa: Wydawnictwo Prawnicze, 1969.

Postulaty 1970–71 i 1980. Materiały źródłowe do dziejów wystąpień pracowniczych w latach 1970–1971 i 1980 (Gdańsk i Szczecin). Eds. Beata Chmiel, Elżbieta Kaczyńska Warszawa: Niezależna Oficyna Wydawnicza "Nowa," Stowarzyszenie "Archiwum Solidarności," 1998.

Rakowski, Mieczysław F. *Dzienniki polityczne 1958–1962.*Warszawa: Iskry, 1998.

________. *Dzienniki polityczne 1963–1966*, Warszawa: Iskry, 1999.

"Relacja Artura Starewicza p nastrojach społecznych na wsi w sierpniu 1948 r." Ed. Dariusz Jarosz. *Dzieje Najnowsze* 2 (1993).

Rocznik Statystyczny GUS 1959. Warszawa: GUS, 1959.

Rocznik Statystyczny GUS 1961. Warszawa: GUS, 1961.

Rocznik Statystyczny GUS 1965. Warszawa: GUS 1965.

Rocznik Statystyczny GUS 1967. Warszawa: GUS, 1967.

Rocznik Statystyczny GUS 1969. Warszawa: GUS, 1969.

Rocznik Statystyczny GUS 1971. Warszawa: GUS, 1971.

Rocznik Statystyczny GUS 1982. Warszawa: GUS, 1982.

Rolniczy Rocznik Statystyczny 1945–1965. Warszawa: GUS, 1966.

Rocznik Statystyki Międzynarodowej GUS 1970. Warszawa: GUS, 1970.

Rocznik Statystyki Międzynarodowej GUS 1977. Warszawa: GUS, 1977.

Rocznik Statystyki Międzynarodowej GUS 1991. Warszawa: GUS, 1991.

Rocznik Statystyki Międzynarodowej GUS 2003. Warszawa: GUS, 2003.

Rosenbusch, Adam. *Śmiech zakazany. Antologia dowcipu politycznego Polski Ludowej*. Melbourne: Harold Press, 1987.

Statisticzieskij jeżegodnik stran-czlienow Sowieta Ekonomiczeskoj Wzaimopomoszczi 1976. Moskwa, 1976.

Uchwały Komitetu Centralnego Polskiej Zjednoczonej Partii Robotniczej od II do III Zjazdu. Warszawa: Książka i Wiedza, 1959.

4. Published Secondary Sources

Adamus, Anna. "Problemy wsi w Polsce w latach 1956–1980 w świetle listów do władz centralnych." *Dzieje Najnowsze* 1 (2017).

________. *Problemy wsi w Polsce w latach 1956–1980 w świetle listów do władz centralnych*. Warszawa: Instytut Pamięci Narodowej, 2017.

Andrejew, Igor. *Polskie prawo karne w zarysie*. Warszawa: PWN, 1980.

Bafia, Jerzy. *Odpowiedzialność karna za przestępstwa przeciw własności społecznej. Z problematyki zmian wprowadzonych przez ustawę z 18 czerwca 1959*. Warszawa: Wydawnictwo Prawnicze, 1960.

________. Hochberg Leo. *Przestępstwa gospodarcze. Komentarz*. Warszawa: 1960.

________. Hochberg Leo, Siewierski Mieczysław. *Ustawy karne PRL. Komentarz*. Warszawa: Wydawnictwo Prawnicze, 1965.

Beskid, Lidia. "Sytuacja materialna i potrzeby robotników w 1983 r. (wyniki badania ankietowego)." In *Położenie klasy robotniczej w Polsce*, vol. 3: *Warunki bytu robotników*. Warszawa: IPPML, 1984.

Błaszkiewicz, Anna. "Prawda i konwencja. Analiza poezji robotniczej okresu napięć społecznych (grudzień 1970 i sierpień 1980)". *Studia nad ruchami społecznymi*. Eds. Ewa Lewicka-Banaszak, Piotr Marciniak, Wojciech Modzelewski. Warszawa: Uniwersytet Warszawski, 1987.

Brzostek, Błażej. *Robotnicy Warszawy. Konflikty codzienne (1950–1954)*. Warszawa: TRIO, 2002.

Burrel, Kathy. "The Political and Social Life of Food in Socialist Poland." *Anthropology of East Europe Review*, no 21 (2003).

Bywalec, Czesław, *Wzrost gospodarczy a poziom życia społeczeństwa polskiego*, Warszawa: Instytut rynku Wewnętrznego i Konsumpcji, 1991.

Chumiński, Jędrzej. "Formy obrony interesów pracowniczych w warunkach totalizacji życia społecznego (1949–1956)." *Studia Historyczne* 1 (1999).

________. *Ruch zawodowy w Polsce w warunkach kształtującego się systemu totalitarnego 1944–1956*. Wrocław: Wydawnictwo Akademii Ekonomicznej, 1999.

Crowley, David. "Warsaw's Shops: Stalinism and the Thaw". In *Style and Socialism: Modernity and Material Culture in Post-War Eastern Europe*. Eds. Susan E. Reid, Susan Emily and Crowley, David. Oxford: Berg, 2000.

Cyprian Tadeusz. *Przestępstwa gospodarcze*. Warszawa: PWN, 1960.

Czerny, Zofia. *Książka kucharska*. Warszawa: Polskie Wydawnictwa Gospodarcze, 1954.

________. Strasburger, Maria. *Gotuj smacznie i zdrowo*. Warszawa: Państwowy Zakład Wydawnictw Lekarskich, 1957.

________. Strasburger, Maria. *Żywienie rodziny. Wiadomości ogólne. Przepisy potraw*. Warszawa: Czytelnik, 1948.

Cziomer, Erhard. *Zarys historii Niemiec powojennych 1945–1995*. Warszawa – Kraków: Wydawnictwo Naukowe PWN, 1997.

Danowska Bogumiła. *Grudzień 1970 roku na Wybrzeżu Gdańskim*. Pelplin: Bernardinum, 2000.

Drążkiewicz, Jerzy, Rychard. "Strajki w regionie warszawskim w lecie 1980 r.," in *Studia nad ruchami społecznymi*. Ed. Kulpińska Jolanta. Warszawa: UW, PTS, 1990.

Dudek, Antoni, Marszałkowski, Tomasz. *Walki uliczne w PRL 1956–1989*. Kraków: Krakówska Oficyna Wydawnicza, 1992.

Dudzik, Maria [et al.]. *Praktyczna kuchnia.* Warszawa: Państwowe Wydawnictwo Rolnicze i Leśne, 1959.

Dyka, Sławomir, Urban, Roman. "Uboje gospodarcze i niezorganizowany rynek mięsa." *Badania Rynku Żywca i Mięsa* 2 (1964).

Evielson Evgenija. *Sudebnyje prociessy po ekonomiceskim dielam w SSSR.* London: Overseas Publ. Interchange, 1986.

Felbur, Stefan. *Analiza układu cen produktów rolnych w Polsce.* Warszawa: Państwowe wydawnictwo Naukowe, 1962.

Ferriéres, Madeleine, *Histoire des peurs alimantaires. Du Moyen Âge à l'aube du XXe siècle.* Paris: Edition du Seuil, 2002.

Fidelis, Małgorzata. *Kobiety, komunizm i industrializacja w powojennej Polsce.* Warszawa: W.A.B., 2015.

________. *Women, communism, and industrialization in postwar Poland.* Cambridge: Cambridge University Press 2010.

Fiedorczyk, Piotr. *Komisja Specjalna do Walki z Nadużyciami i Szkodnictwem Gospodarczym 1945–1954. Studium historycznoprawne.* Białystok: Temida 2, 2002.

Fuszara, Małgorzata. "Prawne aspekty reglamentacji." In *Umowa o kartki.* Ed. Kurczewski, Jacek. Warszawa: TRIO, 2004.

________. Jakubowska, Iwona, Kurczewski. "Sprawiedliwość czasów reglamentacji." In *Umowa o kartki.* Ed. Kurczewski. Warszawa: Trio, 2004.

Górecki, Wojciech, "Strajki robotnicze w Łodzi w latach 1948–1949," *Polska 1944/45–1989. Studia i materiały* IV (1999).

Górniok, Oktawia. *Przestępczość gospodarcza (Wybrane przejawy i uwarunkowania).* Katowice: Uniwersytet Śląski, 1986.

Grabarczyk, Grażyna. *Przestępczość gospodarcza na tle przemian ustrojowych w Polsce.* Toruń: Towarzystwo Naukowe Organizacji i Kierownictwa "Dom Organizatora," 2002.

Grosse, Tomasz, Grużewski, Jarosław, Kozak, Michał, Kula, Marcin, Meller, Marcin, Piasecki, Konrad, Piskorski, Paweł, Salak, Piotr, Woźniak, Marcin, Zalewski, Piotr. "Szarzy ludzie zaplątani w codzienności komunizmu." *Przegląd Historyczny* 3 (1993).

Grześkowiak, Alicja. *Kara śmierci w polskim prawie karnym.* Toruń: Uniwersytet Mikołaja Kopernika, 1982.

Gulbicka, Bożena. *Zmiany w spożyciu żywności w grupach społeczno-ekonomicznych gospodarstw domowych w latach 1981–1990.* Warszawa: IERiGŻ, 1991.

________. Sztarbałło, Wanda, Chmielewska, Barbara, Dyka, Aleksandra. *Samowystarczalność żywnościowa Polski*. Warszawa: Instytut Ekonomiki Rolnictwa i Gospodarki Żywnościowej, 1990.

Holzer, Jerzy. "*Solidarność*" *1980–1981. Geneza i historia*. Paryż: Instytut Literacki, 1984.

Jagiełło, Jerzy. "Przestępczość w przemyśle i handlu mięsem w świetle warszawskiej afery mięsnej." *Problemy Kryminalistyki* 53 (1965).

Jarosz, Dariusz. "Akta Biura Listów i Inspekcji KC PZPR jako źródło do badań rzeczywistości społecznej w Polsce w latach 1950–1956." *Polska 1944/45–1989. Studia i materiały* II (1997).

________. "Chłopskie oswajanie Polski Ludowej". In *Dzieje i przyszłość ruchu ludowego*, vol. 2: *Polska Ludowa (1944/45–1989)*. Eds. Waldemar Paruch, Stefan Pastuszka, Romuald Turkowski. Warszawa: Ludowa Spółdzielnia Wydawnicza, 2002.

________. "Citizens of communist Poland as 'small individualists.'" *Acta Poloniae Historica* 105 (2012).

________. "Listy do centralnych instytucji państwa stalinowskiego jako źródło do badań życia codziennego w Polsce." *Kwartalnik Historii Kultury Materialnej* 3 (1996).

________. "Listy do centralnych instytucji państwa stalinowskiego jako źródło do badań życia codziennego w Polsce." *Kwartalnik Historii Kultury Materialnej* 3 (1996).

________. "Oswajanie wrogiej rzeczywistości. Chłopi polscy a instytucje państwowe w latach 1948–1956". *Pamiętnik Instytutu Macieja Rataja* 3 (1996).

________. "Poles and the collapse of communism: in search of a new paradigm. Not only social resistance and political opposition." *Divinatio* 39–40 (2015).

________. *Polityka władz komunistycznych w Polsce w latach 1948–1956 a chłopi*. Warszawa: Wydawnictwo DiG, 1998.

________. "POST-1989 historiography's distorted image of the relation between authorities and society in Poland during the period from 1944 to 1989." *Revue d'études comparatives Est-Ouest* 45 (2014).

________. M. Pasztor. *W krzywym zwierciadle. Polityka władz komunistycznych w Polsce w świetle plotek i pogłosek z lat 1949–1956*. Warszawa: Fakt, 1995.

________. Wolsza, Tadeusz. "Komisja Specjalna do Walki z Nadużyciami i Szkodnictwem Gospodarczym (1945–1954)." *Biuletyn Głównej Komisji Badania Zbrodni przeciwko Narodowi Polskiemu"* 36 (1993).

Jastrząb, Michał. *Puste półki. Problem zaopatrzenia ludności w artykuły powszechnego użytku w Polsce w latach 1949–1956.* Warszawa: Wydawnictwo Szkoły Przedsiębiorczości i Zarządzania im. Leona Koźmińskiego, 2004.

Juźwik, Aleksander. "Zagraniczna pomoc charytatywna dla dzieci i młodzieży w Polsce w latach 1945–1950". *Polska 1944/45–1989. Studia i materiały* 11 (2013).

Kaliński, Janusz. *Bitwa o handel 1947–1948.* Warszawa: Książka i Wiedza, 1971.

Kallas, Marian, Lityński, Adam. *Historia ustroju i prawa Polski Ludowej.* Warszawa: Wydawnictwo Lexis Naxis, 2003.

Kamiński, Łukasz. Lingua securitatis. *Pamięć i Sprawiedliwość* 1 (2003).

________. "Plotka i pogłoska polityczna w Polsce w świetle akt Ministerstwa Informacji i Propagandy (1945–1947)". Ed. Wojciech Wrzesiński. *Wrocławskie studia z historii najnowszej*, IV (1997).

________. *Polacy wobec nowej rzeczywistości 1944–1948: formy pozainstytucjonalnego, żywiołowego oporu społecznego.* Toruń: Wydawnictwo Adam Marszałek, 2000.

________. "Strajki robotnicze w Polsce w latach 1945–1948." Wrocław: Gajt, 1999.

________. "Strajki robotnicze w Polsce 1945–1948. Próba bilansu." *Dzieje Najnowsze* 4 (1997).

Kenney, Padraic. *Rebuilding Poland. Workers and Communists 1945–1950.* Ithaca and London: Cornell Univeristy Press, 1997.

Kierlik, Jan. *O przestępczości w przetwórstwie mięsnym.* Warszawa: Departament Szkolenia i Doskonalenia Zawodowego MSW, 1974.

Kochanowski, Jerzy. "Do uboju." *Polityka* 33 (2002).

________. "Das 'Problem Nummer 1' und seine Protagonisten. Fleisch und Fleischspekulanten in Polen 1944 bis 1989." *Unsere Feinde. Konstruktionen des Anderen im Sozialismus.* Lepzig: Leipziger Universitätsverlag, 2004.

________. Kochanowski, Jerzy. " 'Serdelki oczywiście zostają', czyli jeszcze jeden dowód na polityczną rolę kiełbasy (w 1956 r.)." *Kuchnia władzy. Księga pamiątkowa z okazji 70-tej rocznicy urodzin Andrzeja Garlickiego.* Eds. Borodziej, Włodzimierz and J. Kochanowski. Warszawa: Czytelnik, 2005.

________. *Tylnymi drzwiami. "Czarny rynek" w Polsce 1944–1989.* Warszawa: Wydawnictwo Neriton i Instytut Historyczny UW, 2010.

________. "Zmagania ze smokiem. . .: działalność Centralnej Komisji do Walki ze Spekulacją (1981–1987)". *Przegląd Historyczny* 4 (2010).

Kołakowska-Przełomiec Helena, Syzduł, Edward. "Przestępstwa gospodarcze w Polsce w świetle statystyki milicyjnej za lata 1962–1965". *Państwo i Prawo* 9 (1966).

Komarow, W.E., Czierniawskij, U.G. Dochody i potrieblienije nasielienija SSSR, Moskwa 1973.

Kordos, Jan, Kubiczek, Agata. "Warunki bytu rodzin robotniczych w latach 1980–1983." *Warunki bytu robotników*. Ed. Przemysław Wójcik. Warszawa: IPPML, 1984.

Kornai, János. *Economics of shortage*. New York: North-Holland Pub. Co, 1980.

________. *Niedobór w gospodarce*. Warszawa: Państwowe Wydawnictwo Ekonomiczne, 1985.

Kos, Czesław, Nowak, Jan. *Tendencje spożycia żywności w wybranych krajach RWPG i EWG*. Warszawa: IRWiR PAN, 1988.

Kozlov, V. A., *Massovyje besporiadki w SSSR pri Khrushchevie i Brezhnevie (1953 - naczalo 1980-ch gg.)*. Novosibirsk, 1999.

Kuchnia polska. Warszawa: Państwowe Wydawnictwo Ekonomiczne, 1974.

Kurczewski, Jacek. *Umowa o kartki*. In *Umowa o kartki*. Ed. J. Kurczewski. Warszawa: Trio, 2004.

Lernell, Leszek. *Przestępczość gospodarcza. Zagadnienia społeczno-ekonomiczne*. Warszawa: Wydawnictwo Prawnicze 1965.

Lesiakowski, Krzysztof. *Strajki robotnicze w Łodzi 1945–1976*. Łódź: IPN, 2008.

Leszczyński, Adam. *Sprawy do załatwienia. Listy do "Po prostu" 1955–1957*. Warszawa: TRIO, 2000

Lorek, Elżbieta. *Zmiany w strukturze konsumpcji w Polsce w układzie przestrzennym*. Katowice: Akademia Ekonomiczna, 1993.

Luszniewicz, Andrzej. *O metodach badania budżetów rodzinnych w Polsce w latach 1920–1957 (Szkic historyczny)*. Warszawa: Polskie Wydawnictwa Gospodarcze, 1959.

Łoś, Maria. *Communist Ideology, Law and Crime. A Comparative View of the USSR and Poland*. Houndmills, Basingstoke, Hampshire, London: Macmillan Press, 1988.

Łukasiewicz, Piotr. *Pogłoski i dowcip polityczny w PRL*. Warszawa: In Plus, 1987.

Łysiak, Wojciech. *Wielka kontestacja. Folklor polityczny w PRL*. Poznań: PSO, 1998.

Machcewicz, Paweł. *Polski rok 1956*. Warszawa: "Mówią Wieki," 1993.

Madej, Krzysztof. "Kara śmierci za mięso". *Biuletyn Instytutu Pamięci Narodowej* 11 (2002).

Majchrzak, Irena. *Pracownicze przestępstwo gospodarcze i jego sprawca*. Warszawa: Wiedza Powszechna, 1965.

Małkiewicz, Andrzej. "Demonstracje robotnicze w Brnie w 1951 r." In *Studia i materiały z dziejów opozycji i oporu społecznego*. Ed. Kamiński. II (1999).

________, Ruchniewicz, Krzysztof, *Pierwszy znak solidarności. Polskie odgłosy powstania ludowego w NRD w 1953 r.* Wrocław: Arboretum, 1998.

Marecki, Jacek. *Ekonomiczne i organizacyjne problemy przestępczości gospodarczej*. Warszawa 1962 (manuscript).

________. "Na niekorzyść konsumenta". *Życie Gospodarcze* 28 (1964).

Marciniak, Piotr. "Horyzont programowy strajków w 1980 r." In *Studia nad ruchami społecznymi*. Eds. Piotr Marciniak, Wojciech Modzelewski. Vol. II. Warszawa: UW, PTS, 1989.

Marody, Mirosława. "Przemiany postaw ideologicznych i przystosowanie w systemie komunistycznym." In *Komunizm. Ideologia, system, ludzie*. Ed. Tomasz Szarota. Warszawa: Neriton, 2001.

________. *Warunki trwania i zmiany ładu społecznego w relacji do stanu świadomości społecznej*. Warszawa: Instytut Socjologii UW, 1986.

Mazurek-Łopacińska, Krystyna. "Modelowanie konsumpcji żywności". In *Polski model konsumpcji, cz. 2. Problemowe modele konsumpcji lat osiemdziesiątych – wybrane techniki*. Eds. Józefa Kramer, Zofia Kądzior. Katowice: Akademia Ekonomiczna Instytut Rynku i Konsumpcji, 1990.

Mieczkowski, Bogdan. *Personal and Social Consumption in Eastern Europe. Poland, Czechoslovakia, Hungary, and East Germany*. New York Washington London: Praeger Publishers, 1975.

Miernik, Grzegorz. "Dzień powszedni robotników w województwie kieleckim w okresie stalinowskim." Ed. Jacek Wijczak. *Z przeszłości regionu świętokrzyskiego od XVI do XX wieku*. Kielce: Jard, 2003.

Murzynowski, Andrzej and Rezler, Jan. *Wymiar sprawiedliwości w Polsce w latach 1944–1970. Ustawodawstwo, organizacja i działalność*. Warszawa: Wydawnictwo Uniwersytetu Warszawskiego, 1972.

Nalepa, Edward J. "Wojskowe bataliony górnicze w Polsce w latach 1949–1959." *Przegląd Historyczny* 1–2 (1994).

Narojek, Winicjusz. *Perspektywy pluralizmu w upaństwowionym społeczeństwie*. Warszawa: ISP PAN, Toruń: Adam Marszałek, 1994.

Naumiuk, Jan. *Na początku trudnej drogi. Ruch zawodowy w Polsce Ludowej w latach 1944–1949*. Kielce: Wydawnictwo Łódzkie, 1985.

Naumowicz, Z. "Przestępstwa w handlu." *Biuletyn Generalnej Prokuratury* 12 (1964).

Paczkowski, Andrzej. *System nomenklatury kadr w Polsce (1950–1970)*. Warszawa: Instytut Studiów Politycznych PAN, 2000.

Pawełko, Witold. *Zapobieganie przestępstwom gospodarczym*. Warszawa: PWN, 1971.

Piotrowski, Paweł. "Reforma walutowa 1953 r. w Czechosłowacji i jej skutki społeczne." In *Studia i materiały z dziejów opozycji i oporu społecznego*. Ed. Kamiński. III (2000).

Poznański Czerwiec 1956. Eds. Jarosław Maciejewski, Zofia Trojanowiczowa. Poznań: Wydawnictwo Poznańskie, 1990.

Poznański Czerwiec 1956 w dokumentach. Ed. Stanisław Jankowiak, Edmund Makowski. Poznań: IPN, 1995.

Ruzikowski, Tadeusz. "Tajni współpracownicy pionów operacyjnych aparatu bezpieczeństwa 1950–1984," *Pamięć i Sprawiedliwość* 1 (2003).

Rychard, Andrzej. "Konflikt i przystosowanie: dwie koncepcje ładu społecznego w Polsce." In *Rzeczywistość polska i sposoby radzenia sobie z nią*. Eds. Mirosława Marody, Antoni Sułek. Warszawa: UW, 1987.

Rzepliński, Andrzej. "Przystosowanie ustroju sądownictwa do potrzeb państwa totalitarnego w Polsce w latach 1944–1956." In *Przestępstwa sędziów i prokuratorów w Polsce lat 1944–1956*. Eds. Witold Kulesza and Andrzej Rzepliński, Warszawa: Instytut Pamięci Narodowej, 2000.

Sasanka, Paweł. *Czerwiec 1976. Geneza przebieg konsekwencje*. Warszawa: Instytut Pamięci Narodowej, 2006.

Skazani bez wyroku. Warszawa: Krajowy Zarząd Związku Represjonowanych Żołnierzy Górników, 1999.

Skórzyński, Zygmunt. *Podstawowe zajęcia mieszkańców Warszawy w codziennym budżecie czasu*. Warszawa: OBOP, 1962.

Spożycie artykułów żywnościowych w gospodarstwach domowych w latach 1983–1986. Warszawa: Zarząd Wydawnictw Statystycznych i Drukarni, 1987.

Starzyńska, Feliksa, Zawistowska, Zofia. *Nowoczesne żywienie rodziny*. Warszawa: Państwowy Zakład Wydawnictw Lekarskich, 1966.

Strzelecka, Maria. *Zmiany w konsumpcji gospodarstw domowych w latach 1980–1983*. Warszawa: IRWiK, 1984.

Stan wojenny w Polsce 1981–1983. Ed. Antoni Dudek. Warszawa 2003.

Sylwestrzak, Andrzej. *Najwyższa Izba Kontroli*. Warszawa: Zakład Narodowy im. Ossolińskich, 1990.

Szarota, Tomasz. "Śmiech zakazany – kawał (dowcip) polityczny jako informacja o postrzeganiu peerelowskiej rzeczywistości". *Polska 1944/45–1989. Studia i materiały* V (2001).

Szostkiewicz, Stefan. *Zaopatrzenie w żywność w opinii społecznej.* Warszawa: Wydawnictwa Radia i Telewizji, 1974.

Sztompka, Piotr. *Socjologia. Analiza społeczeństwa.* Kraków: Znak, 2002.

Świda, Witold. *Wpływ zmiany ustroju na przestępczość (w świetle przestępczości w Kaliszu i powiecie kaliskim).* Wrocław: Zakład Narodowy im. Ossolińskich, 1960.

Świda - Ziemba, Hanna. "Robotnicy lat pięćdziesiątych." In *Elity władzy w Polsce a struktura społeczna w latach 1956–1981.* Ed. Przemysław Wójcik. Warszawa: Uniwersytet Warszawski, Polskie Towarzystwo Socjologiczne, 1994.

Świetlik, Krystyna. *Znaczenie reglamentacji w procesie racjonalizacji wyżywienia.* Warszawa: Instytut Ekonomiki Rolnictwa i Gospodarki Żywnościowej, 1991.

Tymiński, Maciej. "Malwersacje w przedsiębiorstwach socjalistycznych (1950–1970)." *Dzieje Najnowsze* 4 (2002).

Witkowska-Krych, Agnieszka. "Coś z niczego, czyli przepisy kulinarne w dobie kryzysu. Analiza treści wybranych książek kucharskich wydanych w ostatniej dekadzie PRL." *Wyzwoleni, ale nie wolni. Studia z historii najnowszej* 2 (2015).

Wolle, Stefan, *Wspaniały świat dyktatury. Codzienność i władza w NRD 1971–1989.* Warszawa: Wiedza Powszechna, 2003.

Wójtowicz, Norbert. "Dowcip polityczny w Polsce Ludowej w latach 1944–1956." In *Studia i materiały z dziejów opozycji i oporu społecznego.* Ed. Kamiński. I (1998).

Zaremba, Marcin. "Gdzie jest mięso." *Polityka* 8 (1988).

________. *Społeczeństwo polskie lat sześćdziesiątych – między "małą stabilizacją" a "małą destabilizacją."* In *Oblicza Marca 1968.* Ed. Konrad Rokicki, Sławomir Stępień. Warszawa: Instytut Pamięci Narodowej, 2004.

________. *Wielka trwoga. Polska lat 1944–1947. Ludowa reakcja na kryzys.* Kraków: ZNAK, 2012.

Zawistowska, Zofia. *Potrawy bezmięsne i półmięsne.* Warszawa: Wydawnictwo Przemysłu Lekkiego i Spożywczego, 1965.

________. Krzyżanowska, Małgorzata, *Książka kucharska,* Warszawa: Watra, 1982.

Zawistowski, Andrzej. *Bilety do sklepu. Handel reglamentowany w PRL.* Warszawa: PWN, 2017.

Zblewski, Zdzisław. *Leksykon PRL-u.* Kraków: ZNAK, 2001.

Ziemba, Zdzisław A. *Prawo przeciwko społeczeństwu. Polskie prawo karne w latach 1944–1956*. Warszawa: Uniwersytet Warszawski, 1997.

Zubok, Vladislav, Pleszakov, Konstantin. *Zimna wojna zza kulis Kremla. Od Stalina do Chruszczowa*. Warszawa: Książka i Wiedza, 1999.

Życki, Wojciech. *Spożycie artykułów żywnościowych w Polsce. Przemiany w latach 1945–1966*. Warszawa: Wydawnictwa Naukowo-Techniczne, 1970.

5. Interviews

Andrzej Werblan, 24 January 2003.

6. Unpublished Works

Juźwik, Aleksander. *Od ratownictwa do etatyzacji. Opieka nad dziećmi i młodzieżą w działalności organizacji społecznych w Polsce w latach 1944–1950*. PHD thesis defended at the Institute of History of the Polish Academy of Sciences, supervised by D. Jarosz, Warszawa 2017.

Kwiecień, R. *Kielecka Delegatura Komisji Specjalnej do Walki z Nadużyciami i Szkodnictwem Gospodarczym (1946–1954)*. MA thesis defended at the Institute of History of the former Świętokrzyska Academy (today Jan Kochanowski Univesity in Kielce), supervised by D. Jarosz, Kielce 2003.

Index

L

Geschichte - Erinnerung - Politik
Studies in History, Memory and Politics

Edited by Anna Wolff-Powęska & Piotr Forecki

Bd./Vol. 1 Machteld Venken: Stradding the Iron Curtain? Immigrants, Immigrant Organisations, War Memories. 2011.

Bd./Vol. 2 Anna Wolff-Powęska / Piotr Forecki: Der Holocaust in der polnischen Erinnerungskultur. 2012.

Bd./Vol. 3 Marta Grzechnik: Regional Histories and Historical Regions. The Concept of the Baltic Sea Region in Polish and Swedish Historiographies. 2012.

Bd./Vol. 4 Lutz Niethammer: Memory and History. Essays in Contemporary History. 2012.

Bd./Vol. 5 Piotr Forecki: Reconstructing Memory. The Holocaust in Polish Public Debates. 2013.

Bd./Vol. 6 Marek Słoń (ed.): Historical Atlas of Poland in the 2nd Half of the 16th Century. Voivodeships of Cracow, Sandomierz, Lublin, Sieradz, Łęczyca, Rawa, Płock and Mazovia. Volume 1-4. Translated by Agata Staszewska, Editorial Assistance Martha Brożyna. 2014.

Bd./Vol. 7 Maciej Janowski: Birth of the Intelligentsia 1750-1831. A History of the Polish Intelligentsia - Part 1. Edited by Jerzy Jedlicki. Translated by Tristan Korecki. 2014.

Bd./Vol. 8 Jerzy Jedlicki: The Vicious Circle 1832-1864. A History of the Polish Intelligentsia - Part 2. Edited by Jerzy Jedlicki. Translated by Tristan Korecki. 2014.

Bd./Vol. 9 Magdalena Micińska: At the Crossroads 1865-1918. A History of the Polish Intelligentsia - Part 3. Edited by Jerzy Jedlicki. Translated by Tristan Korecki. 2014.

Bd./Vol. 10 Anna Wolff-Powęska: Memory as Burden and Liberation. Germans and their Nazi Past (1945-2010). Translated by Marta Skowrońska. 2015.

Bd./Vol. 11 Thomasz Szarota: On the Threshold of the Holocaust. Anti-Jewish Riots and Pogroms in Occupied Europe. Warsaw - Paris - The Hague - Amsterdam - Antwerp - Kaunas. Translated by Tristan Korecki. 2015.

Bd./Vol. 12 Anna Wolff-Powęska / Piotr Forecki (eds.): World War II and Two Occupations. Dilemmas of Polish Memory. Translated by Marta Skowrońska and Blanka Zahorjanova. 2016.

Bd./Vol. 13 Elżbieta Katarzyna Dzikowska / Agata Handley / Piotr Zawilski (eds.): The Great War. Insights and Perspectives. 2016.

Bd./Vol. 14 Jerzy Jedlicki: A Degenerate World. Translated by Tristan Korecki. Edited by Elena Rozbicka. 2016.

Bd./Vol. 15 Miroslaw Matyja: Zwischen Krieg und Hoffnung. Internierung der 2. polnischen Infanterieschützen-Division in der Schweiz 1940-45. 2016.

Bd./Vol. 16 Adam Leszczyński: Leap into Modernity - Political Economy of Growth on the Periphery, 1943-1980. 2017.

Bd./Vol. 17 Antoine Marès / Wojciech Prażuch / Inga Kawka (eds.) : Les exilés polonais en France et la réorganisation pacifique de l'Europe (1940-1989). 2017.

Bd./Vol. 18 Dominika Gortych / Guido Hinterkeuser / Łukasz Skoczylas: Erinnerungsimplantate – Der (Wieder-)Aufbau der Schlösser in Posen und Berlin im interdisziplinären Vergleich. Unter Mitwirkung von Karsten Holste. 2017.

Bd./Vol. 19 Elżbieta Katarzyna Dzikowska / Agata G. Handley / Piotr Zawilski (eds.): Beyond the Trenches – The Social and Cultural Impact of the Great War. 2017. Second Edition 2019.

Bd./Vol. 20 Marcin Zaremba: Communism – Legitimacy – Nationalism. Nationalist Legitimization of the Communist Regime in Poland. 2019.

Bd./Vol. 21 Klaus Bachmann: Genocidal Empires. German Colonialism in Africa and the Third Reich. Edited by Barbara Kurowska. 2018.

Bd./Vol. 22 Krzysztof Trybuś / Michael Düring / Maciej Junkiert (Hrsg.): Polen und Deutsche in Europa. Polacy i Niemcy w Europie. Beiträge zur internationalen Konferenz, 16. und 17. November 2015, Poznań. Tom podsumowujący międzynarodową konferencję, 16 i 17 listopada 2015, Poznań. 2018.

Bd./Vol. 23 Monika Jaglarz / Katarzyna Jaśtal (Hrsg.): Bestände der ehemaligen Preußischen Staatsbibliothek zu Berlin in der Jagiellonen-Bibliothek. Forschungsstand und -perspektiven. 2018.

Bd./Vol. 24 Zuzanna Bogumił / Małgorzata Głowacka-Grajper: Milieux de mémoire in Late Modernity. Local Community, Religion and Historical Politics. 2019.

Bd./Vol. 25 Bruno Kamiński: Fear Management. Foreign Threats in the Post-War Polish Propaganda. The Influence and the Reception of the Communist Media (1944-1956). 2019.

Bd./Vol. 26 Anna Wylegała: Displaced Memories. Remembering and Forgetting in Post-War Poland and Ukraine. 2019.

Bd./Vol. 27 Iwona Zamkowska: Religious Liberty in the Educational System of the United States. From the 1980s to the Present. 2019.

Bd./Vol. 28 Sylwia Bykowska: The Rehabilitation and Ethnic Vetting of the Polish Population in the Voivodship of Gdańsk after World War II. 2019.

Bd./Vol. 29 Aleksander Łupienko: Order in the Streets. The Political History of Warsaw's Public Space in the First Half of the 19th Century. 2019.

Bd./Vol. 30 Josef Vladár / Egon Wiedermann (eds.): The World behind the World. Intercultural Processes in the Prehistory of European Civilization. 2020.

Bd./Vol. 31 Krzysztof Brzechczyn: Historical Distinctiveness of Central Europe.A Study from Philosophy of History. 2020.

Bd./Vol. 32 Jacek Surzyn: Return to the Promised Land. The Birth and Philosophical Foundations of Zi-onism. 2020.

Bd./Vol. 33 Ryszard Kaczmarek: Poles in Kaiser's Army. On the Front of the First World War. 2020.

Bd./Vol. 34 Tomasz Wiślicz: Earning Heavenly Salvation. Peasant Religion in Lesser Poland. Mid-Sixteenth to Eighteenth Centuries. 2020.

Bd./Vol. 35 Zbigniew Tucholski: Polish State Railways as a Mode of Transport for Troops of the Warsaw Pact. Technology in Service of a Doctrine. Translated by Marek Ciesielski. 2020.

Bd./Vol. 36 Paweł Kras: The System of the Inquisition in Medieval Europe. Translated from Polish by Magdalena Panz-Sochacka. 2020.

Bd./Vol. 37 Maria Pasztor / Dariusz Jarosz: Increase Supply, Reduce Demand and Punish Severely. A Contextual History of Meat in Communist Poland. Translated by Alex Shannon. 2020.

www.peterlang.com

www.ingramcontent.com/pod-product-compliance
Ingram Content Group UK Ltd.
Pitfield, Milton Keynes, MK11 3LW, UK
UKHW041825100926
8556IPUK00002B/29

9 783631 825907